New Hampshire
Marriage Licenses and Intentions
1709-1961

Pauline Johnson Oesterlin

HERITAGE BOOKS
2007

HERITAGE BOOKS
AN IMPRINT OF HERITAGE BOOKS, INC.

Books, CDs, and more—Worldwide

For our listing of thousands of titles see our website
at
www.HeritageBooks.com

Published 2007 by
HERITAGE BOOKS, INC.
Publishing Division
65 East Main Street
Westminster, Maryland 21157-5026

Copyright © 1991 Pauline Johnson Oesterlin

Other Heritage Books by the author:

Hillsborough County, New Hampshire Court Records, 1772-1799

Hopkinton, New Hampshire Vital Records, Volume 1

Hopkinton, New Hampshire Vital Records, Volume 2

New Hampshire 1742 Estate List

Rockingham County, New Hampshire Paupers

Surname Guide to Massachusetts Town Histories
Pauline J. Oesterlin and Phyllis O. Longver

All rights reserved. No part of this book may be reproduced or transmitted in any form or by any means, electronic or mechanical, including photocopying, recording or by any information storage and retrieval system without written permission from the author, except for the inclusion of brief quotations in a review.

International Standard Book Number: 978-1-55613-530-0

CONTENTS

Foreword by Frank Mevers v

Early Marriage Intentions (1709-1911) 1

Wentworth Marriage Licenses (1742-1776) 35

Concord, Jaffrey, and Stratham
  Marriage Intentions (1791-1960) 43

Out-of-state Minister Licenses (1921-1961) 93

Cross Index to Brides 233

FOREWORD

One of the first laws promulgated by the New Hampshire legislature in 1679 required that intentions of marriage be published openly at least three times or posted in a conspicuous spot in the community for fourteen days prior to the event [*New Hampshire Laws*, I, 26]. Many of these notices have survived the ravages of time, weather, and man and so remain in the State Archives to be used by today's researchers.

This listing of brides and grooms reveals many names quite possibly not saved in any other public records and hence should make an excellent source for genealogical research. The records of the eighteenth century--those signed by Benning and John Wentworth--probably rested at length in the old state house in Portsmouth and then in the office of the province treasurer in Exeter with other important documents throughout the Revolution and early statehood period. Those papers were moved to Concord in 1820 when the statehouse was completed. They remained in its various vaults, under the eye of the secretary of state, until the New Hampshire Historical Society agreed to house them with many other of the state's records. In the 1960s, with the establishment of the state's Division of Records Management and Archives some of those materials were transferred to the Records and Archives building. Even more--some of these marriage intentions among them--were transferred to the Archives during the 1980s and those particularly from Stratham and Concord arrived only in 1991. The intention is that they remain here for the duration of time.

The twentieth-century items resulted from the necessity to register with the secretary of state when the marriage was to be performed by a clergyman from out of state, a situation brought about by any number of reasons, but principally owing to relationship to the bride or groom or friendship on the part of either. Just as the intentions signed by the Wentworths in the eighteenth century are directed to "Either of the Ordained Ministers of the

Gospel" in New Hampshire, it was necessary that the secretary of state issue a temporary authorization for a non-resident ordained minister to perform the marriage within the state. In 1919 and 1921 the legislature ordered that such "special licenses" be issued by the governor and council [*Laws*, 1919, Chapter 56; 1921, Chapter 79] but amended the law in 1925 to concur with the actual practice by which the secretary of state issued the license [*Laws*, 1925, Chapter 27]. The provision remains in force today [*New Hampshire Revised Statutes Annotated*, 457:32]. Fortunately for us the legislature was careful to instruct that this be kept as a permanent record.

Certainly this listing does not even approach a complete listing of all marriages in New Hampshire. If the name sought is not in the following list, the researcher's next source for marriage information should be the New Hampshire Bureau of Vital Records and Health Statistics, Department of Health and Human Services, Hazen Drive, Concord, NH 03301. Not finding a record there one should next inquire to the clerk of the town in which the marriage was solemnized for it has always been required that the parties register with the town clerk. Those of us who keep the records, who index them, and who publish or broadcast the index commit our time, efforts and resources in the hope that you the user will find the information helpful.

Frank C. Mevers
New Hampshire State Archivist

EARLY MARRIAGE INTENTIONS

These marriage intentions were filed in New Hampshire primarily in the late 18th century and the early 19th century. The earliest date given is 1709, and the latest is 1911. The entries are arranged alphabetically by groom, and give the name and residence of both the bride and groom, the date the intention was filed, and the origin of the report.

ABBOTT James H of Pembroke & CONNORS Susan of Pembroke int 12 Jun 1857 rept from Pembroke
ABBOTT Rufus L of Candia & WILLARD Nancy A of Candia int 24 Sep 1848 rept from Candia
ADAMS Benjamin of Sutton & WHITE Nancy of Bow int 3 Sep 1832 rept from Sutton
ADAMS Benjamin F of Sutton & WHITE Nancy N of Bow int 24 Sep 1832 rept from Bow
ADAMS Joseph of Dublin & EMERY Betsey of Jaffrey int 15 May 1805 rept from Dublin
ADAMS Stephen Jr of Jaffrey & CHADWICK Rebecca of Rindge int 4 Mar 1813 rept from Rindge
ADAMS William of Henniker & FELCH Angetial of Hopkinton int 5 Oct 1848 rept from Henniker
ADAMS William of Henniker & FELCH Angelia S of Hopkinton int 4 Nov 1848 rept from Hopkinton
ALBEE Alexander of Littleton & CHANDLER Dolly of Concord int 27 Aug 1832 rept from Littleton
ALDRICH Aaron of Salem & HUMPHREY Sarah Jane of Salem int 4 Jul 1829 rept from Salem
ALEXANDER William of Dover & CAREY Elizabeth of Dover int 15 May 1866 rept from Dover
ANDERSON Evans Jr of Pembroke & FRENCH Sarah of Pembroke int 25 Sep 1878 rept from Pembroke
ANDREWS Isaac of Hillsboro & BEARD Sarah of Peterborough int 10 Dec 1820 rept from Peterborough

ARNOLD Edward of Rindge & SPOFFORD Sally O of Jaffrey int 3 May 1804 rept from Rindge
AVERY Eliphalet of Greenland & CATE Mary of Greenland int 25 Feb 1775 rept from Greenland
AYER John J of Hooksett & FOX Harriet of Jaffrey int 8 Oct 1827 rept from Hooksett
BACHELDER Thomas of Candia & CLEAVES Rhoda of Candia int 11 Feb 1849 rept from Candia
BAGDER Abner of Marborough & CROSBY Nancy of Jaffrey int 10 Dec 1827 rept from Marborough
BAGLEY Elijah of New Town & SANBORN Hannah Wid of New Town int 9 Aug 1795 rept from New Town
BAGLEY Layfaette of Thornton & HANSON Betsy of Boscawen int 9 Jan 1862 rept from Thornton
BAILEY Joshua of Hopkinton & CLEMENT Sarah of Haverhill int 3 Nov 1788 rept from Hopkinton
BAKER Charles W of Epping & LIBBEY Hannah of Epping int 15 Jan 1852 rept from Epping
BAKER Samuel D of Bow & GLOVER Eliza A of Concord int 13 Mar 1832 rept from Bow
BAKER Silas of Hampstead & DAVIS Lydia of Hampstead int 9 Oct 1791 rept from Hampstead
BALCH Leonard of Bradford MA & PARSON Hannah of Durham int 24 Jan 1850 rept from Durham
BALCH Walter of Manchester & DEMERITT Augusta of Durham int 10 Nov 1860 rept from Durham
BALLADE William of Nashua & VIRGIN Caroline of Concord int 18 Jan A1846 rept from Nashua
BALLARD William H of Lee & WENTWORTH Annie of Lee int 1 Sep 1862 rept from Lee
BANKS Edwin of Rockland ME & WILLEY Julia M of Durham int 14 Aug 1864 rept from Durham
BARRETT Enoch L of Mason & SPAULDING Elizabeth of Jaffrey int 9 Sep 1824 rept from Mason
BARTLETT Daniel of Plaistow & CHANEY Abigial of Plaistow int 20 May 1768 rept from Plaistow
BARTLETT Eliphelet of Newtown & EMERSON Mary of Haverhill int 14 Dec 1791 rept from Newtown
BATCHELDER John of Candia & GRIFFIN Lattice of Candia int 2 Aug 1856 rept from Candia
BATCHELDER Newton of Durham & OTIS Abby J of Durham int 27 Nov 1862 rept from Durham
BAYLEY Richard of Haverhill & EMERSON Mehitable of Haverhill int 30 Jun 1769 rept from Haverhill

BEAN Benjamin of Raymond & PAGE Naomi of Raymond int 9 Jan 1802 rept from Raymond
BEAN Benjamin of Raymond & PAGE Naomi of Raymond int 19 Jan 1802 rept from Raymond
BECKER George S of Sanford ME & THOMPSON Abbott E of Lee int 7 Oct 1856 rept from Lee
BECKLEY George A of Manchester & HOYT Sarah L of Manchester int 19 Oct 1849 rept from Manchester
BEEM Joseph of Deerfield & CRAM Nancy of Raymond int 12 Apr 1806 rept from Raymond
BELL John A of Hooksett & BLAKE Sarah of Lowell MA int 15 Nov 1835 rept from Hooksett
BELL Louis of Farmington & BOUTON Mary A P of Farmington int 30 May 1859 rept from Farmington
BENSON William S of Newfield ME & HIGLE Mary Ann of Candia int 13 Jan 1850 rept from Candia
BERRY Walter of Loudon & POTTER Sarah of Concord int 24 Jun 1827 rept from Loudon
BICKFORD Robert of Durham & CLARK Sarah of Durham int 4 Nov 1867 rept from Durham
BLAISDELL Gilman of Goffstown & BLAISDELL Cynthia of Goffstown int 5 Jun 1848 rept from Goffstown
BLANCHARD James P of Durham & DAME Martha of Durham int 20 May 1850 rept from Durham
BLASDELL John of New Chester & FORBES Ruth of New Chester int 4 Dec 1828 rept from New Chester
BLOOD Samuel of Bradford & BATES Lucy of Bradford int 7 Nov 1814 rept from Bradford
BLY Benjamin of Plaistow & ORDWAY Hannah of Plaistow int 2 Oct 1769 rept from Plaistow
BOND Chas A of Concord & KIDDER Conneli of Bristol int 17 Oct 1866 rept from Bristol
BOWIN Jonathan of Dublin & NOYS Elizabeth of Dublin int 8 Apr 1816 rept from Dublin
BOYCE Benjamin of Haverhill & PEPEN Susanna of Haverhill int 18 Sep 1770 rept from Haverhill
BOYS Alexander of Londonderry & STEVENS Susanna of Plaistow int 23 Oct 1786 rept from Plaistow
BRACKETT Leonard W of Gorham & ADAMS Mary J of Henniker int 15 Nov 1848 rept from Henniker
BRADLEY Benjamain of Haverhill MA & NOYES Sarah of Plaistow int 30 Mar 1769 rept from Plaistow
BRADLEY Benjamin of Haverhill MA & CURRIER Elizabeth of Plaistow int 4 Apr 1801 rept from Plaistow

BRADLEY Benjamin of Haverhill & NOYCE Sarah of Plaistow int 3 Apr 1769 rept from Haverhill

BRADLEY Charles E of Providence RI & BATCHELDER Abby of Canterbury int 2 Jun 1855 rept from Canterbury

BRADLEY John of Haverhill MA & FOLENSBEY Elizabeth of Plaistow int 14 Dec 1780 rept from Plaistow

BRADLEY Stephen of Haverhill MA & STONE Abiah of Atkinson int 6 Sep 1784 rept from Atkinson

BRALEY Cornelious of Northfield & COLLINS Almeda of Northfield int 24 May 1861 rept from Northfield

BRIANT John of Jaffrey & POOR Sally of Dublin int 19 Jan 1807 rept from Dublin

BRICKETT Charles of Pembroke & MOORE Weltha of Pembroke int 19 Mar 1856 rept from Pembroke

BRIDGES James of Wilton & FISKE Sally of Jaffrey int 20 Aug 1825 rept from Wilton

BRIGHAM Eli of Jaffrey & RUSSELL Abigial of Dublin int 22 Dec 1819 rept from Dublin

BRIGHTMAN George E of Fall River Mas & SNELL Lydia A of Lee int 4 Feb 1865 rept from Dover

BROWN Albert of Northfield & LEIGHTON Nellie of Andover int 1 Jan 1866 rept from Northfield

BROWN Anson of Loudon & POTTER Alvira of Concord int 1 Nov 1834 rept from Loudon

BROWN Cyrus of Sharon & SEVERANCE Milla of Jaffrey int 10 Dec 1810 rept from Sharon

BROWN Freeman M of Candia & McDUFFIE Elizabeth of Candia int 18 Jan 1851 rept from Candia

BROWN James of New Town & GREENOUGH Moley of Plaistow int 24 Apr 1781 rept from Plaistow

BROWN James of Bridgewater & HARRAN Judith B of Bridgewater int 12 Sep 1830 rept from Bridgewater

BROWN Joseph of Canterbury & CLEASBY Hannah W of Concord int 25 Sep 1828 rept from Canterbury

BROWN Nathaniel of Candia & PIPER Mary Ann of Manchester int 25 Nov 1848 rept from Candia

BROWN Stephen Jr of Candia & PILLSBURY Abby Y of Candia int 26 Mar 1848 rept from Candia

BRUCE Cyrus of Troy & WILDER Sara of Troy int 23 Mar 1823 rept from Troy

BRYANT Andrew of Plaistow & BARTLETT Maribah of Plaistow int 6 Jun 1772 rept from Plaistow

BRYANT David of Plaistow & GILMAN Molly of Plaistow int 23 Jan 1783 rept from Plaistow

BRYANT David of Haverhill MA & GILMAN Moley of Plaistow int 4 Sep 1783 rept from Plaistow

BRYANT James of Plaistow & JOHNSON Nabby of Plaistow int 19 Feb 1795 rept from Plaistow

BULLARD Ebenezer of Dublin & PHILLIPS Olive of Dublin int 13 Oct 1805 rept from Dublin

BULLARD Timothy of Dublin & BOWERS Lydia of Dublin int 29 Jul 1813 rept from Dublin

BUNELL John D of Durham & DOEG Mary E of Durham int 22 Apr 1867 rept from Durham

BUNKER Daniel C of Durham & TWILIGHT Helen D of Kittery ME int 14 Mar 1865 rept from Durham

BUNKER John of Durham & CLOUGH Louise V of Durham int 14 Jun 1860 rept from Durham

BURBANK Samuel of Groveland & DOE Emily of Durham int 23 Nov 1854 rept from Durham

BURNHAM John of Manchester & DANINSON Harriet of Manchester int 3 Jul 1844 rept from Manchester

BURROUGH Joseph of Hampstead & EMERY Edna of Hampstead int 23 Dec 1788 rept from Hampstead

BURROUGHS Joseph Wilson of Hampstead & EMERY Ebner of Hampstead int 10 Feb 1789 rept from Hampstead

BUSWELL John Jr of Rindge & HORTON Sarah of Jaffrey int 3 Jul 1803 rept from Rindge

BUZSWELL Edward of Hopkinton & ANSDEN Sarah A of Hopkinton int 12 May 1865 rept from Hopkinton

BUZZELL Semuel of Lee & JEAN Emma of Lee int 23 Dec 1856 rept from Lee

CAEFER (servant) of Greenland & VILOT (servant) of Greenland int 6 May 1777 rept from Greenland

CALEF James of Hampstead & KIMBALL Anne of Plaistow int 17 Mar 1804 rept from Plaistow

CALF Joseph of Hampstead & KIMBALL Nabby of Plaistow int 22 Mar 1802 rept from Plaistow

CALTON Samuel of Plaistow & BARTLETT Sarah of Plaistow int 2 Oct 1780 rept from Plaistow

CARLETON Joseph M of Methuen MA & MILLS Lucy Ann of Durham int 17 Sep 1817 rept from Durham

CARLTINER David of Plaistow & STEVENS Ruth of Plaistow int 23 Nov 1773 rept from Plaistow

CARR Jonathan of New London & MARTHES Sarah of Durham int 30 Dec 1857 rept from New London

CARSON Charles H of Durham & ELLISON Sarah of Durham int 9 Jan 1857 rept from Durham

CARTER James of Peterborough & BATES Mary of Jaffrey int 17 Apr 1819 rept from Peterborough
CARTER Jude of Rindge & PIERCE Abigial of Jaffrey int 31 Jan 1812 rept from Rindge
CASS Levi of Epsom & OSGOOD Mahetable of Raymond int 29 Aug 1803 rept from Raymond
CATER William of Barrington & PIERCE Mary of Barrington int 21 Jul 1814 rept from Barrington
CHANDLER Josiah of Grafton & MERRILL Mehitable of Grafton int 13 Jan 1829 rept from Grafton
CHANEY Giles of Plaistow & PEASLEY Hannah of Plaistow int 29 Jul 1791 rept from Plaistow
CHANEY Richard of Plaistow & CHASE Ann of Haverhill MA int 5 Jun 1771 rept from Plaistow
CHASE Caleb of Hawke & STRAW Moley of Plaistow int 17 Dec 1781 rept from Plaistow
CHASE Charles of Hopkinton & EVANS Mary of Hopkinton int 10 Mar 1835 rept from Hopkinton
CHASE Charles of New Chester & CASS Sally of New Chester int 4 Dec 1824 rept from New Chester
CHASE Daniel of New Town & EATON Hannah of Plaistow int 7 Nov 1791 rept from Plaistow
CHASE Enoch of Somersworth & LORD Maria of Somersworth int 15 Jan 1822 rept from Somersworth
CHASE J Hazelton of Loudon & PALMER Belinda of Lowell MA int 24 May 1847 rept from Loudon
CHELLIS John S of Manchester & LITTLE Emma A of Concord int 22 Oct 1852 rept from Manchester
CHENEY John of Plaistow & STEVEN Lucy Fair of Plaistow int 29 Feb 1788 rept from Plaistow
CHENEY Richard of Plaistow & CHAFE Anne of Haverhill int 15 Apr 1771 rept from Haverhill
CHESLE Israel of Lee & GLASS Elizabeth of Nottingham int 25 Sep 1849 rept from Lee
CHESLEY Israel of Lee & CLAPS Elizabeth of Nottingham int 27 Sep 1847 rept from Nottingham
CHESLEY John S of Loudon & SANBORN Addie of Durham int 22 Oct 1861 rept from Durham
CILLEY Abraham of Northwood & CILLEY Julia A of Nottingham int 29 Jan 1849 rept from Northwood
CILLEY Jacobs of Manchester & BOUTON Martha C of Concord int 26 Jan 1861 rept from Manchester
CLAGGETT William of Sunapee & MORRILL Sarah K of Concord int 11 Apr 1831 rept from Sunapee

CLARK Amos of Plaistow & BRADLEY Hannah of Plaistow int 5 Jan 1789 rept from Plaistow
CLARK Amos of Plaistow & PEASLEY Elizaabeth of Plaistow int 10 Mar 1802 rept from Plaistow
CLEMENT Benaiah of Haverhill MA & SAWYER Abigial of Atkinson int 9 Sep 1782 rept from Atkinson
CLEMENT David of Haverhill MA & LADD Dille Mrs of Atkinson int 10 Nov 1769 rept from Atkinson
CLEMENT Philip of Haverhill & CONCERN Phebe of Haverhill int 21 Nov 1766 rept from Haverhill
CLIFFORD Hiriam of Dunbarton & ROY Mary Ann of Dunbarton int 2 May 1845 rept from Dunbarton
CLIFFORD T Israel of Dunbarton & STEVENS Achea Mrs of Atkinson int 19 Oct 1772 rept from Atkinson
COLBATH Jothan of Exeter & JONES Sarah D of Exeter int 31 Jan 1842 rept from Exeter
COLBEY Daniel of Hampstead & TRUSSELL Sarah of Plaistow int 10 Oct 1769 rept from Plaistow
COLBURN Lenoard of Plaistow & FLOOD Elizabeth of Plaistow int 23 Mar 1767 rept from Plaistow
COLBY Benajamin of Hawke & POLLARD Mary of Plaistow int 11 Nov 1779 rept from Kingstown
COLBY Elijah S W of Hooksett & HARTFORD Mahala R of Candia int rept from Candia
COLBY Timothy of Plaistow & DAVIS Sophia of Plaistow int 10 Mar 1804 rept from Plaistow
COLCORD Joseph O of Candia & WORTHEN Adaline of Candia int 17 May 1851 rept from Candia
COLLINS Jonathan of Hampstead & PLAMER Ellen of Hampstead int 12 Jun 1792 rept from Hampstead
COLLINS Jonathan of Hampstead & PLUMMER Alice of Hawke int 4 Jun 1792 rept from Kingstown
COLLINS Joseph of Brentwood & NORRIS Ruth of Epping int 5 Mar 1789 rept from Epping
COMINGS Joseph G of Lee & DAVIS Sarah E of Lee int 25 Apr 1864 rept from Lee
COMMING Thattias of Fitzwilliam & COLLINGS Amy of Fitzwilliam int 23 Apr 1803 rept from Fitzwilliam
COMSTOCK William of Sullivan & JEWETT Patty of Jaffrey int 17 Feb 1801 rept from Sullivan
COOPER John B of Newport & MOODY Mary O of Newport int 21 Aug 1862 rept from Newport
COPP Josiah of Plaistow & EDWARDS Elizabeth of Haverhill MA int 25 Jan 1779 rept from Plaistow

COTTEN Icahob Shaw of New Town & CARLTON Agibial of New Town int 16 Oct 1795 rept from New Town
COTTON Albert of Dover & TWOMBLY Hannah of Madbury int 23 Nov 1854 rept from Madbury
COTTON Albert W of Dover & TWOMBLY Hannah of Madbury int 25 Nov 1854 rept from Dover
CRAM Abner of Raymond & WOODMAN Hannah of Raymond int 2 Nov 1801 rept from Raymond
CRAM Ebenezer of Raymond & OSGOOD Jane of Raymond int 6 Jul 1805 rept from Raymond
CRANE William of Candia & EATON Lucy W of Dedham MA int 11 Nov 1849 rept from Candia
CRITCHERSON Charles M of Lee & GLOVER Sarah E of Lee int 26 Mar 1864 rept from Lee
CRITCHETT John W of Candia & CLIFFORD Martha of Allenstown int 19 Nov 1848 rept from Candia
CROMMITT Joseph B of Bedford & FIFIELD Louise of Lowell MA int 24 Sep 1838 rept from Bedford
CROSBY Alphons of Troy & FOSS Mary of Jaffrey int 20 Mar 1822 rept from Troy
CROSS Charles of Canterbury & HOLT Rebeckah M of Concord int 9 Mar 1830 rept from Canterbury
CURRIER Gideon of Raymond & SMITH Louisa of Candia int 24 Oct 1852 rept from Candia
CURRIER John W of Manchester & HUBBARD Elizabeth B of Candia int 19 Sep 1852 rept from Candia
CURRIER Samuel of Hampstead & STEVENS Dameris of Hampstead int 5 Mar 1789 rept from Hampstead
CURRIER Stephen of Amesbury MA & DOWN Ann of Plaistow int 4 Feb 1804 rept from Plaistow
CUTLER Edgar of Conway & COFFIE Judith of Conway int 1 Feb 1833 rept from Conway
DANFORD Orrin of Webster & MORRILL Abra Ann of Webster int 13 Feb 1862 rept from Webster
DANIEL Benjamin of Newmarket & ROLLINS Anna of Newmarket int 6 Apr 1859 rept from Newmarket
DARLING Benjamin of Dublin & AMES Fanny of Dublin int 6 Jun 1803 rept from Dublin
DARLING Robart of Hampstead & GUILE Judith of Plastow int 29 Jan 1784 rept from Hampstead
DART Eli of Gilson & FARRAR Eleanor of Marborough int 30 Jan 1875 rept from Marborough
DART Eli of Gilsum & FARRAR Eleanor of Marborough int 6 Feb 1815 rept from Gilsum

DAVIDSON Benjamin of Fitzwilliam & MARSHALL Nabby of Jaffrey int 31 May 1813 rept from Fitzwilliam

DAVIS Amos of Plaistow & HARISSON Sarah of Atkinson int 16 Nov 1788 rept from Plaistow

DAVIS Amos of Plaistow & HUNKINS Sarah of Haverhill MA int 26 Jun 1788 rept from Plaistow

DAVIS Benjamin of Bradford & TODD Janette L B of New London int 28 Aug 1854 rept from New London

DAVIS Benjamin F of Bradford & TODD Janette L B of New London int 24 Aug 1854 rept from Bradford

DAVIS Charles H of Durham & WILLEY Sarah of Durham int 29 Jul 1855 rept from Durham

DAVIS Charles S of Durham & BUTLER Sarah A of Durham int 23 Apr 1854 rept from Durham

DAVIS Ephrain of Amesbury MA & DOW Polly of Plaistow int 9 Apr 1803 rept from Plaistow

DAVIS Gideon of Amesbury MA & CHANEY Ruth of Plaistow int 30 Nov 1772 rept from Plaistow

DAVIS Moses of Atkinson & DAVIS Sophia of Plastow int 10 Mar 1802 rept from Atkinson

DAVIS Sam Francis of Dover & TUTTLE Mary F H of Dover int 14 Jul 1852 rept from Dover

DAVIS Webster of Kingstown & POLLARD Betty of Kingstown int 30 Jul 1789 rept from Kingstown

DAVIS William of Amesbury MA & DOW Lydia of Plaistow int 21 Jan 1765 rept from Plaistow

DAVY Moses of Plaistow & HOYET Judith of Amesbury MA int 5 Nov 1783 rept from Plaistow

DEMERITT Ezra E of Madbury & DEMERITT Louisa of Madbury int 30 May 1855 rept from Madbury

DEMORY James of Rindge & PAGE Olive of Rindge int 25 Jun 1822 rept from Rindge

DERLING Robart of Hampstead & GILE Judith of Plaistow int 29 Jan 1784 rept from Plaistow

DICKINSON William of Candia & OAKES Martha of Landaff int 4 Sep 1852 rept from Candia

DICKMAN Amos of Manchester & BENNETT Ruth M of Manchester int 9 Dec 1848 rept from Manchester

DIMAN Oliver Jr of Fitzwilliam & POTTER Polly of Fitzwilliam int 26 Sep 1803 rept from Fitzwilliam

DINSMORE Daniel of Meredith & STARK Caroline of Goffstown int 10 Nov 1835 rept from Meredith

DODD James of Milton & CHANDLER Lucia of Milton int 12 Feb 1858 rept from Milton

DODGE Joseph of Haverhill MA & WHITE Nabby of Atkinson int 20 Jul 1773 rept from Atkinson

DODGE Joseph of Haverhill MA & WHITE Nabby of Atkinson int 27 Aug 1773 rept from Plaistow

DOE Elbert F of Durham & FOLSOM Lucy M of Durham int 13 Feb 1852 rept from Durham

DOE Henry of Durham & CHAPMAN Fanny of Durham int 7 Feb 1857 rept from Durham

DOLF William of Haverhill MA & HARRIMAN Levina of Plaistow int 22 Mar 1770 rept from Plaistow

DOLLOFF Benjamin of Raymond & WASSON Elizabeth of Raymond int 3 May 1800 rept from Raymond

DOLLOFF William of New Hampton & HAMILTON Maria of Conway int 8 Jul 1844 rept from New Hampton

DOW Cyrus H of Canterbury & CHARLES Deborah S of Canterbury int 5 Dec 1843 rept from Canterbury

DOW Joshua of Plaistow & HARRIAM Acsah of Plaistow int 30 Mar 1769 rept from Plaistow

DOW Obid A of Weare & COGSWELL Sarah P of Weare int 5 Dec 1861 rept from Weare

DRAKE Oliver of E Boston MA & KNOWLTON Sarah L of Chichester int 12 Aug 1862 rept from Chichester

DREW Gamalriel of Candia & WORTHEN Hannah of Candia int 3 May 1852 rept from Canterbury

DREW Henry A of Durham & TUTTLE Sarah of Durham int 14 Dec 1852 rept from Durham

DREW John T of Durham & NUTE Annie E of Dover int 12 May 1860 rept from Durham

DREW John W of New Market & DAVIS Sarah E of Durham int 9 Sep 1869 rept from Durham

DREW Nicholas of Durham & JENKINS Hannah of Durham int 18 Jan 1847 rept from Durham

DREW William J Jr of Durham & AYERS Susan L of Dover int 19 Dec 1867 rept from Durham

DUNCAN Hiram of New London & CUTTER Emelen of Jaffrey int 29 Jun 1829 rept from New London

DUNCAN William of Candia & MURPHY Mary of Londonderry int 10 Oct 1801 rept from Candia

DURGIN Henry S of Epping & YOUNG Jeanette of Madbury int 22 Mar 1862 rept from Madbury

DURRELL Charles M of Laconia & HOLT Susan J of Loudon int 12 Jul 1859 rept from Laconia

DUSTIN Cyrus of Hopkinton & FISK Ednah of Hopkinton int 12 Apr 1834 rept from Hopkinton

DUSTIN David G of Enfield & FOGG Sarah A of Enfield int 7 Mar 1853 rept from Enfield

DUSTON Timothy of Haverhill & CELMENT Abigial of Haverhill int 9 Jun 1766 rept from Haverhill

DUTTON Asa S of Chester & HASELTON Sylvania of Candia int 17 Oct 1852 rept from Candia

EASTMAN Benjamin of Kingstown & ROLAND Mary of Kingstown int 18 Apr 1773 rept from Kingstown

EASTMAN James of Boston MA & SEVERANCE Moley of Hawke int 16 Apr 1783 rept from Hawke

EATON Benjamin of Plaistow & STEVENS Tamar of Plaistow int 15 Sep 1794 rept from Plaistow

EATON Henry S of Candia & SMITH Mary A of Candia int 3 Nov 1850 rept from Candia

EATON Samuel of Landraff & NOYES Susanna of Plaistow int 5 Apr 1786 rept from Plaistow

EATON Samuel of Plaistow & DOW Lydia of Plaistow int 12 Jul 1780 rept from Plaistow

EATTON Timothy of Methuen MA & DOLTON Mary of Plaistow int 22 Oct 1766 rept from Plaistow

EDGERLEY Joseph of Durham & RAND Susan of Durham int 18 Sep 1856 rept from Durham

ELIOT John of Dublin & BIXBY Deborah of Dublin int 5 Dec 1809 rept from Dublin

ELLSWORTH Oliver of Epping & JANVIN Mary of Epping int 13 Aug 1868 rept from Exeter

EMERSON Abraham of Haverhill & EATON Hannah of Haverhill int 27 May 1769 rept from Haverhill

EMERSON Robert of Hampstead & LITTLE Abigail of Hampstead int 18 Dec 1727 rept from Hampstead

EMERSON Smith of Alton & BEACHMAN A E of Wolfeborough int 24 May 1862 rept from Alton

EMERY Jacob of Pembroke & CUSHING Elizabeth of Haverhill int 17 Jul 1769 rept from Haverhill

EMERY Jacob of Pembroke & CUSHING Elizabeth of Haverhill MA int 10 Jul 1762 rept from Pembroke

ESTERBROOKS Benjamin of Rindge & STREETER Sarah of Rindge int 5 Jan 1829 rept from Rindge

EVANS Elijak S of Candia & HUBBARD Mary of Candia int 5 May 1850 rept from Candia

EVELETH William of Dublin & LAWRENCE Sarah of Jaffrey int 2 Apr 1830 rept from Dublin

FARNUM Israel of Manchester & GOODWIN J Annette of Newbury VT int 29 Apr 1857 rept from Manchester

FARNUM W B of Plymouth & KENNEDY Hannah of White River Jct VT int 25 May 1861 rept from Plymouth

FARRINGTON Ebenezer of Amesbury MA & AYER Mary of Plaistow int 24 Jan 1777 rept from Plaistow

FIFE George F of Chichester & CHASES Hannah of Candia int 23 Apr 1848 rept from Candia

FIFIELD Asa of Loudon & HOIT Sophia of Loudon int 30 Sep 1835 rept from Loudon

FIFIELLD John of Candia & HARRIS Rebecca of Candia int 24 Oct 1849 rept from Candia

FLAND Oscar of Albany VT & MCCOY Elizabeth of Bow int 24 Dec 1843 rept from Bow

FLANDERS Ezra of Kingstown & BLASDEL Sarah of Kingstown int 16 Mar 1768 rept from Kingstown

FLETCH Philip of Greenfield & FORTIN Peneope of Jaffrey int 11 Apr 1911 rept from Greenfield

FLINT Joseph of Plaistow & HARRIMAN Moley of Plaistow int 22 Apr 1767 rept from Plaistow

FLINT Luther of Candia & SMITH Sarah Lane of Newmarket int 13 Feb 1853 rept from Candia

FLOOD Joseph of Marborough & PRIST Betty of Jaffrey int 27 Apr 1802 rept from Marborough

FOLLINSBY Nathan of Plaistow & SAWYER Anna of Plaistow int 5 Nov 1783 rept from Plaistow

FORBES S B of New Chester & WELLS Ruth of New Chester int 19 Nov 1802 rept from New Chester

FORSAITH Matheu 2nd of Manchester & GAY Cyntha of Manchester int 4 Apr 1848 rept from Manchester

FOSTER Adams of Canterbury & EASTMAN Sarah B of Concord int 17 Nov 1832 rept from Canterbury

FOSTER Denise H of Chichester & LeJOY Mercy of Newmarket int 3 Jul 1858 rept from Newmarket

FRECHMAN Samuel of Dover & BLAKE Sara of Dover int 29 Jan 1827 rept from Dover

FRENCH Charles C of Deerfield & EMERSON Clarrissa of Candia int 11 May 1851 rept from Candia

FRENCH John L of Hopkinton & CURRIER Viola L of East Unity int 21 Feb 1866 rept from Hopkinton

FRENCH Moses of Atkinson & HASELTINE Mary of Haverhill MA int 25 Sep 1778 rept from Atkinson

FRENCH Truman of Candia & SWAIN Lavinia of Candia int 28 Apr 1850 rept from Candia

FRENNCH David of New Ipswich & HUNT Sarah of Jaffrey int 1 Mar 1826 rept from New Ipswich

GAGE John C of Boscawen & STEVENS Hannah of Loudon int 4 Dec 1853 rept from Loudon

GAGE John C of Boscawen & SARGENT Elizabeth of Canterbury int 30 Oct 1843 rept from Canterbury

GAGE Pierce of Pelham & EATON Eunice of Haverhill MA int 9 Sep 1787 rept from Pelham

GARFIELD John of Marborough & DAVIS Lucy of Jaffrey int 24 Jan 1803 rept from Marborough

GEAR John W of Barrington & BOODY Susan H of Barrington int 11 Jul 1863 rept from Barrington

GEROGE King of Plymouth & EATON Ruth of Plaistow int 9 Jan 1797 rept from Plaistow

GIBBS Ira of Dublin & PIPER Susanna of Dublin int 19 Jun 1820 rept from Dublin

GIBBS John F of Dover & THURLIN? Temperance of Dover int 14 Jul 1852 rept from Dover

GILCHRIST John of Dublin & STANLEY Margaret of Dublin int 15 Mar 1818 rept from Dublin

GILE David of Plaistow & AYER Sally of Plaistow int 25 Oct 1791 rept from Plaistow

GILE Reuben of Plaistow & HARRIMAN Sallay of Plaistow int 25 Feb 1793 rept from Plaistow

GLIDDEN Howard M of Lee & WIGGIN Mabelle of Durham int 24 Nov 1865 rept from Lee

GOODWIN Smith of Hampstead & COLBY Mary of Hampstead int 5 Nov 1768 rept from Hampstead

GORING Almerin of Dublin & SANDERS Sally of Jaffrey int 4 Sep 1826 rept from Dublin

GOWING Joseph of Dublin & FAIRBANKS Hepisibath of Dublin int 27 Oct 1807 rept from Dublin

GRANT George of Lanesborough M & HARRIMAN Molley Wid of Plaistow int 27 Apr 1793 rept from Plaistow

GREEN John of Sandown & DOW Mehitebel of Plaistow int 12 Mar 1781 rept from Plaistow

GREEN Wiliam of Plymouth & KIMBALL Harriet of Concord int 10 Mar 1828 rept from Plymouth

GREENOUGH A C of Concord & SANBORN Maria L of Canterbury int 15 Mar 1845 rept from Canterbury

GREENOUGH Joseph of Boston MA & KELLEY Elizabeth of Hopkinton int 13 Dec 1833 rept from Hopkinton

GREENOUGH Joseph of Hopkinton & STANWOOD Lydia of Hopkinton int 25 Apr 1836 rept from Hopkinton

GREENWOOD Jackson of Dublin & GOWIN Eleanor of Dublin int 11 Mar 1818 rept from Dublin

GRIFFIN John of Chichester & SARGENT Clarenda of Chichester int 7 Jan 1854 rept from Chichester
GROVER Henry of Millbury MA & GROVER Sarah E of Durham int 24 Jul 1862 rept from Durham
GUTTERSON James of Atkinson & EATON Sarah of Haverhill MA int 31 Aug 1795 rept from Atkinson
GUTTERSON James of Atkinson & EATON Sarah of Haverhill MA int 31 Aug 1795 rept from Atkinson
HADLEY Thomas of Goffstown & SARGENT Phebe of Plaistow int 23 Mar 1796 rept from Plaistow
HAGER John C of Manchester & TUFTS Sophionia of Concord int 4 Sep 1840 rept from Manchester
HALE Alonzo of New Chester & FOLLANSBEE Anne of New Chester int 14 Dec 1828 rept from New Chester
HALE Benjamin of Rindge & PIERCE Miriam of Jaffrey int 10 Oct 1812 rept from Rindge
HALE Nathan of Rindge & WHITCOMB Sarah of Rindge int 24 May 1809 rept from Rindge
HALL John of Allenstown & BROWN Susan P of Candia int 17 Aug 1851 rept from Candia
HALL Peter of Chester & ATWOOD Lois of Haverhill int 15 Feb 1774 rept from Chester
HALL Thomas of Plaistow & CHASE Elizabeth of Haverhill MA int 12 Jul 1781 rept from Plaistow
HAM Daniel of Barrington & BICKFORD Sarah of Rochester int 12 Mar 1829 rept from Barrington
HAM Daniel Jr of Barrington & BICKFORD Sarah of Rochester int 12 Mar 1829 rept from Barrington
HANAFORD John of Northfield & FLANDERS Nancy of Concord int 15 Nov 1830 rept from Northfield
HAND Orre of Albany VT & MCCOY Eliza of Bow int 9 Jan 1844 rept from Bow
HARDY Benjamin 3rd of Hopkinton & PUTNEY Lydia of Hopkinton int 5 Sep 1835 rept from Hopkinton
HARDY William G of Hopkinton & MORGAN Priscilla M of Hopkinton int 2 Apr 1838 rept from Hopkinton
HARIMAN Joseph Lt of Plaistow & HUNKINS Moley of Haverhill MA int 21 Nov 1801 rept from Plaistow
HARRIMAN Benjamin of Plaistow & PERRY Hannah of Haverhill MA int 6 Nov 1798 rept from Plaistow
HARRIMAN Benjamin of Plaistow & PERRY Hannah of Haverhill MA int 20 Nov 1798 rept from Plaistow
HARRIMAN Benjamin of Plaistow & CHANEY Mary of Plaistow int 10 Jan 1791 rept from Plaistown

HARRIMAN James of Plaistow & HARRIMAN Abigial of Plaistow int 23 Jan 1799 rept from Plaistow

HARRIMAN John of Plaistow & DOW Moley of Plaistow int 19 May 1784 rept from Plaistow

HARRIMAN Joseph of Plaistow & HEATH Abigial of Plaistow int 13 Oct 1772 rept from Plaistow

HARRIMAN Peter of Plaistow & PLUMMER Lydia of Plaistow int 27 Nov 1778 rept from Plaistow

HARRIS H D Jr of Chicago IL & DENNISON Jennie A of Enfield int 19 Mar 1867 rept from Enfield

HARTFORD John H of Dover & HAYES Elizabeth S of Dover int 12 Jul 1850 rept from Dover

HARVEY Charles of Nottingham & LANGLEY Sophronia of Durham int 26 Jan 1861 rept from Durham

HARVEY Daniel of Nottingham & COVERS Sarah of Concord int 10 Mar 1835 rept from Nothingham

HASTTINE Jonathan of Springfield & WEBSTER Esther S of Hooksett int 21 Sep 1843 rept from Hooksett

HAYNES Oliver S of Candia & LANY Lydia W of Candia int 18 Mar 1849 rept from Candia

HAZELTON Richard of Westmortland & BARKER Mehitabel of Pelham int 27 Jan 1787 rept from Pelham

HAZEN Moses of Haverhill & JACKMAN Jemima of Plaistow int 12 Dec 1784 rept from Plaistow

HEALEY Benjamin of Raymond & STEPHEN Sarah of Raymond int 29 Jun 1802 rept from Raymond

HEALY Nathan of ? & FROOG ? of ? int 30 Oct 1751 rept from Plymouth

HEALY Warren I of Candia & TAYLOR Elizabeth of Candia int 1 Apr 1849 rept from Candia

HEATH Daniel S of Conway & DAVIDSON Hana of Conway int 28 Nov 1831 rept from Conway

HEATH David of Raymond & CLIFFORD Tabitta of Raymond int 4 Oct 1802 rept from Raymond

HEATH Enoch of Plaistow & STEVENS Elizabeth of Plaistow int 5 Mar 1783 rept from Plaistow

HEATH Isaac of Plaistow & HALL Elizabeth of Plaistow int 10 Oct 1768 rept from Plaistow

HEATH Job of Plaistow & STEVENS Susanna of Plaistow int 22 Jan 1771 rept from Plaistow

HEATH Jonathan of Plaistow & CARLETON Marrian of Plaistow int 13 Oct 1778 rept from Plaistow

HEATH Lewis of Bristol & EDWARDS Sally W of Bristol int 13 Apr 1832 rept from Bristol

HEATH Nathaniel of Plaistow & PEASLEE ? of Plaistow int 12 Feb 1798 rept from Plaistow

HEMPHILL J D of New London & LITTLEFIELD S S of Grantham int 14 Oct 1857 rept from New London

HENRY George of Hollis & GILMORE Mary Ann of Jaffrey int 3 Nov 1806 rept from Hollis

HERBERT C D Rev of Mont Vernon & FLANDERS Sarah A of Durham int 19 Sep 1853 rept from Mont Vernon

HERBERT Charles D of Mt Vernon & FLANDERS Sarah A of Durham int 2 Sep 1853 rept from Durham

HERSEY Nathaniel of New Chester & WADLEIGH Achsak of New Chester int 18 May 1828 rept from New Chester

HEWIN Otis of Durham & DAME Charlotte of Durham int 12 Jan 1861 rept from Durham

HOISE Haselton of Loudon & PALMER Belinda of Lowell MA int 25 May 1849 rept from Loudon

HOLT Daniel 2nd of Pembroke & LEAVITT Hannah of Candia int 22 Oct 1848 rept from Candia

HOLT Simeon of Wilton & BROOKS Esther of Jaffrey int 9 Mar 1801 rept from Wilton

HOLT William H of Loudon & VIRGIN Eliza of Concord int 21 Aug 1835 rept from

HOOK George C of Sandown & BARTHOLOMEN Hearriett of Sandown int 17 Mar 1863 rept from Sandown

HOYT Ebenzer of Grafton & CLEMENT Abigail of Atkinson int 26 Nov 1790 rept from Atkinson

HOYT Ethan of Hopkinton & SCALES Emily of Hopkinton int 12 Feb 1834 rept from Hopkinton

HOYT Henry N of Henniker & HOYT Olive P of Henniker int 5 Mar 1866 rept from Henniker

HUBBARD John H of Plaistow & SMITH Salley of Plaistow int 26 Aug 1799 rept from Plaistow

HUSE James of Plaistow & AYER Abigial of Plaistow int 29 Mar 1768 rept from Plaistow

HUTCHENS Richard of Hampstead & BRADLEY Patty of Plaistow int 22 Mar 1802 rept from Plaistow

HUTCHINSON E D of Derry & WOOD Elviar of Derry int 19 Mar 1866 rept from Derry

INGALLS Moses of Atkinson & EATON Betty of Haverhill int 12 Sep 1781 rept from Atkinson

JACKMAN Noah of Plaistow & NOYES Prudence of Plaistow int 1 Dec 1790 rept from Plaistow

JAMES Andrew D of Lee & BUNKER Lillis of Durham int 22 Feb 1847 rept from Lee

JAMES Andrew D of Durham & BUNKER Lilles of Durham int 27 Feb 1847 rept from Durham

JAQUITH Collins H of Chester & TOWERS Merriam of Peterborough int 12 Mar 1816 rept from Peterborough

JEFFERS John of Plaistow & FOSTER Cyvil of Plaistow int 10 Jul 1776 rept from Plaistow

JENKINS Ephraim of Madbury & JACKSON Abbie of Durham int 20 Nov 1854 rept from Durham

JENKINS Ephraim of Madbury & JACKSON Abby T of Durham int 21 Nov 1854 rept from Madbury

JENKINS John S of Lee & OTIS Maria of Newmarket int 18 Nov 1865 rept from Lee

JENNINGS Thoedore of Waverly NY & SMITH Almira of Durham int 7 Sep 1853 rept from Durham

JEWEL Alvin of Winchester & PIERCE Kezia of Jaffrey int 2 Feb 1806 rept from Winchester

JOFLIN Josiah of Hopkinton & FISK Mary of Dublin int 16 Feb 1805 rept from Dublin

JOHNSON John of Hampstead & EMERSON Ruth of Haverhill int 10 Jan 1772 rept from Hampstead

JOHNSON Lewis of Handock & DINSMORE Jane of Jaffrey int 20 Dec 1836 rept from Handcock

JOHNSON Noah of Hampstead & JEFFERS Mary of Hampstead int 5 Feb 1781 rept from Hampstead

JOHNSON Noah of Hampstead & JEFFERS Moley of Plaistow int 12 Feb 1781 rept from Plaistow

JOHNSON William of Plaistow & CHANEY Sarah of Plaistow int 10 Oct 1770 rept from Plaistow

JOHNSON William of Epping & CIFFORD Sarah J of Epping int 6 Oct 1856 rept from Epping

JOHNSON Zacheriah of Salem & WHITTAKER Esther of Salem int 2 Jun 1768 rept from Plaistow

JONES Frank M of Lee & STEVENS Etta of Boston MA int 12 Apr 1872 rept from Lee

JONES Richard H of Gilmanton & VARNEY Anna J of Gilmanton int 26 Apr 1841 rept from Gilmanton

JONSON Jonathan of Plaistow & BRYANT Anna of Plaistow int 12 Jun 1780 rept from Plaistow

JUDKINS Seth of Bow & ABBOTT Phebe of Concord int 17 Jan 1831 rept from Bow

JUNKINS Millville of Allentown & FERNALD Susan of Madbury int 24 Dec 1861 rept from Newmarket

KELLEY George of Madbury & STACKPOLE Annie of Madbury int 6 Jan 1867 rept from Madbury

KELLEY George W of Durham & STACKPOLE Annie L of Durham int 16 Jan 1867 rept from Durham
KENT Eben Jr of Durham & NUTE Annie M of Durham int 2 Oct 1858 rept from Durham
KEZAR Samuel of Haverhill MA & STEVENS Lucy of Plaistow int 25 Oct 1781 rept from Plaistow
KIMBALL Alvah of Dunstable & MARDEN Lydia of Dunstable int 14 May 1832 rept from Nashua
KIMBALL David of Pembroke & CLEMENT Mehitable of Haverhill MA int 12 Dec 1774 rept from Pembroke
KIMBALL George O of Loudon & WATSON Elizabeth of Chichester int 4 Jun 1862 rept from Loudon
KIMBALL Jonathan of Pembroke & EATON Salley of Plaistow int 28 Mar 1801 rept from Plaistow
KIMBALL Joshua of Plaistow & NOYES Betty of Plaistow int 9 Jan 1776 rept from Plaistow
KIMBALL Nathaniel of Plaistow & KNIGHT Sally of Atkinson int 1 May 1803 rept from Plaistow
KIMBALL Nathaniel of Plaistow & SAWYER Susanna of Haverhill MA int 26 May 1772 rept from Plaistow
KIMBALL William Jr of Rindge & SHED Ruth of Rindge int 23 Feb 1820 rept from Rindge
KNIGHT Benjamin of Landraff & JACKMAN Sarah of Plaistow int 1 Jan 1787 rept from Landraff
LADD William D of Candia & LANG Lucinda of Candia int 4 May 1851 rept from Candia
LAKE Ira of Rindge & WELLINGTON Adaline of Rindge int 1 May 1825 rept from Rindge
LANCASTER Samuel of Marborough & MOODY Lucy A of Manchester int 8 Apr 1850 rept from Manchester
LANCASTER Samuel T of Lowell & MOODY Lucy of Manchester int 22 Apr 1850 rept from Milford
LANE Isaac of Raymond & DAVIS Joanna of Raymond int 4 Dec 1803 rept from Raymond
LANE Jonathan of Raymond & EMERSON Susanna of Raymond int 16 Jun 1785 rept from Raymond
LANE Samuel of Lee & DURGIN Susan of Nottingham int 27 Sep 1860 rept from Nottingham
LANE Samuel of Lee & DURGIN Susan of Nottingham int 27 Sep 1860 rept from Lee
LANG Gilman C of Nashua & BARKER Sarah Ann of Candia int 9 Apr 1848 rept from Candia
LANG Isaiah of Candia & LADD Martha A of Raymond int 13 Aug 1848 rept from Candia

LANG Jacob B of Candia & BROWN Adaline R of Candia int 3 Oct 1852 rept from Candia

LANGLEY George E of Durham & PALMER Lydia of Durham int 16 Oct 1861 rept from Durham

LANGMAID Alonzo of Lee & WIGGINS Isella of Lee int 28 Jan 1866 rept from Lee

LAW John of Temple & DEAN Susanna of Jaffrey int 29 Sep 1810 rept from Temple

LAWRENCE Joseph F of Lee & PEASE Sarah F of Meredith int 29 Oct 1858 rept from Lee

LAWRENCE Smith of Meredith & WILSON Maranna of New Boston int 9 Feb 1829 rept from New Boston

LAWRENCE Smith of Meredith & WILSON Maranda of Meredith int 17 Jan 1830 rept from Meredith

LEAVIT John of Candia & SHANNON Hannah of Candia int 6 Aug 1803 rept from Raymond

LEAVITT Thomas of Raymond & BLASDEL Lucy of Raymond int 26 Sep 1803 rept from Raymond

LEE John of Barrington & LEATHERS Clairssa of Barrington int 5 Jul 1829 rept from Barrington

LESLIE Samuel H of Warner & CLARK Emaline of Warner int 16 Nov 1861 rept from Warner

LEWIS Rufus Esq of New Hampton & SMITH Sally of New Hampton int 23 Sep 1828 rept from New Hampton

LIBBEY Abram of Pembroke & HILDRETH Jane E of Pembroke int 11 Jul 1837 rept from Pembroke

LITTLE Enoch of Atkinson & NOYES Sally of Atkinson int 8 Dec 1828 rept from Atkinson

LITTLE Jonathan of Hampstead & HALE Maribak of Plaistow int 27 Mar 1773 rept from Plaistow

LITTLE Jonathan of Hampstead & FARNHAM Meribam of Hampstead int 2 Apr 1793 rept from Hampstead

LITTLE Samuel of Atkinson & BOND Sally of Atkinson int 2 May 1828 rept from Atkinson

LITTLE Thomas B of Boscawen & CUTLER Nettie M of Boscawen int 7 Sep 1864 rept from Boscawen

LITTLEFIELD Thomas of Kennebunk ME & TWOMBLEY Mary E of Durham int 16 Dec 1857 rept from Durham

LOCKE Simeon of Epsom & PENDEXTER Lydia K of Durham int 5 Apr 1855 rept from Durham

LONG Stephen of Kingstown & BATCHELDER Mehitable of Kingstown int 5 Oct 1778 rept from Kingstown

LOVELL Henry R of Boston & PATTEN Mehitable of Candia int 4 Nov 1849 rept from Candia

LOVERIN Moses H of Springfield & GROSS Nancy L of Springfield int 21 Jul 1851 rept from Springfield

LOVERING Ture of Durham & SMITH Lucy A of Barrington int 24 Jun 1861 rept from Durham

LOWELL Timothy of Mason & CARLTON Olive of Haverhill int 19 Jan 1778 rept from Mason

LUND John Q of Boston MA & PERKINS Sarah of Allenstown int 4 Jan 1858 rept from Allenstown

MARDEN Edward of Candia & DAVIS Mary Ann of Candia int 25 Jul 1852 rept from Candia

MARDEN Mark of Epsom & SILVER Ruth J of Concord int 9 Mar 1840 rept from Epsom

MARDEN Samuel of Epsom & SILVER Deborah of Concord int 8 Mar 1840 rept from Epsom

MARSHAL Silas of Sandown & FELLER Ruth of Sandown int 6 Dec 1791 rept from Sandown

MARSTON Joseph of Gilmanton & LADD Olive Marie of Loudon int 30 Mar 1840 rept from Loudon

MARSTON Joseph B of Gilmanton & LADD Olive Marcia of Loudon int 24 May 1840 rept from Gilmanton

MARTIN Moses of Deerfield & CLIFFORD Betsy of Kensington int 30 Jun 1800 rept from Kensington

MARTIN Nanson C of Dunstable & DICKERSON Mary of New Chester int 4 Feb 1829 rept from New Chester

MASCALLY Stephen of Beverly MA & CHASE Beverly of Loudon int 2 Oct 1830 rept from Loudon

MASCOLL Stephen Jr of Beverly MA & STEVENS Mary of Loudon int 3 Oct 1830 rept from Loudon

MATHES Augustus of Durham & HOITT Rosabelle of Lee int 3 Dec 1867 rept from Durham

MATHES Burham of Durham & STEVENS Elizabeth of Durham int 26 Apr 1862 rept from Durham

MEAD John C of Candia & BUSWELL Clarunda of Chester int 6 Jan 1850 rept from Candia

MEADER John G of Barnstead & TASKER Lydia of Barnstead int 9 Aug 1840 rept from Barnstead

MEGOON Moses Cliffor of Candia & LANE Hannah of Raymond int 8 Sep 1803 rept from Raymond

MERRILL Daniel Y of Candia & HOLT Mary K of Pembroke int 8 Apr 1849 rept from Candia

MERRILL Haskill B Lt of Atkinson & KNIGHT Maria of Atkinson int 3 Aug 1831 rept from Atkinson

MERRILL Samuel of Manchester & CARPENTER Clara A of Concord int 13 Sep 1859 rept from Manchester

MERRILL Steven of Warner & NOYSE Mary of Kingstown int 23 Jul 1792 rept from Kingstown
MERRILL Stevens of Warren & NOYS Mary of Kingston int 19 Jul 1792 rept from Warren
MESSER Silas of Bow & HADLEY Nancy T of Dunbarton int 15 Apr 1841 rept from Dunbarton
MIED Jessa of Jaffrey & BULLARD Mary of Dublin int 25 Mar 1809 rept from Dublin
MILLIKEN Alexander of Sharon & BATES Nancy of Jaffrey int 7 Feb 1803 rept from Sharon
MILLIKIN Alexander of Peterborough & BIXBY Julia of Dublin int 27 Oct 1804 rept from Dublin
MILLS George of Dunbarton & SARGENT Abigial of Dunbarton int 14 Jul 1829 rept from Dunbarton
MOODY Daniel Jr of Raymond & SWAIN Charlotte of Raymond int 12 Mar 1803 rept from Raymond
MOOR Nathan of Sharon & NEWELL Sarah of Jaffrey int 19 Jan 1832 rept from Sharon
MOORE Coffins D of Candia & SARGENT Mary E of Candia int 25 Aug 1850 rept from Candia
MOORE Joseph of Ossipee & BENNETT Martha of So Berwick ME int 12 Feb 1864 rept from Newmarket
MOORE Stephen of Loudon & BERRY Mary Mrs of Loudon int 8 Sep 1866 rept from Loudon
MOORE Willima Cpt of Chester & ABBOTT Judith of Concord int 5 Sep 1835 rept from Chester
MORGAN Asa of Bow & ELLIOT Martha of Bow int 15 Nov 1854 rept from Bow
MORRILL Gilman M of Concord & ELLIOTT Martha J of Bow int 3 Feb 1841 rept from Bow
MORRILL John J of Gilford & SANBORN Nancy of Gilford int 22 Mar 1845 rept from Gilford
MORRISON Abraham of Sanbornton & LIBBEE Mary of Dandia int 28 Oct 1849 rept from Candia
MORRS Josiah Jr of Chester & WEBSTER Lois of Chester int 17 Feb 1773 rept from Chester
MORSE Edmund of Hampstead & EATON Mehitabel of Plaistow int 26 Nov 1800 rept from Hampstead
MORSE Levi of Loudon & POTTER Ann of Loudon int 6 Jan 1828 rept from Loudon
MOULTON William of Northampton & PAGE Molly of Northampton int 9 Oct 1797 rept from Northampton
MOULTON Henry of Hooksett & PAGE Hanah of Hooksett int 9 May 1830 rept from Hooksett

MUZZY Reuben of Dublin & HAMILTON Betsey of Dublin int 7 Feb 1804 rept from Dublin
McCLINTOCK Mark of Hillsboro & BUTMAN Maria of Hillsboro int 24 Oct 1867 rept from Hillsboro
McCONNELL Moses of Pembroke & DOW Rachel of Plaistow int 26 Mar 1781 rept from Pembroke
McCRILLIS John of Nottingham & EMERSON Mary of Durham int 18 May 1862 rept from Durham
McLEOD David of Hill & SARGENT Laventum of Hill int 18 Nov 1865 rept from Hill
McMILLEN Gilbert of Conway & McFARLAND Susan K of Concord int 24 Feb 1838 rept from Conway
NEALLEY Sylvester of Newmarket & HANSON Sarah of Newmarket int 10 Aug 1857 rept from Newmarket
NEEHAM Nicanor of Jaffrey & CUTTER Rhoana of Jaffrey int 8 Mar 1808 rept from Peterborough
NICHOLAS Warren of Loudon & MORRILL Anna of Concord int 18 Sep 1833 rept from Loudon
NORRIS Dudley of Epping & FOGG Ann of Epping int 17 Oct 1839 rept from Epping
NOYES Aaron of Bow & LADD Betty of Goffstown int 3 Aug 1773 rept from Goffstown
NOYES John W of Chester & BOUTON Harriettie of Concord int 16 Jan 1835 rept from Chester
NOYES Joseph of Newbury MA & PEASLEE Ruth of Plaistow int 12 Nov 1776 rept from Plaistow
NOYES Oliver of Plaistow & EATON Mehitabel of Plaistow int 18 Mar 1783 rept from Plaistow
NOYES Tappan W of Warner & FRENCH Sally of Warner int 8 Jan 1827 rept from Warner
NOYES Thomas Cpt of Dorchester & JACKSON Hannah of Concord int 12 Feb 1833 rept from Dorchester
NOYS Favor of Bow & LADD Betty of Goffstown int 26 Jul 1773 rept from Bow
NUDD Benjamin of Wolfeboro & GRIFFIN Mary A of Lee int 6 Apr 1851 rept from Wolfeboro
NUDD Benjamin S of Wolfeboro & GRIFFIN Mary A of Lee int 12 Apr 1851 rept from Lee
ORDWAY Joel of Loudon & WIGGINS Sarah Jane of Loudon int 20 Jan 1858 rept from Loudon
ORDWAY John of Lyndeboro & DOW Mary of Lyndeboro int 9 Mar 1767 rept from Lynberough
ORDWAY John of Lyndeboro & DOW Mary of Plaistow int 10 Mar 1767 rept from Plaistow

ORDWAY Moses of Loudon & CARRIER Mary of Haverhill int 6 Jun 1780 rept from Loudon

OSGOOD Chase of Raymond & CRAM Elizabeth of Raymond int 27 Sep 1800 rept from Raymond

PAGE Daniel of Atkinson & NOYES Dolly of Atkinson int 10 Dec 1792 rept from Atkinson

PAGE David of Raymond & FULLINTON Rachel of Raymond int 25 Oct 1800 rept from Raymond

PAGE Joseph of Lee & LEIGHTON Hannah of Lee int 7 Nov 1849 rept from Lee

PAGE Josiah of Haverhill & PATEE Lydia of Haverhill int 15 Aug 1769 rept from Haverhill

PAGE Moses R of Hooksett & BUNZELL Clymena of Dunbarton int 5 Oct 1820 rept from Hooksett

PAIGE George of Bradford & SILVER Elizabeth of Bradford int 1 May 1849 rept from Bradford

PALMER Aaraon of Hopkinton & GEORGE Sarah of Concord int 23 Dec 1828 rept from Hopkinton

PALMER Joseph of Candia & CARR Batey of Raymond int 17 Oct 1803 rept from Raymond

PALMER Joshua of Raymond & SWEATT Sarah of Raymond int 2 Mar 1801 rept from Raymond

PALMER Thomas of Rye & BLOZO Mehitabel of Greenland int 3 Mar 1773 rept from Greenland

PALMER Thomas A of Candia & DUTTON Abby S of Candia int 25 May 1851 rept from Candia

PALMER William of Greenland & BLAZO Mehitabel of Greenland int 13 Feb 1778 rept from Greenland

PARKER Samuel Cpt of Mason & STEWART Batrex of Mason int 30 Sep 1813 rept from Mason

PARMER James of Bradford & SMITH Abigial of Plaistow int 13 Jan 1795 rept from Plaistow

PARSONS Ebenezer of Durham & TASKER Mary of Strafford int 23 May 1862 rept from Durham

PATRICK Joel Oatis of Fitzwilliam & BRIGHAM Salley of Jaffrey int 21 Oct 1817 rept from Fitzwilliam

PATTEN George H of Candia & POOR Julia G of Candia int 3 May 1852 rept from Candia

PATTEN William of Candia & McCURDY Mary P of Manchester int 2 Oct 1850 rept from Candia

PATTERSON J A of Hopkinton & BOUTON Sarah C of Hopkinton int 11 Nov 1867 rept from Hopkinton

PAYNE William of Cornish & HUGGINS Bridget of Greenland int 3 Mar 1777 rept from Greenland

PEASLEY Edward of New Town & WHITE Abigial of Plaistow int 23 Apr 1778 rept from Plaistow
PEASLEY Nicholas of Dover & TITCOMB Hannah of Dover int 12 Oct 1807 rept from Dover
PEAVEY Hudson of Strafford & YOUNG Hannah of Durham int 23 Nov 1857 rept from Durham
PECKHAM George T of Newmarket & ODELL Caroline E of Durham int 22 Apr 1850 rept from Durham
PERRY Ebenezer of Plaistow & DORRITY Salley of Plaistow int 28 May 1803 rept from Plaistow
PERRY John of Rindge & WESTON Lucy of Rindge int 14 Feb 1820 rept from Rindge
PERRY Wm G of Exeter & FISKE Lucretia of Concord int 13 Aug 1849 rept from Exeter
PICKERING William of Greenland & FABYAN Abigial of Greenland int 16 Dec 1776 rept from Greenland
PIERCE Eliphia of Rindge & HENRY Anna of Rindge int 20 Apr 1815 rept from Rindge
PIERCE Nancy of Peterborough & HOSMER Sewell of Peterborough int 31 Mar 1823 rept from Peterborough
PIKE Frederick of Newmarket & SMALL Mary of Newmarket int 27 Nov 1856 rept from Newmarket
PIKE Robert Jr of Brookfield & JOHNSON Elizabeth of Durham int 4 Mar 1854 rept from Durham
PILSBURY Caleb of Candia & DOLLOFF Elizabeth of Raymond int 8 Oct 1803 rept from Raymond
PIPER Ruben of Dublin & GOWING Anna of Dublin int 30 Mar 1817 rept from Dublin
POLLY Amos S of Hooksett & ROWE Evaline F of Candia int 11 Jul 1852 rept from Candia
POOR Daniel Jr of Plaistow & NOYES Sarah of Plaistow int 26 Dec 1764 rept from Plaistow
POOR Jonathan of Atkinson & KIMBALL Sarah of Plaistow int 15 Mar 1785 rept from Plaistow
POTTER Josiah of Fitzwilliam & WOSTER Sarah of Jaffrey int 8 Aug 1810 rept from Fitzwilliam
PREFSE Peter of Kingston & MOULTON Elizabeth of Sandown int 29 May 1786 rept from Kingstown
PRESCOTT James W of Portsmouth & CUNNINGHAM Mary E of Portsmouth int 23 Dec 1827 rept from Portsmouth
PRESCOTT John H of Gilmanton & MESERVE Sall C of Northwood int 31 Mar 1820 rept from Northwood
PRICE Harold of Barrington & WOODMAN Sarah A of Lee int 29 Oct 1870 rept from Lee

PRICE Jacob of Alstead & PRICE Betsy of Jaffrey int 13 Jan 1818 rept from Alstead

PROCTOR Hail of Dunstable & HAYNES Louis of Dunstable int 15 May 1879 rept from Nashua

RAMSEY Hugh of Manchester & WORTHLEY Angeline of Manchester int 24 Mar 1855 rept from Manchester

RAND Stephen of Durham & EMERSON Saraha of Durham int 4 Jul 1863 rept from Durham

RANDELL Jeremiah of Lee & BARTLETT Susan of Lee int 10 Apr 1862 rept from Lee

REED W Tilly of Acworth & BYAM Deliverance of Jaffrey N int 27 Dec 1810 rept from Acworth

REMICK Daniel of Kennebunk ME & TWOMBLEY Annie of Durham int 4 Jun 1854 rept from Durham

RICHARDS John Jr of Rindge & PAGE Candace of Jaffrey int 25 Sep 1821 rept from Rindge

RICHARDSON Abijah of Dublin & HAY Mary of Dublin int 21 Apr 1819 rept from Dublin

RICHARDSON Augustus of Madbury & DAVIS Lydia P of Madbury int 5 Mar 1848 rept from Madbury

RICHARDSON Augustus of Dover & DAVIS Lydia P of Madbury int 12 Mar 1848 rept from Dover

RICHARDSON Eliphalet of Canaan & PLUMMER Abi of Plaistow int 20 Feb 1794 rept from Plaistow

RICHARDSON Enoch of Hampstead & GREENOUGH Eunice of Atkinson int 15 Aug 1780 rept from Atkinson

RICHARDSON John A of Durham & MURDOCK Frances J of Concord int 3 Feb 1835 rept from Durham

RICHARDSON Moses of Hampstead & DAM Martha of Hampstead int 3 Nov 1790 rept from Hampstead

RILBURY Henry W of Andover & HERSEY Sophrona of Hill int 17 Mar 1862 rept from Andover

ROACH Guy Lt of Hooksett & NICHOLS Ann of Hooksett int 10 Mar 1829 rept from Hooksett

ROBERTS John of Candia & BARTLETT Loraine of Raymond int 2 Oct 1850 rept from Candia

ROBERTS Sewall T of Alton & BEACHAM A E of Wolfborough int 24 May 1862 rept from Amherest

ROBIE Charles F of Candia & CARR Abby Ann of Candia int 26 Apr 1852 rept from Candia

ROBINSON Thomas of Candia & CASS Sarah of Candia int 9 Nov 1851 rept from Candia

ROGERS Alfred of Boston MA & MESERVE Lucinda of Barrington int 27 Nov 1827 rept from Barrington

ROLFE William of Haverhill & HARRIMAN Levina of Plaistow int 10 Apr 1770 rept from Plaistow
ROLLINS Joseph of Dublin & RUSSELL Mary of Dublin int 12 Sep 1819 rept from Dublin
ROTCH Francis O of Chilmark MA & WILKINS Elizabeth of Derring int 20 Jul 1845 rept from Derring
ROWE Andrew M of Hooksett & KEMP Mary of Candia int 22 Aug 1847 rept from Candia
ROWE David P of Candia & PERKINS Sarah E of Manchester int 2 Jun 1850 rept from Candia
ROWE John Jr of New Chester & MURRAY Jane of New Chester int 17 Feb 1828 rept from New Chester
ROWE Smith of Andover & SANBORN Caroline of Andover int 18 Dec 1835 rept from Andover
ROWELL Edmund R of Candia & REYNOLDS Olive of Candia int 5 Nov 1848 rept from Candia
RUSSELL Leonard of Bow & HALL Sarah of Concord int 10 Mar 1829 rept from Bow
SAMSON Oliver of Ashburnham & HOWE Lydia of Rindge int 24 Oct 1820 rept from Rindge
SANBORN Abraham of Kingstown & DOW Martha of Kingstown int 1 Sep 1789 rept from Kingstown
SANBORN Moses of Epping & FOGG Nancy of Raymond int 20 Mar 1801 rept from Raymond
SANBORN Moses of Epping & FOGG Nancy of Raymond int 9 Mar 1807 rept from Epping
SANBORN Peter of Sandown & DOW Martha of Sandown int 9 Oct 1775 rept from Kingstown
SANBORN Ture Jr of Chichester & SEAVEY Ruth L of Concord int 26 Nov 1857 rept from Chichester
SANDERS John of ? & LACY Sally of Jaffrey int 10 Apr 1826 rept from Dublin
SANDERS Robert Lt of Ossipee & LOCKE Abigial of Concord int ? rept from Ossipee
SANDS John of Jaffrey & JONES Ruthey of Dublin int 13 Jul 1812 rept from Dublin
SARGENT Hazen 2nd of New Chester & DUSTIN Eliza Ann of New Chester int 28 Feb 1826 rept from New Chester
SARGENT John B of Pittsfield & BROWN Harriett of Pittsfield int 14 Jan 1851 rept from Pittsfield
SARGENT Joshua of Amesbury MA & POLLARD Polley of Plaistow int 2 Jul 1789 rept from Plaistow
SARGENT Moses of Candia & VARNUM Enlalia of Candia int 11 Apr 1852 rept from Candia

SARGENT Starling Cpt of Allenstown & DAVIS Mehitable Mrs of Amesbury MA int 25 Nov 1785 rept from Allenstown
SARGENT Zebediak of Haverhill MA & STEVENS Moley of Plaistow int 18 Dec 1780 rept from Plaistow
SAVAGE William of Greenfield & HODGE Joanna of Jaffrey int 11 Nov 1813 rept from Greenfield
SAWYER Chester N of Dover & BALL Ella M of Dover int 7 Dec 1861 rept from Dover
SAWYER H E of Francestown & FRENCH Julia A of Candia int 9 Nov 1851 rept from Candia
SAWYER John of Hampstead & TOWNSEND Susannah of Hampstead int 1 Mar 1790 rept from Hampstead
SAWYER John of Plaistow & KNIGHT Molley of Kingstown int 15 Nov 1791 rept from Kingstown
SAWYER Moses of Sharon & HATHORN Hipsebeth of Jaffrey int 22 Nov 1795 rept from Sharon
SAWYER Stephen of Hampstead & HEATH Polly of Hampstead int 9 Mar 1709 rept from Hampstead
SAWYER Stephen of Plaistow & HEATH Moley of Hampstead int 4 Mar 1789 rept from Plaistow
SHATTUCK Enos of Plymouth & SHUTE Erebecca of Concord int 28 Aug 1828 rept from Plymouth
SHAW Andrew of Kensington & GILES Mary E of Durham int 9 Jun 1867 rept from Kensington
SHAW Charles C of Boston & PICKERING Sarah A H of Durham int 5 Jun 1848 rept from Durham
SHAW Nathaniel of Raymond & WATSON Hanah of Nottingham int 5 Jun 1802 rept from Raymond
SILSBY Thom of Walpole & BURNHAM Mary A of Boston MA int 26 Oct 1847 rept from Walpole
SIMONS Harrison of Weare & FOSTER Lydia Ann of Concord int 25 Oct 1846 rept from Weare
SIMPSOM Lafayette Dr of Hopkinton & COLBY Arline of Henniker int 28 Dec 1856 rept from Hopkinton
SLATE Lyman of Manchester & WORTHEN Abby B of Candia int 2 Oct 1850 rept from Candia
SLEEPER James M of Epping & SMART Abby S of Epping int 13 Oct 1851 rept from Epping
SMART Amos of Durham & GAGE Elizabeth M of Boston MA int 28 Nov 1860 rept from Durham
SMITH French R of Candia & QUIMBY Laura of Candia int 25 May 1851 rept from Candia
SMITH Albert of Peterborough & STEARNS Tidilea of Jaffrey int 11 Feb 1828 rept from Peterborough

SMITH John of Durham & SEAVY Ann of Rye int 2 Apr 1776 rept from Durham
SMITH John A of Loudon & BROWN Sarah of Loudon int 14 May 1854 rept from Loudon
SMITH John C of Franklin & SHAW Vesta S of Franklin int 4 Dec 1861 rept from Franklin
SMITH John H of Candia & BARKER Mary B of Candia int 15 Apr 1849 rept from Candia
SMITH Joseph of Plaistow & CHANEY Mary of Plaistow int 10 Jan 1791 rept from Plaistow
SMITH Joseph of Plaistow & SAYER Moley of Plaistow int 1 Dec 1784 rept from Plaistow
SMITH Joseph Jr of Plaistow & HEATH Nabey of Plaistow int 2 Mar 1798 rept from Plaistow
SMITH Samuel of Durham & DEMERITT Ann of Durham int 26 Nov 1856 rept from Durham
SNELL Alfred of Lee & PAGE Emily of Lee int 19 Jun 1853 rept from Lee
SNOW James of Haverhill MA & HALL Ruth of Plaistow int 25 Sep 1778 rept from Plaistow
SOMERS Alfred of Rye & LONG Patience of Greenland int 17 Mar 1774 rept from Greenland
SPAULDING David of Jaffrey & FOSTER Hannah of Fitzwilliam int 10 Apr 1821 rept from Fitzwilliam
SPAULDING Rueben of Jaffrey & PRATT Polly of Dublin int 12 Nov 1795 rept from Dublin
SPAULDING Soami of Temple & MARSHALL Esther of Jaffrey int 22 Sep 1818 rept from Temple
STARBIRD Stephen of Durham & DAVIS Caroline of Durham int 23 Nov 1851 rept from Durham
STEARNS William of Temple & CHADWICK Sally of Temple int 19 Oct 1818 rept from Temple
STEBBENS Hiel of Winchester & BLODGETT Lucinda of Jaffrey int 10 Apr 1822 rept from Winchester
STEPHEN William of Raymond & HEREMAN Sarah of Raymond int 12 Nov 1801 rept from Raymond
STEVENS Calef of Hampstead & HARRIMAN Elizabeth of Hampstead int 16 Feb 1791 rept from Hampstead
STEVENS David Jr of Plaistow & STEVENS Betty of Plaistow int 25 Oct 1782 rept from Plaistow
STEVENS John W of Gilford & TOWLE Mario of Laconia int 3 Dec 1857 rept from Manchester
STEVENS Joshua of Plaistow & SLOWLEY Sarah of Plaistow int 14 Dec 1790 rept from Plaistow

STEVENS Paul of Plaistow & HARRIMANA Moley of Plaistow int 15 Jan 1799 rept from Plaistow
STEVENS Soloman of Plaistow & EATON Hannah of Plaistow int 7 Jul 1784 rept from Plaistow
STICKNEY David of Lancaster & HOIT Betsey of New Chester int 1 Oct 1826 rept from New Chester
STICKNEY John of Jaffrey & GRAGG Phebe of Rindge int 1 May 1812 rept from Rindge
STILSON Daniel of Newmarket & DAVIS Ellen of Newmarket int 17 Apr 1855 rept from Newmarket
STIMPSON Richard of Durham & WENTWORTH Sally of Barrington int 24 Aug 1822 rept from Barrington
STONE Jonathan of Fitzwilliam & MILLER Sophia of Jaffrey int 11 Sep 1809 rept from Fitzwilliam
STONE Samuel of Fitzwilliam & GREEN Hannah of Fitzwilliam int 28 Nov 1803 rept from Fitzwilliam
STRAW John of Plaistow & HALE Hannah of Atkinson int 22 Mar 1775 rept from Plaistow
STREETER Thomas of Rindge & LOCKE Paulina of Jaffrey int 12 Oct 1826 rept from Rindge
STUART Samuel of New Town & SAWYER Polly of Plaistow int 4 Sep 1802 rept from Plaistow
SWEAT Joseph of Kingstown & SEVERANCE Salley of Kingstown int 11 May 1795 rept from Kingstown
SWEET George J of E Andover & CALLEY Abby S of E Andover int 25 Jan 1864 rept from Andover
SWEET Moses of Manchester & RICE Mary A of Manchester int 15 Aug 1845 rept from Manchester
SWEETSER Isaiah of Bennington & QUIGLEY Marsh of Francestown int 4 Dec 1861 rept from Francestown
SWEETSER Isiah W of Bennington & QUIGLEY Mary of Francestown int 21 Oct 1848 rept from Bennington
TAPEN S S of Conway & DANA Hannah of Conway int 11 Jan 1851 rept from Conway
TARBOX Mark of Stoddard & ABBOTT Susan of Concord int 12 May 1830 rept from Stoddard
TASKER Andrew B of Northwood & SNELL Louisa N of Lee int 30 Sep 1862 rept from Northwood
TASKER Ezra of Northwood & HILLIARD Eunice L of Concord int 3 Nov 1859 rept from Northwood
TAYLOR Elivis of Jaffrey & BULLARD Abigial of Mason int 1 Mar 1831 rept from Mason
TENNEY Sarah R of Weare & WHITAKER Peter of Weare int 24 Feb 1862 rept from Weare

TEUXBURY Isaac of Hampstead & HALE Susanna of Hampstead int 14 Feb 1792 rept from Hampstead

THAYER William of Manchester & ALLISON Sarah A of Concord int 18 Jan 1843 rept from Manchester

THOMPSON Job of Lee & DEMERITT Emma of Lee int 13 Apr 1856 rept from Lee

THOMPSON Solomon of Barrington & HAM Nancy of Barrington int 30 Nov 1823 rept from Barrington

THURSTON Ebenezer of Hopkinton & MERRILL Molly of Hopkinton int 16 Dec 1799 rept from Hopkinton

TICKERING William of Newington & FABYAN Abigial of Newington int 16 Dec 1776 rept from Newington

TILDEN Joseph of Hanover & VIRGIN Mary E of Concord int 27 Sep 1842 rept from Hanover

TILTON Samuel of Raymond & DUDLEY Susanna of Raymond int 5 Jan 1800 rept from Raymond

TINNO Alma of Rindge & REED Hepzibah of Rindge int 2 May 1813 rept from Rindge

TODD John of Freeport MA & TODD Jean of Raymond int 24 Apr 1802 rept from Raymond

TOWLE Jonathan of Andover & EMERY Almira of Loudon int 18 Apr 1842 rept from Loudon

TOWLE Parker M of Candia & BROWN Hannah R of Candia int 7 Jan 1849 rept from Candia

TOWNE Joshua of Rindge & CHADWICK Polley of Jaffrey int 14 Apr 1810 rept from Rindge

TRULL Phenihas Dr of Newmarket & JENESS Nancy of Raymond int 6 Jul 1805 rept from Raymond

TUCKER Cyrus of Loudon & HOIT Fanny Jane of Concord int 30 Sep 1835 rept from Loudon

TUCKER Stephen of Raymond & ROBIE Nancy of Raymond int 27 Aug 1806 rept from Raymond

TUFFS Charles A of Dover & SOUTHEN Anne B of Concord int 15 Apr 1848 rept from Dover

TURNER Adam J of Nashua & SHEDD Mary J of Merrimack int 26 Sep 1853 rept from Nashua

TWIP John of New Boston & TWIP Arcenith of Jaffrey int 3 Feb 1825 rept from New Boston

TWITCHELL Gerham Jr of Dublin & BAILEY Sally of Jaffrey int 12 Nov 1812 rept from Dublin

TWITCHELL John of Dublin & PARKER Lucey of Rindge int 2 Feb 1810 rept from Dublin

TWITCHELL John of Dublin & PARKER Susan of Rindge int 2 Feb 1818 rept from Rindge

TWITCHELL Samuel Jr of Dublin & BAILEY Abigial of Jaffrey int 16 Jun 1813 rept from Dublin
TYLER Lucien of Hopkinton & ANSDEN Sarah of Hopkinton int 26 Apr 1852 rept from Hopkinton
UPTON David Jr of Sharon & SCRIPTURE Mary of Nelson int 28 Apr 1826 rept from Nelson
UPTON Eli of Peterborough & UPTON Mary of Sharon int 27 Sep 1825 rept from Peterborough
UPTON Eli Jr of Jaffrey & SNOW Abagail of Jaffrey int 11 May 1809 rept from Peterborough
UPTON Thomas of Peterborough & SNOW Lydia of Jaffrey int 25 Dec 1809 rept from Peterborough
VARNUM James M of Candia & BICKFORD Susank of Lowell MA int 19 Mar 1848 rept from Candia
VITTAM David of Meredith & HALL Mary E of Concord int 27 Nov 1850 rept from Meredith
VOSE George of Amherst & EATON Elise of Hillsboro Bridge int 14 Apr 1804 rept from Amherest
WALLACE Alonzo of Epsom & WHITE Satura of Epsom int 13 Aug 1855 rept from Epsom
WARNER Stephen of Peterborough & LAWRENCE Rebecca of Jaffrey int 6 Sep 1818 rept from Peterborough
WASHBURN David of Roxbury MA & DAVIS Lydia of Bradford int 2 Jun 1849 rept from Bradford
WATERTOWN George of Barrington & TWOMBLY Elizabeth of Barrington int 16 Mar 1828 rept from Barrington
WATSON Joseph H of Hooksett & TOWLE Mary Ann of Candia int 4 Sep 1852 rept from Candia
WEBBER John H of Peterborough & DINSMORE Lucy of Peterborough int 10 Oct 1838 rept from Peterborough
WEBBER Maxamilian of Hopkinton & SWEATT Clarissa of Concord int 20 Nov 1831 rept from Hopkinton
WEBBER Nathaniel of Methuen MA & PEABODY Rebecca of Atkinson int 8 Jul 1775 rept from Atkinson
WEBSTER Jonathan of New Ipswich & STREETER Abigial of Jaffrey int 7 Apr 1828 rept from New Ipswich
WEBSTER Moses K of Lyme & KIMBALL Mary C of Boston MA int 18 Feb 1856 rept from Lyme
WEBSTER William G of Rochester & AMBROSE Susan of Salem int 7 Jun 1829 rept from Rochester
WEEKS J Frank of East Boston Ma & SMITH Lizzie of Meredith int 29 Sep 1854 rept from Meredith
WEEKS James of Columbia & SAWYER Mary F of Columbia int 11 Aug 1856 rept from Columbia

WEEKS Nathan H of Thornton & PHILBRICK Martha of Sanbornton int 29 Jun 1859 rept from Thornton

WELCH Aaron of Kingstown & BRADBURY Betsey of Haverhill East MA int 28 Jul 1788 rept from Kingstown

WELCH Joseph of Kingstown & DOLTON Mary of Plaistow int 29 Sep 1770 rept from Kingstown

WELCH Joseph of Kingstown & POLLAND Mary of Plaistow int 24 Sep 1770 rept from Plaistow

WELCH Samuel of Plaistow & CHANEY Elizabeth of Plaistow int 23 Mar 1776 rept from Plaistow

WELCH Samuel of Plaistow & CHENEY Ann of Plaistow int 14 Jun 1779 rept from Plaistow

WELLS Thomas F of Goffstown & CURRIER Lucy of Goffstown int 17 Aug 1835 rept from Goffstown

WENTHWORTH Hiram S of New Durham & REYNOLDS Hannah of Madbury VT int 28 Oct 1864 rept from Dover

WENTWORTH John 2nd of Somersworth & GOODWIN Stattira of Berwick ME int 15 Nov 1824 rept from Somersworth

WENTWORTH Russell of Rochester & WIGGIN Mary J of Durham int 4 May 1864 rept from Dover

WENTWORTH William of Boston MA & GRIFFITH Martha of Durham int 20 Jan 1849 rept from Durham

WHIGHT Samuel of Peterborough & GOWING Theresa of Dublin int 27 Oct 1807 rept from Dublin

WHITAKER Moses of Salem & DUSTON Mary of Salem int 12 Jan 1792 rept from Salem

WHITCOMB George of Rindge & SMITH Sarah of Jaffrey int 9 Nov 1829 rept from Rindge

WHITCOMB James of Newport & EMERSON Georgia of Barnstead int 5 Mar 1868 rept from Newport

WHITCOMB James of Henniker & HALE Polly of Jaffrey int 14 Dec 1808 rept from Henniker

WHITE Daniel of Bow & CARTER Mary of Concord int 11 Jan 1815 rept from Bow

WHITE John of Plaistow & KIMBALL Elizaabeth of Plaistow int 15 Mar 1785 rept from Plaistow

WHITE Samuel of Peterborough & GOING Thisa of Dublin int 20 Oct 1807 rept from Peterborough

WIGGIN John of Loudon & BATCHELDER Hannah of Loudon int 12 Oct 1854 rept from Loudon

WIGGIN John A of Epping & HANSON Abby S of Epping int 28 Oct 1862 rept from Epping

WIGGINS Andrew of Portsmouth & SWEAT Dorothy of Portsmouth int 1 Aug 1751 rept from Portsmouth

WIGGINS Joseph of Lee & BEARDSLEE Hannah of Salem int 17 Dec 1863 rept from Lee
WIGGINS Joseph N of Dover & MORRISON Jennie N of Madbury int 10 Jun 1867 rept from Madbury
WIGHT Eli of Dublin & CHAPLIN Fanny of Dublin int 31 Dec 1812 rept from Dublin
WIGHT Joel of Dublin & MOOR Mary of Jaffrey int 27 May 1808 rept from Dublin
WILDER Ezra of Jaffrey & HODGE Jerusha Wid of Peterborough int 13 Oct 1804 rept from Peterborough
WILDER James of Peterborough & TURNER Lydia of Jaffrey int 6 Sep 1802 rept from Peterborough
WILDER Joseph of Peterborough & TURNER Susanna of Jaffrey int 10 Jul 1806 rept from Peterborough
WILDER Simson of Peterborough & TURNER Joanna of Jaffrey int 20 Jan 1807 rept from Peterborough
WILLEY Farnum of Newmarket & PIKE Ellin M of Newmarket int 7 Jan 1854 rept from Newmarket
WILLEY Silas of Gilmanton & GREENLEAF Betsy of Raymond int 26 Mar 1802 rept from Gilmanton
WILLIAMS John of Hampstead & STEVENS Alice of Hampstead int 6 Oct 1778 rept from Hampstead
WILLIAMS Thomas of Hampstead & JOHNSON Susanna of Hampstead int 15 Sep 1785 rept from Hampstead
WILLIAMS Washington of Dover & AYER Charlotte of Concord int 18 Feb 1834 rept from Dover
WILLIS Joseph N of Northfield & FLANDERS Sarah of Concord int 15 Apr 1850 rept from Northfield
WILSLOW George W of Epping & SANBORN Harriet of Epping int 21 May 1829 rept from Epping
WILSON Levi T of Lee & BROWN Harriett of Nottingham int 12 May 1858 rept from Newmarket
WINSLOW Jacob of Kingston & SEVERANCE Tryphena of Kingston int 15 Oct 1778 rept from Hawke
WITHAM Walter of Portsmouth & HILARD Mary of Portsmouth int 7 Oct 1747 rept from Portsmouth
WOOD Eben Thurston of Jaffrey & BOYNTON Rebecah of Temple int 26 Jan 1808 rept from Temple
WOODBRIDGE Thomas of New Castle & AYER Lydia of Plaistow int 12 Feb 1778 rept from Plaistow
WOODMAN Dana of New Hampton & WILSON Jane of New Boston int 20 Jan 1834 rept from New Boston
WOODMAN Dana of New Hampton & WILSON Jane of New Boston int 23 Jan 1834 rept from New Boston

WOODWARD Eliphalet of Plaistow & GAGE Martha of Haverhill MA int 28 Jul 1779 rept from Plaistow

WOODWARD Stephen of Plaistow & GAGE Lydia of Haverhill MA int 24 Dec 1782 rept from Plaistow

WOODMAN Jonathan of Candia & LANE Saley of Raymond int 16 Sep 1815 rept from Raymond

WRIGHT Thomas of Portsmouth & MORRIS Deborah of Portsmouth int 3 Sep 1765 rept from Portsmouth

WYMAN Daniel of Amesbury & DAVIS Hannah of Amesbury int 25 Sept 1787 rept from Amesbury

YEARDLEY William of Dublin & BROOKS Rhoda of Jaffrey int 17 Dec 1804 rept from Dublin

YEATON Nathaniel of New Castle & BERRY Hannah of Durham int 12 Mar 1854 rept from Durham

YORK Daniel of Durham & SMART Susan of Durham int 18 Nov 1854 rept from Durham

YOUNG Aaron of Candia & HALL Laura of Candia int 28 Jan 1850 rept from Candia

YOUNG Andrew of Barrington & MILES Susan E of Madbury int 2 May 1853 rept from Madbury

YOUNG Andrew H of Barrington & NILES Susan E of Madbury int 10 May 1853 rept from Barrington

YOUNG Cleazon of Madbury & MESENIE Sophia of Durham int 29 Nov 1817 rept from Durham

YOUNG Edwin of Durham & DREW Lizzie of Durham int 22 Mar 1862 rept from Durham

YOUNG John T of Newmarket & THOMPSON Mary Ann of Newmarket int 24 Nov 1865 rept from Newmarket

WENTWORTH MARRIAGE LICENCES

The following marriage licences were issued at Portsmouth, New Hampshire by Gov. Benning Wentworth (BW), or his successor Gov. John Wentworth (JW), between 1742 and 1776. The licenses are arranged here alphabetically by groom, and give the bride's name, the date of the license, and by whom it was issued. Some of these certificates are numbered while others are not; when the number is known, it is given as the last item in each entry.

ALEN Thomas & BULLOCK Hannah 19 Jun 1765 by BW
ALLEN David & NEWELL Margaret 12 Sep 1775 by JW #349
ASH Gilbert & BLUNT Elizabeth 24 Apr 1769 by JW #555
ATKIN James & TITCOMB Mary 12 Apr 1743 by BW
AUBIN Philip & GREENLIEF Abigail 10 May 1775 by JW #320
BAILEY William & CHASE Anna 6 Jan 1773 by JW #123
BALLINGALL Roger & DAVENPORT Elizabeth 24 Feb 1766 by BW
BARNARD Timothy & BAGLEY Mary 23 May 1774 by JW #5678
BARNES Thomas & DRIVER Hannah 16 Sep 1774 by JW
BARSTOW Michael & CUNINGHAM Agnes 4 Apr 1775 by JW #306
BARTLET Richard & GEORGE Abigail 23 Nov 1769 by JW #746
BARTLET William & LASCOMB Betty 15 Jun 1775 by JW #916
BARTLETT John & GREELEY Hannah 3 May 1773 by JW #152
BATCHELDER John & RAY Mary 27 Aug 1745 by BW
BATTLE Ebenezor & DURANT Nancy 3 Oct 1775 by JW #352
BEAVEANON Alexander & WARNER Mehitable 11 Aug 1774 by JW #242
BEAVER William & PEPPER Mary 6 Oct 1743 by BW
BENNETT Spencer & CARR Sarrah 2 Jan 1766 by BW
BICKFORD Thomas & VISCOUNT Abigail 12 Nov 1746 by BW
BLADWIN Samuel & WHITCHER Elizabeth 5 Mar 1752 by BW
BLODGETT Caleb & WAYMAN Elizabeth 6 Aug 1744 by BW
BOARDMAN Francis & HODGS Mary 6 Sep 1774 by JW #249
BOARDMAN Thomas & BROWN Hannah 6 Dec 1775 by JW #358
BOARDMAN Thomas & MORSE Anna 2 Aug 1775 by JW

BROWN Benjamin & CHATMAN Martha 16 Jul 1770 by JW
BROWN Edmund & SANBORN Mary 16 Jul 1746 by BW
BROWN Nathaniel & FOX Mary 4 Sep 1767 by JW
BROWNE William & SAVAGE Margarett 7 Jun 1769 by JW #587
BUROS John & RIMINGATON Mary 21 May 1774 by JW #227
BYRN Simon & VUALPY Hannah 26 Apr 1775 by JW
CALL Daniel & SWAN Sarah 11 Sep 1746 by BW
CAMPBELL Andrew & ARCHER Sarah 31 Aug 1769 by JW #644
CARREL John & ROADS Jane 7 Aug 1744 by BW
CHACE John & GOVE Rachel 5 Dec 1751 by BW
CHASE Somerby & TITCOMB Sarah 3 Nov 1774 by JW #5794
CHURCHILL Joseph & NORTHY Anna 14 Jul 1768 by JW #324
CLARK Benjamin & FARRAR Anna 6 Dec 1769 by JW #754
CLARK William & COLLINS Mary 17 Jun 1746 by BW
CLEMENT Benjamin & PILSBURY Sarah 16 Feb 1764 by BW
CLEVELAND Stephen & JEFFRY Margaret 27 Oct 1772 by JW #4806
CLOUSTON Thomas & COLLINS Elizabeth 24 May 1769 by JW #576
COLES John & BOHON Anne 21 Oct 1769 by JW #716
COLLINS Richard & CROOMS Eleanor 15 Nov 1768 by JW #429
COLLSON Adam & BRIDGE Christian 10 Nov 1774 by JW
CONEN Thomas & ATTWOODEE Sarah 8 Jun 1765 by BW
CONERY William & GROVER Elizabeth 8 Dec 1747 by BW
COOK Chandler & CASWELL Mary 25 Sep 1744 by BW
COULBY John & LUNT Betty 19 Jul 1773 by JW #169
CRAVEN Nicholas & HOLMS Bridget 8 Sep 1749 by BW
CROCKER James & MARCH Abigial 10 Apr 1750 by BW
CROSMAN Edward & INGERSELL Polly 12 Oct 1772 by JW #109
DABNEY Nathanael & GARDNER Elizabeth 8 Mar 1773 by JW #133
DALESHALL Richard & MILFORD Ann 6 Oct 1748 by BW
DAVIS Benjamin & BOX Sarah 27 Aug 1774 by JW #247
DAVIS Hoen & STOCKMAN Anne 30 Dec 1767 by JW
DAVIS Joseph & HARRIS Martha 12 Sep 1746 by BW
DAVIS Samuel & SWAIN Hannah 11 Nov 1752 by BW
DEAGGCON John Adam & WAIT Sarah 29 Jul 1765 by BW
DEARBORN Levi & SWEET Sarah 27 Mar 1751 by BW
DEARBORN Nathaniel & GODFREY Hannah 13 Feb 1771 by JW #131
DENNIS Frances Borden & GRANT Elizabeth 25 Jul 1774 by JW #238
DENNIS Nathaniel & STANIFORD Mary 10 Apr 1773 by JW #147
DEVERE Joseph & NEWHALL Lydia 17 Jun 1746 by BW

DODGE Thomas & STANFORD Hannah 23 Apr 1770 by JW #850
DOLE Stephen & ENILSEY Abigial 14 Oct 1773 by JW #170
DOW Moses & DOW Elizabeth 3 Nov 1772 by JW #60439
DOWNEE Henry & COOMBS Susanna 28 May 1764 by BW
DWYER William & SMITH Rebecah 4 Apr 1775 by JW #307
EATON William & ARNOL Nancy 24 Jun 1766 by BW
EDWARD Thomas & CRADOCK Ann 22 Jun 1759 by BW
ELIOT Skippes & BLAKE Mjoanna 15 May 1752 by BW
ELLERY William & BARROW Relief 24 Oct 1748 by BW
FARLEY John & DENNIS Sarah 14 Jun 1770 by JW #876
FELENAHIAS Nathan & ORRMAN Elizabeth 12 Dec 1766 by BW
FELLYPLACE Edward & WILLIAMS Jane 18 Jul 1775 by JW #340
FISHER Daniel & DODGE Anna 11 Apr 1775 by JW #309
FLANDERS Hopkins & FITTS Mehitable 9 Nov 1768 by JW #422
FLECH Henry & DOW Phebe 3 May 1756 by BW
FOULLER Solomon & CANT Mary 3 Nov 1774 by JW #254
FRENCH Amos & SWEET Judah 20 Apr 1774 by JW #5658
FRENCH Benjamin & JACKMAN Joanna 4 Oct 1748 by BW
FRENCH Nathaniel & BLANCHARD Sarah 9 Dec 1773 by JW #211
GEORGE Benjamin & JACKSON Sarah 31 Oct 1768 by JW #414
GIGORY William & HARPPER Hannah 29 Sep 1775 by JW #351
GILL William & NEEDHAM Elizabeth 29 Dec 1775 by JW #362
GLOVER John & LEE Fanny 15 Dec 1775 by JW #360
GOALL John & PICKERING Lois 11 May 1772 by JW
GODSILL Hugh & CHENEY Anne 16 Sep 1765 by BW
GOODHUE Joseph & STICKNEY Anna 1 Jan 1773 by JW #121
GOZART John & NICHOLLS Margaret 15 Jul 1773 by JW #168
GRANT James & TUCKER Mary 2 Jul 1764 by BW
GRAVES Mark & BRIANT Sarah 31 Jan 1774 by JW #216
GREENLEAF William & PEARSON Ruth 30 Oct 1744 by BW
GREENOUGH Symond & CHADWICK Abigailo 27 Jul 1748 by BW
GROVES Freeborn & BORVEN Mary 27 Sep 1756 by BW
HALE John & GREEN Mary 21 Nov 1774 by JW #269
HALL Ephrain & SANBORN Molly 19 Nov 1772 by JW #641339
HARRISON Peter & PELHAM Elizabeth 6 Jun 1746 by BW
HARROD Benj Jr & HAZZEN Mary 18 Jan 1769 by JW #498
HASKET Thomas & FLANDERS Anna 16 Oct 1767 by JW
HAY John & FARNHAM Katharine 6 Aug 1774 by JW #241
HAYNS John & THWING Hannah 17 Jun 1774 by JW #230
HEATH Samuel & MANNING Priscilla 21 Dec 1769 by JW #767
HEWIT Charles & ALLEN Rebecca 11 Nov 1769 by JW #723
HICKLING William & HUDSON Elizabeth 8 Nov 1769 by JW #721
HIDE David & BUTFINCH Abigail 9 Jan 1768 by JW
HIDE Ephraim & DORR Abigail 2 Feb 1775 by JW #297

HILL Samuel & EMMONS Hannah 7 Jul 1766 by BW
HODGE Michael & SEVALL Sarah 11 Sep 1769 by JW #658
HODGOON Alexander & BUTLER Mary 19 Apr 1774 by JW #224
HOLLIDAY Benjamin & PILLSBURY Mary 1 Jun 1774 by JW #5686
HOMAN Richard & SABMAN Sarah 25 Jul 1774 by JW #239
HULL Thomas & PICK Mary 3 Nov 1765 by BW
HUNTER Thomas & LYON Agnes 19 Oct 1743 by BW
INGERSALL Samuel & HARTHAN Susanah 19 Oct 1772 by JW #135
JACKSON Jonathan & TRACEY Hannah 13 May 1772 by JW #327672
JAMES Samuel & PRECSCOT Meribah 5 Mar 1767 by BW
JILLINGS Joseph & CLEMENS Mary 1 Oct 1767 by JW
JOHONNOT Gabriel & BRADSTREET Sarah 4 Nov 1774 by JW
JOHONNOT William & BAYLEY Sally 2 Jul 1775 by JW #336
KENNEDY William & FROSTER Margaret 3 Nov 1742 by BW
KILBORN Eliphalet & FRASEY Jane 31 Aug 1745 by BW
KIMBALL Benjamin & LEE Johannah 6 Nov 1755 by BW
KNOWLTON Ebenezer & DODGE Mary 2 May 1755 by BW
LAMB Thomas & GOLDSMITH Sarah 17 Sep 1750 by BW
LAMSON Joseph & SANBORN Rachel 28 Apr 1769 by JW #560
LANDERS William & MATTON Bathsheba 10 Jul 1767 by JW
LEE Joseph & CABOT Elizabeth 9 Jun 1769 by JW #593
LEFEBURE Samuel & CARPENTER Sarah 30 Sep 1769 by JW 669
LITTLETON Benjamin & SHACKFORD Sarah 16 Jul 1747 by BW
LOCK Thomas & COLLINS Elizabeth 7 Mar 1768 by JW
LONG Robert & WHITE Ruth 26 Aug 1773 by JW #183
LOVERING Thomas & BACON Sarah 19 Apr 1774 by JW #223
LOWELL Ezra & ARNOLD Sarah 8 Aug 1775 by JW
LUNT Cutting & GERRISH Mary 9 Nov 1774 by JW #5796
LUNT David & WELLS Susanna 31 Oct 1765 by BW
MACCOY Charles & MOULTON Mary 3 Feb 1753 by BW
MACE Barnard & MARCH Elizabeth 22 May 1766 by BW
MAHANEY Philip & TABB Mary 3 Dec 1745 by BW
MARGRY Benjamin & CUMMINS Elizabeth 7 Dec 1769 by JW #757
MARSHAL Moses & THIMPLE Elizabeth 3 Mar 1753 by BW
MARSHALL John & THOMSON Mary 7 Mar 1744 by BW
MARSTON John & BLAKE Mary 12 Aug 1750 by BW
MARSTON John & BROWN Abigail 31 Oct 1765 by BW #28
MARTON John & ANDERSON Isabella 3 Apr 1746 by BW
MASNORY David & LAKEMAN Hannah 12 Jan 1769 by JW #9999
MASSY George & COFFIN Sarah 6 Feb 1749 by BW

MCLEAD Alexander & STARLING Christian 17 Jan 1768 by JW
MELOON Jonathan & NORRIS Ruth 31 Oct 1765 by BW
MILLER Robert & STANYEN Mehitable 29 Oct 1743 by BW
MITCHELL John & LOWELL Lydia 11 Jan 1754 by BW
MOOR William & PHILBRICK Martha 18 Nov 1753 by BW
MORSS Stephen & BAILEY Sarah 28 Oct 1773 by JW #200
MOTTEY Joseph & KING Mehitable 7 Aug 1769 by JW #627
NEEDHAM Edmund & SANDERS Sarah 11 Jan 1770 by JW #781
NESS John & JENISON Jane 28 Jan 1773 by JW #127
NEWCOMB John & CHASE Anna 10 Jan 1776 by JW #363
NEWELL Andrew & HASKEL Olive 24 Jan 1775 by JW #293
NEWTON Nonah & RICHARDSON Rebecca 21 Feb 1750 by BW
NORRIS Edward & LEE Sarah 19 Jul 1775 by JW #342
NUT John & BLACKLEY Sarah 6 Oct 1748 by BW
OLIVER Joseph & OLDRIDGE Elizabeth 27 May 1769 by JW #579
OSBORN John & SEGOURNEY Susanna 11 Jul 1765 by BW
PAGE Samuel & ATKINS Ruth 21 Jul 1748 by BW
PAINE William & ORNE Lois 24 Sep 1772 by JW #100
PALMER Joseph Pierce & HUNT Elizabeth 22 Oct 1772 by JW #5009
PARSON John & WALLACE Hannah 6 Oct 1773 by JW #2000
PARSON Moses & DAVENPORT Sarah 27 Apr 1774 by JW #5665
PATTIN John & HEWLIN Elizabeth 12 Jun 1775 by JW #330
PEDRICKY John Esq & SWASEY Hannah Mrs 10 Nov 1774 by JW
PERKIN John & OBBEY Elizabeth 17 Oct 1765 by BW
PERKINS Robert & CHAPMAN Sarah 8 Nov 1767 by JW #419
PIKE Adonak & DOLE Mary 6 Jun 1752 by BW
PILSBURY Eliphalet & CROSS Elizabeth 12 Jan 1775 by JW #287
POLAND Daniel & BISHOP Sarah 7 Oct 1747 by BW
PUTNAM Belings & ALLEN Hannah Wear 19 Apr 1775 by JW #312
QUILLIG William & NEWHALL Elizabeth 15 Aug 1744 by BW
RANDAL Benjamin & LONG Hannah 30 May 1774 by JW #228
RAWLINGS John & LONGFELLOW Anna 21 Mar 1774 by JW #21
RAYMOND Edward & STERNS Mary 24 Jul 1754 by BW
REVELL John & WORMSEADE Hannah 13 Sep 1774 by JW #255
RHODES William & STANNEY Mary 5 May 1745 by BW
RING Moses & TARBOX Abigial 3 Oct 1750 by BW
ROBERTS Peter & GREENLEAF Margery 15 Jan 1776 by JW #365
ROBINSON Benjamin & PERKINS Mary 6 Jul 1751 by BW
ROGERS Jacob & BARBER Ann 22 Dec 1774 by JW #283
ROWLINGS Eliphalet & GLIDDEN Abey 2 Sep 1756 by BW
RYAN Bryan & FANAN Mary 28 Apr 1773 by JW #148
SALLEDGE Timothy & DAVIS Elizabeth 7 Aug 1745 by BW
SEBER Jacob & LOVIT Elizabeth 1 Nov 1748 by BW

SHAW Benjamin & GOODWIN Betsy 12 Jan 1775 by JW #188
SHEPPARD William Esq & MILLER Deborah 11 Jan 1769 by JW #490
SIMOND Joseph & ANDREWS Jerusha 5 Feb 1755 by BW
SKEET Richard Barnsley & SKEET Elizabeth 5 Oct 1766 by BW
SMITH Samuel & LEE Libby 27 Sep 1744 by BW
SMITH Simon & LEE Elizabeth 18 Feb 1744 by BW
STACEY John & GOODWIN Nancy 11 Apr 1775 by JW #308
STEPHENSON William & BUTLER Mary 8 Jul 1766 by BW
STICKNEY John & WOODWELL Sarah 21 Dec 1773 by JW #212
STICKNEY Moody & PIKE Sarah 18 Jan 1775 by JW #271
STICKNEY William & PERKINS Welthen 19 Dec 1752 by BW
SWETT David & KIAH Dorotha 1 Sep 1746 by BW
SWINNERTON Jasper & SWINNERTON Elizabeth 9 Mar 1742 by BW
TAPPIN Amos & CLARKSON Lydia 4 Mar 1775 by JW #5871
TENNEY James & GARLAND Mary 4 Feb 1767 by BW
THOMAS Enoch & LUCAS Mary 23 Jun 1774 by JW #358320
TILDEN Job & VINER Elizabeth 14 Sep 1742 by BW
TILLEY Goerge & TUTTLE Mary 1 Jul 1747 by BW
TILTON David & CLOUGH Meriam 1 Jul 1767 by JW
TOWLE Robert & HOWARD Judith 9 May 1775 by JW #319
TOWN Nathan & POOLE Unice 12 Nov 1743 by BW
TRACY Nicholas & TITCOMB Miriam 30 Apr 1752 by BW
TREADWELL William & CARBOTT Mary 22 Jan 1776 by JW
TYLER John Steel & WHITWELL Sarah 6 Jun 1775 by JW #327
VANS William & CROWNINGSHIELD Eunice 12 Jul 1775 by JW #5920
VINCENT Anthony & TIMMINS Dorothy 25 Jun 1770 by JW #99894
WALDRON Edward & CROCKER Hannah 14 Nov 1775 by JW #356
WARD Samuel & COLBY Abigial 1 Mar 1756 by BW
WARNER Nathaniel & TITCOMB Anna 7 Jul 1746 by BW
WATSON Andrew & SANBORN Sarah 19 Oct 1765 by BW
WEARE Daniel & TRUE Mary 19 Oct 1750 by BW
WEBB Thomas & ROGERS Ann 4 Sep 1756 by BW
WEBSTER Eliphatet & PRESCUTT Hannah 26 Jan 1774 by JW #5007
WELCH John & BRYANT Sarah 6 Aug 1746 by BW
WELD Edmund Grindell & WILD Sarah 1 Mar 1776 by JW #371
WENDNIK Leasor & MILLER Susanah 20 Sep 1773 by JW #186
WHITE Abel & POOL Rebecca 7 Dec 1769 by JW #756
WHITON Moses & WHITON Martha 13 Jan 1775 by JW #289
WILCOM William & COFFIN Mary 18 Sep 1769 by JW #667

WILLAIMS Samuel & PORTER Sarah 27 Oct 1756 by BW
WILLCOM William & MOODY Jane 14 Oct 1773 by JW #169
WILLIAM Adam & STEVENS Marey 6 Feb 1776 by JW #369
WOOD Joseph & PERKINS Sarah 14 Mar 1769 by JW #530
WOODS Colidge Plimpton & HAGER Marg 21 Apr 1774 by JW #226
WRIGHT John & WHEELER Elizabeth 27 Oct 1774 by JW
YORK John & PILSBERY Anna 8 Apr 1773 by JW #148
YOUNG David & ELIOT Amy 15 Oct 1767 by JW
YOUNG William & MARCH K 15 May 1750 by BW
ZACHARY John & WOODMAN Judith 11 Nov 1766 by BW

CONCORD, JAFFREY, AND STRATHAM INTENTIONS

These marriage intentions were recently acquired by the state archives. The earliest date given in these records is 1791; the latest is 1960. The entries are arranged alphabetically by groom, and give the name and residence of both the bride and the groom, the date the intention was filed, the date of marriage if known ("nd" after "mar" or "int" indicates that no date of marriage or intention is given in the record), and the source of the record.

ABBOT Elias of Northfield & WINSLOW Sarah of Concord int 6 Aug 1826 mar nd Concord Records
ABBOT Alfred C of Concord & KNOWLS Sarah B of Concord int 9 Dec 1830 mar nd Concord Records
ABBOT Charles of Concord & CARTER Sarah of Concord int 4 Nov 1827 mar nd Concord Records
ABBOT Ira of Concord & CAPEN Hannah of Concord int 14 Feb 1831 mar nd Concord Records
ABBOT Jeremiah S of Concord & KNOWLTON Adaline A of Concord int 12 Jun 1848 mar nd Concord Records
ABBOT John D of Concord & BARTLETT Elizabeth of Concord int 27 Aug 1826 mar nd Concord Records
ABBOT William of Concord & CARTER Dorcas of Concord int 16 Jan 1820 mar nd Concord Records
ABBOTT Aaron of Concord & BADGER Nancy of Concord int 22 Aug 1824 mar nd Concord Records
ABBOTT Amos S of Concord & WILLIAMS Harriet A E of Concord int 30 Jun 1860 mar nd Concord Records
ABBOTT Calvin of Barnard VT & BURNHAM Polly of Concord int 19 Dec 1819 mar nd Concord Records
ABBOTT George of Concord & CARTER Clarissa of Concord int 21 Dec 1861 mar nd Concord Records
ABBOTT Hazen E of Concord & GILE Emma S of Concord int 2 Jun 1862 mar nd Concord Records

ABBOTT Hazen of Concord & ELA Ruth M of Hooksett int 16 Nov 1828 mar nd Concord Records

ABBOTT Isaac K of Concord & SMITH Martha of Hopkinton int 12 Nov 1862 mar nd Concord Records

ABBOTT Jeremiah S of Concord & KNOWLTON Rhoda A of Concord int 10 Mar 1859 mar nd Concord Records

ABBOTT Jese of Concord & CHANDLER Rebeccah of Concord int 25 Mar 1821 mar nd Concord Records

ABBOTT Joseph S of Concord & FARNUM Esther of Concord int 3 Dec 1827 mar nd Concord Records

ABBOTT Nathaniel of Bedford & BUTTERS Abi of Jaffrey int 1 Jan 1823 mar 25 Mar 1823 Jaffrey Records

ABBOTT Robert B of Concord & FOX Elizabeth of Lebanon int 26 Mar 1824 mar nd Concord Records

ABBOTTS Amos of Concord & GOULD Sally of Concord int 1 Oct 1820 mar nd Concord Records

ADAMS Charles of Stratham & PORTER Emory Sarah of Rye int 6 Jul 1833 mar nd Stratham Records

ADAMS David of Jaffrey & HODGE Elmira of Jaffrey int 30 Dec 1819 mar nd Jaffrey Records

ADAMS Jonathan of Jaffrey & ADAMS Hannah of Jaffrey int 1922-1925 mar nd Jaffrey Records

ADAMS Joseph of Dublin & EMERY Betsey of Jaffrey int 9 May 1805 mar 19 May 1805 Jaffrey Records

ADAMS Samuel of New York & WRIGHT Sally of Jaffrey int 28 Jan 1816 mar 28 Jan 1816 Jaffrey Records

ADAMS Stephen Jr of Jaffrey & CHADWICK Rebeccah of Rindge int 4 Apr 1813 mar 4 Apr 1813 Jaffrey Records

AIKEN George C of Concord & BAKER Eliza W of Concord int 10 Oct 1832 mar nd Concord Records

AILIN Soloman of Barrington & BALDWIN Ruth of Concord int 1 May 1825 mar nd Concord Records

AILIN Zeuhiriah of Concord & DANIELS Harriet of Haverhill MA int 28 Apr 1822 mar nd Concord Records

ALBE Alexander Esq of Littleton & CHANDLER Dolly of Concord int 1 Sep 1832 mar nd Concord Records

AMBROSE Nathaniel Dea of Concord & EASTMAN Martha of Concord int 2 Jan 1832 mar nd Concord Records

AMES Charles A of Lawrence MA & MARDEN Annie K of Concord int 12 Oct 1865 mar nd Concord Records

ANDERSON Joseph M of Lynn MA & ADAMS Cynthia of Jaffrey int 20 Oct 1817 mar 28 Oct 1817 Jaffrey Records

ANDRUS Joseph of Francestown & ELLIOT Polly of Concord int 29 Aug 1819 mar nd Concord Records

APPLETON Nathaniel of Portsmouth & GREENE Mary C of Concord int 2 Sep 1821 mar nd Concord Records
ARLIN Daniel Jr of Concord & FERRIN Jane of Concord int 23 Jun 1829 mar nd Concord Records
ARLIN Daniel Jr of Concord & SHAW Ann of Concord int 17 Feb 1822 mar nd Concord Records
ARLIN Jeremiah of Concord & CHANDLER Nancy of Concord int 15 Jan 1821 mar nd Concord Records
ARNOLD Edward Dr of Rindge & SPOFFORD Sally of Jaffrey int 10 May 1804 mar 10 May 1804 Jaffrey Records
AVERY Daniel of Stratham & PIPER Betsey of Stratham int 9 Feb 1823 mar 12 Mar 1823 Stratham Records
BABBET William L of Castleton VT & JERDINE Agnes of Concord int 23 May 1859 mar nd Concord Records
BACHELDER Luther C of Concord & WHITTERMORE Jane of Concord int 29 Dec 1822 mar nd Concord Records
BACON Hezikiah of Concord & GEORGE Elizabeth of Concord int 3 Feb 1842 mar nd Concord Records
BACON Jonathan of Jaffrey & PATRICK Sally of Jaffrey int 6 Jul 1818 mar 6 Jul 1818 Jaffrey Records
BAILEY Edward Capt of Jaffrey & MILLIKEN Nabby of Jaffrey int 20 Sep 1820 mar 20 Sep 1820 Jaffrey Records
BAKER Hazael of Concord & WORTHING Esther of Concord int 15 Mar 1865 mar nd Concord Records
BAKER Luke of Bow & CARTER Ann of Concord int 7 Apr 1822 mar nd Concord Records
BAKER Samuel L of Medford MA & PORCTOR Eliza A of Concord int 12 Aug 1833 mar nd Concord Records
BAKER Samuel L of Medford MA & PROCTOR Eliza of Concord int 12 Aug 1833 mar nd Concord Records
BAKER Samuel of Concord & BARRETT Nenpha of Litchfield int 20 Nov 1825 mar nd Concord Records
BAKER Samuel D of Concord & GLOVER Eliza Ann of Concord int 20 Mar 1832 mar nd Concord Records
BALDWIN Benjamin L of Jaffrey & FRENCH Rosaline of Jaffrey int 30 Apr 1838 mar nd Jaffrey Records
BALDWIN William T of Jaffrey & FELCH Charlote of Jaffrey int 9 Nov 1825 mar nd Jaffrey Records
BALLARD Char's E of Concord & DUNLAP Cynthia V of Concord int 1 Dec 1866 mar nd Concord Records
BALLARD Ezra of Concord & FLANDERS Mary of Concord int 15 May 1825 mar nd Concord Records
BALLARD Nathan of Brooklyn NY & GODDARD Emily of Newburyport MA int nd mar 20 Sep 1851 Concord Records

BALLOU David J of Deerfield & BARTLETT Mary F of Concord int 10 May 1855 mar nd Concord Records

BARKER Benjamin of Exeter & SCAMMON Lydia of Stratham int 24 May 1823 mar nd Stratham Records

BARKER Levi of Stratham & CLARK Mehitable of Stratham int 30 Mar 1823 mar nd Stratham Records

BARLEY John of Concord & KNEELAND Eliza of Concord int 18 Jan 1829 mar nd Concord Records

BARNARD Josiah of Peru VT & BRAM Hannah of Jaffrey int 27 Jan 1807 mar nd Jaffrey Records

BARRETT Enoch of Mason & SPAULDING Eliza of Jaffrey int 23 Nov 1824 mar 23 Nov 1824 Jaffrey Records

BARRETT Henry of Brattleborough VT & LAWRENCE Lucy P of Jaffrey int nd mar 18 Nov 1823 Jaffrey Records

BARRON Dickinson of West Lebanon & HARTFORD Orline of Concord int 12 Nov 1856 mar nd Concord Records

BARROWS John Stuart of Fryburg ME & BRADLEY Ann Ayer of Concord int 6 Sep 1820 mar nd Concord Records

BARTLETT Chauncy of Concord & BOISE Sarah C of Concord int 27 Sep 1841 mar nd Concord Records

BARTLETT James of Concord & SEAVEY Catharine of Concord int 22 Jul 1833 mar nd Concord Records

BARTLETT Josiah Jr of Stratham & THOMPSON Hannah of Stratham int 23 Jul 1827 mar nd Stratham Records

BATES Samuel of Jaffrey & CUTTER Jenney of Jaffrey int 11 Jun 1810 mar 21 Jun 1810 Jaffrey Records

BAULDWIN David of Fitchburg MA & JACQUITH Abigail of Jaffrey int 12 Sep 1791 mar nd Jaffrey Records

BAYLEY Abner of Jaffrey & GILLMORE Caroline of Jaffrey int 1824 mar 4 Nov 1824 Jaffrey Records

BEAN Amos of Concord & POTTER Phebe A of Concord int 2 Dec 1836 mar nd Concord Records

BEATLEY Spencer of Boston MA & PORTER Mary B of Concord int 7 Apr 1830 mar nd Concord Records

BELKNAP Josiah of Jaffrey & SMILEY Sally of Jaffrey int 13 Jun 1791 mar nd Jaffrey Records

BENSON Walter of Concord & SMITH Mary of Concord int 28 Jun 1850 mar nd Concord Records

BERRY Walter of Loudon & POTTER Sarah F of Concord int 10 May 1827 mar nd Concord Records

BERRY Washington of Concord & DALE Maria of Danvers MA int 4 Apr 1822 mar nd Concord Records

BIGELOW Levi of Jaffrey & CUTTER Mary of Jaffrey int 1822-1825 mar nd Jaffrey Records

BIGELOW Perkins of Farmingham MA & PATRICK Relief of Jaffrey int 21 Nov 1825 mar 24 Nov 1825 Jaffrey Records

BINGHAM James H of Alstead & KENT Charlotte M of Concord int 9 Jan 1820 mar nd Concord Records

BINGHAM John of London England & GANELL Emma of London England int 23 May 1852 mar nd Concord Records

BISHOP Jewett of Concord & HAZLETINE Mary of Concord int 21 Jun 1823 mar nd Concord Records

BLAISDELL Samuel of Providence RI & SHACKFORD Harriet N of Concord int 21 Oct 1854 mar nd Concord Records

BLAKE Michael of Concord & KNOWLES Ruth Anne of Concord int 3 Dec 1833 mar nd Concord Records

BLASDELL Joseph of Stratham & PIPER Nancy of Stratham int 25 Jan 1823 mar nd Stratham Records

BLODGETT Nathan of Jaffrey & FRENCH Nancy of Jaffrey int 18 Sep 1815 mar 10 Oct 1815 Jaffrey Records

BOARDMAN Benjamin of Ossipee & STICKMEY Benjamin of Concord int 16 Apr 1826 mar nd Concord Records

BOARDMAN George S of Concord & SMART Betsey S of Concord int 12 Dec 1855 mar nd Concord Records

BOHONNON Benjamin of Lowell MA & CAPEN Maria L of Concord int 25 Oct 1835 mar nd Concord Records

BORWN John of Concord & SHUTE Clara A of Concord int 12 Nov 1840 mar nd Concord Records

BOWLEY Charles E of Exeter & BUTLER Melissa of Lebanon ME int nd mar nd Stratham Records

BOYDEN Abner Esq of Jaffrey & CROSBY Nancy of Jaffrey int 22 Oct 1827 mar nd Jaffrey Records

BRACKET Joseph of Newmarket & BRACKET Eliza of Stratham int nd mar 23 Nov 1823 Stratham Records

BRACKET Joshua of Stratham & DANE Mary of Stratham int 27 Jul 1828 mar nd Stratham Records

BRACKET Thomas Capt of Stratham & KEASEY Sarah W of Stratham int 9 Aug 1828 mar nd Stratham Records

BRADLEY Asa F of Concord & HOIT Rachel T of Concord int 16 Feb 1835 mar nd Concord Records

BRADLEY Moses H of Concord & ROBY Lucy M of Concord int 22 Dec 1858 mar nd Concord Records

BREED Thomas Andrews of Lynn MA & HAINES Harriet of Concord int 18 Nov 1827 mar nd Concord Records

BRIANT John of Jaffrey & POOR Sally of Jaffrey int 12 Jan 1807 mar 24 Feb 1807 Jaffrey Records

BRIDGES James of Wilton & FISH Sally of Jaffrey int 22 Aug 1825 mar 6 Sep 1825 Jaffrey Records
BRIDGES Richard B of Greenland & FRENCH Lydia of Stratham int 9 Apr 1825 mar nd Stratham Records
BRIGGS John of Boston MA & WEST Mary E of Concord int 30 Oct 1843 mar nd Concord Records
BRIGHAM Levi of Boston MA & AYER Nancy of Concord int 7 Jan 1821 mar nd Concord Records
BRIGHAM Love of Jaffrey & BRONSDON Ann L of Concord int 26 Aug 1821 mar nd Concord Records
BROADHEAD John M Dr of Deerfield & WATERMAN Josephine of Concord int 26 Mar 1826 mar nd Concord Records
BROOKS Patrick of Acton MA & BALDWIN Elizabeth of Jaffrey int 9 Nov 1818 mar 18 Nov 1818 Jaffrey Records
BROUGHTON Daniel of Stratham & ROBINSON Betsy of Stratham int nd mar 5 Sep 1819 Stratham Records
BROWN Anson of Loudon & POTTER Elvira W of Concord int 6 Oct 1834 mar nd Concord Records
BROWN Cyress of Sharon & LAWRENCE Milly of Jaffrey int 18 Dec 1810 mar nd Jaffrey Records
BROWN Daniel of Rye & GARLAND Sarah Ann of Rye int nd mar 2 Nov 1834 Stratham Records
BROWN Eliphalett of Concord & WILLEY Eliz of Concord int 31 Oct 1819 mar nd Concord Records
BROWN Greenleaf of Stratham & BROWN Abigail of Hampton Falls int 2 Feb 1828 mar 5 Mar 1828 Stratham Records
BROWN John W of Hanover & ROLFE Harriet W of Concord int 25 Feb 1850 mar nd Concord Records
BROWN Joseph of Canterbury & CLEASLEY Hannah W of Concord int 17 Aug 1828 mar nd Concord Records
BROWN Melvin of Jaffrey & FISKE Bathsheba of Jaffrey int 14 Jan 1815 mar 14 Jan 1815 Jaffrey Records
BROWN Nathan of Deering & AILIN Sarah of Concord int 17 Feb 1822 mar nd Concord Records
BROWN Richard N of Concord & PERKINS Sarah T of Dunbarton int 7 May 1826 mar nd Concord Records
BROWN Samuel Jr of Concord & BUNTIN Elizabeth of Concord int 11 May 1823 mar nd Concord Records
BROWN Stephen of Norwich VT & WILKINS Fanny of Concord int 5 Sep 1824 mar nd Concord Records
BROWN Thomas of Deerfield & MOORE Mary of Concord int 21 SEP 823 mar nd Concord Records
BROWNING Thomas of Barre VT & ROSS Persis of Jaffrey int 21 Jan 1812 mar nd Jaffrey Records

BRUCE Cyrus of Troy & WILDER Sarah of Jaffrey int 1823 mar nd Jaffrey Records

BULLARD Ebenezer of Dublin & PHILIPS Olive of Dublin int 13 Oct 1805 mar nd Jaffrey Records

BUNKER Andrew of Concord & PENDERGAST Mariam of Barnstead int 16 Jul 1855 mar nd Concord Records

BUNTON Robert of Boston MA & HASKELL Emily V of Concord int 28 Aug 1848 mar nd Concord Records

BURLEY Walter of Franklin & DANFORD Augusta R of Franklin int 27 Nov 1856 mar nd Concord Records

BURMHAM John A of Manchest & DAVIDSON Harriet W of Concord int 27 May 1843 mar nd Concord Records

BURNHAM Andrew of Concord & WEST Sarah of Concord int 5 Dec 1853 mar nd Concord Records

BURPE Moses of Jaffrey & KEYES Janet of Jaffrey int 26 Jan 1807 mar nd Jaffrey Records

BURPEE Moses Jr of Jaffrey & KEYS Hannah of Jaffrey int 25 Jan 1808 mar 26 Jan 1808 Jaffrey Records

BURPEE Samuel of New York & CROSBY Esther of Jaffrey int 5 Oct 1820 mar nd Jaffrey Records

BURT Charles of Dunteith IL & BLANCHARD Marianna of Concord int 11 Sep 1861 mar nd Concord Records

BUSS Samuel of Jaffrey & EMERY Lucy of Dublin int 23 Nov 1801 mar nd Jaffrey Records

BUSWELL Andrew of Concord & DIMOND Zelphia of Concord int 13 Nov 1819 mar nd Concord Records

BUSWELL Carter of Hopkinton & ABBOTT Mary of Concord int 29 Apr 1821 mar nd Concord Records

BUSWELL Hammond of Concord & CONNER Martha H of Concord int 7 Dec 1828 mar nd Concord Records

BUSWELL James of Concord & DAVIS Judith of Concord int 27 Feb 1832 mar nd Concord Records

BUSWELL John of Jaffrey & HORTON Sarah of Jaffrey int 15 Jul 1803 mar 1 Sep 1803 Jaffrey Records

BUTTENS Thomas of Concord & DUNCKLEY Sarah of Concord int 15 Sep 1834 mar nd Concord Records

BUTTER Warren of Wilmington MA & STICKNEY Rebecca of Jaffrey int 22 Jan 1806 mar 30 Mar 1806 Jaffrey Records

BUXTON Edward Rev of Boscawen & McFARLAND Elizabeth of Concord int 27 May 1838 mar nd Concord Records

CABAN Samuel of Exeter & THOMAS Phebe of Exeter int nd mar 4 Nov 1827 Stratham Records

CALEF Joseph of Boscawen & ABBOTT Nancy B of Concord int 12 Jan 1823 mar nd Concord Records

CALEF Samuel of Concord & FARNUM Sarah W of Concord int 18 Feb 1857 mar nd Concord Records
CALF Nathaniel of Springfield & PAGE Rhoda S of Concord int 9 Apr 1826 mar nd Concord Records
CALL Horace of Concord & SMART Emma S of Concord int 29 Oct 1850 mar nd Concord Records
CAPEN Albert G of Lowell MA & HALL Mary of Concord int 15 Apr 1838 mar nd Concord Records
CAPEN Thomas C of Concord & CORLISS Mary of Concord int 19 Dec 1832 mar nd Concord Records
CAPON Silas of Concord & JONES Dolly of Concord int 5 Dec 1819 mar nd Concord Records
CAPRON Isaac of Jaffrey & PRIEST Sally of Jaffrey int 1 Oct 1810 mar nd Jaffrey Records
CAREY Joseph W of Danvers MA & FIFE Abigail of Concord int 26 Mar 1826 mar nd Concord Records
CARTER Aaron of Concord & HAZLETINE Eliza of Concord int 30 Mar 1823 mar nd Concord Records
CARTER Abiel of Concord & FARNUM Patty of Concord int 13 Nov 1819 mar nd Concord Records
CARTER Amariah of Concord & DODGE Susan of Hanover int 12 Feb 1826 mar nd Concord Records
CARTER Hiram I of Concord & GILL Sarah K of Concord int 9 Jul 1866 mar nd Concord Records
CARTER James of Peterborough & BATES Mary of Jaffrey int 17 Apr 1819 mar nd Jaffrey Records
CARTER John F of Corinth VT & DAMON Polly B of Concord int 29 Mar 1856 mar nd Concord Records
CARTER Jude of Rindge & PIERCE Abigail of Jaffrey int 3 Feb 1812 mar 6 Feb 1812 Jaffrey Records
CARTER Nathan of Concord & FLANDERS Ruth C of Concord int 20 Jul 1857 mar nd Concord Records
CARTER Nathaniel of Concord & ROBERTSON Elizabeth of Bow int 6 Feb 1820 mar nd Concord Records
CARTER Simon of Concord & ABBOT Eliza of Concord int 4 Nov 1827 mar nd Concord Records
CARTER William M of Concord & MORSE Lucy of Concord int 2 Sep 1827 mar nd Concord Records
CASS Simon of Cancord & INGALLS Almeda C of Canterbury int 10 May 1866 mar nd Concord Records
CATE John G of Stratham & WIGGIN Martha of Stratham int 18 Mar 1833 mar nd Stratham Records
CATE Nathan H of Concord & WORTH Abighail T of Concord int 20 Jan 1828 mar nd Concord Records

CATE Nathan of Stratham & LANE Mary M of Stratham int 27 Feb 1825 mar nd Stratham Records

CAYRS Joseph H of Boston MA & WHITTERMORE Emily T of Concord int 1 Jan 1855 mar nd Concord Records

CHADWICH David of Jaffrey & STACY Hannah of Jaffrey int 23 May 1809 mar nd Jaffrey Records

CHAFFIN John F of Concord & POLLARD Rebeccah of Harvard MA int 20 Apr 1823 mar nd Concord Records

CHAFFIN Willia F of Concord & SHATTUCK Louisa of Concord int 8 Feb 1829 mar nd Concord Records

CHAMBERLAIN David of Jaffrey & CHADWICK Nabby of Jaffrey int 23 Jun 1812 mar 7 Jul 1812 Jaffrey Records

CHANDLER Ezra Jr of Concord & WOOD Charlotte of Concord int 22 Feb 1824 mar nd Concord Records

CHANDLER Jeremiah of Concord & CHASE Fidilia of Concord int 9 Dec 1829 mar nd Concord Records

CHANDLER Josiah of Grafton & MERRILL Mehitabel of Concord int 11 Jan 1829 mar nd Concord Records

CHASE Timothy W of Fisherville & SHAW Elvira J of Pittsfield int 1 Jul 1861 mar nd Concord Records

CHASES Moses Jr of Concord & WELLS Louisa of Concord int 25 Feb 1827 mar nd Concord Records

CHENEY Enoch of Concord & DUN Phebe of Concord int 1 Apr 1821 mar nd Concord Records

CHESLEY Trueworth of Concord & ABBOTT Judith of Concord int 4 Sep 1825 mar nd Concord Records

CHOATE Thomas of Hopkinton & SWAN Harriet of Concord int 8 Jan 1826 mar nd Concord Records

CLAGGGETT William of Wendell MA & MORRILL Sarah K of Concord int 14 Apr 1831 mar nd Concord Records

CLARK Aaron of Concord & MARSTON Mary E of Concord int 22 Sep 1855 mar nd Concord Records

CLARK Benjamin F of Stratham & WINGATE Elizabeth of Stratham int 19 Feb 1831 mar nd Stratham Records

CLARK John of Stratham & NEAL Elizabeth of Stratham int 22 Feb 1823 mar 21 Mar 1823 Stratham Records

CLARK Satihel of Concord & STEVENS Priscilla of Concord int 4 Nov 1827 mar nd Concord Records

CLARK Thomas J of Stratham & LANG Priscilla C of Stratham int 7 Sep 1823 mar nd Stratham Records

CLEMENT Moses of Concord & WILKINS Cynthia of Concord int 24 Nov 1830 mar nd Concord Records

CLIFFORD Samuel Jr of Concord & KIMBALL Mary B of Concord int 22 Jan 1826 mar nd Concord Records
CLOUGH Charles H of Concord & LANG Mary C of Concord int 14 Sep 1840 mar nd Concord Records
COCHRAN Samuel C of Concord & DEARBORN Elizabeth of Concord int 6 Oct 1834 mar nd Concord Records
COFRAN George B of Concord & DREW Anna of Concord int 17 May 1856 mar nd Concord Records
COLBATH Eliphalet of Stratham & ROLLINS Esther of Stratham int 12 Apr 1823 mar nd Stratham Records
COLBY David of Concord & COLBY Judith of Concord int 11 Apr 1819 mar nd Concord Records
COLBY Elijah of Concord & EASTMAN Susan of Concord int 26 Oct 1829 mar nd Concord Records
COLBY Moody of Bradford VT & TAYLOR Elizabeth of Jaffrey int 10 Jan 1832 mar 17 Jan 1832 Jaffrey Records
COLBY Moses of Hopkinton & ABBOT Ely of Concord int 3 Dec 1820 mar nd Concord Records
COLLETT J F of Burlington VT & BROWN H A of Concord int 3 Nov 1851 mar nd Concord Records
COLLINS Benjamin of Nortfield & DEARBORN Comfort of Concord int 14 Apr 1825 mar nd Concord Records
COLLYER William S of Derby VT & THORN Sarah L of Concord int 9 May 1819 mar nd Concord Records
CONNER John of Exeter & THURSTON Hannah of Stratham int 7 Sep 1828 mar nd Stratham Records
COOK William R of Hopkinton & COOK Lovicy M of Lowell MA int 22 Jan 1861 mar nd Concord Records
CRANDELL Charles H of Concord & CHASE Eley of Concord int 6 Mar 1830 mar nd Concord Records
CRIMBELL Abram of Stratham & WIGGINS Mary of Stratham int nd mar 9 Sep 1821 Stratham Records
CRIMBELL Benjamin of N Hampton & NAY Sarah of Notingham int nd mar 29 May 1822 Stratham Records
CROCKER Alvah of Fitchburg MA & FOX Abigail of Jaffrey int 3 Aug 1829 mar 20 Aug 1829 Jaffrey Records
CROCKETT Sanborn M of New Hampton & SANBORN Sarah E of New Hampton int 1 Apr 1865 mar nd Concord Records
CROSBY Abial R of Montgomery AL & CHANDLER Judith of Concord int 27 Jul 1842 mar nd Concord Records
CROSBY Alphus of Troy & FOX Mary of Jaffrey int 1 Apr 1822 mar 3 Apr 1822 Jaffrey Records
CROSBY Asa of Boston MA & HOWE Mary W of Jaffrey int 27 Apr 1829 mar 30 Apr 1829 Jaffrey Records

CROSS Charles of Canterbury & HOIT Rebecca of Concord int 6 Mar 1830 mar nd Concord Records
CROUMMET Robert of Concord & WEEKS Harriet S of Concord int 29 Nov 1827 mar nd Concord Records
CUMINGS Nathaniel of Jaffrey & STICKNEY Salley of Jaffrey int 26 Jan 1803 mar nd Jaffrey Records
CUMMINGS Hiram of Colebrook & STEVENS Hannah of Concord int 25 Feb 1829 mar nd Concord Records
CUMMINGS Thadeus of Jaffrey & COLLINS Anna of Jaffrey int nd mar 25 Apr 1803 Jaffrey Records
CURRIER Adna S of Concord & ATWOOD Fanny G of Concord int 15 Aug 1859 mar nd Concord Records
CURRIER Benjamin H of Concord & TOWNER Martha of Concord int 4 Mar 1821 mar nd Concord Records
CURTIS Samuel of Concord & CHASE Sally of Concord int 18 Jul 1819 mar nd Concord Records
CURTISS Samuel Jr of Concord & ELLINGWOOD Nancy D of Boston MA int 13 May 1827 mar nd Concord Records
CUTLER Daniel of Jaffrey & JONES Sally of Jaffrey int 18 Nov 1806 mar nd Jaffrey Records
CUTLER Tara of Epsom & COFFIN Judith of Concord int 30 Nov 1833 mar nd Concord Records
CUTTER John Jr of Jaffrey & CROSBY Betsey of Jaffrey int 7 Jan 1811 mar 7 Feb 1811 Jaffrey Records
CUTTER Luther of Jaffrey & CUTTER Caroline of Jaffrey int 23 Aug 1830 mar 15 Sep 1830 Jaffrey Records
CUTTER Stephen of Jaffrey & KIMBALL Mehittabell of Jaffrey int 29 Mar 1814 mar nd Jaffrey Records
DANFORD John of Concord & SWEATT Maria Ellen of Concord int 16 Nov 1860 mar nd Concord Records
DARLING Benj of Dublin & AMES Fanny of Dublin int nd mar 10 Jun 1803 Jaffrey Records
DARLING Benjamin of Jaffrey & WILDER Lydia of Jaffrey int 1922-1925 mar nd Jaffrey Records
DAVIS Eleazer of Concord & ELLIOTT Lydia C of Concord int 11 Mar 1823 mar nd Concord Records
DAVIS Amos of Stratham & WIGGING Deborah of Stratham int 3 Mar 1832 mar nd Stratham Records
DAVIS Benjamin of Boston MA & FARNUM Phebe A of Concord int 7 Oct 1838 mar nd Concord Records
DAVIS Eliser of Concord & DOW Hannah of Concord int 19 Mar 1820 mar nd Concord Records
DAVIS James of Concord & CLEASBY Melinda of Concord int 1 Sep 1835 mar nd Concord Records

DAVIS John O of Concord & BROWN Lucy S of Hopkinton int 8 Jan 1826 mar nd Concord Records
DAVIS John of Concord & DEMERITT Susan of Concord int 16 Jun 1822 mar nd Concord Records
DAVIS Mose of Concord & MARTIN Esther of Concord int 11 Dec 1825 mar nd Concord Records
DAVIS R Lewis of Concord & MOORE Harriet of Concord int 11 Sep 1848 mar nd Concord Records
DAVIS Richard Jr of Jaffrey & GARFIELD Sally of Jaffrey int 18 Dec 1801 mar nd Jaffrey Records
DAVIS Samuel of Concord & GEORGE Betsey of Concord int 18 Dec 1826 mar nd Concord Records
DEARBORN Samuel H of Hampton Falls & WIGGIN Sarah W of Stratham int 9 Mar 1867 mar nd Stratham Records
DEVON Lewis of Concord & LaBONTE Margaret of Concord int 4 Sep 1842 mar nd Concord Records
DIEFENDORF J W of Concord & STEARANS Helen P of Concord int 12 Jun 1862 mar nd Concord Records
DIMAN Oliver Jr of Fitzwilliam & POTTER Polly of Fitzwilliam int nd mar 7 Nov 1803 Jaffrey Records
DIMON David K of Stratham & PIPER Nancy of Stratham int 17 Mar 1822 mar nd Stratham Records
DIMOND John of Concord & BENNET Betsey of Andover int 22 Feb 1824 mar nd Concord Records
DINMOND Samuel of Concord & BLANCHARD Susan of Concord int 7 Jul 1822 mar nd Concord Records
DODGE John of Jaffrey & BURPEE Polly of Jaffrey int 1 Mar 1807 mar 1 Mar 1807 Jaffrey Records
DOE Warren of Stratham & LANG Clarrissa of Stratham int 28 Sep 1823 mar 26 Oct 1823 Stratham Records
DOLDT James of Milton & CHANDLER Lucia of Concord int 15 Feb 1858 mar nd Concord Records
DOW Isaac Jr of Concord & AUSTIN Nancy of Concord int 1 Jan 1825 mar nd Concord Records
DOW Samuel of Concord & HARVEY Nancy of Concord int 2 Nov 1823 mar nd Concord Records
DOWNING Alonzo of Concord & SANBORN Marianne M of Concord int 30 Oct 1848 mar nd Concord Records
DOWNS Henry of Stratham & PETTINGILL Elizabeth of Stratham int 21 Jul 1827 mar nd Stratham Records
DUKE Milton M of Concord & WOODBURY Sarah A of Concord int 19 Jan 1851 mar nd Concord Records
DUNCAN Hiram of New London & CUTTER Emeline of Jaffrey int 30 Jun 1829 mar 21 Jul 1829 Jaffrey Records

DUNIB Davud R of Stratham & PIPER Nancy of Stratham int nd mar 1 Apr 1822 Stratham Records

DUNLAP John of Concord & ASLIN Nancy of Concord int 9 Nov 1820 mar nd Concord Records

DUNN Asa of Concord & WOOD Maria B of Keene int 12 Apr 1827 mar nd Concord Records

DURGIN Fred W of Fisherville & JAMESON Mary H of Fisherville int 31 Aug 1864 mar nd Concord Records

DURGIN Jesse of Concord & BAKER Clarrissa of Concord int 15 Aug 1824 mar nd Concord Records

DUTTON Nathan of Jaffrey & BALDWIN Sally of Jaffrey int 18 May 1804 mar 20 May 1804 Jaffrey Records

DUTTON Thomas of Jaffrey & SMITH Betsy of Jaffrey int 3 Jan 1815 mar 3 Jan 1815 Jaffrey Records

DWIGHT Francis of Shirley MA & BLANCHARD Maria of Jaffrey int 31 Mar 1805 mar nd Jaffrey Records

EASTMAN Amos of Andover & TRUE Susanna of Concord int 30 Apr 1820 mar nd Concord Records

EASTMAN Amos of Concord & HILYARD Mary P of Concord int 1 Feb 1829 mar nd Concord Records

EASTMAN Charles B of Sanbornton & CLARK Nancy S of Sanbornton int 26 Mar 1863 mar nd Concord Records

EASTMAN Ebenezer Jr of Concord & HOIT Ruth of Concord int 13 May 1833 mar nd Concord Records

EASTMAN Ebenezer of Concord & UNDERWOOD Mary D of Portsmouth int 14 Nov 1824 mar nd Concord Records

EASTMAN Ezra of Greensborough VT & ELLIOTT Lois of Concord int 6 Feb 1820 mar nd Concord Records

EASTMAN George of Concord & ELLIOT Judith of Concord int 14 Jun 1820 mar nd Concord Records

EASTMAN Hiriam of Concord & KIMBALL Mary of Concord int 20 Jan 1828 mar nd Concord Records

EASTMAN John of Concord & FOUST Dorothy of Canterbury int 17 Nov 1823 mar nd Concord Records

EASTMAN Philip Esq of No Yarmouth ME & AMBROSE Mary of Concord int 1 Jul 1827 mar nd Concord Records

EASTMAN Philip of Fryeburg ME & LOVEJOY Martha of Concord int 15 Jan 1838 mar nd Concord Records

EASTMAN Seth Capt of Concord & COFFIN Sarah of Concord int 12 Jul 1830 mar nd Concord Records

EASTMAN William of Hopkinton & HOIT Ruth of Concord int 26 Nov 1820 mar nd Concord Records

EATON Charles F of Cambridge MA & HILL Marianne S of Concord int 25 Aug 1844 mar nd Concord Records

EATON Charles of Cambridge MA & HILL Mariann of Concord int 23 Aug 1847 mar nd Concord Records

EATON Jeremiah B of Haverhill MA & ROLLINS Martha J of Stratham int 25 May 1833 mar nd Stratham Records

EATON John of Concord & JOHNSON Judith of Concord int 6 Jul 1833 mar nd Concord Records

EDMUNDS Jonathan of Chichester & MEHIER Mary of Concord int 3 Jan 1866 mar nd Concord Records

ELKINS Peter of Concord & HALL Harriet of Concord int 19 Oct 1823 mar nd Concord Records

ELKINS William E of Weare & CHASE Antoinette of Concord int 25 Dec 1853 mar nd Concord Records

ELKINS William of Concord & CHANDLER Phebe of Concord int 3 Jan 1828 mar nd Concord Records

ELLIOET James C of Concord & BLAKE Abigail of Concord int 6 May 1821 mar nd Concord Records

ELLIOT Ephraim C of Concord & BLASDELL Sarahann of Concord int 28 Dec 1828 mar nd Concord Records

ELLIOT Jeremiah of Concord & CURRY Polly of Canterbury int 12 Sep 1819 mar nd Concord Records

ELLIOT Nathaniel of Concord & AUSTIN Sophia of Concord int 2 Apr 1830 mar nd Concord Records

ELLIOTT Alfred of Concord & ORDWAY Louisa M of Concord int 8 Nov 1862 mar nd Concord Records

ELSWORTH Samuel of Boscawen & ABBOT Ruth of Concord int 15 Feb 1829 mar nd Concord Records

EMERSON Henry L of Concord & ARLIN Hannah of Concord int 14 Aug 1825 mar nd Concord Records

EMERSON John of Concord & STEVENS Mary Ann of Concord int 6 Jun 1829 mar nd Concord Records

EMERY David Dr of Jaffrey & JAQUITH Esther (widow) of Jaffrey int nd mar 29 Nov 1804 Jaffrey Records

EMERY Isaac Jr of Concord & EASTMAN Eloise of Concord int 22 Dec 1836 mar nd Concord Records

EMERY Joseph H of Concord & DOYEN Sarah S of Concord int 28 Sep 1823 mar nd Concord Records

EMERY Joseph of Dover & MOORE Sophoria of Concord int nd mar 21 May 1826 Stratham Records

EMERY Joshua of Loudon & EASTMAN Eliza of Concord int 11 Dec 1826 mar nd Concord Records

EMERY Samuel of Jaffrey & BAILEY Mary of Jaffrey int 6 Jul 1821 mar nd Jaffrey Records

EMERY Timoth W of Concord & POTTER Comfort of Concord int 29 Nov 1840 mar nd Concord Records

EMERY William T of Concord & ELLIOTT Jennette of Concord int 24 Apr 1843 mar nd Concord Records

EMERY Zackiniah of Jaffrey & MOWER Rebecah of Jaffrey int 16 Nov 1819 mar nd Jaffrey Records

ESTABROOK John of Concord & ABBOT Emeline of Concord int 6 Jul 1829 mar nd Concord Records

ESTABROOK William of Concord & DAMON Ann H of Concord int 6 Jul 1833 mar nd Concord Records

EVANS Asash of Montomery AL & FISK Clarrisa N of Concord int 2 May 1836 mar nd Concord Records

EVANS Franklin of Concord & DAVIS Sara E of Concord int 12 Nov 1840 mar nd Concord Records

EVANS Ralph of Concord & DAVIS Almira of Concord int 20 Jun 1831 mar nd Concord Records

EVANS Samuel of Hopkinton & MARTIN Sarah of Concord int 1 Jan 1825 mar nd Concord Records

EVELETH Asahel of Jaffrey & GILLMAN Mary of Jaffrey int 13 Apr 1808 mar nd Jaffrey Records

FAIRBANKS Windsor of Concord & BROWN Eliza W of Concord int 11 Sep 1843 mar nd Concord Records

FARLEY Henry of Harvard MA & TYLER Mary of Concord int 19 Nov 1826 mar nd Concord Records

FARNUM Edwaard of Concord & DOW Abby M of Concord int 22 Jul 1865 mar nd Concord Records

FARNUM Hazen K of Concord & FAVOR Narcissa of Concord int 15 Dec 1840 mar nd Concord Records

FARNUM Isaiah of Concord & MOONEY Clarissa of Concord int 21 Sep 1834 mar nd Concord Records

FARNUM Simon of Concord & SMITH Clarissa of Hopkinton int 24 Jan 1820 mar nd Concord Records

FARRINGTON Thomas F of Farmington Miss & DODGE Hannah S of Concord int 31 Oct 1830 mar nd Concord Records

FASSETT John of Jaffrey & BURPEE Margaret of Jaffrey int 4 Mar 1827 mar nd Jaffrey Records

FAY Gershom of Concord & BALDWIN Cynthia of Jaffrey int 30 May 1826 mar nd Jaffrey Records

FELCH Samuel of Weare & SCALES Sarah of Concord int 5 Oct 1828 mar nd Concord Records

FELLOWS Jonathan of Concord & HAINES Louisa of Concord int 26 Jan 1857 mar nd Concord Records

FELT Peter of Jaffrey & GILLMORE Polly of Jaffrey int 21 Mar 1809 mar nd Jaffrey Records

FERRIN Henry L of Concord & ELLIOTT Ruth A of Fisherville int 18 Oct 1862 mar nd Concord Records

FERRIN Isaac of Concord & KNOWLES Betsey of Concord int 21 Feb 1825 mar nd Concord Records

FERRIN Philip of Concord & SMITH Dolly W of Concord int 13 Jan 1828 mar nd Concord Records

FIELDS Silas C of Concord & MEARS Abby S of Concord int 17 Oct 1857 mar nd Concord Records

FIFIELD George B of Northampton & SMITH Mary of Northampton int nd mar 6 Apr 1820 Stratham Records

FININ Jonathan of Concord & TANDY Jane of Concord int 17 Aug 1828 mar nd Concord Records

FISH Jr of Jaffrey & MANN Cynthia of Jaffrey int 4 Aug 1800 mar nd Jaffrey Records

FISHER Samuel of Concord & ADAMS Susan of Andover MA int 11 Mar 1823 mar nd Concord Records

FISK Abna of Concord & ABBOTT Eunice of Concord int 25 Nov 1826 mar nd Concord Records

FISK Ephramin of Concord & DOW Margarett of Concord int 29 Feb 1824 mar nd Concord Records

FISK Joel of Jaffrey & PIERCE Sally of Jaffrey int 26 Feb 1812 mar 17 Mar 1812 Jaffrey Records

FISK William of Concord & WALKER Hannah of Concord int 13 Nov 1819 mar nd Concord Records

FISSENDEN Moses of Concord & CHAFFIN Nancy of Concord int 1 Sep 1822 mar nd Concord Records

FITCH Paul of Jaffrey & WALKER Sally of Jaffrey int 22 Nov 1802 mar nd Jaffrey Records

FLANDERS Jacob of Concord & ABBOTT Huldah of Concord int 21 Mar 1819 mar nd Concord Records

FLEMMING David of Stratham & WILLIAMS Eunice of Hampton Falls int 12 Oct 1832 mar nd Stratham Records

FLETCHER Samuel Esq of Concord & BOARDMAN Nancy of Reading MA int 30 May 1819 mar nd Concord Records

FOLLENSBEE John B of Enfield & WILLIS Elizabeth M of Cannan int 9 Jan 1867 mar nd Concord Records

FOLSOM John D of Stratham & WIGGIN Olive of Stratham int 11 Aug 1827 mar nd Stratham Records

FOSS Augustus of Concord & FOSS Jowsha of Franfort ME int 5 Aug 1844 mar nd Concord Records

FOSTER Adams of Canterbury & EASTMAN Sarah B of Concord int 20 Nov 1832 mar nd Concord Records

FOSTER Samuel of Jaffrey & SPOFFORD Sophia of Jaffrey int 4 Oct 1817 mar 9 Oct 1817 Jaffrey Records

FOX John of Concord & KIMBALL Cerra of Concord int 21 Apr 1834 mar nd Concord Records

FOX John of Jaffrey & HOWE Eloisa M of Jaffrey int 3 Aug 1829 mar 20 Aug 1829 Jaffrey Records

FRENCH Cummings of Jaffrey & SHEDEL Sally of Jaffrey int 9 Feb 1819 mar 11 Feb 1819 Jaffrey Records

FRENCH David of New Ipswich & HUNT Sarah of Jaffrey int 13 Mar 1826 mar nd Jaffrey Records

FRENCH David of Stratham & BURLEY Susan of Newmarket int 12 Sep 1830 mar nd Stratham Records

FRENCH Henry S G Rev of Concord & ALLISON Sarah C of Concord int 6 Jul 1839 mar nd Concord Records

FRENCH James R of Jaffrey & EMERY Mary of Jaffrey int 17 May 1827 mar 17 May 1827 Jaffrey Records

FRENCH Jonathan B of Jaffrey & LICOLN Betsey of Jaffrey int 22 Mar 1816 mar 22 Mar 1816 Jaffrey Records

FRENCH Theoror of Concord & POLLARD Lydia of Dunstable int 12 Sep 1819 mar nd Concord Records

FRENCH Thomas Jr of Jaffrey & JEWELL Sophia of Jaffrey int 7 Mar 1816 mar 8 Mar 1816 Jaffrey Records

FRENCH Timothy of Stratham & CHAPMAN Mary J of Newmarket int 1 Sep 1833 mar nd Stratham Records

FRENCH Walter of Hopkinton & HERRICK Asenith of Concord int 27 Mar 1825 mar nd Concord Records

FRENCH Zechariah of Greenland & PEARL Abigail L of Stratham int 27 Nov 1834 mar nd Stratham Records

FROST Thomas of Jaffrey & BUTTERS Betey of Jaffrey int 13 Feb 1806 mar nd Jaffrey Records

FROST Thomas of Jaffrey & NUTTER Betsey of Jaffrey int 22 Jan 1806 mar 13 Feb 1806 Jaffrey Records

FULLER Thadeus Muzzy of Greenfield & DEAN Betsy Sampson of Dubliny int nd mar 24 Feb 1804 Jaffrey Records

GARFIELD Moses of Prinston MA & PAGE Polly of Jaffrey int 2 Dec 1821 mar 2 Dec 1821 Jaffrey Records

GARLAND Samuel of Hampton & TOWLE Sara Ann of Hampton int nd mar 27 Feb 1833 Stratham Records

GARVIN Benjamin of Concord & STAYAN Sally of Chichester int 11 Sep 1825 mar nd Concord Records

GARVIN Jeremiah of Concord & HUTCHINSON Mary F of Andover MA int 23 Jul 1826 mar nd Concord Records

GARVIN Nathaniel of Concord & ROGERS Mary of Bow int 21 Mar 1824 mar nd Concord Records

GAULT Samuel of Concord & EASTMAN Sarah of Concord int 3 Oct 1824 mar nd Concord Records

GAULT William of Concord & STICKNEY Harriet of Concord int 7 Jan 1820 mar nd Concord Records

GEAR John Jr of Dover & STOCKBRIDGE Martha of Stratham int 7 Sep 1833 mar 6 Oct 1833 Stratham Records

GEARFIELD John of Marlboro & DAVIS Lucy of Jaffrey int 31 Jan 1803 mar nd Jaffrey Records

GEORGE John H of Concord & BRINGHAM Ann L of Concord int 24 Sep 1849 mar nd Concord Records

GIBSON Charles of New York & STICKNEY Mary Frances of Concord int 22 Dec 1834 mar nd Concord Records

GIBSON John of Francestown & GALE Ruth E of Concord int 13 May 1827 mar nd Concord Records

GIBSON Royal of Canterbury & THORN Harriet of Concord int 6 Aug 1826 mar nd Concord Records

GILBERT Harvey J of Savannah GA & MORRILL Priscilla H of Concord int 26 Sep 1842 mar nd Concord Records

GILCHRIST Albert of Andover & CORLIS Abigail of Concord int 13 Apr 1842 mar nd Concord Records

GILLMORE David Lt of Jaffrey & POWERS Muriel of Jaffrey int 14 Apr 1806 mar 1 May 1806 Jaffrey Records

GILLMORE David Jr of Jaffrey & WELLINGTON Lucy of Jaffrey int 10 Oct 1800 mar 12 Nov 1800 Jaffrey Records

GILLMORE Henry of Jaffrey & BYAM Mary of Jaffrey int 30 Dec 1824 mar 30 Dec 1824 Jaffrey Records

GILLMORE Jonathan of Jaffrey & MILLIKEN Betsey of Jaffrey int 15 Aug 1803 mar nd Jaffrey Records

GILMAN Daniel of Jaffrey & STICKNEY Mary of Jaffrey int 5 Nov 1804 mar 1 Dec 1804 Jaffrey Records

GILMAN James of Jaffrey & BUSS Nancy of Jaffrey int 15 Jul 1803 mar 27 Nov 1803 Jaffrey Records

GLAZIER Aaron of Vergenes VT & BUSS Lydia of Jaffrey int 8 Feb 1825 mar nd Jaffrey Records

GLEASON Simion of Mexico ME & OSGOOD Lydia of Concord int 8 Sep 1830 mar nd Concord Records

GLEASON Zebediah of Concord & SHATTUCK Mary of Concord int 28 Nov 1819 mar nd Concord Records

GLINES Joseph of Concord & PUFFER Polly of Concord int 27 Feb 1825 mar nd Concord Records

GLINES Peter B of Canterbury & ELLIOT Dorcas F of Concord int 22 Apr 1827 mar nd Concord Records

GOFF Robert of Jaffrey & BRIANT Sally of Jaffrey int 23 Oct 1810 mar nd Jaffrey Records

GOFFIN Enoch of Concord & PLUMMER Achsa of Dunbarton int 17 Mar 1822 mar nd Concord Records

GOODELL William F of Concord & HALL Sarah of Concord int 26 Oct 1834 mar nd Concord Records

GOODHUE Nathaniel of Concord & MORRILL Lydia P of Salem int 27 Aug 1852 mar nd Concord Records
GOODWIN James of Concord & HOLT Sally of Pembroke int 12 Feb 1826 mar nd Concord Records
GOODWIN Rueben of Concord & WEBBER Betsey (Mrs) of Concord int 3 Dec 1826 mar nd Concord Records
GOWING Almerin of Dublin & SANDERS Sally of Jaffrey int 11 Sep 1826 mar nd Jaffrey Records
GOWING Rodney of Jaffrey & SAWTELL Rebecca of Jaffrey int 20 Jan 1833 mar 23 Apr 1833 Jaffrey Records
GOWNING Simeon of Jaffrey & FROST Mary of Jaffrey int 29 Aug 1803 mar 4 Sep 2803 Jaffrey Records
GRAHAM George of Concord & THORN Luvia of Concord int 1 Jan 1825 mar nd Concord Records
GRAHAM Joseph of Concord & LOVERING Lucinda of Concord int 24 Nov 1830 mar nd Concord Records
GRAHAM Thomas of Quincy MA & STEVENS Jane Morrill of Concord int 13 Sep 1834 mar nd Concord Records
GRANT Andrew M of Concord & MORRILL Nancy C of Concord int 16 Dec 1850 mar nd Concord Records
GRANT Joshua Jr of Concord & TUTTLE Nancy of Concord int 4 Jan 1824 mar nd Concord Records
GRAVENS Louis of Boston MA & ELLIOTT Emma D of Fisherville int 13 Oct 1866 mar nd Concord Records
GRAVES William F of Moultonbough & EMERSON Susan of Concord int 31 Aug 1826 mar nd Concord Records
GRAY Jethro of Stratham & POTTLE Lucretia M of Stratham int 13 Apr 1826 mar nd Stratham Records
GREEN William of Concord & KIMBALL Harriet of Concord int 2 Mar 1828 mar nd Concord Records
GREENE Ephraim of Concord & BABB Amelia of Sanborton int 13 Aug 1820 mar nd Concord Records
GREENOUGH E A of Concord & SANBORN Maria L of Canterbury int 17 Mar 1845 mar nd Concord Records
GRIFFIN Peter of Concord & ALLIN Hannah of Concord int 17 Oct 1824 mar nd Concord Records
GUTHRIE George N of Putnam OH & McFARLAND Sarah A of Concord int 1 Sep 1839 mar nd Concord Records
HADLEY Amos of Concord & PRESCOTT Laura M of Concord int 25 Aug 1851 mar nd Concord Records
HADLEY George of Newmarket & SPEED Martha of Newmarket int 1832 mar nd Stratham Records

HAGAR John C of Manchester & TUFTS Sophronia T of Concord int 6 Sep 1840 mar nd Concord Records

HAINES John S of Loudon & PHILBRICK Mary H of Concord int 28 May 1820 mar nd Concord Records

HAINES Robert of Concord & STEPHENS Mary of Loudon int 26 Feb 1822 mar nd Concord Records

HAINES Samuel of Stratham & BRIMBLOCOM Almira of Stratham int 3 Jan 1829 mar nd Stratham Records

HAINES Thomas F of Stratham & ROLLINS Mary of Stratham int 16 Feb 1828 mar nd Stratham Records

HALE Benjamin of Rindge & PIERCE Miriam of Jaffrey int 26 Oct 1812 mar 29 Nov 1812 Jaffrey Records

HALE Nathan of Rindge & WHITCOMB Sally of Jaffrey int 25 May 1809 mar nd Jaffrey Records

HALL Avory of Concord & DOW Sarah of Concord int 3 Aug 1837 mar nd Concord Records

HALL Daniel of Concord & FELLOWS Elizabeth of Salisbury int 30 Oct 1825 mar nd Concord Records

HALL Daniel of Concord & JOHNSON Sally of Hopkinton int 7 May 1820 mar nd Concord Records

HALL Howard of Windsor NY & GRIGGS A H of Windsor NY int 21 Nov 1856 mar nd Concord Records

HALL Ivory of Concord & CLEMENT Pamelia of Concord int 30 Jun 1822 mar nd Concord Records

HALL Joel of Strafford & HAM Lydia A of Stratham int 23 Feb 1866 mar nd Stratham Records

HALL Robert of Concord & CAPEN Lucinida S of Concord int 20 May 1833 mar nd Concord Records

HALL Stephen of Concord & BRADLEY Charlotte of Concord int 11 Feb 1821 mar nd Concord Records

HAM Charles T of Stratham & THURSTON Jane of Stratham int 27 Sep 1829 mar nd Stratham Records

HAMILTON Irenus of Lymeord & FOSTER Sarah E of Concord int 29 Sep 1864 mar nd Concord Records

HANELY E L of Boston MA & EASTMAN Ruth B of Concord int 2 Nov 1840 mar nd Concord Records

HANNAFORD John of Northfield & FLANDERS Nancy of Concord int 16 Nov 1830 mar nd Concord Records

HARDY Josiah of Concord & COLBY Margarett of Hopkinton int 6 Feb 1820 mar nd Concord Records

HARDY Samuel of Concord & WASHBURN Clarissa of Plainfield VT int 1 Jan 1825 mar nd Concord Records

HARRIS Samuel of Fitchburg MA & ROBBINS Jane of Jaffrey int 22 Nov 1802 mar nd Jaffrey Records

HARVEY Daniel of Nottingham & EWEN Sarah of Concord int 9 Mar 1835 mar nd Concord Records

HARVEY Jesse of Stratham & KELLEY Mary of Stratham int 24 Nov 1822 mar nd Stratham Records

HASELTINE Banes of ? & ROLFE Rebeccah of ? int 9 Apr 1820 mar nd Concord Records

HASKELL Mark of Newbury MA & RUNDLET Mary Ann of Nohampton int 2 Apr 1832 mar nd Stratham Records

HASKELL William M of Boston MA & VIRGIN Emily of Concord int 24 Apr 1832 mar nd Concord Records

HASKELL William M of Concord & VIRGIN Emily of Concord int 15 Apr 1832 mar nd Concord Records

HASLETINE Barnes of Concord & MORSE Hannah of Boscawen int 3 Dec 1820 mar nd Concord Records

HATCH Anthony of Medford MA & CURRIER Mary W of Concord int 27 Jan 1834 mar nd Concord Records

HATCH David W of Stratham & EMERY Sophia of Lynn MA int nd mar 25 Oct 1853 Stratham Records

HATCH Wm W of Concord & LORD Mary I of Brownville ME int 12 Aug 1868 mar 15 AUG 1868 Concord Records

HAWES Amos of Concord & LOCK Frances of Concord int 23 Jun 1846 mar nd Concord Records

HAYNES T C of St Johnsbury VT & BACON Susina of St Johnsbury VT int 186- mar nd Concord Records

HAZELTINE John A of Concord & BAKER Mary of Concord int 1 Oct 1857 mar nd Concord Records

HAZELTON James of Concord & ROLFE Caroline Frances of Concord int 28 Nov 1848 mar nd Concord Records

HAZLETINE Joseph Jr of Concord & WHITMARSH Abigail of Lyndeborouth int 23 May 1824 mar nd Concord Records

HEARD William B of Concord & BLAKE Nancy of Concord int 30 Aug 1840 mar nd Concord Records

HENRY George of Hollis & GILLMORE Mary Ann of Jaffrey int 28 Dec 1806 mar 28 Dec 1806 Jaffrey Records

HERBERT Richard 3rd of Concord & KENDALL Nancy of Concord int 30 Jun 1822 mar nd Concord Records

HIDDIN William of Concord & BELKNAP Lucy of Concord int 21 Sep 1823 mar nd Concord Records

HILL Benjamin of Concord & GILES Martha of Concord int 16 Sep 1821 mar nd Concord Records

HILL Horatio of Concord & EMERY Clara Walker of Concord int 28 Apr 1820 mar nd Concord Records

HILLMAM Moses of Jaffrey & MILLIKEN Polly of Jaffrey int 7 Mar 1805 mar 11 Mar 1805 Jaffrey Records

HOAG Levi of Lynn MA & PHILIPS Louisa of Stratham int 14 Apr 1832 mar nd Stratham Records

HODGDON Carles C of Concord & MERRILL Betsey of Hopkinton int 9 Oct 1825 mar nd Concord Records

HODGDON Charles C of Concord & MERRILL Ruth of Hopkinton int 9 Nov 1828 mar nd Concord Records

HODGDON Phinehus of Concord & CLIFFORD Mary of Loudon int 6 Sep 1820 mar nd Concord Records

HODGDON Thomas of Concord & CARTER Dolly of Concord int 29 Nov 1824 mar nd Concord Records

HODGDON William A of St Louis MO & SANDERSON Abby of Concord int 20 Aug 1856 mar nd Concord Records

HODGE John of Jaffrey & PAGE Polly of Jaffrey int 1922 mar 18 Apr 1822 Jaffrey Records

HODGE Joseph Jr of Jaffrey & TWISS Nabby of Jaffrey int 28 Jul 1830 mar nd Jaffrey Records

HODGE Simpson of Jaffrey & JOHNSON Elmira of Jaffrey int 3 Dec 1822 mar nd Jaffrey Records

HOIT Amos of Concord & ABBOTT Betsey of Concord int 24 Mar 1822 mar nd Concord Records

HOIT Benjamin of Concord & EASTMAN Hannah of Concord int 27 Jul 1819 mar nd Concord Records

HOIT Ethan of Hopkinton & SCALES Emily of Concord int 27 Jan 1834 mar nd Concord Records

HOIT Joseph of Concord & EASTMAN Mary of Concord int 21 May 1820 mar nd Concord Records

HOITE Ezra of Concord & CAULE Fanny of Boscawen int 9 Nov 1823 mar nd Concord Records

HOITE Jedidiah of Concord & DOW Betsey of Concord int 9 Mar 1823 mar nd Concord Records

HOLMES Enos of Springfield VT & ADAMS Louisa of Jaffrey int 2 Sep 1825 mar nd Jaffrey Records

HOLMES Ezra of Boscawen & COLBY Mahala of Concord int 14 Aug 1825 mar nd Concord Records

HOLMES John of Springfield VT & CUTTER Hepsey of Jaffrey int 26 May 1825 mar nd Jaffrey Records

HOLT Horace H of Concord & SMART Caroline H of Concord int 21 Sep 1847 mar nd Concord Records

HOLT John of Suncook & TURNER Eliza of Suncook int 25 Dec 1866 mar nd Concord Records

HOLT Leonard of Concord & HERBERT Marcia of Concord int 17 Jun 1854 mar nd Concord Records
HOLT Simeon of Wilton & BROOKS Esther of Jaffrey int 3 Mar 1801 mar nd Jaffrey Records
HOLT William K of Loudon & VIRGIN Eliza T of Concord int 24 Aug 1835 mar nd Concord Records
HOOK Joseph B of Concord & BEAN Hannah of Loudon int 31 Dec 1849 mar nd Concord Records
HORNE Nathl of Stratham & PIPER Caroline of Stratham int 25 Jan 1823 mar nd Stratham Records
HORNER Elias of Concord & BROWN Eliza of Peeling ? int 26 May 1834 mar nd Concord Records
HORTON Asa of Jaffrey & BREED Susan of Jaffrey int 25 Oct 1806 mar 27 Nov 1806 Jaffrey Records
HORTON Ebenser of Templeton MA & FOSTER Ruth of Jaffrey int 9 Dec 1802 mar 15 Dec 1802 Jaffrey Records
HOWE Abner Dr of Jaffrey & THORNDIKE Sally of Jaffrey int 13 Oct 1806 mar nd Jaffrey Records
HOWE Abner of Jaffrey & THORNDIKE Sarah of Jaffrey int 29 Oct 1806 mar 18 Nov 1806 Jaffrey Records
HOWE Luke Esq of Jaffrey & HOWE Mary of Jaffrey int 25 Jan 1819 mar 11 Feb 1819 Jaffrey Records
HOYT George C of Concord & GRIFFIN Melissa of Candia int 28 Jul 1855 mar nd Concord Records
HUBBARD Benjamin of Stratham & FRENCH Sally of Stratham int 12 Oct 1823 mar nd Stratham Records
HUBERT Samuel of Concord & BRIDGES Nancy of Andover MA int 12 Jan 1823 mar nd Concord Records
HUNTOON John of Hanover & EATON Mary of Concord int 20 Sep 1826 mar nd Concord Records
HUNTRESS Gideon of Concord & TYLER Cylinda of Concord int 25 Dec 1825 mar nd Concord Records
HURD Thomas of Loudon & THOMPSON Melinda of Concord int 18 Jan 1829 mar nd Concord Records
HUTCHINS George of Concord & TUCKER Sarah R of Concord int 30 Mar 1820 mar nd Concord Records
HUTCHINS Josiah of Concord & CLISBY Charlotte S of Concord int nd mar nd Concord Records
HYATT Thomas S of Albany NY & EASTMAN Nancy of Concord int 28 Apr 1839 mar nd Concord Records
INGALLS Josiah Jr of Jaffrey & CAPRON Lois of Jaffrey int 29 Nov 1808 mar nd Jaffrey Records

INGALS Ira of Brandon ? & HODGE Jerusha of Jaffrey int 15 Feb 1809 mar nd Jaffrey Records

JACKSON Andrew of Concord & GILL Rebecca of Concord int 25 Mar 1856 mar nd Concord Records

JACKSON John of Madbury VT & RINGSBURY Abigail of Jaffrey int nd mar 5 Jun 1804 Jaffrey Records

JACKSON John of Sudbury VT & KINGS Abigel of Jaffrey int 5 Jun 1804 mar nd Jaffrey Records

JACKSON Joseph L of Concord & SHUTE Cynthia of Concord int 22 Jun 1835 mar nd Concord Records

JACOBS Eli of Concord & MARDIN Dora of Concord int 29 Mar 1869 mar nd Concord Records

JACOBS Godfrey Jr of Concord & PUMROY Etta Louisa of Lorvell Mich int 14 Jan 1869 mar nd Concord Records

JAMES J of Stratham & WIGGIN Nancy P of Stratham int 11 Jan 1824 mar nd Stratham Records

JAMESON John H of Concord & MOORE Eliza Ann of Concord int 1 Oct 1849 mar nd Concord Records

JAMESON Samuel of Concord & MERRILL Mary P of Concord int 14 Sep 1853 mar nd Concord Records

JAMIESON John of Concord & SEAVEY Sarah of Concord int 23 Aug 1862 mar nd Concord Records

JAQUITH David of Jaffrey & SAWYER Sally of Jaffrey int 27 Dec 1817 mar 31 Dec 1817 Jaffrey Records

JARVIS John of Concord & FARNUM Mary of Allenstown int 9 Jun 1822 mar nd Concord Records

JENNISSON William of Worcester MA & WALKER Mary C of Concord int 10 Oct 1830 mar nd Concord Records

JEWELL Alvin of Winchester MA & PIERCE Keziah of Jaffrey int 22 Jan 1806 mar 6 Feb 1806 Jaffrey Records

JEWELL David of Stratham & LEAVITT Rachel of Stratham int 12 Nov 1832 mar nd Stratham Records

JEWELL Dexter of Jaffrey & MOWER Sarah of Jaffrey int 25 Dec 1829 mar nd Jaffrey Records

JEWELL Harvey of Boston MA & BRADLEY Susan A of Concord int 14 Dec 1849 mar nd Concord Records

JEWELL Levi Esq of Stratham & MARSTON Elizabeth C of Nothampton int 21 Jun 1834 mar nd Stratham Records

JEWETT Ezra of Jaffrey & MAYNARD Elvira of Jaffrey int 10 Feb 1826 mar nd Jaffrey Records

JOHNSON Charles of Concord & CURTIS Lucinda S of Concord int 24 Jan 1847 mar nd Concord Records

JOHNSON Dolliver of Concord & UNDERWOOD Louisa of Billerica MA int 4 Feb 1827 mar nd Concord Records

JOHNSON Lewis of Hancock & DINSMORE Jane of Jaffrey int 20 Dec 1836 mar nd Jaffrey Records

JOHNSON Zenas of Hull Lower Canada & FLANDERS Nancy Parker of Concord int 8 Oct 1826 mar nd Concord Records

JONES Charles A of Stratham & ANDERSON Sarah of Baldwin ME int 5 Jun 1876 mar nd Stratham Records

JONES Freeman of Concord & IRISH Elizabeth W of Concord int 2 Nov 1845 mar nd Concord Records

JONES Gardner of Epping & WHITLAND Ester of Stratham int nd mar nd Stratham Records

JONES Robert E of Brooklyn NY & KIMBALL Priscilla H of Concord int 13 Nov 1848 mar nd Concord Records

JONES Theophilus of Exeter & THURSTON Dorothy M of Stratham int 3 Oct 1830 mar nd Stratham Records

JOSLIN T Esq of Hopkinsville & FISK Nancy of Dublin int nd mar 16 Feb 1805 Jaffrey Records

JOSLIN Thomas of Leominster MA & ADAMS Polly of Jaffrey int 23 Sep 1807 mar 24 Sep 1807 Jaffrey Records

JUDKINS Seth of Bow & ABBOT Phebe of Concord int 17 Jan 1831 mar nd Concord Records

KELLEY Benjamin of Stratham & FELTCH Sarah M of Stratham int 15 Apr 1831 mar 23 Jun 1831 Stratham Records

KELLEY Benjamin of Stratham & WENTWORTH Sally of Barrington int 28 Apr 1827 mar nd Stratham Records

KELLEY Charles of Stratham & KENISTON Olive of Stratham int 8 Nov 1831 mar nd Stratham Records

KELLEY George of Stratham & SPEED Martha of Newmarket int 1 Sep 1832 mar nd Stratham Records

KELLEY Samuel Rev of Gilmanton & SHUBURN Maryann of Concord int 25 Mar 1827 mar nd Concord Records

KELLLEY Frederick of Concord & HOLLAND Harriet N of Concord int 5 Nov 1856 mar nd Concord Records

KELSEA William of Concord & ABBOTT Sarah D of Concord int 19 Sep 1841 mar nd Concord Records

KEMP Petitiah B of Groton & DIMOND Dolly of Concord int 6 Feb 1820 mar nd Concord Records

KENT George of Concord & FARRAN Luvia Anne of Burlington VT int 8 Oct 1820 mar nd Concord Records

KENT William A of Roxbury MA & TUCKER Margarett of Concord int 17 Jun 1821 mar nd Concord Records

KICKER John of So Berwick ME & SIMPSON Nancy N of Stratham int nd mar nd Stratham Records
KIMBAL Hazen of Concord & FIFIELD Nancy of Loudon int 2 Jan 1820 mar nd Concord Records
KIMBALL Cyrus of Boston MA & KIMBALL Charlotte Green of Concord int 30 Nov 1828 mar nd Concord Records
KIMBALL Hazen of Hopkinton & BAKER Mary Ann of Concord int 20 Jan 1828 mar nd Concord Records
KIMBALL Willis G C of Concord & GOVE L Ella of Concord int 28 May 1863 mar nd Concord Records
KITTREDGE Augustus G of Concord & TILTON Bell H of Concord int 16 Jan 1866 mar nd Concord Records
KNOWLTON Nathaniel M of Concord & SARGENT Ruth of Dunbarton int 17 Dec 1820 mar nd Concord Records
KNOWLTON Simon of Seabrook & ROLLINGS Abigail of Seabrook int nd mar 11 Jun 1820 Stratham Records
LANE Charles J of Concord & HILL Sophia of Concord int 17 Oct 1854 mar nd Concord Records
LANE George of Stratham & BARKER Mary L of Stratham int 1 Mar 1822 mar nd Stratham Records
LANE John L of Stratham & WIGGIN Louisa A of Stratham int 27 Sep 1834 mar nd Stratham Records
LANE Samuel of Medford & TUFFTS Fanny of Concord int 14 Apr 1834 mar nd Concord Records
LANG Benjamin of Stratham & SMITH Hannah of East Kingston int 18 Apr 1827 mar nd Stratham Records
LANG Charles W of Concord & PILLSBURY Louis C of Concord int 26 Apr 1865 mar nd Concord Records
LANG David of Stratham & GROVER Irena of Sandown int 1 Jan 1831 mar nd Stratham Records
LANG David of Stratham & SCAMMON Comfort of Stratham int nd mar 2 Dec 1819 Stratham Records
LANG Joseph of Newmarket & FIFIELD Elizabeth of Stratham int 3 Mar 1832 mar 5 Jul 1832 Stratham Records
LANG Stephen Jr of Concord & WALDRON Sally W of Concord int 6 Jan 1822 mar nd Concord Records
LANG Thomas G of Hampton Falls & DANIELS Eunice of Stratham int 26 Mar 1831 mar 14 Apr 1831 Stratham Records
LANGLY Reuben of Stratham & SCAMMON Sally of Stratham int nd mar 18 Apr 1822 Stratham Records
LANGLY Reuben of Stratham & SCAMMON Sarah of Stratham int ? Feb 1822 mar nd Stratham Records

LANGMAID Minot of Stratham & WILLAND Lois of Stratham int 31 Mar 1832 mar nd Stratham Records
LARABEE Jonathan of Jaffrey & GARY Lucy of Jaffrey int 26 Nov 1807 mar 24 Jan 1808 Jaffrey Records
LARY Voltaine of Concord & PILSBURY Mary W of Concord int 11 Mar 1852 mar nd Concord Records
LAW Artemas of Jaffrey & CUTTER Sarah of Jaffrey int 27 Apr 1829 mar nd Jaffrey Records
LAW John of Jaffrey & DEAN Susannah of Jaffrey int 1 Oct 1810 mar nd Jaffrey Records
LAWRENCE Artemas of Jaffrey & ADAMS Lucy of Jaffrey int nd mar 6 Feb 1805 Jaffrey Records
LAWRENCE Ithamer of Jaffrey & JEWELL Betsy of Jaffrey int 12 Sep 1812 mar nd Jaffrey Records
LAWRENCE Joseph of Concord & CAFREY Ann of Concord int 25 Jun 1848 mar nd Concord Records
LAWRENCE Moody of Jaffrey & BRYANT Doris of Jaffrey int 2 Apr 1805 mar nd Jaffrey Records
LAWRENCE Moody of Jaffrey & SPAULDING Polly of Jaffrey int 3 Feb 1811 mar 3 Feb 1811 Jaffrey Records
LAWTON Robert of Concord & KELLEY Catharine of Concord int 2 May 1865 mar nd Concord Records
LEAVIT Jonathan of Stratham & BOYD Charlotte of Stratham int 6 Jul 1828 mar nd Stratham Records
LEAVITT Edmund of Concord & REED Nancy of Exeter int 9 Dec 1820 mar nd Concord Records
LEAVITT Ephraim of Stratham & PIPER Abigail of Stratham int 7 Sep 1822 mar 23 Sep 1822 Stratham Records
LEAVITT John of Allenstown & FOLSOM Martha of Stratham int 14 Nov 1830 mar nd Stratham Records
LEAVITT Walter of Concord & SILVER Clennia of Concord int 18 Mar 1867 mar nd Concord Records
LIBBEY Charles of Concord & TANDY Ruhaman of Concord int 17 Apr 1837 mar nd Concord Records
LITCH Samuel of Jaffrey & STEVENS Patty of Jaffrey int 12 Jun 1809 mar nd Jaffrey Records
LITTLE John of Boscawen & LOVEJOY Miriam of Concord int 22 Aug 1824 mar nd Concord Records
LOCK John of Concord & SANBORN Rachel of Epsom int 7 Jul 1822 mar nd Concord Records
LOCK Josiah of Concord & PHILBRICK Lydia of Concord int 24 Sep 1820 mar nd Concord Records

LOCKE Josiah of Concord & EMERY Clara G of Concord int 10 Mar 1857 mar nd Concord Records
LOCKE Laroy of Loudon & EVES Hannah of Concord int 27 Jan 1868 mar nd Concord Records
LOCKE William of Concord & NEWTON Alina B of Cornish int 5 Mar 1848 mar nd Concord Records
LONG M E of Hopkinton & RUNNELS Almira of Concord int 20 Oct 1859 mar nd Concord Records
LOTHROP David of Concord & COLE Lucy E of Concord int 22 Aug 1862 mar nd Concord Records
LOUGEE Josesph of Loudon & KIMBALL Pamelia of Concord int 29 May 1825 mar nd Concord Records
LOUGER James of Boscawen & CARTER Phebe of Concord int 6 Apr 1823 mar nd Concord Records
LOVEJOY Henry of Concord & THORN Sarah L of Concord int 9 Jun 1822 mar nd Concord Records
LOVEJOY Peter of Concord & SMITH Sophia of Concord int 5 Nov 1832 mar nd Concord Records
LOVJOY Chandler of Concord & VIRGIN Fanny H of Concord int 10 Dec 1826 mar nd Concord Records
LOW John of Concord & VICKERY Sarah of Concord int 20 May 1821 mar nd Concord Records
LYNN William of Concord & PILLSBURY Eliz Ann of Concord int 13 Nov 1819 mar nd Concord Records
MANAHAN Joseph Capt of Concord & MONTGOMERY Ellen D of Concord int 10 Sep 1831 mar nd Concord Records
MANSON William of Concord & AILIN Charlotte of Concord int 22 Jul 1821 mar nd Concord Records
MARDEN Mark of Epsom & SILVER Ruth T of Concord int 7 Mar 1840 mar nd Concord Records
MARDEN Samuel of Epsom & SILVER Deborah of Concord int 7 Mar 1840 mar nd Concord Records
MARSHALL William of Jaffrey & KIMBALL Sally of Jaffrey int 22 Oct 1805 mar nd Jaffrey Records
MARSTON Joseph T of Northampton & CRIMBELL Sally D of Northampton int nd mar 17 Sep 1826 Stratham Records
MARSTON Noah of Greenland & PIPER Polly of Stratham int 20 Jul 1815 mar nd Stratham Records
MARTIN Henry 3rd of Concord & FLANDERS Sarah of Concord int 5 Dec 1819 mar nd Concord Records
MARTIN Jeremiah of Concord & BROWN Nany of Concord int 7 Sep 1823 mar nd Concord Records
MASON Hiram of St John's VT & PERKINS Mary A of Concord int 6 May 1864 mar nd Concord Records

MAVOREY Charles of Greenville & INGALLS Deborah of Jaffrey int 4 Apr 1816 mar nd Jaffrey Records

MAYHEW William of Jaffrey & KIMBALL Sarah of Jaffrey int 16 Oct 1805 mar 22 Oct 1805 Jaffrey Records

MAYHUE Charles of Concord & DAVIS Lydia G of Concord int 12 Jan 1860 mar nd Concord Records

MAYNARD John H of Concord & KIMBALL Jane K of Concord int 20 Mar 1837 mar nd Concord Records

MCCAN Thomas of Stratham & ROBINSON Betsey of Stratham int 20 Jan 1829 mar nd Stratham Records

MCINTIRE David of Dixfield ME & FISK Phily of Concord int 20 Jan 1828 mar nd Concord Records

MCWILLIAM Gilbert of Conway & FARLAND Susan K of Concord int 26 Feb 1838 mar nd Concord Records

MEED Albigenu of Concord & JOHNSON Susan of Canterbury int 1 Mar 1824 mar nd Concord Records

MEEDS Jsesse of Dublin & BULLARD Mary of Jaffrey int 22 Mar 1809 mar nd Jaffrey Records

MELVILLE Jonas of Jaffrey & LACY Betsey of Jaffrey int 1922-1925 mar nd Jaffrey Records

MERRILL Asa (Elder) of Stratham & BABB Susanna of Stratham int nd mar 19 Sep 1831 Stratham Records

MERRILL Nathan L of Exeter & WIGGIN Elizabeth of Stratham int 26 Sep 1829 mar nd Stratham Records

MERRILL Nathaniel of Hopkinton & CHANDLER Mehitable of Concord int 16 Jul 1820 mar nd Concord Records

MILES William of Medford MA & THOMPSON Sally of Medford MA int nd mar 6 Jun 1804 Jaffrey Records

MILLER John of Concord & EMERY Sarah B of Concord int 29 Nov 1824 mar nd Concord Records

MILLIKIN Alexander of Jaffrey & BIXBY Julia of Dublin int nd mar 28 Oct 1991 Jaffrey Records

MILLS Charles of Concord & BROWN Mary of Concord int 30 Sep 1833 mar nd Concord Records

MILLS John of Concord & LEAVITT Rachel of Concord int 17 Nov 1823 mar nd Concord Records

MILLS Nathaniel of Concord & GLOVER Betsey of Pembroke int 9 Dec 1827 mar nd Concord Records

MITCHELL M George of Concord & COGSWELL Lydia B of Concord int 6 Jul 1853 mar nd Concord Records

MITCHELL William E of Belfast ME & McKINLEY Martha A of Concord int 16 Apr 1848 mar nd Concord Records

MIXER Charles T of Concord & MORRILL Eliza Jane of Concord int 2 May 1834 mar nd Concord Records

MOODY Andrew of Rumford ME & WHEELER Ruth Whittermor of Concord int 1 Feb 1829 mar nd Concord Records
MOODY Charles of Concord & GERRISH Maria A of Three Oak MI int 27 Apr 1864 mar nd Concord Records
MOODY George of Concord & GALE Mary of Concord int 15 Apr 1838 mar nd Concord Records
MOODY Silas of Kennebunk ME & TOWNSON Harriet B of Stratham int 26 Nov 1831 mar nd Stratham Records
MOORE Henry E of Plymouth & FARNUM Susan D of Concord int 1 Jan 1825 mar nd Concord Records
MOORE Henry of Concord & BAKER Lydia of Concord int 24 Oct 1831 mar nd Concord Records
MOORE Jacob B of Concord & HILL Mary A of Ashburnham MA int 2 Jul 1820 mar nd Concord Records
MOORE John Jr of Stratham & PARKER Sarah Ann of No Hampton int 5 Dec 1830 mar nd Stratham Records
MOORE John W of Concord & EASTMAN Emily of Concord int 7 Sep 1832 mar nd Concord Records
MOORE Josiah of Canterbury & ARLIN Ruth of Concord int 18 Jan 1829 mar nd Concord Records
MOORE William of Concord & ABBOTT Judith of Concord int 2 Jan 1835 mar nd Concord Records
MOORS Nathan of Sharon & NEWELL Sarah S of Jaffrey int 16 Jan 1832 mar 19 Jan 1832 Jaffrey Records
MOORS William of Jaffrey & BLODGET Sarah of Jaffrey int 18 Dec 1833 mar nd Jaffrey Records
MOREY J T of Concord & SYMONDS Mary E of Concord int 23 Nov 1854 mar nd Concord Records
MORGAN Jesse of Bow & SEAVEY Mary of Concord int 22 Aug 1824 mar nd Concord Records
MORRIL Saban of Canterbury & BRADLEY Susan of Concord int 17 Aug 1823 mar nd Concord Records
MORRILL Benjamin of Concord & SIMPSON Elenor of Concord int 29 Oct 1826 mar nd Concord Records
MORRILL Geo S of Fisherville & MOODY Clara A of Fisherville int 13 Nov 1867 mar nd Concord Records
MORRILL Gilman of Concord & ELLIOT Martha Jane of Bow int 31 Jan 1841 mar nd Concord Records
MORRILL Joel S of Concord & EASTMAN Mary Ann of Concord int 8 Dec 1834 mar nd Concord Records
MORRISON David of Concord & STEVENS Abigail of Concord int 9 Mar 1828 mar nd Concord Records
MORRISON Robert G of Canterbury & CARTER Sarah R of Concord int 24 May 1860 mar nd Concord Records

MORSE Caleb of Concord & MARCH Lydia of Amesbury MA int 11 Dec 1825 mar nd Concord Records

MORSE Isaac of Orange & SPOFFORD Miriam of Jaffrey int 2 Mar 1801 mar nd Jaffrey Records

MORSE St Luke of Rumford & WHEELER Judith of Concord int 1 Dec 1822 mar nd Concord Records

MOULTON Benning of Center Harbor & GEORGE Eliva of Concord int 30 Apr 1820 mar nd Concord Records

MOULTON James Jr of Concord & CHANDLER Rebeca Abbot of Concord int 11 Feb 1828 mar nd Concord Records

MOULTON James Jr Dea of Concord & SOUTHER Betsey of Concord int 26 Mar 1846 mar nd Concord Records

MOULTON Joseph of Hampton Falls & BROWN Mary Ann of Hampton Falls int nd mar 9 Dec 1823 Stratham Records

MOULTON Nathan Capt of Hampton Falls & BROWN Sarah of Stratham int nd mar 17 Jun 1830 Stratham Records

MOULTON Nathan of Hampton Falls & BROWN Sarah of Stratham int 26 May 1830 mar nd Stratham Records

MOWD Ephraim of Rye & COMBS Olive of Stratham int 14 Sep 1824 mar nd Stratham Records

MOWER Gilman of Jaffrey & JEWELL Roseana of Jaffrey int 5 May 1825 mar 7 May 1825 Jaffrey Records

MOWER Liberty of Jaffrey & BUSS Emily of Jaffrey int 25 Dec 1829 mar 29 Dec 1829 Jaffrey Records

MURRAY John of Stratham & PINDER Fanny of Stratham int 6 Jun 1823 mar nd Stratham Records

MUTHIKEN Alexander of Sharon & BATES Nancy of Jaffrey int 1 Jan 1803 mar 24 Apr 1803 Jaffrey Records

MUVEY John of Greenland & PINDER Fany B of Stratham int nd mar nd Stratham Records

MUZZY Reuben of Dublin & HAMBLETON Betsey of Dublin int nd mar 24 Feb 1804 Jaffrey Records

NARY Daniel of Northfield VT & CHANDLER Charlotte F of Concord int 6 Nov 1856 mar nd Concord Records

NASON Joshua of Stratham & ROBINSON Deborah of Stratham int 19 May 1822 mar 18 Jun 1822 Stratham Records

NEAL Darius of Meredith & MOODY Frances S of Concord int 27 Aug 1855 mar nd Concord Records

NEAL Samuel of Boston MA & VIRGIN Sarah Ambrose of Concord int 21 Aug 1833 mar nd Concord Records

NEAL William A W of Concord & MOORE Comfort of Concord int 31 Jul 1831 mar nd Concord Records

NEEDHAM Nicanor Dr of Peterborough & CUTTER Roanna of Jaffrey int 4 Mar 1808 mar nd Jaffrey Records

NEWMAN Samuel P of Brunswick ME & KENT Caroline of Concord int 3 May 1821 mar nd Concord Records
NICHOLS Alexander of Concord & STOW Eleanor of Hopkinton int 6 Feb 1820 mar nd Concord Records
NICHOLS Warren Rev of Loudon & MORRIL Ann Maria of Concord int 23 Sep 1833 mar nd Concord Records
NISKSON John of Concord & GLOVER Mary of Canterbury int 6 Nov 1825 mar nd Concord Records
NORTON John of Stratham & HEATH Ruth of Stratham int 6 Jul 1823 mar nd Stratham Records
NORTON Winthrop B of Oxford ME & SYMONDS Sally of Concord int 28 Apr 1832 mar nd Concord Records
NOYES David of Enfield & CARTER Polly of Concord int 5 Apr 1821 mar nd Concord Records
NOYES John W of Concord & BOUTON Harriette of Concord int 7 Jun 1855 mar nd Concord Records
NUTTING Abel of Jaffrey & CUTTER Rachel of Jaffrey int 1 Jan 1815 mar 1 Jan 1815 Jaffrey Records
NUTTING Ebenezer of Jaffrey & BYAM Sophia of Jaffrey int 15 Mar 1827 mar 18 Mar 1827 Jaffrey Records
NUTTING Jonas of Jaffrey & TURNER Jean of Jaffrey int 30 Dec 1799 mar nd Jaffrey Records
ORDWAY John C of Concord & BOHANON Louisa W of Concord int 28 Apr 1829 mar nd Concord Records
ORDWAY Moses of Concord & CHASE Sarah N of Concord int 6 Sep 1834 mar nd Concord Records
ORDWAY Plummer of Concord & ELLIOTT Dolly F of Concord int 23 Dec 1843 mar nd Concord Records
OSGOOD Oliver of Jaffrey & STICKNEY Polly of Jaffrey int 1791 ? mar nd Jaffrey Records
PAGE Bracket of Concord & BRADLEY Eliza of Plymouth int 1 Jan 1825 mar nd Concord Records
PAGE Elias of Rindge & SMITH Olive of Fitzwilliam int nd mar 9 Jul 1803 Jaffrey Records
PAGE George of Bradford & SILVER Elizabeth of Concord int 27 Apr 1849 mar nd Concord Records
PAGE James H of Concord & FARNUM Mary F of Concord int 11 Jun 1825 mar nd Concord Records
PAGE Reuben of Rindge & WHEELER Polly of Jaffrey int 15 Sep 1807 mar nd Jaffrey Records
PALMER Aaron A of Hopkinton & GEORGE Sarah of Concord int 30 Nov 1828 mar nd Concord Records

PALMER Dudley of Concord & WILKINS Esther of Concord int 30 Dec 1829 mar nd Concord Records

PALMER Isaac K of Concord & CLEMENT Almira of Concord int 23 May 1836 mar nd Concord Records

PALMER Samuel of Hopkinton & EMERY Hannah B of Concord int 29 Apr 1823 mar nd Concord Records

PARGE Jeremiah of Concord & SHADDUCK Mehitable of Pembroke int 12 Mar 1826 mar nd Concord Records

PARISH Obadiah of Gilmanton & KENISTON Elizabeth of Concord int 13 Feb 1825 mar nd Concord Records

PARKER Caleb of Concord & VIRGIN Abigail D of Concord int 28 Oct 1835 mar nd Concord Records

PARKER Jeremiah of Concord & LANG Mary of Concord int 6 Oct 1922 mar nd Concord Records

PARKER Samuel of Mason & STEWART Beatrice of Jaffrey int 2 Nov 1813 mar 2 Nov 1813 Jaffrey Records

PARKER Stephen H of No Andover MA & ABBOTT Ann M of Concord int 23 Jan 1842 mar nd Concord Records

PARKMAN Asa of Palmyra ME & WINGATE Sally of Stratham int 26 Apr 1833 mar nd Stratham Records

PATTERSON I N of Concord & BOUTON Sarah C of Concord int 12 Nov 1867 mar nd Concord Records

PAYNE Solomon of Concord & BARKER Sarah of Canterbury Ct int 12 Dec 1824 mar nd Concord Records

PEARSON Jonas N of Stratham & YEATON Lueasa P of Stratham int 8 Nov 1864 mar nd Stratham Records

PEAVEY Edward H of Stratham & JEWELL Emeline of Stratham int 14 Aug 1834 mar nd Stratham Records

PECKER R C of Concord & ESTABROOK Emeline A of Concord int 20 Dec 1847 mar nd Concord Records

PECKER Rober E Capt of Concord & LANG Esther Johnson of Concord int 1 May 1832 mar nd Concord Records

PECKER William of Concord & CHANDLER Susan D of Concord int 4 Oct 1834 mar nd Concord Records

PERCIVEL Lyman of Nashville (Nashua) & BLODGETT Hepsy E of Jaffrey int 10 Sep 1845 mar nd Jaffrey Records

PERKINS Jacob of Exeter & EATON Harriet of Concord int 20 Sep 1826 mar nd Concord Records

PERKINS John of Concord & ELA Mary of Conway int 17 Oct 1819 mar nd Concord Records

PERRIN Stephen of Salisbury & EASTMAN Priscilla of Concord int 5 Jun 1825 mar nd Concord Records

PERRY Amos of Concord & LABONTIE Priscilla of Concord int 7 Jun 1820 mar nd Concord Records

PERRY William G of Exeter & FISKE L M of Concord int 20 Aug 1849 mar nd Concord Records

PERU Simons of Jaffrey & BYAM Anna of Jaffrey int 7 Jan 1811 mar 26 Feb 1811 Jaffrey Records

PETERS J F of Concord & HEATH Harriet of Concord int 26 Oct 1857 mar nd Concord Records

PETINGIL Amos Rev of Jaffrey & WHITFIELD Agigail of Jaffrey int 23 Oct 1807 mar nd Jaffrey Records

PETTINGILL Amos Rev of Champlain NY & WAKEFIELD Abigail of Jaffrey int 22 Oct 1807 mar 23 Oct 1807 Jaffrey Records

PETTINGILL David of Concord & SARGENT Martha of Concord int 26 Dec 1841 mar nd Concord Records

PETTINGILL James of Concord & RYAN Hannah of Concord int 7 Mar 1831 mar nd Concord Records

PETTINGILL Jefferson of Concord & QUIMBY Maryann of Concord int 12 Dec 1828 mar nd Concord Records

PETTINGILL Lorenzo of Concord & MERRILL Rosette Jane of Concord int 26 Dec 1841 mar nd Concord Records

PHELPS Samuel W of Cincinnati OH & DRAKE Harriet E of Concord int 18 Apr 1836 mar nd Concord Records

PHILBRICK Edward of Concord & EDGERLY Nancy of Epping int 22 Jul 1821 mar nd Concord Records

PICKERING William of Concord & WALKER Susan B of Concord int 8 Jan 1826 mar nd Concord Records

PIERCE Abijah of Jaffrey & MAYNARD Sally of Jaffrey int 19 Feb 1817 mar 20 Feb 1817 Jaffrey Records

PIERCE Augustine C of Danville VT & CARTER Sarah of Concord int 1 Jan 1826 mar nd Concord Records

PIERCE Jacob of Alstead & PIERCE Betsy of Jaffrey int 15 Jan 1818 mar 16 Jan 1818 Jaffrey Records

PIERCE Jonas of Jaffrey & BAILEY Lucinda of Jaffrey int 23 Aug 1811 mar 24 Aug 1811 Jaffrey Records

PIERCE of Jaffrey & PIERCE Esther (Mrs) of Jaffrey int 12 Dec 1821 mar nd Jaffrey Records

PIERCE Samuel of Jaffrey & BROOKS Kitty of Jaffrey int 24 Feb 1806 mar 25 Feb 1806 Jaffrey Records

PILLSBURY Amos of Concord & HEATH Emily of Bow int 20 Sep 1826 mar nd Concord Records

PILLSBURY John C of Concord & ABBOTT Elizabeth of Littleton MA int 23 May 1824 mar nd Concord Records

PILSBURY Thomas A of Concord & DAY Emma of Concord int 9 Mar 1865 mar nd Concord Records

PINDER of Stratham & KELLEY Joanna of Stratham int 15 Oct 1826 mar nd Stratham Records

PIPER John Jr of Stratham & FRENCH Eliz Ann of Stratham int 22 Mar 1828 mar 13 Apr 1828 Stratham Records

PITMAN Gideon C of Somersworth & CHASE Mary Anne (Mrs) of Stratham int nd mar nd Stratham Records

PITMAN Gideon C of Stratham & CHASE Mary Ann of Stratham int 23 Nov 1833 mar nd Stratham Records

POOL Ebenezer of Concord & LEBOSQUET Eliza of Concord int 30 Jul 1826 mar nd Concord Records

POTTER Henry H of Concord & HILL Deresca of Concord int 25 Aug 1854 mar nd Concord Records

POTTER Jacoba of Concord & MOORE Sophronia of Loudon int 19 Nov 1826 mar nd Concord Records

POTTER Josiah of Fitzwilliam & WORSTER Sarah of Jaffrey int 28 Aug 1810 mar nd Jaffrey Records

POTTER Samuel G of Concord & STEPHENS Pamilia of Loudon int 1 Apr 1821 mar nd Concord Records

POTTER Thomas D of Concord & MARDIN Eunice of Chichester int 4 Jun 1820 mar nd Concord Records

POURLEY Josiah of Stratham & PIPER Theodatia of Stratham int nd mar 17 Dec 1826 Stratham Records

POWELL James of Concord & SARGENT Pamael of Concord int 24 Aug 1830 mar nd Concord Records

POWELL Moses of Concord & CHANDLER Eliza of Concord int 30 May 1824 mar nd Concord Records

PRESCOTT Albert H of Kensington & BROWN Elizabeth of Kensington int nd mar 22 Aug 1826 Stratham Records

PRESCOTT Eldad Capt of Jaffrey & HUNT Betsey of Jaffrey int 3 Jun 1829 mar 10 Jun 1829 Jaffrey Records

PRIEST Jacob of Jaffrey & HODGE Eunice of Jaffrey int 16 Oct 1840 mar 26 Nov 1840 Jaffrey Records

PRIEST John of Jaffrey & HADLEY Deborah of Jaffrey int 25 Feb 1806 mar 25 Feb 1806 Jaffrey Records

PRIEST Nathan of Jaffrey & PEAK Sarah of Jaffrey int 28 May 1829 mar 3 Jun 1829 Jaffrey Records

PROCTER Wm Porter of Jaffrey & CHEVEN Mehitable of Jaffrey int 23 Oct 1815 mar 28 Oct 1815 Jaffrey Records

PROCTOR Solomon Capt of Cavendish VT & HOW Lydia of Jaffrey int 21 Sep 1818 mar 22 Sep 1818 Jaffrey Records

PUFFER Thomas Jr of Concord & CHANDLER Dorcas of Concord int 14 Nov 1841 mar nd Concord Records

PURINGTON Josiah R of Lowell MA & RICHARDSON Eliza P of Lowell MA int nd mar 10 May 1827 Stratham Records

PUTNAM Allen of Reading MA & FOSS Martha of Stratham int 8 Aug 1835 mar nd Stratham Records
PUTNAM Nehimrah of Rumford ME & WHEDDEN Hannah of Concord int 31 Dec 1826 mar nd Concord Records
PUTNEY Alexander of Portland ME & ABBOT Mary W of Concord int 4 Jan 1829 mar nd Concord Records
PUTNEY John of Concord & BACHELDER Sally of Loudon int 18 Feb 1821 mar nd Concord Records
QUIMBY Daniel H of Concord & HUTCHINSON Deborah H of Concord int 24 May 1848 mar nd Concord Records
QUIMBY Hanson of Concord & SMART Abigail Jane of Concord int 10 Nov 1864 mar nd Concord Records
QUIMBY Moses M of Concord & CENTER Lydia Jane of Concord int 23 Aug 1862 mar nd Concord Records
RAND Oliver J of Cambridge MA & HILL Sarah W of Concord int 22 Feb 1858 mar nd Concord Records
RANSOM Calvin Rev of Jacksonville OH & CLARK Anne E of Concord int 17 Aug 1846 mar nd Concord Records
REED Tilly of Acworth & BYAM Deliverance of Jaffrey int 3 Dec 1810 mar nd Jaffrey Records
REYNOLDS Joseph of Concord & PRESCOTT Lucy of Cambridge MA int 6 Apr 1828 mar nd Concord Records
REYNOLDS Martin L of Sidney ME & CONY Frances of Augusta ME int 18 Jan 1866 mar nd Concord Records
RICHARDSON John A of Durham & MULRDOCK Frances of Concord int 19 Jan 1835 mar nd Concord Records
RIDER Moses of Jaffrey & WORSTER Hepzebath of Jaffrey int 9 Mar 1801 mar nd Jaffrey Records
RIPLEY John S of Jaffrey & GILLMORE Lucy of Jaffrey int 23 Jan 1826 mar nd Jaffrey Records
ROBB Joseph of Chichester & WHITNEY Sophia of Concord int 22 Apr 1821 mar nd Concord Records
ROBBINS Hervey of Jaffrey & EMERY Nancy Ann of Jaffrey int 19 Apr 1831 mar 28 Apr 1831 Jaffrey Records
ROBERTS Mark of Stratham & WIGGINS Sally of Stratham int 17 Nov 1832 mar 9 Dec 1832 Stratham Records
ROBERTSON Alva of Concord & BEAN Lucy of Springfield int 9 Mar 1821 mar nd Concord Records
ROBERTSON Nathaniel of Concord & GILMAN Deborah of Exeter int 29 Aug 1819 mar nd Concord Records
ROBERTSON Samuel P of Bow & TAYLOR Belinda of Concord int 20 Jan 1828 mar nd Concord Records
ROBINSON Asa C of Stratham & DOWNS Mary B of Rye int 28 Sep 1823 mar nd Stratham Records

ROBINSON Charles N of Fisherville & HOLT Jennie of Fisherville int 24 May 1867 mar nd Concord Records
ROBINSON Isacah of Concord & COLBY Abigail of Warner int 29 Apr 1826 mar nd Concord Records
ROBINSON David Jr of Stratham & COMBS Nancy of Stratham int 9 Nov 1823 mar nd Stratham Records
ROBINSON Timothy K of Jaffrey & FAY Sarah of Jaffrey int 29 Nov 1816 mar nd Jaffrey Records
ROBY Harison A of Concord & SARGENT Sophrona Bedger of Concord int 15 Apr 1861 mar nd Concord Records
ROBY Luther of Concord & CURTIS Nancy of Amherest int 19 Jan 1823 mar nd Concord Records
ROBY Luther of Concord & KIMBALL Mary Ann of Concord int 21 May 1828 mar nd Concord Records
ROGERS Francis of Bow & GARVIN Miriam of Concord int 24 Nov 1822 mar nd Concord Records
ROGERS Robert of Concord & CAULE Abigail of Concord int 19 Aug 1821 mar nd Concord Records
ROGERS Wm H of Concord & WEEKS Martha I of Concord int 19 Mar 1867 mar nd Concord Records
ROLFE Hiram of Concord & COOMBS Georgiana of Billerica MA int 25 Feb 1850 mar nd Concord Records
ROLFE Nathaniel of Concord & MOODY Mary Jane of Concord int 25 Dec 1838 mar nd Concord Records
ROLLARD William of Concord & VIRGIN Carolin E D of Concord int 9 Jan 1847 mar nd Concord Records
ROLLINGS James Capt of Stratham & MOORE Sophia of Stratham int 21 Sep 1823 mar Nov 1823 Stratham Records
ROLLINGS Jeremiah of No Hampton & SHAW Mary Ann of No Hampton int nd mar 19 Jan 1832 Stratham Records
ROLLINS Obed of Exeter & FIFIELD Sarah of Stratham int 5 Jul 1828 mar nd Stratham Records
ROLLINS Phinehas of Stratham & POTTLE Jane of Stratham int 11 Jan 1824 mar nd Stratham Records
ROLLINS William of Stratham & STOCKBRIDGE Sally of Stratham int 8 Dec 1827 mar nd Stratham Records
ROPES Joseph of Salem & TUTTLE Zurviah of Concord int 19 Oct 1834 mar nd Concord Records
ROSS John of Jaffrey & MIRIAM Nabby of Jaffrey int 27 Dec 1803 mar 8 Jan 1804 Jaffrey Records
ROSS Jona of Jaffrey & WORTEN Abigail of Jaffrey int 20 Oct 1807 mar 20 Oct 1807 Jaffrey Records
ROSS Jonas of Jaffrey & WORSTER Abigail of Jaffrey int 22 Jan 1807 mar nd Jaffrey Records

ROSS Phinchas of Winchendon & MARSHALL Betsey of Jaffrey int 11 Oct 1815 mar 19 Oct 1815 Jaffrey Records

ROWELL Ira of Concord & KIMBALL Rebekah of Pembroke int 15 Mar 1828 mar nd Concord Records

ROWELL Ira of Concord & THOMPSON Elizabeth of Concord int 5 Dec 1824 mar nd Concord Records

ROWELL John R Mr of Exeter & DOLLOFF Irene of Exeter int nd mar 11 May 1826 Stratham Records

ROWELL John S of Brentwood & BELKNAP Rose of Exeter int 15 Feb 1864 mar nd Concord Records

ROWELL Thomas of Concord & FARNUM Bridget of Concord int 9 Mar 1828 mar nd Concord Records

ROWLEL Joshua of Concord & MOSES Sally of Concord int 27 Oct 1822 mar nd Concord Records

ROWLEY Moses of Stratham & FOSS Caroline of Stratham int nd mar 26 Feb 1821 Stratham Records

RUNDLETT Simeon of Stratham & TIBBETS Betsy of Stratham int nd mar 6 Mar 1827 Stratham Records

RUNEL Leonard of Bow & HALL Sarah of Concord int 18 Jan 1829 mar nd Concord Records

RUNNELLS Osmyn C of Hopkinton & EATON Eliza Jane of Concord int 5 Nov 1856 mar nd Concord Records

RUNNELS Farnum of Concord & WEBBER Jerusha of Boscawen int 2 Mar 1823 mar nd Concord Records

RUNNELS Hazen of Concord & CORLIS Sarah E of Concord int 13 Apr 1842 mar nd Concord Records

RUNNELS Hazen of Concord & FISK Sarah B of Concord int 22 Mar 1832 mar nd Concord Records

RUNNELS Isaac of Concord & RUNNELS Anna of Concord int 18 Jul 1821 mar nd Concord Records

RUNNELS Samuel of Concord & HARDY Abigail of Warner int 15 Jan 1826 mar nd Concord Records

RUSSELL Daniel of Roxbury MA & STICKNEY Clarie of Jaffrey int 10 Jan 1801 mar nd Jaffrey Records

RUSSELL Isaac of Portsmouth & MARSTON Rooksbury of Stratham int 10 Dec 1853 mar nd Stratham Records

RUSSELS Samuel of Concord & ABBOT Anner of Concord int 13 May 1827 mar nd Concord Records

SALISBURY William H of Jaffrey & HUNT Fanny of Jaffrey int 3 Dec 1834 mar nd Jaffrey Records

SAMPSON Mendell of Concord & ABBOTT Alice of Concord int 26 Aug 1821 mar nd Concord Records

SANBORN Abraham Jr of Concord & ROGERS Mary K of Concord int 4 Jul 1819 mar nd Concord Records

SANBORN Abraham of Bow & EMERSON Margaret of Concord int 5 Mar 1820 mar nd Concord Records
SANBORN Jonathan of Concord & NOYES Lucy J of Concord int 4 Jan 1827 mar nd Concord Records
SANBORN Oliver L of Concord & SHERBURNE Mary of Concord int 2 Nov 1829 mar nd Concord Records
SANBORN Samuel of Exeter & JEWELL Elizabeth of Stratham int 27 Oct 1832 mar 15 Nov 1832 Stratham Records
SANBORY John of Concord & FRYE Huldah of Concord int 29 Jun 1828 mar nd Concord Records
SANDERS George of Stratham & TWOMBLY Polly of Stratham int 5 Aug 1832 mar nd Stratham Records
SANDERS John of Dublin & LUCY Sally of Jaffrey int 10 Apr 1826 mar nd Jaffrey Records
SANDERS John of Jaffrey & JONES Ruth of Dublin int 15 Jul 1812 mar 11 Aug 1812 Jaffrey Records
SARGENT Asa of Concord & SCALES Bridget W of Concord int 26 Nov 1826 mar nd Concord Records
SARGENT John P of Glouster MA & ARLIN Charlotte G of Concord int 30 Oct 1825 mar nd Concord Records
SARGENT Jonathan of Canterbury & EASTAM Phebe of Concord int 1 Jan 1825 mar nd Concord Records
SARGENT Thomas B of Concord & PUFFER Levina W of Saco ME int 14 Jul 1839 mar nd Concord Records
SAUNDERS Robert of Ossipee & LOCKE Abigail R of Concord int 16 Oct 1837 mar nd Concord Records
SAUNDERS Willard of Concord & CAPEN Rosannah of Concord int 29 Nov 1837 mar nd Concord Records
SAVAGE William of Jaffrey & HODGE Joanna of Jaffrey int 18 Oct 1813 mar 11 Nov 1813 Jaffrey Records
SAWYER Josiah of Jaffrey & FRENCH Margaret of Jaffrey int nd mar 30 Dec 1823 Jaffrey Records
SAWYER Moses of Jaffrey & HATHORN Hepsey of Jaffrey int 20 Nov 1795 mar nd Jaffrey Records
SAWYER Rufus of Jaffrey & DARLING Eunice of Jaffrey int 25 Nov 1811 mar 25 Nov 1811 Jaffrey Records
SCAMMON Ira J of Stratham & LYFORD Ann of Stratham int 24 May 1828 mar nd Stratham Records
SCAMMON Stephen of Stratham & GORDON Maria R of Epping int 27 Sep 1834 mar nd Stratham Records
SCHOLLY John of Boscawen & URAN Polly of Concord int 21 May 1820 mar nd Concord Records
SCRIBNER Gilman of Henniker & ABBOTT Harriet of Concord int 14 Oct 1859 mar nd Concord Records

SEAVEY Andrew of Concord & FISK Betsey of Concord int 27 Apr 1828 mar nd Concord Records
SEAVEY Shadrach of Concord & HERBERT Belinda of Concord int 13 Jan 1834 mar nd Concord Records
SERGANT Samuel of Weare & BURPEY Elizabeth of Jaffrey int 21 Oct 1801 mar nd Jaffrey Records
SHATTCUK Edmund P of Pepperell MA & CUTTER Rachel R of Jaffrey int 16 May 1837 mar nd Jaffrey Records
SHATTUCK Enos of Plymouth & SHUTE Rebecah of Concord int 3 Aug 1828 mar nd Concord Records
SHATTUCK Jacob of Andover MA & CHANDLER Elizabeth of Concord int 1 Aug 1819 mar nd Concord Records
SHEDD Abel of Jaffrey & JEWETT Mary of Jaffrey int 13 Jun 1825 mar 16 Jun 1825 Jaffrey Records
SHEDD John H of Boston MA & GILLMORE Eliza Ann of Jaffrey int 27 Apr 1829 mar 30 Apr 1829 Jaffrey Records
SHEPARD James M of Concord & ELLIOT Catharine J C of Concord int 26 Apr 1852 mar nd Concord Records
SHERBURN Robert H of Concord & EATON Ruth of Sutton int 14 Aug 1825 mar nd Concord Records
SHUTE John Jr of Concord & FLANDERS Hannah K of Concord int 19 Nov 1826 mar nd Concord Records
SHUTE Moses Capt of Concord & DUNKLEE Sophia of Concord int 25 May 1846 mar nd Concord Records
SILVER Joseph of Concord & SANBORN Sophia C of Exeter int 26 Nov 1855 mar nd Concord Records
SILVER Richard of Bow & SANBORN Elizabeth of Concord int 2 Jan 1820 mar nd Concord Records
SIMONS Harrison of Weare & FOSTER Lydia Ann of Concord int 20 Oct 1840 mar nd Concord Records
SIMPSON John of Concord & CHANDLER Ruamah of Concord int 1 Feb 1824 mar nd Concord Records
SINCLAIR James of Stratham & LEAVITT Mary of Stratham int 24 Aug 1828 mar nd Stratham Records
SINELER Samuel of Stratham & LANE Elizabeth of Stratham int 14 Sep 1823 mar nd Stratham Records
SKINNER Saban of Jaffrey & GREEN Polly of Jaffrey int 14 Dec 1795 mar nd Jaffrey Records
SLACK D Augustus Rev of Concord & ROBY Ann of Concord int 8 Oct 1850 mar nd Concord Records
SMART Calvin of Concord & PIPER Susan of Concord int 11 Mar 1839 mar nd Concord Records

SMART Charles of Concord & PRESCOTT Mary H of Concord int 5 May 1847 mar nd Concord Records
SMART Durell Newman of Concord & BROWN Mary Anne of Hopkinton int 19 Feb 1826 mar nd Concord Records
SMART Geo C of Concord & GLIDDEN Nellie M of Sandwich int 10 Oct 1867 mar nd Concord Records
SMART Peter of Concord & HARRIS Hannah of Cneterbury int 12 Oct 1828 mar nd Concord Records
SMILEY Hugh of Jaffrey & HARPER Elizabeth of Jaffrey int 25 Dec 1805 mar nd Jaffrey Records
SMITH Albert of Peterborough & STEARNS Fidelia of Jaffrey int 11 Feb 1828 mar nd Jaffrey Records
SMITH Daniel of Lee & WILSON Nancy of Newmarket int nd mar 8 Sep 1834 Stratham Records
SMITH Horace O of Newmarket & BRUAMT Alice of Newmarket int nd mar nd Stratham Records
SMITH Moses of Concord & CLARK Laura of Concord int 12 Apr 1833 mar nd Concord Records
SMITH Russell of Dover & PUTNAM Addie of Newmarket int 8 Nov 1879 mar nd Stratham Records
SMITH Theophilus W of Exeter & ROBINSON Sarah J of Stratham int nd mar nd Stratham Records
SMITH Zebulina of Concord & SARGENT Hannah of Loudon int 20 Sep 1826 mar nd Concord Records
SOUTHEN Nathaniel of Concord & GILMAN Margarett of Exeter int 8 Dec 1822 mar nd Concord Records
SPALDING T C ? of Somerville MA & FARNUM Nellie of Concord int 17 Mar 1865 mar 19 Apr 1865 Concord Records
SPAULDING David of Jaffrey & FOSTER Hannah of Fitzwillaim int 18 Apr 1821 mar 20 Apr 1821 Jaffrey Records
SPAULDING Loammi of Jaffrey & MARSHALL Esther of Jaffrey int 20 Sep 1818 mar 22 Sep 1818 Jaffrey Records
SPAULDING Phinehas of Jaffrey & FISH Sally of Jaffrey int 16 Feb 1802 mar nd Jaffrey Records
SPAULDING Rueben of Jaffrey & PRATT Polly of Dublin int 21 Nov 1795 mar nd Jaffrey Records
SPOFFORD Abner of Jaffrey & LITCH Betsey of Jaffrey int 17 Nov 1803 mar 17 Nov 1803 Jaffrey Records
SPOFFORD Abraham of Jaffrey & BROOKS Betsy of Jaffrey int 29 Sep 1806 mar 27 Nov 1806 Jaffrey Records
SPOFFORD Jeremiah Jr of Rowley MA & SPOFFORD Ayer of Jaffrey int 4 Oct 1813 mar 15 Oct 1813 Jaffrey Records

SPOKESFIELD George of Concord & LAWRENCE Carrie M of Concord int 4 Jul 1859 mar nd Concord Records
STANLEY Jedwiah of Jaffrey & ROSS Prudence of Jaffrey int 11 Jul 1809 mar nd Jaffrey Records
STEARNS Lafayette of Concord & WHITTAKER Marietta E of Concord int 21 Nov 1859 mar nd Concord Records
STEARNS Moses of Lexington MS & HATHORN Peggy of Jaffrey int 6 Nov 1809 mar nd Jaffrey Records
STEARNS Samuel of Newtown & LAWRENCE Gracy of Jaffrey int 9 Apr 1829 mar nd Jaffrey Records
STEBBINS Hial of Jaffrey & BLODGETT Lucinda of Jaffrey int 1 Apr 1822 mar 3 Apr 1822 Jaffrey Records
STEPHENS Amos of Concord & THOMPSON Susan of Concord int 15 Sep 1822 mar nd Concord Records
STEPHENS James of Concord & WASHER Tsminia of Concord int 10 Nov 1822 mar nd Concord Records
STEPHENS Simion of Concord & CARPENTER Nancy of Chichester int 6 Oct 1822 mar nd Concord Records
STEVENS David of Loudon & BROWN Hannah of Concord int 24 Oct 1824 mar nd Concord Records
STEVENS Henry of Hopkinton & GOVE Dorothy of Concord int 16 Feb 1828 mar nd Concord Records
STEVENS Theodore of Concord & HAINES Eunice of Concord int 24 Jun 1833 mar nd Concord Records
STEVENS William Esq of Andover VT & HARKNESS Sarah (widow) of Jaffrey int 25 May 1809 mar nd Jaffrey Records
STEWART Benjamin of Jaffrey & THOMPSON Susan of Jaffrey int 28 Dec 1812 mar 28 Dec 1812 Jaffrey Records
STICKNEY Jeremiah of Jaffrey & WEED Esther of Jaffrey int 20 Feb 1806 mar 20 Feb 1806 Jaffrey Records
STICKNEY John of Concord & ABBOT Dorcas M of Concord int 5 Feb 1848 mar nd Concord Records
STICKNEY John of Rindge & BRAGG Phebe of Jaffrey int 16 Jun 1812 mar 17 Jun 1812 Jaffrey Records
STICKNEY Norman of Lancaster & STICKNEY Susannah of Jaffrey int 8 Aug 1812 mar 11 Aug 1812 Jaffrey Records
STOCKBRIDGE James of Stratham & LANG Olive Ann of Stratham int 20 Sep 1815 mar nd Stratham Records
STONE John of Jaffrey & PERKINS Ruth of Jaffrey int nd mar 23 Dec 1804 Jaffrey Records
STONE Jonathan of Fitzwilliam & MILLER Sophia of Jaffrey int 10 Oct 1809 mar nd Jaffrey Records
STONE Saml Jr of Fitzwilliam & GREEN Hannah of Fitzwilliam int nd mar 29 Nov 1803 Jaffrey Records

STRATTON Samuel of Jaffrey & GILLMAN Sally of Jaffrey int 20 Jul 1819 mar 2 Aug 1819 Jaffrey Records
STRAW Daniel of Concord & DIMOND Sally of Concord int 26 Jun 1824 mar nd Concord Records
STRAW James of Concord & SHUTE Sarah of Concord int 27 Mar 1825 mar nd Concord Records
STREETER Thomas of Rindge & LOCK Paulina of Jaffrey int 16 Oct 1826 mar nd Jaffrey Records
STUART John H of Concord & TOWLE Susan T of Concord int 28 Jun 1855 mar nd Concord Records
SWEAT Ephraim of Concord & PHILBRICK Susan of Concord int 18 Jan 1829 mar nd Concord Records
SYMONDS Charles F of Concord & HODGDON Mary Jane of Concord int nd mar nd Concord Records
SYMONDS David of Concord & FLANDERS Nancy P of Concord int 7 Dec 1828 mar nd Concord Records
TAPPAN Samuel S of Conway & DANA Hannah of Concord int 14 Jan 1851 mar nd Concord Records
TARBOX Markinson of Stoddard & ABBOTT Susanah of Concord int 26 Apr 1820 mar nd Concord Records
TARLETON James N of Montgomery Alba & FISK Sarah W of Concord int 11 Aug 1834 mar nd Concord Records
TAYLOR Elias of Jaffrey & MASON Abigail Bullard of Jaffrey int 7 Mar 1831 mar nd Jaffrey Records
TAYLOR Joseph of Stratham & WEEKS Sukey Ann of Stratham int 4 Aug 1822 mar nd Stratham Records
TAYLOR William W of Franklin & TANDY Sarah Jane of Franklin int 11 Feb 1861 mar nd Concord Records
TEMPLETON Charles of Chelmsford MA & MARDEN Mary Jane of Concord int 24 May 1845 mar nd Concord Records
TENNEY Gardner of Concord & SEAVEY Lydia of Concord int 16 Jul 1832 mar nd Concord Records
TENNEY Jacob B of Newbury VT & CRAM Caroline of Concord int 1 Jan 1828 mar nd Concord Records
THAYER William of Manchester & ALLISON Sarah A of Concord int 15 Jan 1843 mar nd Concord Records
THOMAS Moor G Rev of Concord & KENT Mary Jane of Concord int 12 Jul 1830 mar nd Concord Records
THOMPSON Abiele of Concord & BROWN Margarett Eliz of Roxbury MA int 27 Jan 1822 mar nd Concord Records
THOMPSON Asa of Jaffrey & COOLIDGE Sophia of Jaffrey int 10 Dec 1813 mar 10 Dec 1813 Jaffrey Records
THOMPSON Ebenezer of Chester & MAYNARD Hannah of Jaffrey int 4 Jun 1805 mar 4 Jun 1805 Jaffrey Records

THOMPSON George W of Barington & WINGATE Mary of Stratham int 23 Mar 1833 mar nd Stratham Records
THOMPSON Henry of Jaffrey & JAQUITH Betsey of Jaffrey int 18 Dec 1805 mar 18 Feb 1806 Jaffrey Records
THOMPSON J T of Concord & HOOK Abby C of Concord int 10 Oct 1860 mar nd Concord Records
THOMPSON John of Stratham & HOAG Nancy of Stratham int 30 Nov 1828 mar nd Stratham Records
THORNTON Henry of Concord & HANCOCK Margaret of Concord int 21 Feb 1842 mar nd Concord Records
TILDEN Joseph Jr of Hanover & VIRGIN Mary E of Concord int 9 Oct 1842 mar nd Concord Records
TILTON Joseph of Concord & CHANDLER Maria of Concord int 20 May 1853 mar nd Concord Records
TILTON Joseph of Jaffrey & BROOKS Abigail of Jaffrey int 9 Nov 1802 mar 22 Nov 1802 Jaffrey Records
TITCOMB John of Concord & CARR Eliza W of Hopkinton int 5 Sep 1824 mar nd Concord Records
TOAD Henry of Concord & RUSS Sarah of Concord int 17 Nov 1822 mar nd Concord Records
TOMSON Ebnezer of Jaffrey & STICKNEY Eunice of Jaffrey int 19 Apr 1791 mar nd Jaffrey Records
TOWLE Eben S of Concord & EMERY Esther W of Concord int 25 Mar 1827 mar nd Concord Records
TOWLE Jonathan Jr of Hampton & LANE Sarah of Hamptonm int nd mar 5 Sep 1830 Stratham Records
TOWNS Joshua of Rindge & CHADWICK Polly of Jaffrey int 13 Apr 1810 mar 17 APR 11810 Jaffrey Records
TREFETHREN William Capt of Rye & PIPER Susanna of Stratham int nd mar 1 Feb 1821 Stratham Records
TRUE John of Concord & PARKER Anne of Hampstead int 26 Nov 1820 mar nd Concord Records
TUCKER Cyrus Esq of Loudon & HOIT Fanny Jane of Concord int 5 Oct 1835 mar nd Concord Records
TUCKER Francis W of Concord & HOIT Prudence of Concord int 21 Sep 1830 mar nd Concord Records
TUFTS Charles A of Dover & SOUTHEN Anna B of Concord int 24 Apr 1848 mar nd Concord Records
TURNER Elish of Harvard MA & GREEN Caroline of Concord int 26 Nov 1826 mar nd Concord Records
TURNER Joseph of Peterborough & WATTS Polly of Jaffrey int 12 Sep 1801 mar nd Jaffrey Records
TUTTLE Thomas of Stratham & STOCKBRIDGE Mary of Stratham int nd mar 22 Jul 1821 Stratham Records

TWIS John of New Boston & TWISS Apenith of Jaffrey int nd mar 10 Feb 1825 Jaffrey Records
TWISS Timothy of Jaffrey & WILDER Mary of Jaffrey int 11 Feb 1834 mar nd Jaffrey Records
TWITCHELL Gershom Jr of Dublin & BAILEY Sally of Jaffrey int 6 Nov 1812 mar 12 Nov 1812 Jaffrey Records
TWITCHELL John of Dublin & PARKER Susan of Rindge int nd mar 3 Feb 1818 Jaffrey Records
TWITCHELL Samuel of Dublin & BAILEY Abigail of Jaffrey int 21 Jun 1813 mar nd Jaffrey Records
UNDERHILL Charles W of Concord & KIMBALL Susan E of Concord int 25 May 1835 mar nd Concord Records
UNDERWOOD Levi of Watertown NY & CUTTER Eunice of Jaffrey int 6 Sep 1819 mar nd Jaffrey Records
UPTON Eli Jr of Peterborough & SNOW Abigail of Jaffrey int 14 Apr 1809 mar nd Jaffrey Records
UPTON Isaac of Hombolottbo CA & PILLSBURY Augusta of Concord int 9 Nov 1858 mar nd Concord Records
UPTON Thomas of Peterborough & SNOW Lydia of Jaffrey int 25 Dec 1809 mar nd Jaffrey Records
UTLEY Samuel Rev of Middleboro MA & EASTMAN Mary J of Concord int 7 Apr 1834 mar nd Concord Records
VIRGIN Jonathan A of Maron GA & GOODWIN Judith of Concord int 29 Jun 1835 mar nd Concord Records
VIRGIN Leavitt C of Rumford ME & VIRGIN Hannah of Concord int 9 Jan 1820 mar nd Concord Records
VIRGIN Simon of Concord & BLACKBURN Abigail of Concord int 8 Oct 1833 mar nd Concord Records
VIRGIN William M of Concord & TYLER Lavina of Concord int 1 Jan 1826 mar nd Concord Records
VITTUM D S of Baraboo Wis & HALL A T of Concord int 18 Oct 1856 mar nd Concord Records
VITTUM D S of Meredith & HALL Mary E of Concord int 21 Apr 1851 mar nd Concord Records
WAKEFIELD Peter W of Jaffrey & WHHITCOMB Esther of Jaffrey int 26 Feb 1810 mar nd Jaffrey Records
WALKER Abiel of Concord & THORNDIKE Mary of Concord int 17 Nov 1823 mar nd Concord Records
WALKER Amasa of Boston MA & AMBROSE Hannah of Concord int 8 Jun 1834 mar nd Concord Records
WALKER Charles of Rutland VT & AMBROSE Lucitia of Concord int 31 May 1823 mar nd Concord Records
WALKER Frank of Concord & DEROSSEAU Lydia of Concord int 27 Jan 1863 mar nd Concord Records

WALKER Hazen of Berwick ME & KIMBALL Eliza R of Concord int 6 Jun 1824 mar nd Concord Records

WALKER Joseph of Concord & SAWYER Anne of Salisbury int 6 Feb 1820 mar nd Concord Records

WALKER Lyman A of Concord & PRATT Lucy Ann of Concord int 13 Nov 1843 mar nd Concord Records

WALKER Timothy of Concord & GRIFFIN Abigail of Concord int 5 Sep 1846 mar nd Concord Records

WARD Carleton of Concord & BROWN Betsy of Concord int 11 Jan 1830 mar nd Concord Records

WARD Henry S of Roxbury MA & ROSS Nabby of Jaffrey int 16 Aug 1830 mar 25 Aug 1830 Jaffrey Records

WARNER Stephen of Peterborough & LAWRENCE Rebeccah of Jaffrey int 5 Sep 1818 mar 6 Sep 1818 Jaffrey Records

WARREN Charles of Warren ME & FOGG Lavertia of Concord int 3 Sep 1866 mar nd Concord Records

WATSON Philip of Concord & RUSSELL Mary of Concord int 3 Oct 1819 mar nd Concord Records

WATTS Nathaniel of Jaffrey & BALDWIN Polly of Jaffrey int 13 Dec 1813 mar 19 Dec 1813 Jaffrey Records

WEAVER G W of White Post VA & BALLARD Eunice B of Concord int 6 May 1853 mar nd Concord Records

WEBBER Edmund of Boscawen & LYFORD Betsey of Concord int 23 Apr 1820 mar nd Concord Records

WEBBER John H of Peterborough & DINSMORE Lucy of Jaffrey int 11 Oct 1838 mar nd Jaffrey Records

WEBBER Maximillian of Concord & SWEAT Clarsissa of Concord int 7 Dec 1831 mar nd Concord Records

WEBSTER Atkinson of Concord & SMART Rebeccah of Concord int 28 Feb 1820 mar nd Concord Records

WEBSTER Ezekiel of Concord & POLLARD Achsah of Concord int 11 Jun 1825 mar nd Concord Records

WEBSTER James W of Concord & CARPENTER Sarah L of Concord int 28 Nov 1860 mar nd Concord Records

WEBSTER John C of Hopkinton & BOUTIN Elizabeth R of Concord int 12 Dec 1847 mar nd Concord Records

WEBSTER John F of Concord & CUTTING Mary J of Concord int 10 Jun 1856 mar nd Concord Records

WEBSTER Jonathan of New Ipswich & STREETER Abigail of Jaffrey int 7 Apr 1828 mar nd Jaffrey Records

WEBSTER William G Esq of Concord & AMBROSE Susan of Concord int 8 Jun 1829 mar nd Concord Records

WEEKS Ira of Stratham & NORIS Mehitable C of Stratham int 19 May 1823 mar nd Stratham Records

WEEKS Joseph of Greenland & HILTON Nancy R of Greenland int nd mar 1 Feb 1824 Stratham Records

WELCH Chas H of Parsonsfield ME & HILL Abby P of Sanbornton int 1 Jan 1866 mar nd Concord Records

WELLS Charles of Concord & WIGGINS Mary G of Concord int 1 Mar 1824 mar nd Concord Records

WENTWORTH John Mr of Stratham & POTTLE Judith Ann of Stratham int nd mar nd Stratham Records

WEST John D A of Concord & HOYT Mary E of Concord int 8 Nov 1844 mar nd Concord Records

WHEELER Benjamin Jr of Concord & ORDWAY Eliza of Concord int 17 Aug 1828 mar nd Concord Records

WHEELER Daniel of Jaffrey & POWERS Mary of Jaffrey int 2 Mar 1812 mar 3 Mar 1812 Jaffrey Records

WHEELER Jeremiah Jr of Concord & WHIDDEN Sarah of Concord int 6 Feb 1820 mar nd Concord Records

WHITCOMB George of Rindge & SMITH Sarah of Jaffrey int 18 Nov 1829 mar nd Jaffrey Records

WHITCOMB Zaucheus of Henniker & HALE Moley of Jaffrey int 25 Nov 1801 mar nd Jaffrey Records

WHITE Sumner P of Charlestown MA & ROWELL Mary E of Concord int 2 Nov 1845 mar nd Concord Records

WHITTEMOR Samuel Jr of Concord & WHEELER Shuah F of Concord int 22 Dec 1822 mar nd Concord Records

WHITTIMORE James C of Concord & HOIT Elizabeth of Concord int 29 Jul 1833 mar nd Concord Records

WIGGIN Benjamin of Tuftonborough & PIPER Sally of Stratham int 24 Dec 1831 mar nd Stratham Records

WIGGIN Bradbury of Stratham & BENNET Mary of Newmarket int 2 Jun 1832 mar nd Stratham Records

WIGGIN George of Stratham & ROLLINS Nancy of Stratham int 5 Dec 1829 mar nd Stratham Records

WIGGIN Ira of Stratham & JEWETT Sophia of Stratham int 23 Feb 1833 mar nd Stratham Records

WIGGIN Thomas of Stratham & AVERY Mary of Stratham int 18 Jun 1826 mar nd Stratham Records

WIGGIN Walter of Stratham & O'DELL Charlotte of Stratham int 18 Jan 1824 mar 1 Feb 1824 Stratham Records

WIGGINS Ira W of Stratham & JEWELL Sophia of Stratham int nd mar 11 MAR 183 Stratham Records

WILDER Ezra of Jaffrey & HODGE Jerusha (Mrs) of Peterborough int 15 Oct 1804 mar 15 Oct 1804 Jaffrey Records

WILDER James of Peterborough & TURNER Lydia of Jaffrey int 7 Sep 1802 mar 9 Sep 1802 Jaffrey Records

WILDER Joseph of Jaffrey & TURNER Susanna of Jaffrey int 19 Jul 1806 mar 19 Jul 1806 Jaffrey Records

WILDER Oliver of Jaffrey & HODGE Betsey of Jaffrey int 6 Jul 1803 mar 17 Nov 1803 Jaffrey Records

WILDER Simpson of Jaffrey & TURNER Joanna of Jaffrey int 22 Jan 1807 mar 22 Jan 1807 Jaffrey Records

WILKINS Asa of Concord & WHITE Francis of Concord int 17 Oct 1832 mar nd Concord Records

WILKINS George of Concord & SHUTE Nancy of Concord int 16 Apr 1826 mar nd Concord Records

WILLARD George A of Ashby MA & HUNT Elvira of Jaffrey int 9 Oct 1828 mar nd Jaffrey Records

WILLEY Alvin of Concord & BACHELDER Eliza H of Bilerica MA int 18 Dec 1825 mar nd Concord Records

WILLEY Andrew of Hopkinton & CARTER Betsey of Concord int 22 Dec 1822 mar nd Concord Records

WILLEY Jeremiah of Concord & STEVENS Basha of Concord int 10 Nov 1827 mar nd Concord Records

WILLEY John of Concord & URAN Huddah of Concord int 23 Nov 1828 mar nd Concord Records

WILLIAM Andrew, Capt of Newburyport MA & WIGGIN Sarah (Bartlett) of Stratham int nd mar nd Stratham Records

WILLIAM Isaac of Concord & AYER Mary of Concord int 14 Jan 1827 mar nd Concord Records

WILLIAMS Geo W of Concord & STEVENS Jennie P of Concord int 30 Nov 1865 mar nd Concord Records

WILLIAMS Jubile of Westminster VT & KELLEY Hannah B of Concord int 15 Nov 1840 mar nd Concord Records

WILLIAMS Washington of Dover & AYER Charlotte of Concord int 3 Jan 1834 mar nd Concord Records

WILLIS Joseph N of Northfield & FLANDERS Sarah A of Concord int 15 Apr 1850 mar nd Concord Records

WILLMAN Jubilee Rev of Westminster VT & KELLY Hannah B of Concord int 16 Nov 1840 mar nd Concord Records

WITCOMB James Jr of Concord & HUNT Nancy of Guilford int 18 Mar 1821 mar nd Concord Records

WITT Charles of Jaffrey & WOOD Huldah of Jaffrey int 2 Dec 1805 mar 11 Dec 1805 Jaffrey Records

WOOD Amos of Concord & WILLINGTON Louisa of Keene int 15 Aug 1824 mar nd Concord Records

WOOD Daniel of Jaffrey & WELLINGTON Abby of Jaffrey int 17 Aug 1813 mar 17 Aug 1813 Jaffrey Records

WOOD Eben T of Jaffrey & BRYANT Rebecca of Temple int 3 Feb 1807 mar nd Jaffrey Records

WOOD Ebenezer of Jaffrey & BOYNTON Rebeccah of Temple int 3 Feb 1808 mar 23 Feb 1808 Jaffrey Records

WOOD Jonathan Jr of Jaffrey & DAVISON Betsey of Jaffrey int 25 Mar 1816 mar 28 Mar 1816 Jaffrey Records

WOODBURY Louis of Jaffrey & CROSBY Mary of Jaffrey int 9 May 1822 mar nd Jaffrey Records

WOODS John of Newport & BAKER Achsah of Concord int 29 Feb 1824 mar nd Concord Records

WOODWARD Isaac of Jaffrey & MELENDY Polly of Jaffrey int 22 Feb 1813 mar 23 Feb 1813 Jaffrey Records

WOODWARD John of Jaffrey & CHADWICK Hannah of Jaffrey int 15 Feb 1804 mar 21 Feb 1804 Jaffrey Records

WOODWORTH George of Greenville Mich & WALLACE Fanny of Concord int 17 Oct 1859 mar nd Concord Records

WOOLSON Ebenezer of Concord & WHITNEY Nancy of Concord int 4 Jul 1819 mar nd Concord Records

WORCESTER John of Jaffrey & KIMBALL Sally of Jaffrey int 26 Nov 1815 mar 27 Nov 1815 Jaffrey Records

WORTHEN E E of Concord & SHACKFORD Celeste of Concord int 6 Jun 1860 mar nd Concord Records

WRIGHT Oliver of Jaffrey & HADLEY Eunice of Jaffrey int 13 Aug 1803 mar 28 Aug 1803 Jaffrey Records

WRIGHT Saml of Peterboro & GOWING Thirza of Dublin int nd mar 30 Nov 1807 Jaffrey Records

YEARDLEY William of Dublin & BROOKS Rhoda of Jaffrey int 19 Dec 1804 mar 20 Dec 1804 Jaffrey Records

YEATON John S of Exeter & LEAVITT Elizabeth of Stratham int 31 Mar 1832 mar nd Stratham Records

YOUNG Charles A of Hudson OH & MIXER Augusta of Concord int 10 Aug 1857 mar nd Concord Records

OUT-OF-STATE MINISTER LICENSES

These licenses were granted by the state of New Hampshire to out-of-state ministers, permitting them to perform certain marriages within the state. The entries are listed by groom, and give the name and residence of the bride and groom, the date the intention was filed if known, and the name and residence of the minister who received a special license to perform their marriage in New Hampshire. The earliest license listed here was issued in 1921; the latest was in 1961.

AALTO Waino Wm of Fitchburg MA & KIVISTO Tyyne Maria of Fitchburg MA int 9 Jun 1949 by SUMNER Wm A of Fitchburg MA
ABENETHY George C of Shawnee OK & DRAPER Janet of Canton MA int 12 Aug 1937 by SLEEPER H D of Ferribury VT
ABRAHAM Sargon Y of Springfield MA & PENNINGTON Joyce of Springfield MA int 22 Jun 1951 by PRESCOTT E G out of Malden MA
ACKLEY Wallace Edward of E Templeton MA & GRUMMAN Ethel Sterling of New Haven CT int 1 Apr 1960 by E Fay Campbell of Swarthmore PA
ADAMOWICZ Walter of Enfield NH & MOYNIHAN Eleanor of Enfield NH int 20 May 1938 by MOYNIHAN James F of Weston MA
ADAMS Charles Streeter of Jersey City NJ & STEWART Pauline Frances of Worcester MA int 8 Aug 1934 by McALLISTER Francis B of Lexington MA
ADAMS Douglas of Cambridge MA & STANWOOD Marian H of Boston MA int 9 Jul 1937 by IVOL Curtis of Boston MA
ADAMS Elmer C Rev of Madison NH & PARKER Norma B of Madison NH int 13 Jun 1927 by SWIFT Selby of New York NY
ADAMS Louis Charles R of Melrose MA & LARLEE Donna Ann of Melrose MA int 19 Oct 1955 by LEA Fergus of Brighton ME

ADAMS William Austin of Manchester NH & PARKER Anne Patricia of Fitchburg MA int 18 Jul 1949 by PAUL J Bowman of Fitchburg MA

ADAMSKY Robert Francis of Auburn MA & HOLLOWAY Ruth Elizabeth of Pittsfield NH int 29 Aug 1953 by GORDON E Hermonson of Harrisburg PA

ADRIEN Richard N of Wells Beach ME & TURCOTTE Jacqueline of Somersworth NH int 7 Oct 1955 by TANGUAY Ovid of Biddeford ME

AHLMAN Edward of Tewksbury MA & MILTON Rosemarie of Malden MA int 22 Sep 1959 by EDEARD G Johnston of Medford MA

AINSWORTH John Labin of Claremont NH & PATTEN Martha A of Claremont NH int 10 Feb 1949 by TOPPAN Louis C of Amherst MA

AJEMIAN Charles of Salem NH & GARABEDIAN Mary of Salem NH int 30 Apr 1929 by EGHIAZAR Ashjuar of Boston MA

ALBERT E Page of Pittsfield NH & MAXFIELD Ella A of Manchester NH int 27 May 1935 by PERCY R Batcheldor of Bridgeport CT

ALDRIDGE Franklin H of Woodstock NH & WILLETT Pauline Ann of Lincoln NH int 18 May 1955 by ROSAIRE Croteau of CAN

ALEXANDER William Marsh of E Providence RI & TYDEMAN Nancy Eliz of New York NY int 15 Jul 1948 by ARTHUR H Bradford of Providence RI

ALLAN Thomas Frederick of No Conway NH & KLOCK Carol Louise of No Conway NH int 27 May 1955 by BARTH Jos of Miami FL

ALLARD Joseph Gerard of Manchester NH & PANNENTON Lucille of Manchester NH int 28 Mar 1957 by PANNETON Paul E of Wakefield MA

ALLEN Edwin Joseph of Pittsfield MA & FERNALD Margaret Louise of Milford NH int 3 Sep 1931 by J Varror Garton of Bedford MA

ALLEN Fred H Jr of Holyoke MA & BROWN Frances of Dover NH int 13 Jul 1938 by DAVID P Hatch of Fairfield CT

ALLEN Lloyd Edward of Boston MA & PARKER Frances C of Meriden CT int 17 Aug 1939 by NOBLE Chas C of Glen Falls NY

ALLEY Ralph David of Loudonville NY & DEROCHEMONT Jane Y of Newington NH int 11 Aug 1956 by NELSON John E of Somerville MA

ALLIN Lewis Raymond of North Stratford NH & WILLIS Patricia Luella of North Stratford NH int 16 Jun 1959 by ROBERT M Brown of St Johnsbury VT

ALLISON Charles of Manchester NH & STEELE Barbara Frances of Manchester NH int 10 Jul 1948 by ROULANDS William D of Chelsea MA

ALMOVE Harry J of Gilmanton NH & KITCHEN Beverly Ann of Gilmanton NH int 26 Aug 1946 by RYLAARSDAM J Coert of Chicago IL

AMBROSE Robert Dyer of Deerfield NH & LINNALL Constance Ruth of Northwood NH int 31 May 1945 by RALPH G Barnes of Boston MA

AMEN John H of New York NY & DOWN Marion C of New York NY int 19 Jul 1926 by CALVIN P Erdams of Pasadena CA

AMES H Thurlon of Pittsfield NH & COLEMAN Mary F of Pittsfield NH int 12 May 1954 by FRANK J Coleman of Cranston RI

AMES John Willard of Belfast ME & MARTIN Susan of Francestown NH int 19 Jun 1956 by FREDERICK D Hayes of Auburn ME

AMYOT Omer H of Manchester NH & BOIVIN Gilberte I of Manchester NH int 8 Jun 1929 by ROLAND G Amyot of Suffern NY

ANASTASI Nicholas Richad of Newbury NH & BUNKER Jessie Elaine of Bradford NH int 16 Sep 1946 by GEORGE E Cary of Bradford MA

ANDERSON Arvid Emil of Lynn MA & MANLEY Elizabeth of Arlington MA int 29 Sep 1958 by OSBORN Donald L of Randolph VT

ANDERSON Elliott L of Boston MA & ELLIOTT Georgia Ann of Rumney NH int 29 May 1948 by HAROLD R Elliott of Chicago IL

ANDREWS Charles Titus of Cambridge MA & McDUFFEE Doris of Alton NH int 19 Aug 1929 by GETCHELL Wm H of No Berwick ME

ANDREWS Neal Davis of Durham NH & WILLIAMS Elizabeth W of Grafton Ctr NH int 19 Aug 1948 by PHILIP H Havener of Brattleboro VT

ANGERS William of Manchester NH & BOISVERT Rachel of Manchester NH int 16 Aug 1952 by DONAT Boisvert of CAN

ANNIS Frank Robinson of Braintree MA & SCRUTON Susie Blanche of Rochester NH int 20 Aug 1946 by PENT Arnold V of York Beach ME

ANNIS Wm Henry of N Conway NH & FORREST Elizabeth of Silver Bay NH int 13 Aug 1956 by WITHAM Winfield of N Bridgton ME

ANTONELLIS Benjamain Jr of Nashua NH & GRANGER Sheila A of Nashua NH int 10 Dec 1957 by MULLIGAN W R of Fairfield VT

APPLEFORD George B of No Andover MA & BOYD Jean Stuart of No Andover MA int 13 Jun 1941 by D C Boyd of Belleville IL

APPLETON Jude Marc of Croton NY & SMITH Gale of Tilton NH int 1 Dec 1952 by EDWARD G Ernst of Bangor ME

ARANA Thomas of Tucson Ariz & JETTE Helen of Exeter NH int 15 May 1953 by OMER L Dufault of Morrisville VT

ARETAS James of Hyde Park MA & LESSARD Pauline of Manchester NH int 29 Oct 1957 by LYONNAIES Emery of Lowell MA

ARMSTRONG Robert G of Windham NH & BOULGER Shirley M of Windham NH int 25 Apr 1947 by JOHN G Gaskill of Andover MA

ARNER Robert of Washington DC & HAHN Charlotte of Wolfeboro NH int 18 Jul 1956 by W Leroy Haven of Westminster VT

ARSEAULT Raymond A of Berlin NH & LaPOINTE Enita Alice of Berlin NH int 10 Jan 1955 by LEMIEUX Arthur E of Montreal CAN

ARSENAULT George R of Berlin NH & BERGERON Isabelle L of Berlin NH int 24 Mar 1955 by LEMIEUX Arthur E of Montreal CAN

ARSENEAULT Alfred T of Berlin NH & LAVIGNE Gertrude of Berlin NH int 12 Jun 1948 by LAVIGNE Sabin of St Jean CAN

ARTHER Gordon G Jr of Grafton VT & STEPHENS Arlyne of Ashuelott NH int 12 Nov 1957 by ROGERS Walter Allyn of E Dover VT

ASH Clifford of Loudon NH & RUGGLES Elizabeth of Loudon NH int 10 Jan 1959 by WILLIAM Ash of Augusta ME

ASTTEY Hardman A of Wilder VT & WING Joan R of Lyme Ctr NH int 2 Jun 1959 by DONALD W Henderson of Windham ME

ATKINSON Edward of Durham NH & CRITTENDON Lorraine of Springfield Ms int 7 Aug 1944 by JOSEPH Atkinson of Brookline MA

ATWATER David H Jr of Barrington RI & SEYBOLD Nina H of Providence RI int 9 Aug 1960 by NOBLE Chas C of Syracuse NY

ATWOOD Daniel Stickney of Pelham NH & GAZES Georgia of Pelham NH int 5 Mar 1958 by REESE William J of Lowell MA

ATWOOD Raymond P of Newton MA & MILLER Doris A of Brookline MA int 12 Sep 1932 by SAUNDERSON Henry of Brighton MA

ATWOOD Wayne of New London NH & CARTER Phyllis of New London NH int 21 Jul 1948 by HAROLD H Buker of Lynn MA

AUSTIN Ralph of So China ME & HUFF Myrtle of So China ME int 26 Jun 1940 by LIPPINCOTT Joseph T of E Vassalboro ME

AUSTIN Robert of Webster NH & SMITH June of Webster NH int 22 Aug 1946 by J Osborne Crowe of Pepperell MA

AVERY Newton Bert of Woodstock NH & SMALL Christine Arlin of Pittsfield NH int 30 Jul 1940 by JOSEPH P C Johsnon of Waterbury CT

AVERY Walter W of Laconia NH & LOUGEE Elizabeth of Laconia NH int 25 Jul 1938 by EMERY L Bradford of Boxford MA

BABBITT Will C of Farmington NH & ALLEN Ruth of Farmington NH int 19 Aug 1925 by WILLIAM A Babbitt of So Bend IN

BACKE Donald Erik of Holderness NH & TAYLOR Claire Elaine of Laconia NH int 16 Aug 1958 by BAXTON William M of Washington DC

BADGER David of Dover MA & BOWDITCH Sue of Rye Beach NH int 12 Aug 1958 by A Graham Baldwin of Andover MA

BADGER Thedore L of Brookline MA & WETHERBEE Alice of Boston MA int 22 Jul 1936 by ALLEN W Clark of Brookline MA

BAGHDASARIAN Paromaz of Nashua NH & HILL Carol Ann of Nashua NH int 10 Jul 1959 by WEEKS Herbert of Auburn ME

BAHLMAN Mipon Fuller of Cotuit MA & GATH Barbara of Manchester NH int 28 Mar 1951 by LEWIS A Jones of Falmouth ME

BAILEY Herbert of Peterboro NH & NELSON Edna M of Peterboro NH int 2 Aug 1932 by ERNEST W Eldridge of Ashby MA

BAILEY Kenneth Otis of W Lebanon NH & PUDVAH Beverley Eloise of W Lebanon NH int 3 Aug 1950 by SULLIVAN Joseph L of Hartford VT

BAILEY Richard T of Haverhill MA & TABOR Janice Marion of Haverhill MA int 25 Jul 1940 by NELSON Harley R of Willimantic CT

BAILEY Stephen Kemp of Evanston IL & BROWN Cornelia of Newton Highland MA int 19 Aug 1940 by ROBERT Bean of Newton Highland MA

BAILLIE Arlan Andrew of Boston MA & DELAHANTY Margaret of Hanover NH int 4 May 1942 by BERRY Wilbur F of Vassalboro ME

BAKER Edwin R of Epping NH & NOYES Betsy of Exeter NH int 23 Jul 1956 by MARTIN Paul T of Manhasset NY

BAKER Floyd M of Nashua NH & SINCLAIR Poly of Nashua NH int 28 Mar 1960 by MAURICE W Baker of Schenectady NY

BAKER Henry of Baltimore MD & CLARK Joyce of Baltimore MD int 7 Aug 1959 by HENRY H Crane of Detroit MI

BAKER Myles Pierce of Boston MA & BREMER Mabel Farnsworth of Dublin NH int 20 Jun 1929 by POMEROY Vivian T of Milton MA

BAKER Sidney L M of Exeter NH & BARTOW Ann of Lancaster NH int 18 May 1960 by LOVETT Sidney A of New Haven CT

BAKIAN Dickvan of Nashua NH & WHITNEY Shirley of Nashua NH int 10 Sep 1947 by STANLEY J Keach of Palmer MA

BALDWIN Arthur B of Canaan NH & BALCH Katharine of Boston MA int 21 Sep 1936 by FRANK O Holmes of Jamaica Plain MA

BALDWIN Mark W of Langdon NH & DREW Grace E of Wilmington MA int 20 Aug 1952 by MARSH George B of Grafton VT

BALDWIN Sherman of New York NY & RANTOUL Harriet C of Jamaica Pl MA int 21 Aug 1930 by McKEE Elmore M of New Haven CT

BALLOU Leo Bernard of Lexington MA & NORTON Iola of Portsmouth NH int 19 Oct 1953 by DONALD G Ballou of Walpole MA
BAPTIST Charles of Tilton NH & MOSES Agnes of Stamford CT int 4 Apr 1946 by SNOW Arthur J of Stoneham MA
BARBER Harold W of Hartland VT & CLARK Letty Ella of West Cannan NH int 17 Aug 1948 by RICHARD A Babock of Cambridge MA
BARBER Harry C of Exeter NH & TODD Rachel Gorst of Newton MA int 25 Jun 1931 by THOMPSON J West of Winchester MA
BARBER Richard Arnold of Peterboro NH & BELLVUE Mary Dow of Peterboro NH int 1 Aug 1951 by FREDERICK R Griffin of Petersham MA
BARBIN Robert of Berlin NH & CARBONNEAU Marie Louise of Berlin NH int 1 Sep 1939 by ALBERT Carbonneau of CAN
BARDIS James Ezekiel of Bellows Falls VT & HALL Katarine of Walpole NH int 12 Aug 1927 by HENRY B Bryan of Jersey City NJ
BAREHAM Ernest of Oswego NY & CHUTTER Ruth Eleanor of Pittsford VT int 28 May 1949 by BENJAMIN R Andrews Jr of E Northfield MA
BARKER Walter L of Nashua NH & HYMAN Irene of Nashua NH int 25 Jun 1938 by JAMES King of Lowell MA
BARNARD Frank Hardy of Bedford NH & MARTIN Isabelle Dean of Amherst NH int 9 Sep 1937 by WATSON Albert P of Wilton ME
BARNARD Robert Hyland of Keene NH & LIBBEY Hadley Dame of Keene NH int 24 Sep 1930 by WHITCOMB James L of Hoosick NY
BARONDES Earl Derohan of Kittery ME & DOLE Joan of Portsmouth NH int 19 Nov 1955 by MARVIN Ellison F of Yonkers NY
BAROWSKI Edward of Nashua NH & GAGNON Mariette of Nashua NH int 2 Jun 1952 by PAUL J Hean of Franklin PA
BARRATT Raymond W of Durham NH & RUGGLES Helen Louise of Salem NH int 21 Jun 1943 by GUPTILL Nathl W of Rowley MA
BARRETT Clarence E Jr of Somersworth NH & FARRINGTON Mary Jean of Berwick ME int 21 Aug 1953 by ROBERT S Illingworth of Barre MA
BARRON Richard Gilman of Marlboro NH & ARSENAULT Joyce of Marlboro NH int 2 Aug 1951 by L Philip Arsnault of Greensboro AL
BARRY John Stanley of River Edge NJ & MORGAN Erma Elizabeth of Baltimore MD int 15 Aug 1950 by YARROW Ernest A of River Edge NJ
BARRY Joseph P of Newton MA & ROUSSEAU Margaret M of Franklin NH int 11 Nov 1939 by ROBERT P Barry of Boston MA

BARRY Maurice Joseph of Bellows Falls VT & BALDASARO Angela Mae of No Walpole NH int 5 Aug 1959 by PATRICK A Barry of Bellows Falls VT

BARRY Richard of Manchester NH & ALLEN Frances of Manchester NH int 29 Jul 1936 by F E Butler of NC

BARRY William T Jr of Melrose MA & TOBEY Margaret of Hampton NH int 18 Sep 1943 by WARREN C Herrick of Melrose MA

BARTHALEMEW Noyes N of Chicago IL & WHYMAN Doris Marie of Chicago IL int 18 Aug 1937 by WHYMAN Henry C of New York NY

BARTLETT Arthur of Manchester NH & RAY Madelein of Manchester NH int 17 Sep 1952 by GERARD Chouinard of Plattsburgh NY

BARTLETT Clark Orin of E Orange NJ & WHITTERMORE Mariette of Andover MA int 1 Aug 1936 by WINN Arthur H of Houston TX

BARTLETT Eldridge M of Epsom NH & TAYLOR Winifred Louise of Northwood NH int 2 May 1951 by THOMSON Owen D of Danvers MA

BARTLETT Lewis of Boscawen NH & McALISTER Dorothy of Salisbury NH int 9 Nov 1949 by ROGER P Horton of Portland ME

BARTON David of Newport NH & JOHNSON Susan of Newport NH int 28 Aug 1958 by HOWARD L Brown of White River Jct VT

BARTON Donald of Portland ME & CORBETT Helen of Colebrook NH int 14 Jul 1937 by RICHARD A Frye of Brattleboro VT

BARTON Elbert Spaulding of Plainfield NH & HALL Winifred of Brookline NH int 23 Jul 1935 by J Irving Fletcher of Dorchester MA

BARTON Robert B of Pikesville MD & PARKER Sally of Peterboro NH int 2 Sep 1931 by PARK Charles E of Boston MA

BASCOMB Charles H of Alstead NH & GRANT Lois E of Charlestown NH int 6 Jan 1954 by STETSON Cliff R of Springfield VT

BASMAJIAN Vahan of Boston MA & SHATTUCK Sandra E of Nashua NH int 12 Dec 1959 by KRIKOR Keurukian of Watertown MA

BASSAGE Winfield of Athens PA & HAYES Carolyn of Berlin NH int 25 Jul 1955 by DUANE E Ferris of Fairfax MO

BASSETT Samuel Butler of Waterbury CT & BRITLES Rose Eleanor of New Britain CT int 7 Aug 1947 by GREENE Theodore of New Britain CT

BASSON Philip W of Mt Vernon NY & HOLMES Priscilla May of Walpole NH int 28 Apr 1954 by SHEPPARD Walter of Attleboro MA

BATCHELDER Donald of Newburyport MA & HENRY Gwendolyn of Plaistow NH int 2 Sep 1942 by FRANK W Cummings of Worcester MA

BATCHELDER Gary A of Derry NH & PINARD Dorothy L of Sandown NH int 22 Sep 1960 by NICHOLAS William H of Cambridge MA

BATCHELDER Henry Merton of Randolph VT & STONE Barbara Ruth of Fitzwilliam NH int 4 Jul 1951 by LEONARD W Fowler of Athol MA

BATCHELDER Isaac Walker of Pembroke NH & POTTER Ruth Eleanor of Gilmanton NH int 21 Sep 1959 by DONALD L Osborn of Northfield VT

BATCHELDER James Roland of Suncook NH & FERREN Lucy Agnes of Errol NH int 29 May 1940 by EARLE L Buchin of Cedar Grove NJ

BATES Basil A of Northfield OH & POELMAN Carolyn of Wolefboro NH int 9 Aug 1960 by WILLAND Louise A of Groton CT

BATES Bradford of Boston MA & RICHARDSON Lydia Ellen of Newark DE int 2 Mar 1960 by J Donald Johnston of Bethesda MD

BATES Earle E of Laconia NH & SHUTE Dorothy S of Plymouth NH int 30 Jun 1927 by RAYMOND J Bates of Waterbury CT

BEACH Marcus of Seattle WA & YATES Barbara F of Belmont MA int 8 Jul 1960 by PHELPS Morgan of Montclair NJ

BEALS Robert Veronon of Keene NH & CLARK Dorothy Calwell of Keene NH int 2 Jun 1930 by BEALS Chas E of E Taunton MA

BEAN George Clarke of Sumit NJ & DODWELL Pamela Phyllis of Sumit NJ int 11 Aug 1939 by MORGAN Menot C of Greenwich CT

BEANDRY Normand J of Nashua NH & SIROIS Jeannine of Nashua NH int 23 Dec 1950 by PARADIS Robert M of Palisades NJ

BEARCE James of St Petersbury FL & McSKIMMON Mary of Jaffrey NH int 25 May 1959 by ALBERT E Baldwin of St Petersburg FL

BEATON Virginia Austin of Woodsville NH & KIDDER Donald Ernest of Woodsville NH int 2 Nov 1948 by MORTON W Hale of Weybridge VT

BEAUCHESNE Robert of Lowell MA & McGREEVY Dorothy of Newmarket NH int 16 Aug 1948 by NORMAND Beauchesne of Natick MA

BEAUDET Roger of Manchester NH & BRODEUR Germaine of Manchester NH int 2 Apr 1954 by ROBERT Fortier of Natick MA

BEAUDOIN Anthony of Berlin NH & LEMAY Beatrice of Laconia NH int 15 Nov 1932 by MENDARD Herve of Montreal CAN

BEAUDOIN Ernest A of Cambridge MA & LANDRY Evelyn of Concord NH int 8 Apr 1948 by LIONEL F Beaudoin of Haverhill MA

BEAULIEU Raymond Dennis of Gonic NH & CURRAN Alice Cecile of Portsmouth NH int 19 May 1955 by JOSEPH L Curran of Philadelphia PA

BECKETT Charles Louis of Cambridge MA & MOREY Florence of Andover NH int 3 Jul 1929 by McKINNEY W L of Bridgewater MA

BEDARD Albert of Manchester NH & TRAKIMAS Aldona of Manchester NH int 12 Jun 1950 by PAUL A Cote of Natick MA

BEDARD Camille of Manchester NH & PARENT Irene of Manchester NH int 21 May 1952 by PAUL Cote of Natick MA

BEDARD Paul Emile of Manchester NH & LALIBERTE Corona of Auburn NH int 2 May 1947 by ROLAND Bedard of Attleboro MA

BEDARD Rene of Manchester NH & TURGEON Doris of Manchester NH int 2 Apr 1951 by PAUL Cote of Natick MA

BELANGER Richard R of Nashua NH & DUMAINE Guertrude J of Nashua NH int 21 Jul 1958 by GERALD M Cote of No Gales AZ

BELIVEAU Harold E Jr of Concord NH & BEAN Judith of Concord NH int 16 Sep 1950 by MAYNARD Erville of Albany NY

BELL Leon C of Berlin NH & BEAULIEU Alma of Berlin NH int 23 Jun 1937 by OSCAR Beaulieu of CAN

BENNETT Edward of Newport NH & KRUMMES Jean of Newport NH int 26 May 1947 by ROGER W Bennett of Newton Falls MA

BENNETT Raymond Brown of Loudon Ridge NH & DOTSON Thelma Louise of Exeter NH int 15 Aug 1949 by KENNETH E Dotson of Port Clyde ME

BENNETT William T Jr of Cornish ME & COLBY Margaret of Littleton NH int 11 Jun 1940 by W T Bennett of Cornish ME

BENSON Erwin E of Franklin NH & HANCADE Claudette of Webster NH int 18 Aug 1949 by J Osborne Crowe of Pepperell MA

BENSON Roland of Mechanic Fals ME & MARONEY Margaret of Winchester NH int 24 Dec 1951 by STANLEY H King of Ipswich MA

BENTON Corning of Exeter NH & McGRATH Mary Elizabeth of Jamestown RI int 16 May 1956 by LOUNSBURY Walter of Newburport MA

BENWARE George G of Langdon NH & NIMS Ruth K of Sullivan NH int 22 Aug 1925 by W O Conrad of Georgetown MA

BERARD Maurice of Manchester NH & MARQUIS Marie A of Manchester NH int 15 Nov 1943 by MARQUIS Paul E of Manchester NH

BERG Robert Emanuel of Portsmouth NH & SULLIVAN Virginia F of Portsmouth NH int 17 Nov 1931 by MONTGOMERY David K of Lowell MA

BERGERON Antonio of Dover NH & MAYNARD Juleiette of Dover NH int 13 Dec 1955 by MAYRAND Paul of Lowell MA

BERGERON Donat of Bristol CT & DESROCHERS Germaine of Manchester NH int 10 Jun 1929 by LAPOINTE Omer of St Lucie CAN

BERGERON Marcel of Berlin NH & COUTURE Jeannine of Berlin NH int 29 Mar 1955 by ROLAND Coutur of Bucksport ME

BERGHALZ Richard of Manchester NH & GASKILL Alfrieda Mae of Londonderry NH int 2 Jun 1952 by JOHN G Gaskill of Andover MA

BERGQUIST Bealer U of East Lempster NH & CALDWELL Louise E of East Lemster NH int 24 Sep 1942 by THOMAS W Delong of Waltham MA

BERIOND David of Phil PA & MARCY Jeanne of Newton Highland MA int 26 Jun 1951 by MONTGOMERY Marshall of Lake Worth FL

BERNARD Adrien of ? & HEON Germaine of Nashua NH int 10 Nov 1941 by PAUL J Heon of ?

BERNARD Omer Thomas of Manchester NH & MIGNAULT Rolande A of Manchester NH int 3 Jun 1949 by HENRY Bernard of Montreal CAN

BERNARD Roland of Manchester NH & BEERNAERT Doris of Manchester NH int 29 Jul 1946 by HENRY Bernard of Montreal CAN

BERNDT David D of Newton Falls MA & CASWELL Nancy Lee of Concord NH int 26 May 1961 by BERNDT Wm S of Newton Falls MA

BERNIER Leo of Manchester NH & CASEY Catherine of Manchester NH int 1 Apr 1946 by JOHN A King of Fairfield CT

BERRY Edward W Jr of Winchester MA & STEWART Josephine of Manchester NH int 31 May 1938 by RODDY Clyde H of Great Barrington MA

BERRY Raymond of Lowell MA & GREENWOOD Jeanette of Nashua NH int 8 Oct 1940 by ALBERT Curtress of Reading MA

BERRY Russell Parker Jr of Windsor VT & DOLE Mabel Charlotte of Windsor VT int 19 Jun 1945 by MARTIN Morrill O of Taunton MA

BETTS Hugh S of Townsend MA & CALLAHAN Marion of Brooklin NH int 17 Apr 1947 by QUILL Percival J of Waltham MA

BEZANSON Donald Gardner of W Somerville MA & KING Barbara Louise of Concord NH int 16 Aug 1943 by R Marshall Bezanson of Watertown WI

BEZANSON William Henry of Somerville MA & RAND Florence Harriet of Exeter NH int 24 Jul 1941 by EDWIN K Gedney of Stoneham MA

BICKFORD David of Somersworth NH & DUBE Marie Yvette of So Berwick ME int 9 May 1942 by ARTHUR J Dube of Winslow ME

BIGGS Edward Porver of Cambridge MA & LIONNE Colette Josephie of Boston MA int 31 Aug 1933 by GARDNER Wm E Gardner of Boston MA

BILODEAAU Alphonse of Leominster MA & SAINTJEAN Cecile of Dublin NH int 25 May 1933 by JAMES Connors of Lowell MA

BILODEAU Normand of Manchester NH & BRETON Denise of Manchester NH int 25 May 1942 by VERONNEAU A of Lowell MA

BIRD Henry Lonsdale of Cambridge MA & BREWSTER Hildegarde of Kittery Point ME int 16 Mar 1955 by TAYLOR Charles L Jr of Cambridge MA

BIRD Sidney M of Cambridge MA & HARDY Katherine of Arlington MA int 14 Sep 1932 by LAWRENCE L Barber of Arlington MA

BIRON Robert Dr of Manchester NH & TANGUAY Eva of Nashua NH int 19 Nov 1930 by PAUL Demangeleere of Newton MA

BISHOP William Lester of Arlington VA & MARSHALL Frances E of Portsmouth NH int 1 Oct 1957 by LEWIS Wm W of Arlington VA

BISSION Guy W of Manchester NH & BOUCHARD Lorraine R of Manchester NH int 21 Apr 1958 by ALFRED Bouchard of CAN

BISSON David Arthur of Somersworth NH & LARIVIERE Anita of Somersworth NH int 28 Jul 1960 by ROGER L Bisson of Franklin PA

BISSON Maurice of Somersworth NH & ROBERGE Anita of Somersworth NH int 19 Apr 1955 by ROGER L Bisson of CAN

BITOMSKI Thodore of Exeter NH & ROWELL Leila of Exeter NH int 22 Jun 1956 by PENNOCK Gilbert L of Cincinnati OH

BIXBY Earle Wilson of Manchester NH & HUTCHINS Elizabeth Pile of Goffstown NH int 26 Jan 1950 by L Wendell Hughes of Watertown MA

BLACKBURN Woodward of Andover MA & WESTWOOD Florence Ashby of Hingham MA int 21 Jul 1932 by WESTWOOD Horace Jauett of Hingham MA

BLAKE Alvah H of Penacook NH & GOUGH Margaret E of Penacook NH int 16 Jun 1925 by SIDNEY J Willis of Biddeford ME

BLAKE Harry of Bradford NH & GILLINGHAM Martha of So Newbury NH int 17 Nov 1930 by FOWLER Chas L of Lowell MA

BLAKE Joseph of W Medford MA & JEFFERSON Rita of Westwood MA int 15 Aug 1959 by POTTER Lenwood of Dennis MA

BLAKENEY Gordon of Concord NH & THOMPSON Frances of Concord NH int 20 Aug 1949 by ARCHIBALD Black of Montoclair NJ

BLAKESLEE Rollin Q of Cherry Pt NC & SABIN Mary Louise of Wolfeboro NH int 28 Jul 1959 by W Leroy Haven of Amherst MA

BLAN Elza T of Keota OK & WELCH Diana A of Meredith NH int 2 Jul 1943 by VON-DER-SUMP Frederick of Lantan FL

BLISS Howard H of New York NY & WRIGHT Persis Cowan of Flushing NY int 1 Jun 1929 by DANIEL Bliss of Monson MA

BLOUWNEY John Sherman of Schenetady NY & SOMERVILLE Nak of Quincy MA int 11 Jun 1946 by WING Charles A of Quincy MA

BLOWIN Francis Xavier of Somerville MA & DUBE Dagny of Ctr Ossipee NH int 12 Jul 1951 by LEPOLD Braun of New York NY

BLUM Jon of Philadelphia PA & SCHOLNICK Nancy E of Pittsburg PA int 25 Nov 1955 by WILLIMA H Fineshriber of Phil PA

BOGIE Covlot of McIndoe Falls VT & JOHNSON Helen of Monroe NH int 16 Jan 1942 by WOODWORTH Arthur of McIndoe Falls

BOHANON Paul of Shaker Heights OH & BLAKE Eunice Putnam of New York NY int 8 Sep 1939 by MAUREE Oscar E of New Haven CT

BOILARD Donald of Goffstown NH & LEVASSEUR Pauline of Manchester NH int 17 Sep 1953 by LEVANEUR Alphonse of Province of Quebec CAN

BOISVERT Lucien of Manchester NH & PAQUIN Anna of Manchester NH int 17 Dec 1951 by TURCOTTE Albert L of Methuen MA

BOISVERT Roland of Manchester NH & GONTHIER Ivonne of Manchester NH int 27 Jun 1946 by CANNON Ernestine of Dudley Robert M

BOIVIN Armand of Manchester NH & BEAUDOIN Claire of Manchester NH int 25 Sep 1951 by ROLAND Bedard of E Brewster MA

BOIVIN Lionel of Manchester NH & BROCKWAY Marilyn of Manchester NH int 29 Feb 1960 by FREDERICK Brockway of Dennimora NY

BOLDUC Girard Thomas of Laconia NH & JODOIN Jeanette L M of Berlin NH int 2 May 1948 by TARDIF Hilary M of Montreal CAN

BOLSER Ernest Nelson of Manchester NH & CHUTE Alice May of Manchester NH int 21 May 1931 by TREW Charles of Portland ME

BOOTH Robert A of Swampscott MA & McKAY Joyce L of Marblehead MA int 21 Apr 1950 by SMITH Meredith P of Marblehead MA

BORDERS Harold Bee of Springfield VT & BELDEN Grace Jean of Newport NH int 7 Jul 1951 by FRANK M Beach of Lebanon Springs NY

BOTTOMLEY Bruce of Barrington RI & THOMAS Doris of Melvin Village int 5 Sep 1951 by LAISCH Russell T of Melrose MA

BOUCHARD Rene J of Berlin NH & LEMIEUX Priscilla C of Berlin NH int 27 Aug 1948 by LEMIEUX Arthur E of Attleboro MA

BOULAY Henry Ernest of Manchester NH & LaFLAMME Rachel A of Manchester NH int 22 May 1951 by C Edouard Desilets of CAN

BOULAY Robert of Berlin NH & VACHON Dorothy of Berlin NH int 12 Sep 1953 by VACHON Claude of Buckport ME

BOURDEAU Roger of Millbury MA & THIBAULT Aline of Nashua NH int 27 Jun 1953 by THIBAULT Camillis of NY My

BOUTELLE Clifford K of Antrim NH & WEEKS Alice Seaver of Antrim NH int 1 Dec 1949 by LOPER Frank B of Winchendon MA

BOUTWELL Jeffrie Raymond of Newport NH & NICHOLS Charlotte J of Newport NH int 3 Feb 1947 by ERNEST A Brown Jr of Waltham MA

BOWDEN John Warren of Melrose MA & SHARPLES Mary of Cambridge MA int 26 May 1938 by PARK Charles E of Boston MA

BOWDITCH Ebenezer F of Concord MA & HALE Anna Mitchell of Boston MA int 24 Jul 1935 by CURTIS Dickins of Brookfield CT

BOWEN Joseph P of Fort Fairfield ME & LAVOIE Rita Angela of Nashua NH int 5 Aug 1940 by JOHN E Bowen of Quincy MA

BOWER John Warwick of Keene NH & COOK Eleanor Mabel of Keene NH int 26 May 1948 by ROW W Battenhouse of Cambridge MA

BOWHAY George L of Alstead NH & FOSTER Evelyn of Alstead NH int 16 Oct 1934 by FRANCES A Kimball of Bellow Falls VT

BOWKER Harold of Brighton ME & BELL Muriel F of NH int 5 Jul 1940 by MURPHY James J of Brighton MA

BOYNTON Stanley C of Rockland ME & STEVENS Esther N of Rockland ME int 13 Apr 1941 by YOUNG Fred of Duxfield ME

BOZARTH Donald F of Walpole MA & HOOD Rena of Haverhill NH int 3 Feb 1950 by HOWARD P Bozarth of Walpole MA

BRACKETT Donald Burton of Greenland NH & DAVIDSON Claire of Greenland NH int 15 Sep 1947 by C Basil Harris of Kittery Point ME

BRADLEY Stuart of Goffstown NH & FOGG Bessie of Hancock NH int 20 Aug 1928 by SKILLIN Carl D of Peace Dale RI

BRAUNFIELD Frank Jacob of Wollaston MA & FRENCH Marjorie H of Hudson NH int 29 Oct 1940 by STANLEY E Anderson of Danvers MA

BRAZER Richard Bird of Brookline MA & FRANKS Gertrude Louise of Dedham MA int 22 Jul 1930 by HENRY H Crane of Scranton PA

BRETON Richarton R of Somersworth NH & MICHAUD Pauline M of Somersworth NH int 7 May 1954 by TANGUAY Ovid of Biddeford ME

BREWER George of So Lancaster MA & ATWOOD Carrie Muriel of Keene NH int 19 Jul 1933 by SAUNDERSON A E of Warehouse Point CT

BREWSTER Donald Wright of Waltham MA & BEEBE Rose Ellen of Weston MA int 7 Aug 1951 by EKWALL Geo O of Waltham MA

BREWSTER Eugene of Kensington NH & BECKMAN Ruth Ada of Kensington NH int 11 Sep 1947 by SAWYER Roland of Ware MA

BREWSTER George W of Keningston NH & FLANDERS Marjorie of Keningston NH int 4 Jun 1951 by SAWYER Roland of Ware MA

BRIDGES Elmer Hurd of Plaistow NH & HOUGHTON Doris Abbott of Plaistow NH int 30 Oct 1928 by FRANK Crook of Groveland MA

BRIDGES H Styles of Concord NH & CLEMENT Sally of Concord NH int 25 Jun 1928 by ARCHIBALD Black of Montclair NJ

BRIDGES Seth Reynolds of Buffalo NY & SPRAGUE Frances Helen of Hancock NH int 17 May 1957 by SCHACHT Robert H of Providence RI

BRIDGMAN Robert W of Jefferson NH & CARTER Sylvia of Jefferson NH int 20 Aug 1940 by TYLER Samuel of Cambridge MA

BRIGGS Carlton M Jr of Endicott NY & COBB Barbara A of Plainville MA int 30 Jul 1958 by MALLERY Wesley of Winchester MA

BRIGHAM Lyman Henry of Warren VT & SANBORN Thenice Morrill of Tilton NH int 8 Dec 1952 by EDWARD Ernst of Bangor ME

BRILL Willie Nathan of Woodsville NH & MASON Lois Ada of Woodsville NH int 18 Nov 1938 by NICHERSON E H of Groton VT

BRINDIS Eugene of Haverhill MA & ROSEN Evelyn of Laconia NH int 23 May 1941 by ABRAHAM Jackson of Haverhill MA

BRISSE William C of Laconia NH & DUGUAY Lorraine of Laconia NH int 14 Oct 1955 by PIERRE Brisse of Evansville IN

BRISTOL Herman of Collinsville CT & BLOUNT Merle of Littleton NH int 5 Oct 1931 by PERKINS Harry W of Plymouth CT

BROCHU Donald of Manchester NH & COTE Rachel L of Bedford NH int 4 May 1959 by EMILE A Brochu of New York NY

BROCHU Elzebert Clovis of Somersworth NH & DESHARMAIS Alice Yvette of Somersworth NH int 28 May 1946 by PLANTE Octave of CA

BRODIE Arnold Louis of Manchester NH & PORTER Harriet Joan of Manchester NH int 8 Sep 1950 by ABRAHAM I Jacobson of Haverhill MA

BROOKS David of Haverhill MA & MANGIONE Josephine of Lawrence MA int 11 Jul 1955 by T Dowing Bowler of Bradford MA

BROOKS John Elmer of Boston MA & CHENEY Pauline of Meredith NH int 7 Aug 1927 by PAIGE Wesley A of Providence RI

BROOKS Richard James of Alton NH & HALE Wanda of Alton NH int 7 Jul 1950 by CLAYTON Brooks Hale of Boston MA

BROOKS William Tyler of Portsmouth NH & PHILPOT Helen Agnes of Portsmouth NH int 15 Sep 1937 by HERBERT W Brooks of Kittery Point ME

BROUILLARD Richard P of Laconia NH & HOULE Carmen Emelina of Laconia NH int 17 Jul 1954 by PELLETIER Alfred of Natick MA

BROWN Andrew Allerton of Scarsdale NY & FOSS Alice Parker of Cambridge MA int 28 Jun 1948 by LEAMON John H of Cambridge MA

BROWN Arthur A of Manchester CT & CONANT Edith D of Lexington KY int 7 Jul 1945 by FRED Q Blanchard of Manchester CT

BROWN Boardman W of Seattle WA & FREEZE Nancy J of Hamden CT int 12 May 1950 by SCOTT Phil of Washington DC

BROWN David Trent of Milford NH & KELLOWAY Shirley Jane of Nashua NH int 21 Jun 1957 by ERNEST O Kelloway of Camden NJ

BROWN Donald R of Berwick ME & LeHOULLIER Laurette of Somersworth NH int 5 Jan 1946 by LeHOULLIER Alban of Natick MA

BROWN Donnell S of Bingham NY & EATON Miriam Buswell of Salisbaury MA int 3 Jun 1954 by MILLER William B of Cambridge MA

BROWN Edward of Ashland NH & MORRISSEY Helen of New Hampton NH int 25 Sep 1948 by SPEERS Theodore C of New York NY

BROWN Farwell A of ? & LAKE Mary E of ? int 8 Oct 1932 by MINKER Ralph L of Wilmington DE

BROWN Frank of Hinsdale NH & TAYLOR Miriam of Hinsdale NH int 16 Oct 1940 by MILTON S Czatt of Brattleboro VT

BROWN James Bradley of Woodstown NJ & COLLIER Caroline Celest of Lowell MA int 20 Jun 1950 by LAWRENCE H Blackburn of Lowell MA

BROWN James C of Portsmouth NH & BUNKER Sandra Jean of Portsmouth NH int 16 Dec 1960 by RICHARD C Hardy of Kittery ME

BROWN James M of W Hartford CT & REYNOLDS Louise L of Hartford CT int 5 May 1952 by WILLIAM S Gooch of Kittery Pt ME

BROWN Kyial of Putney VT & HENNESSEY Margaret of No Walpole NH int 28 Aug 1943 by MOYNIHAN James F of Newton MA

BROWN Lloyd of Marboro MA & TUCKER Elizabeth of Lawrence MA int 8 Jan 1934 by OSMOND Fred of Boston MA

BROWN Lyle Arthur of Nashua NH & BULLARD Susan Melvin of Cambridge MA int 11 Jun 1931 by SWISHER Waller Samuel of Wellesley MA

BROWN Mervill C of New York NY & SNYDER Margaret of Winchester MA int 8 Aug 1939 by HOWARD Chidley of Winchester MA

BROWN Raymond of Staten Island NY & KNIGHT Dorothy of Nashua NH int 15 Aug 1947 by LEON Merle Flanders of Great Neck NY

BROWN Reynolds D of Phil PA & RUSSEAU Emily P of Milton MA int 4 Sep 1936 by POMEROY Vivian T of Milton MA

BROWN Sylvan G of Concord NH & WINKLER Mildrew of Rockway NY int 20 Jun 1939 by ROBINSON John J F of New York NY

BROWN Winthrop of Washington DC & PECK Lee Gaives of Atkinson NH int 6 Sep 1950 by MERRILL Randolph of Newton MA

BRUCE Burton Lyle of Nashua NH & DUNLAP Helen Sanborn of Nashua NH int 7 Aug 1929 by DANIEL I Gross of Portland ME

BRUNETTE Raymond K of Salem NH & BARRON Mary Alice of Salem NH int 15 Jun 1953 by SEAWARD Carl Albert of Sanford ME

BRUNO Theodore of Boston MA & SAWYER Catherine of W Rindge NH int 26 Sep 1925 by A Z Conrad of Boston MA

BRYAN Kirk of Cambridge MA & BALDWIN Harriet of Hillsboro NH int 9 May 1956 by WILLIAM S Abernethy of Washington DC

BRYANT Cushman A of No Springfield VT & JESSEMAN Erline A of Laconia NH int 26 May 1948 by A C Allen of Springfield VT

BRYANT Max C of Portsmouth NH & SYPHERS Bertha of Greeland NH int 6 Oct 1947 by C Basil Harris of Kittery Point ME

BRYANT Thomas of Staten Island NY & GRANT Ruth of Arlington MA int 29 Jun 1948 by WILLIAM Henry Denney of Boston MA

BUBIER George Chandler of Boston MA & SKILLAR Evelyn Viola of Boston MA int 25 Aug 1953 by ARTHUR W Dewhurst of No Reading MA

BUCK Bailey R Jr of Milwaukee WI & WHITING Margaret of Wilton NH int 24 Jul 1954 by PARK Charles E of Boston MA

BUGBEE Carl I of Newport NH & TRUELL Helen of Newport NH int 17 Jul 1931 by GABRIEL Guedj of Pawtucket RI

BUINICKY Henry Francis of Claremont NH & LANGDON Priscilla of Claremont NH int 15 Aug 1946 by DANIEL A Glamache of Tauton MA

BULLOCK Robert W of Worcester MA & SIEGLER Sarah M of Holliesbury MI int 30 Jun 1948 by A Edwin Keigioin of New York NY

BUNDLETT Brewster of Concord NH & AYERS Prudence of Concord NH int 18 Nov 1941 by CARL Brenton Bare of Newport RI

BUNKER Paul Clark of Lancaster PA & WESTON Elizabeth of Danvers MA int 2 Sep 1937 by PUTNAM Raymond of St Johnsbury VT

BUNTING Bainbridge of Kansas City MO & FEISE Dorelen of Baltimore MD int 14 Aug 1948 by WILLIAM M Crane of Richmond MA

BURBANK Henry of Laconia & FELLOWS Gertrude E of Laconia NH int 26 Aug 1946 by WATSON John of Milton MA

BURDETTE Lowries W Jr of Greenville SC & GOUBERT Jean W of Newbury NH int 6 Sep 1951 by METTERS Robert of Boston MA

BURGES Ralph of Boston MA NH & BURTON Elizabeth of New Ipswich NH int 27 Oct 1954 by LAVERS Norman of Belmont MA

BURKE Edward Joseph of Waltham MA & LALLY Katherine Mary of Manchester NH int 27 Apr 1948 by KING John of Lenox MA

BURKE Laurence of Jefferson NH & SAMSON Mary of Jefferson NH int 12 Sep 1945 by SAMPSON Antoine of Capelton Province of Quebec CAN

BURKE Richard Calvin of San Diego CA & McDONALD Helen A of S Effingham NH int 22 Oct 1956 by SWEENEY Joseph of Weston MA

BURKE William Alvard of New York NY & BENTON Ruth Kingsbury of New York NY int 27 Jun 1928 by APPLETON Grannis of Lowell MA

BURKLAND Robert of Northwood NH & BEAUCHAIN Joan of Northwood NH int 31 May 1956 by ANDREW B Currier of Essex Ctr VT

BURNETT George of Manchester NH & BAGDASARIAU R Ann of Manchester NH int 16 May 1949 by ARTHUR H Burnett of Towanda PA

BURRILL John H of Stafford Spgs CT & PHILLIPS Marion of Winchester NH int 25 Oct 1956 by WHITE W R of Stafford Springs CT

BURTON Carlton of New London NH & GAY Eleanor V of New London NH int 19 Sep 1950 by HAROLD W Baker of Lynn MA

BURTON George King of Georges Mills NH & FLEMING Stella of Georges Mills NH int 1 Jun 1954 by MALCOLM K Burton of Pontiac MI

BUSHOLD Allen G of Boston MA & BURNHAM Natalie of Hampton NH int 14 Sep 1946 by MILLER Ernest A of Groveland MA

BUSSEY Laurence T of Kittery Pt ME & SEAVER Nancy of Stoneham MA int 22 Jun 1959 by E Maurice Bussey of Kittery Pt ME

BUTLER Bradford Henry of Oxford MA & PRINGLE Theresa of Lebanon NH int 6 Dec 1932 by HARRY Grant Butler of Oxford MA

BUTLER Robert Matthew of Manchester NH & JENOVESE Carol Ann of Concord NH int 21 Oct 1960 by MICHAEL A Genovese of Leominster MA

BUTLER William Sherwood of Fremont NH & KELLY Gertrude Ida of Newton NH int 16 Aug 1944 by JOHN E Fickett of Bar Harbor ME

BUXTON Madison J of Nashua NH & BROCHU Theresa of Somersworth NH int 15 Apr 1942 by NADEAU Armond of Danielson CT

BUXTON Roger of Peterboro NH & CLEARY Joyce of Bennington NH int 10 Aug 1959 by RICE William B of Wellesley MA

BUXTON Robert of Hudson NH & BRUNELLE Lorraine of Nashua NH int 1 Sep 1949 by GEORGE L Brunelle of Holyoke MA

BUXTON William of Springfield MA & POTTALA Aila of Springfield MA int 28 Jun 1938 by CHARLES W Jeffras of Springfield MA

BYAM Charles W of Waltham MA & BRYER Harriet Ellen of Peterboro NH int 25 Jun 1934 by PARK Charles E of Boston MA

BYCHOK John of Claremont NH & WOODWARD Betty Lou of Claremont NH int 27 Jul 1953 by NYKIEL John of So Boston MA

BYCZKOWSKI Stanley of Enfield NH & TEMPLE Shirley of W Lebanon NH int 10 Dec 1957 by ROBERT J Harding of Brattleboro VT

CALDER David Alexander of Roselle Park NJ & REID Elizabeth Ann of Jaffrey NH int 28 May 1956 by FRANCIS C Anderson Jr of Braintree MA

CALKINS Rollin Thomson of Chicago IL & BROOKS Ruth Wilder of Hancock NH int 20 Jul 1931 by RIHBANY Abraham M of Brookline MA

CALL Frank of Brentwood NH & SPRAGUE Betty of Brentwood NH int 25 Nov 1959 by TERRY Clay Thomas of Oakdale MA

CALL George William of Chichester NH & MONETTE Beverley of Concord NH int 15 Dec 1945 by WARD Robt of Sherbrooke CAN

CALLAGHAN Gerald J of Rochester NH & BLAIS Joan of Berlin NH int 14 Aug 1956 by GEORGE J Callaghan of Washington DC

CALLENDER Willard D Jr of Melrose MA & HUSSON Beverly Ann of Manchester NH int 25 Nov 1959 by WILLARD D Callender of Melrose MA

CAMBELL David of Cambridge MA & WENTWORTH Ann of Plaistow NH int 3 Sep 1957 by SMITH Henry F of W Medford MA

CAMBELL Warren H of Langdon NH & HASKINS Delinda of Alstead NH int 31 Mar 1955 by MARSH George B of Grafton VT

CAMPBELL Crawford J of Cooperstown NY & HARTSHORN Catharine of Shot Hill NJ int 26 Jun 1939 by SIMPSON Henry J of Flint MI

CAMPBELL Donald F of New Brunswick NJ & MORRIS Charlotte E of Toms River NJ int 27 Aug 1934 by LEWIS A Galbraith of Newark NJ

CAMPBELL Roland B of Watertown MA & HAMILTON Ruth Greenough of Haverhill MA int 3 Jun 1929 by NORMAN D Fletcher of Haverhill MA

CANNING Horace M of Reno Nev & WHITELAY Emma Evelyn of Peaks Isl ME int 17 Sep 1946 by WHITELAY Harry of Peaks Isl ME

CAOUETTE Wilfrid of Greenville NH & OUELLETTE Irene of New Ipswich NH int 30 Jun 1948 by OMER J Chevrette of Fitchburg MA

CAPISTRAN Armand of Manchester NH & RICHARD Cecile of Manchester NH int 28 May 1960 by RICHARD Ferdinand of Lowell MA

CARHART William V of Exeter NH & SCHOFIELD Anne Justina of St Albans Herts England int 2 Oct 1959 by CHARLES Smith of Cambridge MA

CARIGAN Gerard A of Somersworth NH & FOURNIER Marguerite of Somersworth NH int 10 Jun 1959 by PLANTE Georges J of Saco ME

CARLISLE James M of New Haven CT & PERKINS Dorothy of Cambridge MA int 8 Jun 1936 by JAMES H Gorham of Kent CT

CARLSON Carl of Canaan NH & LARDEN Catherine of Concord NH int 17 Jun 1947 by BERNARD Foley of Garrison NY

CARLSON Harold Gustav of New Hampton NH & MATTHEWS Ethel May of Briston NH int 27 Apr 1954 by P W Back of Arlington MA

CARLSON Herbert of Bristol CT & HALL Adelarde of Bristol CT int 11 Jul 1932 by HUBERT D Jones of New Haven CT

CARLTON John L of Greenland NH & BRACKETT Ruth Elizabeth of Greenland NH int 3 Aug 1947 by WILLIAM J Browne of Magolia MA

CARMICHAEL Robert of Winston Salem NC & BIDWELL Florence of Springfield MA int 29 Aug 1931 by WILLIAMSON E E of Madison NC

CARON Albert Ronald of Manchester NH & LASSONDE Ruth Ann of Chelmsford MA int 7 Mar 1951 by ROGER Rosaire Caron of Brooklyn NY

CARON Jean of Shawinigan CAN & GODIN Charlotte of Concord NH int 2 Jun 1958 by RENE Garceau of Montreal CAN

CARON Roger R of Brooklyn NY & THAYER Joan of Manchester NH int 21 Oct 1952 by QUACKENBUSH Colin D of Brooklin Y

CARON Victor of Claremont & POTVIN Florina of Claremont NH int 9 Oct 1946 by POTVIN Alfred of Lewiston ME

CARONIS George Charles of Newport NH & KNEBEL Carol M of Concord NH int 17 Jun 1959 by MacLAIN Norman C of Marlboro MA

CAROS Alec of Nahsua NH & LANGMAID Ottilie Beth of Bethlemen int 14 May 1952 by SEMINERIO Steven of Somerville MA

CARPENTER Edward Wilson of Westfield NJ & DOW Rachel of New Hampton NH int 23 May 1941 by YINGER Clement B of Haverhill MA

CARPENTER George Luther of West Rye NH & SMITH Mary Brown of So Hampton NH int 20 Oct 1954 by BENJAMIN F Bowling of Boston MA

CARPENTER Harry W of Milford NH & ROBY Miriam of Milford NH int 26 Nov 1951 by ERNEST L Converse of Hopkinton MA

CARPENTER Thurston John of Concord NH & TILTON Ann of Concord NH int 1 Jul 1947 by DANA M Greeley of Boston MA

CARPENTER William W of Waltham MA & FIELD Anne Montague of Auburndale MA int 13 Jan 1958 by RUSSELL H Bishop of Newton Ctr MA

CARR Robert of Waddington NY & HAILMAN Velma Eliz of Concord NH int 15 Jun 1949 by B Marshall White Hurst of Roanoke Rapids NC

CARROLL Charles of Concord NH & BRYNE Arlene of Concord NH int 1 Sep 1951 by ADRIAN J Carroll of Louville NY

CARROLL Charles T of Concord NH & WELCH Dorothea T of Concord NH int 31 Mar 1947 by ADRIAN Carroll of Garrison NY

CARRUTH Wm Glen of Bristol NH & BOYCE Dorothy Irene of Hill NH int 7 Sep 1954 by WILLIAMS Ralph W of New Britain CT

CARTER Albert R of Sanford ME & MARCEAU Edna of Somersworth NH int 28 Jun 1946 by MARCEAU V C of Toole UT

CARTER Clinton Irving of Eliot ME & SMITH Gertrude V of Raymond NH int 16 Jul 1946 by JOHN Taylor Holman of Port Clyde ME

CARTER Michael of Williamstown MA & RUSSELL Lillian of Dublin NH int 3 Aug 1949 by SIDNEY W Goldsmith Jr of Williamstown MA

CARTER Robert W of Rochester NH & SESSLER Elizabeth Irene of Rochester NH int 23 Oct 1952 by JAMES H Burns of Auburndale MA

CARTER William Elmer of So Groveland MA & DORAN Patricia E of Lincoln NH int 14 Apr 1959 by MATHIEU Alphonse of Sherbrooke CAN

CARTON Harold Michael of Milton MA & FOSS Jane Kay of Milton MA int 24 Aug 1953 by J M Flanagan of Lowell MA

CARTY Joseph Jr of Manchester NH & NEILAN Jane E of Boston MA int 7 Jul 1960 by FRANCIS L Keenan of Lowell MA

CASBOIAN Harvey T of College Park NJ & TUTTLE Frances E of College Pk NJ int 6 Jul 1942 by COOLIDGE Henry A of Killingley CT
CASHMAN Alfred Vernon of Portsmouth NH & PENNEY Marie Alice of S Berwick ME int 20 May 1944 by BAGGS John W of Portland ME
CASWELL Francis L of Dover NH & CASSILY Claire V of Dover NH int 6 Jun 1947 by LAMOND John J of Lawrence MA
CASWELL Harry P of Boston MA & ARMSTRONG Priscilla of Boston MA int 19 Jun 1947 by MAYWOOD Wm of Haverhill MA
CATE Carl W Jr of Raymond NH & BROWNELL Georgia Lee of Wheaton IL int 18 Aug 1950 by JOHN Kullberg of Wheaton IL
CATE Dexter E of Shelburne Falls MA & BASTILLE Alberta of Lakeport NH int 14 Dec 1950 by THOMAS J Cate of Shelburne Falls MA
CATE Maurice of Dover NH & GARDNER Evelyn E of Nashua NH int 5 Aug 1925 by EARLE B Cross of Rochester NY
CATHERON Allison G of Milan NH & FLINT Shirley of Milan NH int 11 Jul 1957 by WHITE Beverly T of Norfolk VA
CATON W Stuart of Hartford CT & WILLIAMS Millicent of Keene NH int 20 May 1953 by POLHEMUS Oscar M of Haverhill MA
CAVERLY Gardner Arthur of Laconia NH & ROLLINS Abbie Adaline of Alton NH int 11 Apr 1938 by GEORGE Dahl of New Haven CT
CAYFORD James Merritt of Steubenville OH & CROSBY Jeannett of Boston MA int 4 Sep 1936 by ROSE Wm Wallace of Lynn MA
CEDARSTROM Robert C of Quincy MA & WOODMAN Pauline G of Sanbornton NH int 21 Apr 1944 by J G Berry Armstrong of Newton Ctr MA
CENTER Alden C of So Lynboro NH & FISHER Barbara of Walpole NH int 12 May 1954 by WESTNEAT Arthur S of Bayonne NJ
CHABOT Louis G of Manchester NH & ROY Irene A of Manchester NH int 15 Sep 1948 by G Chouinard of Lowell MA
CHACE William Niels of Tiverton RI & JAMESON Isabel Butler of Antrim NH int 22 Sep 1934 by FRANK L Janeway of Buffalo NY
CHADBOURNE Robert Dana of Enfield NH & QUIMBY Alice Mae of New Castle ME int 22 Jul 1958 by WILLIAMS Ralph C of Toronby CAN
CHALMERS Arthur A of Amsterdam NY & FENTON Marion E of Portsmouth NH int 24 Aug 1932 by EDWARD T Carroll of Amsterdam NY
CHALOFF Juluis Louis of Newton MA & LORING Marjorie of Swampscott MA int 13 Aug 1946 by WEARAY Gereald F of Port Washington NY
CHALOUX Paul of Beecher Falls VT & SIDELEAU Irene of Beecher Falls VT int 31 Oct 1960 by SIDELEAU Art of Sherbrook CAN

CHAMBERLAND Alfred G of Nashua NH & CARON Cecile of Nashua NH int 11 Feb 1955 by J Alfred Chamberland of Quebec CAN

CHAMBERLEN Howard A of Pembroke NH & PAGE Clara Perkins of Hooksett NH int 19 Apr 1951 by STAHL Roland of Storrs CT

CHAMPAGNE Antonio of Manchester NH & GAUDREAULT Lauretta of Manchester NH int 4 Jun 1937 by EMERY Champagne of Manchester NH

CHAMPAGNE Howard J of Nashua NH & COTE Lucille Yvelle of Nashua NH int 12 Nov 1960 by NOURY Eugene of Lowell MA

CHAMPLIN William H Jr of Rochester NH & SPAULDING Virginia P of Rochester NH int 6 May 1941 by GEORGE E Gilchrist of Quincy MA

CHANDLER Douglas Raymond of Bartlett NH & INGRAHAM Ruth Eileen of Hampstead NH int 4 Sep 1942 by STRINGFELLOW Leroy W of Haverhill MA

CHANDLER Hugs S of Raymond NH & WOS Yoline Siva of Raymond NH int 9 Sep 1953 by OSBORNE Clifford of Waterville ME

CHANDLER Norman of Hill NH & WILKIN Jean Crawford of Melvin Village NH int 26 Jul 1949 by ROBERT H Gamble of Bryn Marve PA

CHANEY Richard of Newton NH & KIMBALL Constance of Newton NH int 6 May 1950 by LORENZ James F of Columbus OH

CHAPIN Merrick of Nashua NH & PRESTON Dorothea of Contoocook NH int 25 May 1931 by SHERRILL Henry Knox of Nashua

CHAPMAN Cleo Elbert of Charlestown NH & STREETER Helen Maria of Charlestown NH int 2 Nov 1942 by MILLER Fred H of Springfield VT

CHAPMAN Eben Thompson of Farmington ME & WADHAMS Ann Rosette of Torrington CT int 3 Apr 1950 by JOHN Rea Chapman of Leominster MA

CHAREST Maurice of Manchester NH & PAQUET Madeline of Manchester NH int 1 Jul 1960 by LAMBERT Raymond of Hudson MA

CHARRON George E of Manchester NH & OUELLETT Therese M of Nashua NH int 6 Feb 1951 by OULETTE Lucien of Joliette CA

CHARTIER Arthur Alfred of Littleton NH & LaPOINTE Winifred Theresa of Littleton NH int 6 Mar 1954 by RICHARD Ferdinand of Natick MA

CHARTRAIN Paul M of Mancester NH & GOSSELIN Therese F of Manchester NH int 4 Oct 1960 by PENNENTON Paul E of Medford MA

CHASE George Maurice of Henniker NH & FLANDERS Arlene Eleanor of No Weare NH int 31 Dec 1940 by OLIVER M Frazer of Worcester MA

CHASE Harold K of Haverhill NH & HAMMER Hazel M of Salem NH int 25 May 1958 by WEBB Theodore A of Haverhill MA

CHASTNEY Felix Stanley of Lowell MA & UTKA Agnes Ursula of Nashua NH int 25 Nov 1939 by BRUZOS Anthony of Altamount NY

CHENEY Chas H of Grafton NH & ROLLINS Madeline of Manchester NH int 28 Dec 1929 by McKINNEY W L of Bridgewater MA

CHESHOLM James Alan of N Hampton NH & NICHOLS Norma Irene of Concord NH int 9 Jan 1954 by WATSON Albert P of Tyngsboro MA

CHESLEY Myron H Jr of Manchester NH & SCHMIDT Elaine J of Bedford NH int 2 Jul 1951 by PELON J Charles of ?

CHEVARIE Gerard L of Berlin NH & ARGUIN Lucile Lea of Berlin NH int 8 Apr 1946 by LEMIEUX Arthur E of Attleboro MA

CHILD William Spencer of Philadelphia PA & SIDNEY Elizabeth Bayer of Philadelphia PA int 6 May 1936 by JOSE Cullen Ayer of Philadelphia PA

CHOATE Joseph E of Brooklyn NY & DANE Frances C of Brooklyn NY int 1 Sep 1936 by ALLAN K Chalmer of Brooklyn NY

CHOUINARD Ralph (Raoul) of Manchester NH & BELLIVEAU Juliette I of Manchester NH int 19 Apr 1949 by GERARD Chouinard of Lowell MA

CHOWNING Ernest G of Detroit MI & MORRILL Christine of Litchfield NH int 12 May 1950 by HAROLD W Ewing of Nashville TN

CHRETIEN Alfred J of Manchester NH & SYLVAIN Marie Lucienne of Manchester NH int 8 Jun 1929 by BRUNEAN J of Baltimore MD

CHRISHOM William Hussey of Marblehead MA & SMITH Sara Margaret of Hebron NH int 7 Jun 1950 by SCOTT James F of Amesbury MA

CHRISTIAN Milton James of Nashua NH & ROBERTS Charlotte L of Raymond NH int 12 May 1952 by JAMES E Hawkins of Medford MA

CHRISTIANSON J Harold of Worcester MA & LINDQUIST Miriam of Worcester MA int 5 May 1949 by HAROLD A Hopkins of Willow Grove PA

CHRISTIE Welman B of Boston MA & THOMPSON Jean Esther of Boston MA int 17 Jun 1951 by THOMPSON Roy of Sharon MA

CHURCHILL John Dwight of Plainfield NH & HAND Mary Deshon of NY City NY int 4 Jun 1930 by WILSON Robert C of ?

CLARK Allen W Jr of Danvers ME & WENTWORTH Nancy of Reading MA int 15 May 1947 by ALLEN W Clark of ?

CLARK Kenneth Edward of Manchester NH & HUSE Beverly of Manchester NH int 16 Aug 1946 by PALIMEU Elwin of Payson IL

CLARK Oscar of Franconia NH & HILDRETH Doris of Lisbon NH int 15 Aug 1934 by LEEVAN L G of Lisbon NH

CLARK Russell Allen Jr of Pawlet VT & TILTON Sarah Willis of Laconia NH int 16 Jun 1942 by ROUNDY Rodney of Portland ME

CLARK Stuart of Francestown NH & DANIS Priscilla of Reding MA int 19 Sep 1949 by PIERCE Payson of Bruskin NY

CLARKE Russell Gordon of Dennisport MA & WIXON Lorraine of Dennisport MA int 26 Jul 1950 by EUGENE Dismore Dolloff of New Bedford MA

CLAY Cassin M of Paris KY & BERLE Miriam of Boscawen NH int 23 Jul 1935 by A A Berle of New York NY

CLEAVELAND Paul S of Lancaster NH & GARDNER Leora H of Lancaster NH int 22 May 1939 by McCLINTOCK Richard P of Newton MA

CLEMONS Roger Payson of Wakefield MA & WALLACE Katherine G of Wakefield MA int 22 Apr 1941 by SHERMAN Goodwin of Townsend MA

CLEVELAND Gordon V of Fitchburg MA & KAMILA Hilma of Fitchburg MA int 2 Apr 1951 by JOSEPH B Bubar of Fitchburg MA

CLEVELAND Richard of Rindge NH & BUMFORD Marion E of Rindge NH int 18 Sep 1945 by PROUDFOOT Raymond S of Haverhill MA

CLOUGH Harold R of Contoocook NH & SAWYER Raelene R of Contoocook NH int 10 Sep 1926 by FRED M Baker of Anthony RI

CLOUTIER Real of Berlin NH & FILLION Cecile of Berlin NH int 19 May 1947 by MAURICE C Fillion of Natick MA

CLURMAN Rodney Hart of Washington DC & MacVEAGH Adele Merrill of Harrisville NH int 4 Jun 1958 by LICHLITER James M of Akron OH

COAN Howard R of Exeter NH & ROGERS Constance of Exeter NH int 11 Jun 1926 by FREDERICK G Coan of Minneapolis MN

COBLY Wills Everette of St Johnsbury VT & NUTE Mary F of St Johnsbury VT int 7 Jul 1930 by ROBINSON Alson H of Plainfield NJ

COCHRAN George Milton of Detroit MI & PHILLIPS Olive Katherin of Lancaster NH int 12 Jul 1929 by PARSHLEY Anthony of Bristol RI

COCHRAN Olin John of Windham NH & BURRELL Carolyn M of Windham NH int 3 Aug 1943 by SPEAR Stanley G of Beverly MA

COCHRANE Leo W of Bridgewater MA & MARBLE Gladys W of Bridgewater MA int 1 May 1958 by LANE Edwin A of Winchendon MA

CODER Fred Tolen of Whiteplains NY & HOYT Mary Voncille of Laconia NH int 23 Jul 1941 by E Jerome Johnson of W Hartford CT

CODY John of Harisville NH & READ Joyce of Keene NH int 3 Nov 1954 by STONE William E of Walcott CT

COHEOCORESSER Harold L of Litchfield CT & RICE Josephine R of Portsmouth NH int 12 Jun 1941 by HART Oliver J of Boston MA

COHN Harvey of Andover MA & CHENEY Lucia of Lawrence MA int 2 Jul 1941 by JENNIE Clough of Methuen MA

COLARUSSO Robert Allen of Loudon NH & MAXFIELD Janet Harriett of Loudon NH int 9 Nov 1949 by MacNEIL Kate Josephine of No Waterboro ME

COLBOURN Arthur of Holdness NH & CLARKE Mason Sarah of Dorset VT int 30 Jun 1946 by NOYES Morgan P of Montclair NJ

COLBY Solon Baker Jr of Meredith NH & RANDALL Eleanor May of Meredith NH int 7 Aug 1948 by ADAMS Arnold of Roslindale MA

COLCORD Kenneth H of Plaistow NH & RICHARDSON Eleanor M of Plaistow NH int 4 Mar 1946 by McGINNESS Mason F of Lowell MA

COLE Forest B of Lebanon NH & GORDON Miss of Derry NH int 13 May 1947 by EDGAR Folk of Andover MA

COLE Harris R of Haverhill MA & SPOFFORD Ethel Jordan of Haverhill MA int 12 Aug 1937 by HULL Jno D of Haverhill MA

COLE Lawrence S of No Carver MA & GOULD Ruth Jeanette of No Carver MA int 13 Jun 1952 by M Walker of Bridgewater MA

COLE Ralph F of E Providence RI & BOHANAN Ruby A of Contoocook NH int 17 Nov 1938 by CLIFTON R Bohanan of Minerva NY

COLE Stephen C of Lebanon & GORDON Lurlene A of E Derry NH int 24 May 1947 by G Edgar Folk of Andover MA

COLE Warren M of Grafton NH & CHELLIS Irene Louise of Danbury NH int 23 Jun 1960 by SEAWARD Carl A of Sanford ME

COLEMAN Norman E of Goffstown NH & BORDEN Beverly Anne of No Weare NH int 13 Sep 1958 by ROLAND W Junkins of Auburndale MA

COLLINS Edward of New Haven CT & PRICHARD Susan of Nashua NH int 23 Nov 1957 by ROSE Wm Wallace of Lynn MA

COLLINS Oral Edmond of Alton NY & TOWLE Joyce Irene of Rochester NH int 14 Apr 1952 by ROBERTS Carlye B of Brookline MA

CONANT Roger Freeman of Concord MA & BOUTELLE Isabel of Milford NH int 3 Jul 1934 by WILLIS Sidney J of Monson MA

CONDIT Robert Y of Ithaca NY & SARGENT Priscilla of Nashua NH int 26 Jul 1930 by HENRY J Condit of Ithaca NY

CONDRON Carl of Portsmouth NH & SULLIVAN Florence Ada of Exeter NH int 21 Mar 1950 by NICOLL Wm A of Lawrence MA

CONLEY Christopher of Medford MA & FLANAGAN Elizabeth of Medford MA int 29 Aug 1941 by FRANCIS D Flanagan of Buffalo NY

CONNER Allan Burton of Lexington MA & RANTOUL Anne of Greenfield NH int 5 Jun 1956 by DONALD S Ewing of Wayland MA

CONNOR Dwight W of Henniker NH & COOPER Eloise F of Contoocook NH int 12 Nov 1949 by HOBERT W Blanchard of Indian Lake NY

CONNOR John D of Newmarket NH & BASSETT Sandra M of Newmarket NH int 7 Jun 1960 by W D Connor of Montreal CAN

CONRAD Franklin of Pike NH & CASS Kay of Woodsvills NH int 7 Jun 1952 by RUFUS Ansley of Sanford ME

CONRAD Franklyn K of Hanover NH & SILLOWAY Sheila of Hanover NH int 18 Jan 1945 by EDWARD H Hickcox of Chelsea MA

CONROY Robert Gerard of Manchester NH & LAWLOR Elizabeth May of Manchester NH int 23 Sep 1947 by LAWLOR George F of Newton MA

CONVERSE James M of Hanson MA & WATERS Marjorie L of Whitman MA int 6 May 1957 by ROBERT H Heigham of Hanson MA

CONWAY Walter S of Somerville MA & MILNER Marguerite L of Somerville MA int 22 Jun 1933 by WHITCOMB Howard C of Somerville MA

COOK Alvin S of Concord NH & OSBORN Helen of Concord NH int 30 Apr 1956 by OSBORN Donald L of Randolph VT

COOK Clare of Laconia & MERRILL Mildred E of Laconia NH int 29 Aug 1935 by SEAVER James of Methuen MA

COOK Howard of Norwich VT & HUGHES Marian of Etna NH int 20 Aug 1947 by MESSNER Harold K of Norwich VT

COOK James Herbert of Boston MA & PEARSON Jessie E of Boston MA int 20 Jul 1951 by WILLIAMS F Randal of Cambridge MA

COOPER Francis L Jr of Brockton MA & LISTER Rita of New York NY int 15 Jun 1941 by FRANCIS L Cooper of Brockton MA

COOPER Richard Foss of Rochester NH & WENTWORTH Elizabeth H of Somersworth NH int 5 Oct 1940 by TRACY Olin B of Melrose MA

COOPER William of Durham NH & HARRIS Lois of Stratham NH int 15 Jun 1950 by WENDELL L Bailey of Melrose MA

COPELAND Robert A Jr of Boston MA & NUTE Eleanor Cutting of Boston MA int 22 May 1958 by BURNS Raymond E of Stamford CT

CORBIN Richard J of Lowell MA & RIVIERE Patricia of Nashua NH int 18 Jun 1959 by MOUSSETTE Armand of Lowell MA

CORDWELL Clarence A of Berlin NH & COX Mary E of Meredith NH int 20 Aug 1929 by ELMER T Blake of Dorchester MA

CORLBYONS Albert C of NY & LANGLEY Rae V of Dobbs Ferry NY int 23 Jul 1958 by DAVID O Kundall of Dobbs Ferry NY

CORLIN Richard Edward of Merrimac NH & MALITSOS Katherine of Nashua NH int 12 Oct 1955 by KNAPP Wm T of Hartford CT

CORLISS Harold Scott Jr of Keene NH & ADAMS Harriet Emma of Swazey NH int 20 Apr 1954 by MARTIN Kenneth of Spencer IA

CORMIER Leo Joseph of Portsmouth NH & REARDON Dorothy P of Portsmouth NH int 2 Sep 1939 by IRA J Bourassa of Sherebrooke CAN

CORMIER Prosper of Gardner MA & DesBOIS Ruth of Gardner MA int 20 Apr 1954 by PAIGE Donald E of Gardner MA

CORNWELL Paul E of Hillsboro Ct NH & CORNWELL Corinne of Hillsboro Ctr NH int 18 Oct 1948 by SWEET Robert W of Haverhill MA

CORRIVEAU Arthur J of Laconia NH & TARDIF Rose D of Laconia NH int 1 Feb 1939 by TARDIF Hilary M of Montreal CAN

CORSELLI Caral of Everette MA & KENNEDY Margaret of Portsmouth NH int 10 Sep 1940 by SULLIVAN Francis of No Andover MA

COSTANTINO Robert Wm of Rochester NH & COURNING Mary Rubina of Rochester NH int 8 May 1956 by SCRUTON Paul H of Morris NY

COTE A Joseph of Concord NH & DOON Mary of Henniker NH int 5 Jun 1946 by SHEEHAN Alfred C of E Boston MA

COTE Albani Augustin of Manchester NH & SMITH Jeanne of Manchester NH int 17 Nov 1943 by PAUL Cote of Bucksport ME

COTE Arnold of Manchester NH & GAGNON Pauline of Manchester NH int 8 Apr 1957 by GEORGE A Gagnon of Sherbrooke CAN

COTE Ernest of Derry NH & McMAHON Pauline L of Manchester NH int 23 May 1959 by LACROIX Joseph E of Kenogami CAN

COTE Lewis P of Manchester NH & COUREHESUE Irene of Manchester NH int 17 Jan 1936 by GEORGE Cote of CAN

COTE Philippe J Dr of Manchester NH & TESSIER Cecile R of Manchester NH int 20 May 1938 by MARTEL Leroy R of Worcester MA

COUGHLIN Francis Michael of Durham NH & BRAGON Muriel Ann of Amherst NH int 22 Jun 1953 by O'DONNELL John H of Somerville MA

COULIMORE Herbert of Sherman ME & WENTWORTH Bernice of New Durham NH int 27 Nov 1943 by TAYLOR Clyde W of Quincy MA

COURTEMANCHE Lionel of Manchester NH & LeBLANC Elaine of Manchester NH int 17 Oct 1958 by MARQUIS Paul of Lowell MA

COUTU Normand of Manchester NH & GOUDREAU Helen of Manchester NH int 3 Mar 1959 by LUCIEN Cantu of Washington DC

COUTURE Alfred E of Fitchburg MA & LAPLANTE Rita D of Manchester NH int 24 Dec 1959 by FATHER Gabriel of CAN

COVIN Joseph Ducan of Elmira NY & REED Judith of W Alton NH int 19 Mar 1954 by TAYLOR Floyd J of Lexington MA

COWEN Frank Young of Lebanon NH & STICKNEY Elsie of Keene NH int 27 Jul 1930 by MITCHELL H Summer of Burlington VT

COX William C Jr of Cohasset MA & WHITING Martha A of Wilton NH int 4 May 1953 by EDWARD P Daniels of Concord MA

CRAIG Alderman of Bath NY & FISK Dorothy of Whitefield NH int 7 May 1929 by ALBERT W Jefferson of Lynn MA

CRANE Edward J Jr of Holden MA & RITCHIE Patricia of Melrose MA int 1 May 1959 by REDDEN John J of Lowell MA

CRAY Henry of Bellows Falls VT & KELLY Catherine of No Walpole NH int 7 Aug 1941 by McCULIFFE Wm J of No Easton MA

CRAY Paul S of No Walpole NH & KENNEALLY M Patricia of No Walpole NH int 16 Apr 1947 by E F Cray of Barrey VT

CREENWOOD Donald Harvey of Claremont NH & PUTNAM Grace Elizabeth of Claremont NH int 15 Dec 1948 by WILFRID J Bernard of Hallowell ME

CRISTY George F of Rochester NY & MARGRAF Judith of Wilton NH int 16 Jun 1949 by VERNER N Hegg of New York NY

CROFT Joseph of Exeter NH & FOURNIER Theresa of Somersworth NH int 22 Aug 1955 by RUEST Sylvio of Boston MA

CRONIN Francis of Haverhill MA & DUFRESNE Celeste of Haverhill MA int 31 Mar 1952 by DANIEL F Cronin of ?

CRONIN Timothy A of Manchester NH & NOLETTE Yvonne M of Manchester NH int 21 Jun 1938 by SULLIVAN Timothy C of Boston MA

CROOKS James Douglas of Hackensack NJ & HARMON Julie Ann of New York NY int 28 Jun 1950 by HAROLD C Harmon of Cambridge NY

CROSBY Isaiah of Danville NH & TOTTEN Jean Margaret of Plaistow int 22 Jun 1945 by JAMES M Curtice of Haverhill MA

CROSS Carlton G of Sunapee NH & PORTER Caroline A of Langdon NH int 30 May 1951 by MARSH George B of Perkensville VT

CROSS Hershner of New York NY & JOENSSON Daphne Nora of New York NY int 29 Jul 1939 by HATCH Robert of Boston MA

CROTEAU Howard of Marlboro NH & ARSENAULT Jenne of Marlboro NH int 29 May 1950 by L Philip Arsenault of Greensboro AL

CROTEAU Oliva A of Berlin NH & FECTEAU Laurette of Berlin NH int 3 May 1947 by MURPHY Romeo of Berlin NH

CROTEAU Robert of Miami FL & MURPHY Jeannette of Berlin NH int 23 May 1958 by MURPHY Romeo of Manville RI

CROWELL John Newton of Greenland NH & WESTON Mildred of Winthrop MA int 28 Jul 1927 by HARPER Ralph M of Winthrop MA

CROWLEY James Joseph of Springfield MA & DEROCHES Helen Anne of Charlestown NH int 24 Aug 1954 by EDWARD P Humphrey of Binghamton NY

CROZIER Harry Leslie of Quincy MA & COUGLIN Christina B of Lincoln MA int 22 Oct 1946 by BEDROS Baharian of Quincy MA

CUDDY Owen of No Brookfield MA & LEBLANC Theresa of Nahsua NH int 20 Jun 1955 by FRANCIS L Keenan of Lowell MA

CUMMINGS George of Hartford CT & STEELE Norma of Brooklyn NY int 9 Mar 1960 by WADE Kenneth E of Woodstock VT

CUMMINGS Malcolm of Scottsdale PA & CAMPBELL Betty Rae of Gonic NH int 23 May 1954 by MADEAU David of Barrington RI

CUMMINGS Morton Jerome of Manchester NH & LAZARUS Lilian of Brooklyn NY int 2 Jul 1952 by FREEMAN Charles S of Brookline MA

CURRIER George F of Pelham NH & JONES Helen Louise of Lowell MA int 26 Aug 1929 by THOMAS Percy E of Lowell MA

CURTICE C Leslie Jr of Candia NH & SCOTT Jacqueline of Candia NH int 11 Aug 1950 by C Leslie Curtice of Calais ME

CURTIS Charles S of Shrewsbury MA & HOUGHTELING Harriot of Winetka IL int 12 Sep 1928 by THEODORE A Greene of New Britain CT

CURTIS Robert M of Middlebury VT & PARTRIDGE Shirley M of Winchester NH int 20 Dec 1946 by GEORGE Truman Carl of Chicago IL

CURTISS Herwood Walter of Newlond NH & HALL Phyllis Irene of Marlboro NH int 2 Jul 1949 by McINTIRE Barron F of Yarmouth ME

CURY William H of Wyncate PA & FRENCH Priscilla of Bedford NH int 20 Oct 1954 by TESTA Michael P of Richmond VA

CUSHING Samuel T of Monclair NJ & MacKINNON Frances M of Montclair NJ int 10 Jul 1939 by NOYES Morgan P of Montclair NJ

CUSHMAN George of Salisbury NH & CHAFFEE Thelma of Salisbury NH int 4 Sep 1956 by GLENN R Chaffee of E Whitton ME

CUTTER Lawrence Webster of Arlington MA & RUDELL Linda Ellen of Weston MA int 13 Jul 1960 by EMORY Lee Bothas of Boston MA

CUTTS Roy of Newport NH & HINCH Olive of Newport NH int 24 Jun 1948 by PATCHES Peter of Osterville MA

D'ANNOLFO Anthony of Stoneham MA & HANFORD Paula of Stoneham MA int 23 Oct 1953 by JOHN E Colahan of Stoneham MA

DAHL Frank of Winchendon MA & DAHL Lillian of Fitzwilliam NH int 29 Aug 1940 by REEVERS Jos Wilson of Winchendon MA

DAHOOD Kelly P of Salem Depot NH & CARON Pauline E of Salem NH int 14 Mar 1955 by MITCHELL Dahood of Weston MA

DALTON Donald R of Manchester NH & GAGNON Pauline I of Manchester NH int 10 Jun 1959 by MARIANO Gagnon of Florde Pienfa Peru

DAMREN Jerome Henry of Claremont NH & WOODWARD Beverly Jane of Claremont NH int 19 Aug 1947 by ERNEST A Brown Jr of Waltham MA

DAMSELL William Jr of Exeter NH & ROSE Thema C of Dover NH int 13 Nov 1935 by LEACH John D of Grant Jct CO

DANIELS Roy F of E Montpelier VT & BOLTON Betty E of E Haverhill MA int 11 Jan 1960 by SEARS Donald Henry of Manchester NH

DANUE Henry of Arlington MA & CONKLIN Isabel of Arlington MA int 16 Jul 1938 by SIMPSON C O of Arlington MA

DARAT Richard B of Chesham & NEWCOMB Catherine of Chesham int 15 Sep 1947 by NEWCOMB Edward H of Worthington MA

DAROWSKA Adolph of Pittsfield NH & MACEK Helen S of Manchester NH int 29 May 1948 by MACEK Jos of Phoenixville PA

DAVENPORT Harold B of Lantana FL & EDWARDS Mildred Jones of Moultonboro NH int 2 Jul 1959 by VON-DER-SUMP Frederick of Lantan FL

DAVID Nicholas of Concord NH & NOEL Lillie Odelu of Manchester NH int 22 Apr 1946 by SHAKER Aladsella of Boston MA

DAVIDSON John A of Gary Indiana & JONES Gladys of Leominster MA int 14 Sep 1929 by GEORGE E Brown of Leominster MA

DAVIS Allan Van-Voohees of Philadelphia PA & WESTERMAN Jean of Lancaster PA int 29 Jul 1950 by CLARENCE B Gilbert of Haverhill MA

DAVIS Byron C Jr of Greeland NH & DAVIDSON Regina Harris of Greenland NH int 24 Nov 1949 by C Basil Harris of Kittery Point ME

DAVIS Carle A of Norwich CT & WOLLEY Maude E of Norwich CT int 7 Aug 1945 by ALEXANDER H Abbott of Norwich CT

DAVIS Ellsworth M of Northwood NH & RATT Corinda Mae of Northwood int 9 Jul 1943 by BARNES Ralph of Dorchester MA

DAVIS George of Nashua NH & SMITH Elsie A of Chelmsford MA int 17 May 1926 by STUART Oscar W of Rockland ME

DAVIS Henry B of NH & BAMISTER Grace of NH int 14 Oct 1936 by THOMAS E Barker of Arlington MA

DAVIS John Dennett of Norwell MA & ROLLINS Jessie of Dover NH int 13 Sep 1934 by WILSON Alfred J of Norwell MA

DAVIS Kermit Leach of Keene NH & ROBBINS Joan Helen of England int 12 Aug 1946 by ROBBINS Ralph of Northampton MA

DAVIS Leroy of Amherst NH & BOWEN Patricia of Milford NH int 15 May 1940 by CHARLES W Casson of Lynn MA

DAVIS Robert F of Somerville MA & LITTLEFIELD Eleanor of Dover NH int 11 Jun 1930 by SMITH Crawford of Brookline MA

DAVIS Sidney O of Keene NH & BARRETT Sandra I of Gilsum NH int 27 Apr 1960 by C Barnard Champman of Amherst MA

DAVIS Stanley A Ens of Albany NY & PERKINS Clara Jean of Albany NY int 12 Aug 1943 by WELLES Kenneth of Albany NY

DAVIS William James of Exeter NH & LITTLEFIELD Ruth Emira of Rochester NH int 6 Aug 1941 by ROBINSON W R of Donna PA

DAVIS William Joseph of Dorchester NH & HOULE Clare of Laconia NH int 6 May 1958 by PELLETIER Alfred of Natick MA

DAVIS William Selman of Manchester CT & HOLMES Ruth Frances of Manchester CT int 8 Jun 1936 by NEILL James Stuart of Manchester CT

DEAN Charles Emerson of Portsmouth NH & DESROCHERS Laurette of Portsmouth NH int 30 Apr 1958 by OSCAR Giroux of Biddeford ME

DECKER Wilmot of Wakefield MA & BRUCE Glenna of Manchester NH int 10 Jun 1941 by STEWART C Harbinson of Wakefield MA

DECOFF John William of Ashland MA & GRAVES Violet Ellen of Keene NH int 16 Aug 1946 by ROBERT S Hoogland of IL

DEE James of Keene NH & WHITE Catherine of Keene NH int 1 Oct 1937 by NOONAN Matheu J of Tewksbury MA

DEFOSSE Leon of Laconia NH & CARDINAL Marcelle M of Laconia NH int 28 May 1958 by MAURICE Cardinal of Attleboro MA

DELANO John Phillip of Newton MA & FREDERICK Lydia Lee of Newton MA int 13 Jun 1946 by MERRILL Randolph of Newtonville MA

DELUDE Frederick of Manchester NH & BIBEAU Rita Jeanne of Keene NH int 23 May 1931 by DALPE Jos A of Worcester MA

DEMAREST Geo Washington of Daven CT & DOELE Helen Rumsey of Wayne NJ int 14 Jun 1960 by McGUNNESS Mason F of Boston MA

DEMARRIS Edmond J of Hartford CT & ASHE Mary Elizabeth of Nashua NH int 16 Aug 1956 by MELLON Paul of Lynn MA

DEMERS Arthur Louis of Cascade NH & MAROIS Clarire of Berlin NH int 12 Feb 1957 by STANISLAS Bolduc of Montreal CAN

DEMERS Gerard of Manchester NH & MARCOUX Jeannette of Manchester NH int 27 Aug 1942 by A Houle of Lowell MA

DEMERS Linwood E of Manchester NH & LINDH Arlene Mary of Manchester NH int 13 Jun 1955 by ROBERT L Erickson of Iron Mt MI

DEMERS Louis Albert of Laconia NH & OUELLETTE Edna R of Laconia NH int 5 Oct 1937 by ROMEO Demers of Tarrytown NY

DEMING Charles H of Hopedale MA & JEPSON Rutha A of Warner NH int 5 May 1926 by VERNON H Deming of Hopedales MA

DEMING Spencer F of W Roxbury MA & BARRETT Edith Faustina of Boston MA int 20 Jul 1936 by J D Cameron of Trenton NJ

DENEHY Daniel George of Orange MA & RIVERS Hazel Gertrude of Orange MA int 1 Aug 1951 by HIRSCHOFF Ernest H of Orange MA

DENIS Norman Maurice of Claremont NH & THIBAULT Eunice Romona of Claremont NH int 6 Jan 1946 by JOSEPH Denis of CAN

DENISON Floyd T of Twin Mt NH & LYTLE Ellen L of Twin Mt NH int 3 Sep 1932 by LYTLE James A of Monument Beach NC

DENNERLY Duane Lindsey of Concord NH & FITTS Carole Mae of Concord NH int 22 Apr 1955 by FRANK W Ferstead of Rochester NY

DENTINO Angelo Joseph of Berlin NH & ARGUIN Yvette Annette of Berlin NH int 8 Apr 1946 by LEMIEUX Arthur E of Attleboro MA

DERBY John of Plymouth NH & MacDONALD Elizabeth of Hampton NH int 15 Jun 1960 by MAZUR Ronald M of Stow MA

DERSSEAULT Richard of Somersworth NH & SYLVAIN Rita of Rochester NH int 9 Nov 1953 by TANGUAY Ovid of Biddeford ME

DERY Raymond L of Manchester NH & PLODZIK Dorothy G of Manchester NH int 13 Jun 1956 by MACEK Joseph of Phoenixville PA

DESCHNER Roger Neil of Waslaco TX & PLOWMAN Jeanne G of Danbury NH int 11 Aug 1952 by JOHN Deschner of Weslaco TX

DESFOSSES Edward Joseph of Lowell MA & AREL Madeleine T of Hooksett NH int 28 Jul 1941 by IRA J Bourassa of Sherbrooke CAN

DESJARDINS Arthur Aime of Providence RI & TURGEON Marie Amanda of Somersworth NH int 11 Oct 1937 by TURGEON M R of Elwiston ME

DESJARDINS Roland A of Nashua NH & GAMCHE Cecile B of Hudson NH int 29 Mar 1956 by MAURICE A Desjardins of CAN

DESJARDIRIS Albert of Somersworth NH & MORIN Albertins of Somersworth NH int 1 Jul 1931 by EDWARD Lalibert of Sherbrooke Pq

DESMOND Frank of Ctr Harbor NH & HEDRICK Nancy Anne of Newton Ct MA int 23 Jun 1958 by SAM Hedrick of Newton Ctr MA

DESROCHERS Joseph O of Barnford CT & HOLCUME Barbara S of Branford CT int 12 Dec 1956 by WALKERS J Clement of Branford CT

DESROSIER Royal of Keene NH & MAJOR Caroline of Keene NH int 10 Sep 1958 by RIENE J Joyal of Amesbury MA

DEVEREUX Edward R of Boston MA & RITZMAN Barabara B of Durham NH int 16 Aug 1942 by STAFFORD Russell of So Berwick ME

DEVIGNGARET Maurice of Manchester NH & LEVASSEUR Florence A of Manchester NH int 3 Sep 1954 by LEVASSEUR Alphonse of Levi Quebec CAN

DIAS Henry William of Canterbury NH & DUNBAR Ethel May of Canterbury NH int 21 Jul 1947 by TRACY Olin B of Melrose MA

DICK Theodore George of USN Base Portsmouth & KIMBALL Myrtle L of Portsmouth NH int 11 Jun 1952 by MURRAY Alfred of Kittery Point ME

DICKEY Robert of Haverhill MA & EMERY Inamae of Haverhill MA int 21 Jul 1939 by LESTER E Evans of Haverhill MA

DIERKSMIER Charles M of Wilton NH & PEAVEY Mary of Milford NH int 17 Apr 1947 by W Frederick Addison of E Orange NJ

DIETRICK Ira of Pittburg PA & CHETEMAN Elizabeth of Pittsburg PA int 3 Aug 1934 by WHITE Charles L of Hampton Falls NH

DIGGINS Joseph H of Brighton MA & GALLAGHER Margaret E of Nashua NH int 9 Nov 1946 by ALEXANDER G Duncan of Newton MA

DILL Henry W Jr of Schenectady NY & SMITH Grace E of Derry NH int 30 Aug 1939 by CLARENCE W Dunham of Dorchester MA

DILLINGHAM John Albert of Westfield MA & DAVENPORT Carolyn R of Alstead NH int 16 May 1952 by TEALE Arthur E of Granby MA

DILLON C W of Lawrence MA & KENT Margaret of Lawrence MA int 23 Jun 1931 by SWINGAL Clinton W of Lawrence MA

DION Cleophas of Reeds Ferry NH & SIMARD Madeline of Manchester NH int 29 Nov 1944 by SYLVIA Gilbert of Maryknoll? NY

DOCKMAN John of Newmarket NH & BERRY Josephine of Newmarket NH int 8 Sep 1926 by CLINTON W Carvell of No Andover MA

DODGE John Edwin of Storington CT & GAVDENS Carlota of Cornish NH int 22 Jun 1938 by WILLIAMS Wm F of Storington CT

DOHERTY William A of Andover MA & SHAW Muriel C of Kensington NH int 15 Jul 1958 by SYVINSKI Henry B of Villanova PA

DOLLIVER Harvey Richard of Albany NY & TODD Dorothy Winifred of Melrose Highlands MA int 1 May 1952 by MARTIN L Goslin of Evanston IL

DOLLOFF Carl F of Guilford & CROTEAU Ethel Mae of Sunapee int 18 Sep 1939 by EUGENE D Dolloff of W Medford MA

DONAGHEY Manson of Concord NH & HUTCHINS Fay of Concord NH int 3 Jun 1947 by WILSON E B of Concord NH

DONAHUE Daniel of Georgetown MA & SCRIPTURE Betteann of Portsmouth NH int 15 Jun 1959 by RICHARD G Cunningham of Georgetown MA

DONAHUE Richard A of Keene NH & GREGOIRE Elaine A of Keene NH int 4 Sep 1957 by CHARLES A Donahue of Boston MA

DONE Paul Eric of New York & HOWARD Evelyn of New York int 8 Jul 1944 by ALLAN E Chalmers of New York

DONOVAN C John of Washington DC & GIGUERE Lorraine R C of Pelham NH int 11 Feb 1952 by O'CONNOR C T of Mitchell Air Force Base NY

DONOVAN Patrick B of Exeter NH & HOGAN Christin of Newfield NH int 6 Aug 1943 by JEREMIAH J Donovan of Weston MA

DONOVAN William Francis of Dover NH & BOIS Annette Agnes of Dover NH int 16 Jul 1937 by TWOMEY David W of Newton MA

DOOLITTLE Rodney of Winchester NH & BLISS Dorothy of Winchester NH int 16 May 1949 by STANLEY H King of Ipswich MA

DORRANCE Samuel Richard of Norton CT & EVANS Barbara Gosvenor of Belmont MA int 4 Jun 1946 by SAMUEL M Dorrance of Norton CT

DOUGLAS Hammond Burns of Princeton NJ & VON-DER-SUMP Mildred E of Worcester MA int 21 May 1951 by VON-DER-SUMP Frederick of Lantana FL

DOW Paul Francis of Foxboro MA & HAMILTON Miriam Eliz of Hopkinton NH int 27 Dec 1950 by EDWIN K Gedney of Stoneham MA

DOWLING Lawrence Edward of Greenland NH & BENNETT Barbara Lane of Greenland NH int 13 May 1953 by H Osgood Bennett of Cumberland RI

DOWNES Clarence Edgar of Manchester NH & STEWARD Mildred of Manchester NH int 10 Oct 1928 by MILFORD R Foshay of Lynn MA

DOWNING Frank V of Raymond NH & BROWN Jean V of Raymond NH int 19 Aug 1957 by JAMES E Hawkins of Amesbury MA

DOWNS Horace Sewall Jr of Portsmouth NH & FOLSOM Ethel Miriam of Portsmouth NH int 23 Aug 1955 by WALDO M Emery of Alfred ME

DOWNS Walter S Jr of Andover MA & DARLING Esther of Hampstead NH int 7 Sep 1936 by FRANK E Dunn of Peabody MA

DOWNTON Ray E Jr of Manchester NH & ROBERTSON Barbara of Manchester int 29 Jun 1959 by RICHARDS Andw of Lowell MA

DRAKE Philip S of Rye Beach NH & TONIS Joanne of Rye Beach NH int 23 Apr 1949 by FRED I Cairns of Needham MA

DREHER Gerald Wm of Hudson NY & KERRNETT Martha of Madison NH int 1 Oct 1930 by ELMER C Adams of Holden MA

DRESSER Holland Lamb of Andover NH & WOODMAN Shirley of Northfield NH int 26 Aug 1938 by PARK Charles E of Boston MA

DRETLER William of Marblehead MA & KAAN Gloria of Revere MA int 23 Dec 1957 by RUDAVSKY Joseph of Lawrence MA

DREW John of Farmington NH & GRANT Barbara of Manchester NH int 8 May 1941 by MILLER Ernest A of Lawrence MA

DREW Robert of Amesbury MA & MOORE Phyllis of Seabrook NH int 13 Mar 1957 by McANDREWS Walter G of Amesbury MA

DRINKER Philip of Brookline MA & ALDRICH Suzanne of Boston MA int 30 Mar 1925 by HENRY B Washburn of Cambridge MA

DRISCOLL Robert John of Lancaster NH & SAMSON Paulina E of Jefferson NH int 10 Apr 1944 by O'CONNOR Joseph R of No Hadley CAN

DROUIN Norman L of Laconia NH & GRATTON Phyllis M of Derry NH int 29 Jun 1950 by FAY L Gemmell of Lawrence MA

DRYONT Adelard Jr of Manchester NH & GAMACHE Antonette of Manchester NH int 3 Jul 1933 by JOSEPH Dupont of Mont Laurie Province of Quebec CAN

DUBE Claude of Nashua NH & DESJARDINS Therese of Nashua NH int 8 May 1949 by MAURICE S Desjordians of CAN

DUBE Francis Peter of Salem NH & CHAMBERLAIN Janice M of Salem NH int 8 Dec 1955 by TURCOTTE Albert of Methuen MA

DUBOIS Wendell K of Pembroke Ga & NICHOLS Janet of CT Osippee NH int 21 Jun 1958 by C H Dubois Jr of Charlotte NC

DUCHESNEAU Arthur of Keene NH & SMALL Esther M of Swanzey NH int 16 Aug 1940 by PEARSON Roy M of Amherst MA

DUDLEY Robert M of Tilton NH & CANNON Ernestine of Tilton NH int 11 Aug 1947 by HOOPER Goodwin of Bethel VT

DUDLEY Stepen C of Newport NH & RHODES Gwendalyn of Chelmsford MA int 10 Aug 1949 by CLARENCE H Clark of Westbrook ME

DUFAULT Ernest John of Somerville MA & POTTER Eunice Eleanor of Conway NH int 19 Jul 1950 by HOWLARD Chidley of Winchester MA

DUFRESNE Donald R of Berlin NH & HUDON Anita Beatrice of Berlin NH int 23 Mar 1960 by LEMIEUX Arthur of Attleboro MA

DUHAMEL Roger G of Nashua NH & DUCLOS Denise O of Nashua NH int 24 Aug 1959 by MAURICE Gelinas of Washington DC

DUMBEY Louis Henry of St Louis MO & WEBB Martha of Lisbon NH int 14 Jul 1937 by MARSHALL Benjamin of Lexington MA

DUMONT Paul of Salmon Falls ME & LeHOULLIER Pauline of Somersworth NH int 20 Dec 1956 by LeHOULLIER Alban of Natick MA

DUMONT Roland E of Berlin NH & BERTAND Florine of Berlin NH int 26 Jun 1941 by LUICIEN Dumont of Fall River MA

DUNBAR Bernard Lewis of Springfield VT & MARTIN Margaret Ann of Sunapee NH int 7 Jun 1956 by ORRIN Ireson of Springfield VT

DUNBAR Perley Edison of Everett MA & FEWKES Nettie Seba of Ipswich MA int 16 Sep 1947 by ELIZABETH C Brown of Chelmsford MA

DUNCAN William of Boston MA & JUDKINS Margaret N of Boston MA int 29 Aug 1933 by CHARLES O Judkins of Glen Falls NY

DUNCANSON Richard W of Clinton MA & SNOW Joann Marjorie of Nashua NH int 3 Jun 1957 by CLYDE H Cox Jr of Lynn MA

DUNCKLEE Richard of Meriden NH & DRAKE Marion of W Lebanon NH int 5 Aug 1935 by WILLIAM A Estabrook of Thetford VT

DUNHAM Carroll Keith of Swanzey Ctr NH & WRIGHT Janet Whyatt of E Swanzey NH int 25 Jul 1949 by PEARSON Roy M of Lexington MA

DUNLOP J A of Brookline MA & MACHIAN Marie C of Brookline MA int 16 Jul 1938 by EUGENE D Dolloff of W Medford MA

DUNN Gerald Marvin of Durham NH & LOVEJOY Cynthia Anne of Concord NH int 1 Sep 1955 by G Theordore Forsberg of E Longmeadow MA

DUNNING John Westbrook of Nashua NH & WHITTEMORE Elizabeth of Nashua NH int 29 Mar 1949 by MORTON D Dunning of Granby CT

DUNPHY Barry of Cape Cod MA & SEVERANCE Glenna of Raymond NH int 4 Jun 1958 by SWANSON Edward I of Clinton MA

DUNTLEY Earl R Jr of Rochester NH & ELLISON Wilma Mae of Dover NH int 7 Jun 1946 by MITCHELL Lennis of Springfield MA

DUPERE Benoit of Londonderry NH & VEILLEUX Rollande of Manchester NH int 12 Jul 1952 by VEILLEUX Arthur of Sherbrooke CAN

DUPERIE Roger Joseph of Londonderry NH & VEILLEUX Monique of Manchester NH int 26 May 1953 by VEILLEUX Arthur of Sherbrooke CAN

DUPLESSIS Wilfrid of Manchester NH & NADEAU Yvonne D of Manchester NH int 10 Sep 1931 by PEPIN Napoleon of Sherbrooke Province of Quebec CAN

DUPONT Armand of Manchester NH & CHAUVIN Anita of Manchester NH int 1 Jul 1932 by JOSEPH Dupont of Manchester NH

DUPONT Rosaire Armand of Berlin NH & ARSENAULT Therese P of Berlin NH int 23 Oct 1959 by ARTHUR E Lemieux of Attleboro MA

DURANT David Sedgwick of Lee MA & RAYMOND Clare of Woodstock NH int 23 Aug 1935 by DANIEL J Golden of Cambrige MA

DURELL Donald Gregg of Portsmouth NH & O'LEARY Jean Annette of Eliot ME int 8 Jun 1954 by S Blake Ellis of Eliot ME

DURETTE George of Manchester NH & SWEENEY Claire Helen of Manchester NH int 16 Sep 1957 by MARQUIS Paul of Lowell MA

DURETTE Jean Charles of Manchester NH & FAUCHER Jeannette of Manchester NH int 30 Sep 1946 by ARMAND Desautels of Worcester MA

DURETTE Lucien of Manchester NH & PROVENCHER Francoise of Manchester NH int 1 Apr 1948 by SAINT Pierre Gustave of Rimouski CA

DURGIN Clayton F of Rochester NH & HANSON Bethanya of Rochester NH int 29 Aug 1950 by TEWKSBURY Viola G of Malden MA

DURNAN Vincent W of Boston MA & EMERY Jane of Groveton NH int 17 Jun 1959 by AUGUSTINE F Hickey of Cambridge MA

DUROCHEMENT Fred of Portsmouth NH & MAYRAND Therese of Dover NH int 25 Sep 1940 by MAYRAND Paul of Lowell MA

DUSTIN Harold Edwin of Hampstead NH & BUNKER Jessie Mildred of Kingston NH int 21 Jul 1937 by DUNN Frank E of Peabody MA

DUSTON Norman of Danville NH & DELOREY Alyce of Chester NH int 6 Mar 1952 by MATHEWS Hubate of Reading MA

DUVAL Lucien J of Manchester NH & DUHAINE Mary Rose of Manchester NH int 21 Jun 1946 by EMILE Boucher of Montreal CAN

DUVAL Normand of Manchester NH & BISSONNETTE Irene of Manchester NH int 26 Jun 1947 by EDWARD J Duval of CAN

DUVAL Robert G of Manchester NH & POIEIER Olive D of Manchester NH int 31 May 1946 by UBALD Clement of Montreal CAN

DYKE John T of Minneapolis MN & MOSES Arlene of Tilton NH int 12 Jun 1946 by SNOW Arthur J of Stoneham MA

EAMES Harold M of Somerville MA & FLEMING Eleanor M of Somervile MA int 23 Jul 1926 by GEORGE E Heath of Somerville MA

EARL William Allen of Holyoke MA & PEARCE Colenda M of Holyoke MA int 14 Aug 1943 by STOUY Earl E of Norwich CT

EASON Robert of Farmington NH & PERRY Shirley of W Milton NH int 4 Nov 1955 by SHELLEY Charles C of W Townsend MA

EASTMAN Anthony of Pomfret CT & REID Ellen of New London NH int 31 Aug 1938 by CHARLES H Cadigan of Amherst MA

EASTMAN David Gale of Somersworth NH & DREW Esther Stevens of Union NH int 6 May 1954 by ARTHUR O Dewey of Provincetown MA

EASTMAN Lee Earl of Lancaster NH & WHITCOMB Costance of Lancaster NH int 10 Jun 1953 by FOREST L Eastman of Ashton RI

EATHANT Walter of Durham NH & OTIS Mary Grace of Durham NH int 7 Apr 1947 by CLINTON W Carvall of No Andover MA

EATON Louis F Jr of Brockton MA & FERGUSON Elizabeth C of Pittsfield NH int 7 Apr 1942 by HARRIS G Hale of Marblehead MA

EBEN Bartlett of Goffstown NH & MERRITT Ruth of Manchester NH int 1 Jul 1935 by WALLACE W Anderson of Springfield MA

ECCLES David S of Concord NH & KIRKPATRICK Dorothy of Nashua NH int 29 Aug 1935 by KILMINSTER Percy A of Norwich CT

ECKOFF Ed C Corp of Orange CA & PHILIPPY Irene of Manchester NH int 15 Jun 1944 by WENZEL Enwald C of So Norwalk CT

EDDY William B of Baltimore MD & MITCHELL Dorua of Newmarket NH int 20 Aug 1938 by JOHN W Guyer of Granville NY

EDES Francis Presby of Woodsville NH & LUNDSTROM Edna Grace of Woodsville NH int 1 Dec 1951 by ELMER N Granstram of Newbury VT

EDGCOMB Loring Richard of Weirs NH & LAWRENCE Virginia Fay of Tilton NH int 8 Dec 1952 by EDWARD G Ernst of Bangor ME

EDMOUTON Douglas W of New York NY & GRIFFITH Betty Grace of Brooklin NY int 11 Jul 1935 by LATHROP John H of Windsor VT

EDWARDS Robert L of Rye NY & ALEXANDER Sarah C of Randolph NH int 27 Aug 1947 by DEANE Edwards of Rye NY

EKHOLM Lloyd Ernest of Concord NH & SLEEPER Marian Louise of Loudon NH int 9 Jan 1957 by A Theodore Ekholm of Jamaica Plain MA

ELDREDGE Harold N of Pittsfield NY & McCRILLIS Sally E of Burkehaven NH int 7 Aug 1950 by LANDER Wm P S of New London NH

ELDRIDGE Donald M of Keene NH & SYKES Claudia J of Keene NH int 23 Jun 1930 by ERNEST W Eldridge of Ashby MA

ELEDER Samuel A of Providence RI & MAYNARD Sylvia of Concord NH int 14 Dec 1954 by SWETTERLEIN Lawson of Providence RI

ELEIDER Thomas J Jr of Poughkeepsie NY & POOR Marie L of New London NH int 27 Jul 1939 by REID John of Peabody MA

ELLIOTT Ernest L of Claremont NH & POTTER Alice J of Middletown CT int 29 May 1941 by RALPH Christie of Middletown CT

ELLIS Rodney Seaver of Keene NH & KNOX Harriet Emma of Concord NH int 23 Mar 1942 by FREDERICK R Knox of Chester VT

ELLISTON Herbert of Washington DC & PARKER Joanne of Washington DC int 8 Aug 1941 by POMEROY Vivian T of Milton MA

EMERSON Wesley Ormsby of Lyndonville VT & ASHLEY Rosannund of Keene NH int 14 Sep 1927 by CLINTON W Carvell of No Andover MA

EMERY Joseph Henry of W Peterboro NH & JOHNSON Margaret Eliz of W Peterboro NH int 1 Oct 1929 by TOBIN John F of Altamont NY

ENDEAN Milton Herbert of Detroit Michigan & GRANT Grace Ina of Laconia NH int 10 Dec 1956 by ROGER D Blunn of ?

ENEGUESS Daniel F of Arlington MA & CAVANAUGH Ann of Peterboro NH int 10 Jul 1950 by LEO David J of Boston MA

ENGRAEL Charles of Cambridge MA & GORDON Esther of Dublin NH int 21 Jul 1933 by PENNINGTON Leslie T of Ithaca NY

EOULOMBE Charles of Rochester NH & MULLEN Betty M of Rochester NH int 19 Jun 1946 by RILEY George D of Haverhill MA

ERWIN Wayne Albert of Bradford VT & CHATELIER Ann of Lyme NH int 1 Apr 1952 by VANETTEN Erwin J of Boston MA

ESTER Neil Albah of Bath NH & BEATON Jacquelyn Ruth of Haverhill NH int 1 May 1952 by MORTON W Hale of New Haven VT

ESTER Robert Francis of Hodge LA & PRAY Estelle Thomas of Portsmouth NH int 1 Jul 1936 by PRESSEY Ernest A of Portland ME

EUSTIS James of Chester NH & LEIGHTON Gertrude of Chester NH int 19 Jun 1936 by THOMAS J Cate of Malden MA

EVANS David of Elks NV & RUSSELL Dorothy Ann of Putney VT int 10 Jun 1952 by MERRILL Randolph of Newtonville MA

EVANS Roger of W Cannan NH & MERCHETTI Contstance of Enfield NH int 5 Jun 1959 by SCAVO John E of Wilder VT

EVANS Spencer of W Brooksville ME & HEALEY Joan Weedmann of Peterborough NH int 5 Jul 1957 by RICHARDSON Charles O of Weston MA

EVANS William of Bradford MA & FAIRBANKS Pauline of Haverhill MA int 30 Jul 1935 by CHARLES O Brown of Haverhill MA

EVARTS Forrest of Manchester NH & GAGE Mildred of Manchester NH int 5 Feb 1943 by SMALLEY Wellan F of Brockton MA

EVERETTE Henry Dr of Boston MA & WHITE Joan of Boston MA int 7 Jul 1958 by TRIPP Arthur H of Belmont MA

FABEL Donald Criston of Clevland OH & GRIM Sally Jane of New Haven CT int 4 Aug 1941 by SCOTT Philip G of New Haven CT

FAIRNENY Donald of Reading MA & SCHER Jean S of Lynn MA int 22 Aug 1949 by SAKER Abdallal of Rosingdale MA

FAIRWEATHER George Burce of Rahway NJ & DIEHL Emily Claire of Pembroke NH int 18 Aug 1954 by CHESTER M Davis of Rahway NJ

FAIRWEATHER Richard D of Dover NH & PALMER Eleanor Madeline of Dover NH int 13 Aug 1951 by LESTER C Holmes of Alfred ME

FALLGREN Robert Eugene of Nashua NH & BEAUCLAIR Mary Louise of Nashua NH int 15 Oct 1947 by ANDREW P Farina of Providence RI

FARHADIAN Jolin of Lawrence MA & AZARIAN Lucy Mary of Stoneham MA int 21 Jul 1955 by SNOW Arthur J of Ft Lauderdale FL

FARNSWORTH Elgin G of Washington & PAGE Addie R of Washington int 5 Oct 1925 by ROBINSON Asa T of Melrose MA

FARNUM Donald of Pittsfield NH & TIBBETTS Robert A of Loudon NH int 11 Jul 1957 by TIBBETTS Benjamin D of Waterville ME

FARR Maurice E of Webster MA & ERICKSON Verna Mae of Farmington NH int 31 May 1951 by LAURENCE M Farr of Fort Wayne IN

FARR William Sharon of Washington DC & JOHNSTON Janet S of Washington DC int 13 Jul 1936 by NELSON Kellogg of Briston RI

FARRAR Oliver Lawrence of Chester VT & BLISH Rosalind Audrey of Claremont NH int 22 May 1954 by HARRY A Farrar of Chester VT

FASTH Sanforth of Portsmouth NH & WILSON Virginia of Kensington NH int 24 Nov 1958 by ROBERT L Johnston of Saxonville MA

FAUBHT Paul L of Haverhill MA & CAMPBELL Charlotte of Plaistow NH int 18 Nov 1947 by SWEET Robert W of Haverhill MA

FAUCHER Louis of Londonderry NH & PRINCE Jacqueline of Nashua NH int 14 Feb 1958 by J C Faucher of CAN

FAULKNER Charles Stearns of Brookline MA & FLINK Charlotte Hartwel of Pleasantville NY int 30 Apr 1958 by EDWARD I Cambell of Pleasantville NY

FAVOLISE Charles Joseph of New London CT & TANGUAY Edie Ann of Somersworth NH int 1 Jun 1957 by TANGUAY Ovid of Biddeford ME

FAWCETT Randolph of Canton OH & ERKIS Dorothy E of Derring NH int 2 Sep 1930 by POLING Daniel A of New York NY

FAXON Donald of Haverhill MA & MILLER Valerie of Newburport MA int 3 Jun 1957 by MAYBURY Byron of Haverhill MA

FAXON Robert of Haverhill MA & JUDSON Pat of Plaistow NH int 3 Jun 1957 by MAYBURY Byron of Haverhill MA

FEELEY Walter Patrick of Wellesley MA & SMITH Edna Murial of Nashua NH int 14 May 1936 by STUART Oscar W of Kennebunk ME

FENTON Dennis Edward of Andover NH & FROST Margaret S of E Andover NH int 27 Aug 1956 by TUCKER Francis S of Brooklyn NY

FERGUSON William of Fall Rive MA & ROTCH Helen Gilman of Milford NH int 1 Oct 1941 by TWITCHELL Joseph W of Fairfield CT

FERNALD Burleigh of Newton MA & WEST Miriam of Waterloo NH int 23 Jul 1940 by B M Johns of Wilmington DE

FERREIRA Arthur F of Barre VT & MacARTHUR Faith Lorraine of Nashua NH int 11 Mar 1952 by ERNEST Baxendale of Springfield MA

FICKETT Marvis M of Flushing NY & DOUILLETTE Marcia A of Suncook NH int 7 Jul 1942 by ADAMS Z Arnold of Rumford ME

FIELD John Howe III of White Plains NY & MEACHAM Bette Butterworth of White Plains NY int 3 Aug 1955 by WILLIAM V Berg of Piermont NY

FIELDS Tommie E of Manchester NH & WOLFERTZ Caroline E of Nashville AR int 26 Jan 1960 by MEYERS Lester G of So Dartmouth MA

FIESER Louis Frederick of Cambridge MA & PETERS Mary Augusta of Cambridge MA int 13 Jun 1932 by FREDERIC W Felts of Boston MA

FIFE Clarence Leroy of Canterbury NH & FIFIELD Margaret E of Canterbrury NH int 2 Aug 1955 by TRACY Olin B of Buffalo NY

FIFFIELD Stuart D of Canterbury NH & FIFE Pauline Ann of Canterbury NH int 31 Jul 1956 by TRACY Olin B of Snyder NY

FIFIELD Stuart G of ? & AUSTIN Naomi of ? int 11 Oct 1932 by MORGAN Walter A of ?

FINGAIR Bernard of Hudson NY & SCHNEIDER Dorothy of Hudson NY int 27 May 1952 by VAN Dyke Albert H of Hudson NY

FINGER Arthur Ernest Jr of Burnt Hills NY & PARSONS Priscila Locke of Waterville ME int 5 May 1953 by LESTER L Boobar of Waterville ME

FISH Edwin of Charlestown NH & KONISHO Mary Jeanne of Charlestown NH int 18 Jul 1952 by WYSOLMERSKI B of Bellows Falls VT

FISH Robert L of Malden MA & GRAF Sarah D of Manchester NH int 21 Apr 1959 by MUCICH Roy L of Malden MA

FISHER Galen of Fitzwilliam NH & PIERCE Jennie of Fitzwilliam int 2 Jul 1937 by CLIFTON H Brewer of New Haven CT

FISHER Guy of Macon Ga & McSWAIN Marion of Claremont NH int 30 Jul 1950 by WHIPPLE L Bryon of Northampton MA

FISHER Henry J of Somerville MA & BROWN Lillian H of Somerville MA int 3 Aug 1933 by LANG Stephen C of Somerville MA

FISHER James C of Spofford NH & LAMKEY Monique of New York NY int 21 May 1946 by J Harding Fisher of New York NY

FISHER Ralph of Milford NH & FRENCH Marion E of Merrimack NH int 1 Jul 1930 by WESTNEAT Arthur S of Jersey City NJ

FISHER Richard Kaye of Lyme NH & SCHURMAN Margaret Ann of Conway NH int 5 Feb 1959 by LEWIS A Chase of Wells ME

FISKE Donald W of Dedham MA & WOLF Barbara Page of Cambridge MA int 16 Aug 1938 by WALTER F Greenman of West Newton MA

FITCH Nathan Albert of Somerville MA & WILSON Annie Toon of Somerville MA int 29 Jul 1947 by LANG Stepen C of Somerville MA

FITZGERALD George F of Somerville MA & HURLEY Bernice M of Manchester NH int 7 Jul 1928 by FREDERICK E Fitzgerald of Maryknoll NY

FITZGERALD John of New York NY & MERRILL Elizabeth of Columbus OH int 5 Jul 1950 by MERRILL Boynton of Columbus OH

FLAHERTY Robert P of Lakeport NH & COTTON Phyllis of Lakeport NH int 6 Feb 1953 by CUSHMAN A Bryant of Waterbury VT

FLANAGAN Arthur D of Concord NH & GRANT Elizabeth Olive of Concord NH int 12 Jul 1955 by SMITH Henry B of Andover MA

FLANAGAN Robert E of Boston MA & RILEY Mildred L of So Chatham MA int 17 May 1942 by HERVEY H Hoyt of East Hiram ME

FLANDERS Donald Earl of Manchester NH & LUSSIER Ruth Martha of Manchester NH int 27 Aug 1947 by G Chouinard of Lowell MA

FLANDERS Leon of New York NY & CAIRNS Edna of New York NY int 29 May 1930 by A Edwin Keigwin of New York Ciy

FLEMING Clinton Avery of Bath ME & THOMPSON Ruth Jessie of Manchester NH int 8 Oct 1937 by JOSEPH Atkinson of Brookline MA

FLEMING David Arthur of New York NY & KELSEY Alice Agnes of New York NY int 29 May 1935 by WATSON Albert of Wilton ME

FLEMING Hartwell of Rochester NH & MORRISON Irene of Manchester NH int 15 Dec 1941 by EDMUND C Hoffman of Boston MA

FLEMING Roderick G of Vassalboro ME & PEASE Margaret of New Portland ME int 3 Aug 1946 by SAMPSON Wallace of Providence RI

FLEMING Thomas Edmond of Worcester MA & FERLAND Jacqueline of Claremont NH int 26 Jun 1953 by WALSH Edmund B of N Hampton MA

FLETCHER Warren Marshall of Melrose MA & BRIDGE Isabel Marion of Melrose MA int 12 Aug 1938 by TRACY Olin B of Melrose MA

FLINT Norman K of Newport NH & FAIRBANKS Margaret of Newport NH int 9 Sep 1946 by WIETING Gilbert W of Lawrence MA

FLINT Victor of Boscawen NH & DAVIS Ruth of Boscawen NH int 3 Jun 1941 by A A Berle of New York NY

FLOWER Jewell W of Taunton MA & SWAFFIELD Miriam N of Taunton MA int 10 Jun 1942 by SWAFFIELD W Douglas of Taunton MA

FLYNN James T of San Francisco CA & TARBAR Helen M of Haverhill MA int 24 Jul 1946 by NELSON Harley R of Willimatic CT

FOLEY Robert Francis of Framingham MA & SULLIVAN Phyllis Barbaa of Manchester NH int 30 Mar 1957 by JOHN E Foley of Natick MA

FOLGER Nelson Joseph of Medford MA & FAIRCHILD Helen Svenson of Medford MA int 29 Aug 1960 by EGBERT W A Jenkinson of Methuen MA

FOLKSTRA Gerard J Jr of Bridgeport CT & BARNEY Ruth M of Canaan NH int 13 Jul 1955 by G J Folkstra Sr of Bridgeport CT

FOLSOM Harley C of St Johnsbury VT & CLOUGH Helen D of Lisbon NH int 22 Jul 1926 by WALTEN J M of Woonsocket RI

FOLSOM Henry Titus of Orange NJ & PEEK Phyllis C of Montclair NJ int 18 Jul 1949 by SCOTT Philip G of Washington DC

FOLSOM John B of Epping NH & CROSBY Leslia Ann of Chester NH int 28 May 1946 by EDWARD D Johnson of Methuen MA

FORBUSH Ramsey of Appleton WI & SWANSON Dorothy of Chicago IL int 8 Jun 1948 by DASCOMB E Forbush of Appleton WI

FORD Donald of Providence RI & TUTTLE Joan of Peterboro NH int 18 Sep 1948 by H A Coolidge of Killingly CT

FORD Ralph Henry of Nashua NH & HALL Barbara Alice of Nashua NH int 31 Jan 1957 by MYLES D Blanchard of Cartlage NY

FORD Rand C of Danbury & RUSSELL Grace L of Danbury int 12 Sep 1925 by TRACY Olin B of Norway ME

FORD Richard L of Concord NH & FOY Patricia Louise of Concord NH int 1 Sep 1951 by CHRISTIS Foy of Quebec CAN

FORRISTALL William H of Sandwich NH & PEASLEE Helen of No Sandwich int 12 Jul 1945 by JOHN H Evans of Pittsfield MA

FORTIER James Marden of Ctr Conway NH & LYMAN Charlott of Madison NH int 16 Mar 1953 by LEA Fergus of Brigton ME

FORTIER Kenneth Stewart of Concord NH & FARETRA Eleanor M of Concord NH int 15 Jan 1947 by MICHAEL A Jenovese of Worcester MA

FORTIER Leopold of Manchester NH & GAUTHIER Irene of Manchester NH int 2 Sep 1954 by ROBERT Fortier of Lowell MA

FOSS Eugene Nobel 2nd of Washington DC & BROWN Mary Winifred of Washington DC int 30 Aug 1938 by PHILIP L B of Yarmouth MA

FOSTER Eugene L of Barrington NH & HOWARD Mavin of Stafford NH int 28 Jul 1944 by JOHN C Hatch of Lebanon Springs NY

FOSTER Lloyd Arthur of Stamford CT & WOOD Virginia Grace of Glastonbury CT int 28 May 1959 by WOODS Howard M Jr of Glastonbury CT

FOSTER Russell Danforth of Manchester NH & CHASE Muriel Eastman of Rochester NH int 15 Jun 1942 by STRINGFELLOW Leroy W of Haverhill MA

FOSTER William Hoar of Keene NH & BATCHELDER Alice of Keene NH int 20 Jun 1951 by J Donald Johnston of Newport RI

FOSTER William Houghton of Concord NH & HARRIS Carol of Penacook NH int 2 Jun 1936 by DANA Mclean Greeley of Boston MA

FOULKE Richard F of Merion Station PA & CRANE Nancy of Wonalancet NH int 26 Oct 1954 by ALLEN W Clark of Danvers MA

FOURNIER Victor of Laconia NH & LAPOINTE Irene Jeanette of Concord NH int 29 Jul 1953 by MARQUIS Paul E of Lowell MA

FOWLER Thomas P of Washington DC & SMITH Gendolyn F of Washington DC int 3 Aug 1949 by SYDNEY Adams of Aubondale MA

FOX Edward Charles of Columbia CT & FERNALD Edna Doris of Rochester NH int 26 Sep 1960 by WAGGONER J Garland of Storrs CT

FOY John Francis of Washington DC & FRANCIS Margaret Louise of Orange NJ int 19 Jul 1930 by MARSHALL Robert Elliot of Boston MA

FRANCIS Charles R of Arlington MA & MILLER Sally of Arlington MA int 24 Jul 1954 by THOMPSON David of Acton MA

FRANCIS Norman Walton of Manchester NH & BENNETT Barbara of Alton NH int 22 May 1953 by WESTON Lawrence of Maspeth NY

FRANTZ Wilbert Patton of Garden City NJ & SHARPLES Anne of New York NY int 5 Dec 1941 by PARK Charles E of Boston MA

FRANZONI Richard of Rutland VT & LOWELL Virginia of Exeter NH int 12 Nov 1952 by ROBBINS Burton G of Amesbury MA

FRASER Oliver of No Weare NH & MORGAN Catherine of No Weare NH int 20 Aug 1929 by VINCENT Clarence of Winter Park FL

FRAZER W Oscar of Sullivan NH & JEWETT Ethel M of Sullivan NH int 16 Aug 1935 by OLIVER M Frazer of Worcester MA

FRAZIER Ronald Arthur of Winchester NH & CLARK Carlene Anita of Alstead NH int 17 Dec 1952 by MARSH George B of Grafton NH

FREDETTE Gerard of Manchester NH & LABLE Pauline of Manchester NH int 19 Jul 1956 by TURCOTTE J A of Sherbrooke CAN

FREDRICK Leroy Norman of Darby PA & DAVIS Bertha Hazel of No Sutton NH int 3 May 1948 by TERRELLE B Crum of Cranston RI

FREDRICKSON Carl of Lisbon NH & ENRIGHT Carol of Lisbon NH int 14 Aug 1957 by RICHARD H Hall of Lyndonville VT

FREEBURN Robert John of Newton Ctr MA & BECKNER Mary Lorraine of Manchester NH int 27 Jul 1947 by CAROL A Bernhardt of Weston MA

FREEMAN Arthur of Orange MA & PLUMMER Mabel of Keene NH int 6 Aug 1958 by LUCIE Freeman of Whitingham VT

FREENY Lawrence Carl of Salisbury MD & HOYT Lucille of Lakeport NH int 9 Jun 1949 by E Jerome Johnson of W Hartford CT

FREEZE Ronald Leigh of Seattle Wash & GILMAN Ann Marguerite of No Hampton NH int 31 Mar 1960 by VARGA Paul V of Belchertown MA

FREIJE Albert P of Ansonia CT & SAMARA Lillian M of Manchester NH int 9 Aug 1954 by DIMITRI Nicholas of Lawrence MA

FRENCH Carroll W of Concord NH & HALL Edith Lillian of Concord NH int 2 Jun 1947 by WILSON Edgar Bruce of Amherst MA

FRIED Julian L of Brooklyn NY & BECHOK Vera F of Claremont NH int 25 Sep 1937 by HIRAM T Carpenter of Springfield MA

FRIEND Dana of Great Neck NY & MaRAY Olga of Bronxville NY int 11 Jul 1955 by PARKER George G of Manhassett Long Isl NY

FROST Donald E of Winchester NH & KIVELA Bertha of Troy NH int 15 Sep 1945 by WILLIAMS Ralph W of E Dedham MA

FROST Joseph W P of Kittery Point ME & KRAMER Rebecca of Gardner PA int 20 Sep 1946 by JOHN Eldridge Frost of Kittery Pt ME

FULLER Frank H of Kittery ME & McALLISTER Jenatte A of Portsmouth N int 19 Jun 1945 by McALLISTER M V of Kennebunk ME

FULLER Lawrence N of Newbury VT & DENNIS Alice Blossom of No Haverhill int 20 Aug 1928 by J B Brock of Newbury VT

FULLER Walter of Roxbury MA & PERKINS Florence of Westwood MA int 29 Aug 1929 by FREDERIC A Balcon of Somers CT

FULTON Robert of Bridgewater MA & LAWRENCE Lucy Mae of Brookline MA int 5 Aug 1935 by ROBERT W Coe of Brookline MA

FURBUSH Spencer S of Rochester NH & CHAPMAN Mary Leslie of Somersworth NH int 12 Aug 1940 by THORP Almus Morse of Columbus OH

FURLEY Charles of Manchester NH & PERRAULT Charlotte E of Manchester NH int 7 Jun 1931 by J Horace Gelineaus of Northbirdge MA

GABRIEL Robert P of Malden MA & BUSH Jean of Malden MA int 11 May 1948 by MINICH Roy L of Malden MA

GAGE Earl F of Laconia NH & TUTINGER Myrta of Switzerland int 22 Apr 1958 by ROBERT F Drinan of Brighton MA

GAGE James M of Greenville NH & WILSON Ina L of Boston MA int 27 May 1942 by J Edwin Lacount of Cambridge MA

GAGNON Armand W of Manchester NH & JUNEAU Irene Theresa of Manchester NH int 11 Nov 1950 by ANTONIO Gagnon of Calixa CAN

GAGNON Georges-Robert of Manchester NH & BEAILIEU Pauline Louise of Manchester NH int 31 Aug 1959 by ALBERT Martineau of Lowell MA

GAGNON Gerard of Nashua NH & MARQUIS Lucille of Nashua NH int 13 Sep 1954 by PAUL J Heon of Washington DC

GAGNON Russell O of Manchester NH & MANNING Dorothy Ann of Manchester NH int 9 Aug 1952 by J Joseph Kierce of Dorchester MA

GALE Donald of Nashua NH & BOUCHER Rita of Nashua NH int 10 May 1956 by ANTHONY Bruzas of Ipswich MA

GALHEN Florido of Berlin NH & DUGUAY Amedee of Berlin NH int 17 Oct 1927 by ARTHUR Gallien of Petit Rocher New Brunswick

GANNON Paul G of Littleton NH & MAVRIC Rose of Milwaukee WI int 9 Jun 1954 by STANLEY Lawrence J of Long Island NY

GARABEDIAN William E of Campton NH & DOLE Dorothy Elizabeth of Campton NH int 6 Aug 1930 by AUSTER T Kempton of Cambridge MA

GARCEAU Raymond of Haverhill NH & ADAMS Ruby Dunkley of Haverhill NH int 17 Jun 1949 by NICKERSON Ivan L of Cambridge MA

GARDNER A John of Melrose MA & WELLMAN Elizabeth B of Melrose MA int 5 Jun 1936 by MARSH Daniel L of Boston MA

GARIEPY Edmond of Fitchburg MA & DESCLOS Eugenie of Nashua NH int 22 Jul 1935 by E N Gariepy of Lowell MA

GARLAND Buhrman of Bartlett NH & BROWN Margaret Bulkley of Cambridge MA int 27 Apr 1946 by HERBERT S Brown of Bridgeport CT

GARNER Albert H of Syracuse NY & CUMMINGS Audrey S of Newport NH int 10 May 1944 by SANBORN Arthayer of Woonsocket RI

GARRAN Charles S Dr of Rochester NH & FOSTER Marjorie Davison of Rochester NH int 15 Jun 1935 by CHARLES E Gurran of Truro MA

GARRAN Frank W of Hanover NH & DELAHANTY Frances S of Hanover NH int 27 Apr 1943 by WILBUR F Berry of Waterville ME

GATES Forrest P of Johnstown NY & CURRIER Ruth Prentiss of Rye Beach NH int 3 Feb 1940 by NORMAN D Fletcher of Montclair NJ

GATES Richard Tuttle of Brattleboro VT & MORGAN Ann Imelda of Bethlehem PA int 20 May 1955 by ROBERT J Harding of Brattleboro VT

GAUDRAULT Joseph Adrien of Concord NH & RAY Marie Lida of Concord NH int 1 May 1930 by PII M Gaudreault of Ottawa CAN

GAUKSTERN Ferdinand of Maplewood NJ & GUERTIN Ruth L of Nashua NH int 7 Dec 1956 by ? of WORCESTER MA

GAULTHIER Gerard E of Berlin NH & ARSENAULT Pauline J of Berlin NH int 8 Aug 1949 by LEMIEUX Arthur of Attleboro MA

GAUTHIER Albert Joseph of Newport NH & COLBY Ruth Wainwright of Newport NH int 10 Jul 1937 by ROMEYN James H of Norwich NY

GAUTHIER Arthur of Somersworth NH & LEHOULLIER Ida of Somersworth NH int 30 May 1944 by LeHOULLIER Alban of Natick MA

GAY Leon Stearns of Cavendish VT & SQUIER Barbara of Newton Ctr MA int 23 Jul 1941 by POOLE W Gordon of Glen Falls NY

GEAR Russell W of Manchester NH & RLANBOIT Evelyn of Manchester NH int 18 Nov 1929 by ROBERT H Johnson of W Haven CT

GEARAN Merton J of Concord NH & WHALEN Elizabeth Helen of Concord NH int 10 Jun 1938 by GEARAN Jeremiah of Lynn MA

GEBO Clarence Henry of Amesbury MA & BRIEN Aline Lauritte of Exeter NH int 17 Apr 1956 by MORIN Hermann of Sherbrook CAN

GEDDES Jas C of Putney CT & FRENCH Charlotte R of Portsmouth NH int 14 Sep 1944 by MARSHALL Ernest of Hartford CT

GEERS George of Northwood NH & YOUNG Elizabeth of Northwood NH int 15 Apr 1950 by McCULLOUGH Wm J of Wells ME

GEISINGER Karl F of Wilkesberry CT & BROWN Beverly of Epping NH int 15 Jun 1960 by PENDER James E of Jamaica Plain MA

GENDRON Raymond A of Manchester NH & JOLICOEUR Yvonne of Manchester NH int 8 Oct 1935 by ALPHONSE Jolicoeur of CAN

GENDRON Roger of Manchester NH & DESILLETS Georgette of Manchester NH int 14 Nov 1946 by LeMAY Lionel of Attleboro MA

GENEST Edgar of Manchester NH & MICHAUD Fleurette of Manchester NH int 2 Sep 1944 by THIBAULT Ethelbert of Montreal CAN

GENEST Roland of Manchester NH & CHAMPAGNE Doris Theresa of Manchester NH int 7 Aug 1947 by LAROCHELLE Joseph of CAN

GEORGE Herbert Weston of Goffstown NH & LOVELL Mary Virginia of Goffstown NH int 10 Jun 1935 by MANSON George E of N Providence RI

GEORGE Jesse L of Newton Jct NH & PEASLEE Mildred V of Haverhill MA int 24 Nov 1945 by RAYMOND J Bates of Haverhill MA

GERTNER Adolph of New York NY & PUENMAN Arlene of Syacruse NY int 15 Aug 1945 by NOBLE Charles C of Syracuse NY

GEWEHR Hamilton of Washington DC & CRUIKSHANK Francis of Washington DC int 4 Aug 1941 by ABERNATHY William S of Washington DC

GIBB Dale A of Barrington NH & SAWYER Florence L of Franklin NH int 24 Jul 1934 by WOOD Nathan of Arlington MA

GIBBS Ray Albert of New Rochelle NY & COLEMAN Carol of New Rochelle NY int 28 Jun 1947 by JOHN Parker Coleman of Washington DC

GIFFORD Alden I of Lowell MA & PRESTON Eleanor of Manchester NH int 16 Nov 1934 by SARGENT John Henry of Lowell MA

GIFFORD Preston of Fairhaven MA & BOUTWELL Barbara of Concord NH int 29 Mar 1950 by MILLER Wilburn B of Cambridge MA

GILBERT Clayton A of Lebanon NH & HATCH June Louise of Hanover NH int 31 Dec 1958 by SCAVO John E of Wilder VT

GILBERT Euclide of Manchester NH & GILMAN Aurore of Manchester NH int 29 May 1936 by SYLVIO Gilbert of Mary Knoll NY

GILBERT Francois of Manchester NH & CHARPENTIER Evelyn of Manchester NH int 14 Mar 1951 by SYLVIO R Bilbert of Brookline MA

GILBERT Horace D of Peterboro NH & DePIERREFEU Katherine of Hancock NH int 27 Aug 1935 by PARK Charles E of Boston MA

GILCREST John Raymond of Londonderry NH & WATTS Shirley Lavina of Londonderry NH int 7 Jan 1946 by STEEVES Francis K of Elkins Park PA

GILES Ronald P of Concord NH & CHASE Nancy of Concord NH int 24 May 1956 by PHILIP Randall Giles of So Weymouth MA

GILL Thomas of Quincy MA & ROSSI Virginia of Milford NH int 5 Apr 1960 by QUICK Thomas of Mary Knoll NY

GILLIATT James Edward of Milton MA & WATSON Sarah Whitman of Milton MA int 18 Jul 1960 by GOEHRING Norman D of Milton MA

GILMAN Lawrence B of Cambridge MA & WOODNONFF Chamian H of Elizabeth NJ int 4 Jul 1934 by ARCHIBALD Black of Montclair NJ

GILMAN Raymond Jr of Manchester NH & LOWMAN Virginia Claire of Manchester NH int 29 Apr 1958 by JOHN W Braggs of Portland ME

GILMORE Donald M of New Rochelle NY & ROY Jeanne Patricia of Concord NH int 10 Aug 1949 by FRANCIS J Baum of Staten Island NY

GILPATRICK Granville of Boston MA & OLSON Evelyn of Boston MA int 24 Jul 1950 by RUTHREDGE Lyman of Newton MA

GLASER Frederick Edward of Norwood MA & UFFLEMAN Elva of Concord NH int 15 Oct 1952 by H Daniel Hawver of Watertown MA

GLEASON John P of Winchester MA & LUCAS Fannie E of Lancaster NH int 11 Jul 1950 by THISTLE Wm T of Turner Falls MA

GLENDENING Alfred King of Walton NH & WHIPPLE Helen of Lebanon NH int 6 Aug 1938 by JOHN W Barker of Athol MA

GLENNOR Donald Francis of Manchester NH & LYONS Helenor Crossley of Manchester NH int 21 Apr 1950 by JUDE T Cahillane of Newark NJ

GLODE John B of Needham MA & GRAY Linda of Belmont MA int 25 Aug 1960 by POWELL Havey H of Rockville MD

GODFREY James of Worcester MA & KASHULINE Joan of Hudson NH int 15 Sep 1959 by EDWARD S Sheehan of Needham MA

GODIN Conrad Dr of Trois Rivers CAN & NORMAND Emilienne of Manchester NH int 11 Oct 1940 by MARTIN Paul M of Salem MA

GOFFEY Eugene Edward of W Medford MA & WEEKS Elizabeth Jean of Hinsdale NH int 23 Apr 1951 by MORAN Edmund A of Plymouth MA

GOLDEN Paul Franklin of Manchester NH & THOMPSON Lillian Juania of Manchestr NH int 17 Nov 1945 by RALPH S Colvin of Old Orchard ME

GOLDITHWAITE Wendell of Everett MA & HUCKINS Mary Ethel of Stafford NH int 16 Jun 1942 by MONROE W Irving of Malden MA

GOLDTHWAITE Robert A of Mt Vernon NY & BECKMAN Ellen Katherine of Bronxville NY int 20 Aug 1956 by PELON J Charles of Mt Vernon NY

GOLDTHWAITE Willard C of Gloucester MA & RICHARDSON Christine W of New Castle NH int 12 Mar 1940 by RODENMAYER Robert N of Gloucester MA

GOODELL Warren F Jr of Urbana IL & VASSAMILLET Suzanne of Tilton NH int 19 Aug 1946 by HOWARD Hare of New Bedford MA

GOODNOW Lyle C of Alstead NH & SPOONER Edith of Swanzey NH int 19 Sep 1958 by HOWES Robert M of Kennebunkport ME

GOODNOW W Lawrence of Keene NH & RANDALL Pauline Julia of Keene NH int 20 Nov 1944 by ROBBINS Ralph E of Northhampton MA

GOODRICH Ruel Dexter of Epping NH & THYNG Lorraine of Exeter NH int 15 Aug 1945 by WEATHERBEE Howard P of Chicago IL

GOODWIN Frederick Wm of Dover NH & LINGARD Gertrude E of Stafford NH int 24 Aug 1960 by MacNEIL Katie J of Cambridge NY

GOODWIN Gerald I of Worcester NH & GOLDMAN Helen N of Milford NH int 29 Mar 1948 by SIDNEY Gothman of Worcester MA

GOODWIN John F of Piermont NH & JEWELL Ruth of Piermont NH int 6 Sep 1940 by JOHN P Fitzimmons of Belmont MA

GOODWIN John Robert of Enfield NH & MOODY Phyllis B of Enfield NH int 17 May 1943 by GORDON S Kenison of Orange MA

GOODWIN Roscoe Hooper of Mohawk NY & PERKINS Ruth of Franklin NH int 17 May 1946 by HOOKER R Goodwin of Mohawk NY

GORDON Bruce of Somersworth & HODGEDON Lizbeth of Somersworth int 14 Dec 1950 by PENDLETON Charles of Bethel ME

GORDON Donald E of New York NY & PARKER Marion Elizabeth of Exeter NH int 4 Jun 1951 by SMITH Charles W of Wellesley MA

GORDON Peter Upton of Jaffrey NH & SAINTPIERRE Janet Barbara of Rindge NH int 2 Jul 1956 by CHARLES A Engvall of Medford MA

GORGES Donald Austin of Keene NH & PRATT Evelyn Ida of Keene NH int 12 Apr 1943 by PEARSON Roy M of Amherst MA

GORHAM Harold Harvey of Manchester NH & KATZ Maxine Lois of Manchester NH int 13 Feb 1948 by SAMUEL S Coen of Cincinnati OH

GORMAN John Cavelle of Wellesley MA & DONAHOE Rita Mary of Concord NH int 22 Jun 1944 by McHUG Patrick of Edgewood RI

GORMLEY Arthur Owen Jr of Bergenfield NJ & SIMONEAU Armelle Celine of Nashua NH int 13 Sep 1954 by PAUL J Heon of Washington DC

GOSS Ronald of Henniker NH & JOHNSON Kathleen Ann of Hillsboro NH int 21 Jul 1958 by POLIN Daniel K of New York NY

GOSS Sherwood Westley of Northfield NH & VIRGIN Jennie Mae E of Northfield NH int 10 Dec 1947 by HOOKER R Goodwin of Bethel VT

GOSSELIN Maurice L of Manchester NH & ROBIDAS Simonne of Manchester NH int 14 Aug 1955 by PANNETON Paul E of Wakefield MA

GOSSELIN Paul of Manchester NH & ALLARAD Vivian of Manchester NH int 16 Jun 1960 by PANNETON Paul E of Medford MA

GOSSELIN Robert of Manchester NH & BELAND Yvonne of Manchester NH int 26 Aug 1937 by J Albert Brunet of Manitoba CAN

GOUDREAULT Lucien of Manchester NH & ANGER Irene of Manchester NH int 16 May 1934 by HENRI Goudreau of Crowley LA

GOULD Donald E of Concord NH & BACHELDER Marilyn of Concord NH int 4 Jun 1953 by DANA Mclean Greeley of Boston MA

GOULD Douglas R of Sanborton NH & DAVIS Mildrew Clarissa of Sanborton NH int 29 Jan 1947 by SCOTT Wm Strafford of Woburn MA

GOULD Gordon Ernest of Bellows Falls VT & INGALLS Shirley Lu of No Haverhill NH int 20 Jun 1958 by GARDNER D Cottle of Bellows Falls VT

GOULD Harold of Bellows Falls VT & ROBINSON Marion of So Danbury NH int 20 Sep 1928 by SKILLIAN Carl D of Peace Dale RI

GOULD Irving of Hampton NH & BLACK Lorraine Evelyn of Brookline MA int 19 Jul 1954 by SIGEL Louis Joel of Malden MA

GOULD Kingdon Jr of New York NY & THORNE Mary B of Ctr Conway NH int 5 Feb 1946 by SMITH E Harold of NY NY

GOULD Severance F of So Berwick ME & MILLER Marilyn of Dover NH int 22 Dec 1955 by ALMON M Bartholomew of Springfield MO

GOVE David Chandler of Durham NH & CATE Virginia G of Laconia NH int 13 Jun 1950 by CATE Thos J of Shelburne Falls MA

GOVE Stanley George of Brentwood NH & GLIDDEN Elaine Irene of Farmington NH int 12 Nov 1959 by CARLYLE B Roberts of Worcester MA

GOVETON Warren I of Peterboro NH & GALLUP Ruth Eloise of Peterboro NH int 9 Dec 1930 by WALLACE Gallup of Valley Stream NY

GOVEY Charles F of E Rochester NH & JOHNSON Joyce Bessie of Rochester NH int 6 Oct 1959 by ERNEST V Carpenter of Hyattsville MD

GRACE W Ansto Jr of Concord NH & FAIRBANK Dorothy M of Concord NH int 2 Aug 1929 by KILMISTER Percy A of Norwick CT

GRAF Paul W of Elmira NY & JORGENSEN Betty of Laconia NH int 21 May 1957 by HOWELL R Graf of Elmira NY

GRAGON Hugh Henry Jr of Bellows Falls VT & KING Joan Lois of Hinsdale NH int 4 Oct 1950 by GARDNER D Cottle of Bellows Falls VT

GRAMES Francis of Madison NH & SARGEANT Joan of Fryeburg ME int 14 Apr 1959 by ATIRA Hirami of Cambridge MA

GRANT Allister Harris of Portland ME & THOMAS Luetta Margaret of Portland ME int 16 Jul 1945 by WOOD Nathan of Arlington MA

GRANT Leslie W of Concord NH & RAYNO Ruth F of Concord NH int 26 Jul 1926 by HENRY H Crane of Malden MA

GRANT Vergil Eugene of Columbia Falls ME & SCHULTZE Marilyn Dawn of Kittery ME int 3 Aug 1954 by THURMAN B Morris of Warsaw IN

GRAVEL Edward of Manchester NH & DESROCHERS Rachael of Manchester NH int 3 Aug 1935 by POULIN Ubald of Sherbrook CAN

GRAVES David of Keene NH & KAUPPI Judith Mae of Swanzey NH int 28 Jun 1960 by EINAR M Beck of Moose Lake MN

GRAVES James of Keene NH & BREED Lillian Ruth of Keene NH int 3 Sep 1940 by LEONARD W Fowler of Maynard MA

GRAVES James Addison of Washington DC & PENN Constance of Exeter NH int 1 Oct 1951 by SMITH Charles W F of Washington DC

GRAY Clayton Forrest of Manchester NH & MATSON Beverly Joan of Manchester NH int 16 Apr 1946 by LEE Delroy Bergsman of Boston MA

GRAY Clyde Allan of Gloucester MA & GRANT Louise Webster of Hamilton MA int 15 Oct 1952 by LUDEKING Charles W of Amesbury MA

GRAY Douglas Reid of Honolulu HI & GARDNER Joan Aganes of Groton CT int 22 Aug 1957 by SISSON Oliver H of New London CT

GRAY Hamilton of Gardiner ME & JONES Prudence of Brookline MA int 3 Aug 1936 by CLIFTON H Brewer of New Haven CT

GREELEY Roger Elting of Boston MA & PURCELL Catherine Louise of Quincy MA int 1 Jun 1949 by DANA Mclean Greeley of Boston MA

GREEN Joseph of Camp Edwards MA & POTTS Edithe of Brooklyn NY int 19 Jun 1941 by PARSONSON Robt A of Philadelphia PA

GREENLEAF John Stevens of Bethel ME & BABB Louise of Somersworth NH int 3 Jun 1952 by PENDLETON Chas of Bethel ME

GREER William E Dr of ? & CLARKE Ellen May of ? int 17 May 1944 by ARCHIE H Crowley of Methuen MA

GREETMAN Brenton W of Lakeville CT & ROLLINS Elizabeth of Dover NH int 27 May 1940 by LYFORD Richard T of Bala Oynwyd PA

GREGOIRE Charles of Somersworth NH & OUELLETTE Yvonne of Somersworth NH int 21 Jul 1930 by LALIBERTE Edward of Somersworth NH

GREGOIRE Donald Kemler of Manchester NH & CAGNE Annette Claire of Manchester NH int 15 Nov 1951 by ARMAND Desautels of Worcester MA

GREGOIRE Leo Jospeh of Manchester NH & GILL Pauline Doris of Manchester NH int 28 Dec 1948 by MAURICE Desfosses of Nicolet Province of Quebec CAN

GREGORY Carlton of Anthony RI & WHITEHOUSE Thelma of Farmington NH int 14 Jul 1939 by MacDONALD J Charles of Rockland ME

GREGORY John J of Worcester MA & SAMSON Virginia M of Jefferson NH int 18 Jul 1945 by SAMPSON Antoine of Capelton Pq

GRENIER Gerard Raymond of Manchester NH & FORTIER Therese of Manchester NH int 4 Nov 1955 by SARTO Grenier of CAN

GRENIER Paul Andie of Manchester NH & FORTIN Muriel Ceale of Manchester NH int 3 Mar 1957 by TRUDEL Roland G of Montreal CAN

GRIESEMER William of Scotia NY & COSTELLO Geraldine of Manchester NH int 6 May 1952 by JOSEPH A Griesemer of Frankfort NY

GRIFFIN Warren R of Rochester NH & PENROD Donna of Reeds Ferry NH int 22 May 1953 by LINCKS Howard J of Roslindale MA

GRIFFITH Robert F of Nashua NH & BROWN Mabel Gertrude of Nashua NH int 28 May 1938 by WILLIAM B Gold of Jersey City NJ

GRIGOIRE Carmel of Manchester NH & VALLIERES Annetta of Manchester NH int 16 Aug 1941 by VALLIERIES Jean Joseph of Lowell MA

GRIMMETT Dorsey B of Corning NY & HILL Pearl E of Manchester NH int 14 Oct 1942 by MILLER Ernest A of Lawrence MA

GRINNELL George H of Boston MA & LITTLEFIELD Harriet of Hampstead NH int 7 Dec 1942 by FRANK E Dunn of Malden MA

GRISWALD Howard of Lebanon NH & CLARK Arleen of West Canaan NH int 15 Apr 1943 by RICHARD A Babcock of Cambridge MA

GROSS Harold Bancroft of Providence RI & ABBOTT Mary Elizabeth of Cambridge MA int 8 May 1934 by CHARLES Leslie Glenn of Cambridge MA

GROSS Thomas Rich of Boston MA & CRAFTS Carol Cushman of Manchester NH int 22 Sep 1949 by EDWIN P Booth of Westwood MA

GROVER Elliott Edgar of Manchester NH & HOFFSEE Ruth Houghton of Manchester NH int 30 Aug 1933 by G Dewitt Dowling of So Boston MA

GRZESIK Stanley Jr of Dracut MA & CHMIELEWSKI Lillian of Salem NH int 19 Jul 1958 by SLEJZER Ferdinund of Lowell MA

GUAY Robert Alfred of Laconia NH & SUCHOCKI Mary Elizabeth of Laconia NH int 6 May 1950 by IGNATIUS S Kozik of Ramsey NJ

GUETERSLOH Lawrence of New York NY & PATILLO Mary Alys of New York NY int 16 Aug 1939 by WILLIAM D Beach of New Haven CT

GUEVIN Maurice of Manchester NH & GARDNER Jessie of Manchester NH int 14 Jun 1935 by PHILIP Gardner of Altamont NY

GUILMETTE Bernard of Somersworth NH & LAROCHELLE Antoinette of Somersworth NH int 27 May 1955 by ROGER L Bisson of CAN

GUIMOND Napoleon of Manchester NH & DUCHARME Marie Lena of Hooksett NH int 22 Aug 1946 by MARQUIS Paul of Lowell MA

GURNEY Richard C of Brockton MA & ALEXANDER Margaret E of Center Harbor NH int 6 Aug 1931 by HERBERT D Gallandet of Branford CT

GUSTAFRON Carl T Jr of Stafford NH & REINHARDT Sally Anna of Stafford NH int 7 Sep 1960 by MacLEAN Norman C of Marlborough MA

GUSTAFSON Frederic B of Kansas MO & TWITCHELL Eleanor of Concord MA int 28 May 1940 by ARTHUR Howe of Hampton VA

GUSTAFSON Fritz of Concord NH & FOWLER Beulah of Concord NH int 20 Sep 1927 by ELMER T Blake of Boston MA

HACK Bruce Henry of Norwich VT & JOINER Nancy of Hanover NH int 1 Jun 1956 by JOHN H Hatt of Blauvelt NY

HADDEN Arthur Lloyd of New York & LORING Katharine P of Chocorua NH int 25 Jul 1941 by CHURCHILL Gibson of Richmond VA

HAEBERLE Henry of Jamacia Plains MA & MUELLER Lillian Marie of Worcester MA int 8 Aug 1933 by PARK Charles E of Boston MA

HAINE Dennis M of Durham NH & JOHNSON Lois A of Whitefield NH int 11 Jun 1948 by TAYLOR William H H of Bath ME

HAIVES John of Marlboro NH & FRANCE Julia Ethel of Havana Cuba int 28 Sep 1938 by FREDERIC W Fitts of Boston MA

HALL Frederick Wm of Hampton Beach NH & BURBANK Barbara Jean of Dover NH int 12 Nov 1952 by VIALL John S of Cambridge MA

HALL Gordon of Enfield NH & ARMSTRONG Jennie of Enfield NH int 10 Aug 1927 by MARSHALL Harold of Melrose MA

HALL James Lawrence of Nashua NH & ALEXANDER Elizabeth of Nashua int 22 Sep 1927 by EDWARD A Durham of ?

HALL John Reginald of Everett MA & CUMMINS Janet Mackhan of Brookline MA int 6 Aug 1929 by TOMKINS Floyd W of Phil PA

HALL Myron C of Rindge NH & SMILEY Helen M of Waltham MA int 16 Jun 1930 by SMILEY Edmund L of Riverton CT

HALL Robert of Wellesley MA & BENNETT Lois of Franklin NH int 15 Aug 1958 by BOWE Leslie R of Bridgon ME

HALL Robert Ames of Castine ME & WHITCOMB Judith M of Arlington MA int 19 Jun 1947 by HENRY E Helms of Watertown MA

HALSTEAD John of Toronto CAN & WHEELER Natalie of Londonderry NH int 24 Jul 1951 by WHEELER John L of Fredonia NY

HAM Robert of Gonic NH & FROST Eleanor of Gonic NH int 12 Jun 1957 by MADURAS David L of W Barrington RI

HAMEL Edward of Gonic NH & LALIBERTE Noella of Somersworth NH int 4 Oct 1930 by EDOUARD Laliberte of Sherbrooke Pq

HAMEL Raymond Wm Jr of Manchester NH & BROUILLET Mildred Rose of Manchester NH int 11 Dec 1953 by POTHIER Clement of Hyacinth Pq

HAMLEN Charles of Jaffrey NH & DRIGGS Doris of New York NY int 28 May 1934 by RAYMOND Cunningham of Hartford CT

HAMMAR Adolph of Concord NH & DEMPSEY Maina of Concord NH int 29 May 1959 by LINDAHL G E of Pond ME

HAMMOND Lyman Roy Jr of Raymond NH & ROLLINS Faye Ann of Deerfield NH int 4 Apr 1955 by HARRY F Booth of Islington MA

HAMMOND Raymond E of Hillsboro NH & BELCHER Alice E of Hillsboro NH int 21 Aug 1936 by STRUM Roy A of Otterlin IN

HAMPSEY Bernard of Bethel PA & LETORNEAU Jean of Jaffrey NH int 23 Jun 1960 by WRIGHT John P of Pittsburg PA

HANCOCK Norman of Milan NH & HAMLIN Olive of Milan NH int 17 Aug 1948 by DELPHAS S Barnet of Ipsich MA

HANDSPICKER Meredith of Malden MA & WEST Diane E of Lebanon NH int 11 Jun 1955 by MILLER James V of Lewiston ME

HANEY John Clifford Jr of Salem MA & HALLIDAY Patricia Ann of New London NH int 21 Jul 1950 by ALAN Knight Chalmers of Boston MA

HANEY Robert of Franklin NH & ANDREWS Joan of Deering NH int 5 Jul 1955 by PETTY A Ray of Vista CA

HANKAID Albert Joseph of Lexington MA & POIRER Madeline Alma of Lincoln NH int 30 Apr 1957 by JAMES W Fitzgerald of No Cambrige MA

HANLEY Edward E Lt of Portsmouth NH & EDWARD Janice M of Portsmouth NH int 5 Sep 1957 by PAUL H Furfey of Washington DC

HANNA George R of W Swansey NH & GARFIELD Shirley of Hindsdale NH int 16 Jan 1946 by MIRTZ Orvil E of Mt Hermon MA

HANNON Robert L of Derry NH & BISHOP Beth L of Derry NH int 7 Jul 1949 by MacCORKLE Douglas of Newtonville MA

HANSON George F of Lawrence MA & BULLOCK Lila of Metheun MA int 1 Jul 1944 by LAURIN Sven A of Amesbury MA

HANSON John A of Newton NH & RICHARD Margery of Newton NH int 16 May 1950 by WILSON William J of Jay NY

HARALD Franklin Anderson of Milford NH & CEDAR Myrtle Selma of Manchester NH int 5 Jul 1939 by J Woldemar Harald of Milford MA

HARDWICK James of Alliance OH & CROOKS Adena Margaret of Allenton PA int 24 Jul 1925 by JOHN M G Darms of Plymouth Wisconsin

HARDWIG Cliftston S of Portsmouth NH & SMITH Barbara V of Portsmouth NH int 29 Jul 1941 by PRESSEY Ernest A of Portland ME

HARLAN Peter of Manchester NH & McGRATH Marjory of Manchester NH int 18 Jun 1946 by GEORGE B Healey of Orange MA

HARPER Harold Casper of Keene NH & HROYLE Dorothy Elizabeh of Keene NH int 19 May 1948 by ROY W Battenhouse of Cambridge MA

HARRIMAN Stanley of Gardiner ME & CRONK Ruby of Farmington NH int 26 Aug 1925 by HERBERT S Dow of York Village ME

HARRINGTON Howard of Boston MA & MARRITT Edna of Boston MA int 18 Jul 1936 by DANIEL Bliss of Greenwich CT

HARRINGTON Millard L of S Lancaster MA & LARSEN Sylvia Astud of S Lancaster MA int 1 Jun 1956 by PUDLEY Arthur J of Poughkeepsie NY

HARRIS Beouell James of Portsmouth NH & WORTMAN Beulah D of Portsmouth NH int 22 Sep 1950 by C Basil Harris of Kittery Pt ME

HARRIS Frederick E of Woodsville NH & PIPER Gayle of Woodsville NH int 9 Aug 1956 by J Henry Hanhisalo of E Weymouth MA

HARRIS Lawrence Jr of Baltimore MD & ROBINSON Sarah Rogers of Broxville NY int 23 Jun 1956 by LAURENCE H Blackburn of Cleveland OH

HARRIS Richard of Boston MA & FERGUSON Sylvia Lee of Brighton MA int 6 Apr 1953 by CHARLES Dana Chrisman of Nanuet NY

HART Joseph M of Concord NH & DROUIN Marie Alice of Concord NH int 8 Nov 1933 by ROBERT L Ahern of Springfield MA

HART Stanley R of Lynn MA & SMITH Joanna M of Conway NH int 27 Jul 1956 by WEST Fergus Lea of W Falmouth ME

HARTFORD Hollis Maynard of Boston MA & MacPHERSON Helena of Boston MA int 2 Jun 1934 by HERBERT Handel of Somerville MA

HARTOFELIS Andrew of Manchester NH & MAVRILLIS Theodora of Manchester NH int 26 Dec 1935 by THEODORON Theodoros of Lowell MA

HARVEY Floyd C of Hillsboro NH & PUTNAM Gladys P of Derring NH int 25 Jan 1940 by MYER Henry H of Boston MA

HARWOOD Landry Jr of New York NY & DURANT Emily Davies of New London NH int 6 Aug 1935 by ARCHIBALD Black of Monticlair NJ

HASH Howard C Jr of Nashua NH & KELLOWAY Ethel Mae of Nashua NH int 21 Oct 1949 by ERNEST O Kelloway of Bridgeton NJ

HASKELL Cheves of Somersworth NH & GRANT Joan of Farmington NH int 20 May 1951 by BAIRD Wm R Jr of New Haven CT

HASKINS Franklin of Alstead NH & SAVORY Shirley of Alstead NH int 25 Dec 1952 by MARSH George B of Grafton VT

HASWELL Joseph of Meuthen MA & NOWELL Gladys E of Meuthen MA int 26 Dec 1933 by MOORE John Ward of ?

HATCH Herbert Lilden of Milford NH & FARMER Katherine Cookes of Milford NH int 28 May 1958 by MILLER Samuel H of Cambridge MA

HATCH John P of Wakefield MA & CHALMERS Marjorie of Tilton NH int 20 Dec 1945 by MUNICH Roy L of Malden MA

HATCH Lincoln of Cochituate MA & LEDREW Marilyn A of Cochituate MA int 7 Jul 1956 by C Malcolm Keir of Fitchburg MA

HATCH Walter of Wells ME & HERRON Sarah Margaret of Rochester NH int 28 May 1927 by SMITH Howard B of Quinquet ME

HATHAWAY Edward L Jr of Amarillo TX & CARRIER Ruth Hayward of Winchester MA int 20 Jun 1946 by LOBINGIER John L of Boston MA

HAVEN Philip H of Loudon NH & DeFOREST Anith of Loudon NH int 30 Aug 1939 by PAGE Frederick H of Waltham MA

HAWKINS Clarence E of Brookline MA & HASKELL Fayette of Ctr Harbor NH int 13 Apr 1953 by ARTHUR Flayhn Fultz of Boston MA

HAWKINS Elston Gale of Stafford NH & FARNSWORTH Ann Eliz of Stafford NH int 28 Sep 1950 by SMITH Curtis W of Cannan VT

HAYARD Richard Folsmon of Cincinnati OH & FAULKNER Ruth M of Keene NH int 26 Jun 1933 by SNOW Sidney B of Chicago IL

HAYES Frederick of Boscawen NH & EASTMAN Esther B of Concord NH int 1 Jun 1933 by SNEATH Isaciah W of Newton MA

HAYES Milton of Milton NH & LOVER Valna I of Milton NH int 18 Jun 1930 by ARTHUR Jeffries of W Acton MA

HAYNES Philip D of Alstead NH & BLISS Barbara of Keene NH int 20 Jan 1951 by KENNETH R Bliss of Kingsbury IN

HAYWARD Harold Mansfield of Burlington VT & BOLLES Chloe Celeste of West Swanzey H int 21 May 1925 by WILLIAM A Davison of Burlington VT

HEAD Thomas Marshall of Bronxille NY & JOHNSON Nancy of Melrose MA int 24 Aug 1954 by LOESCH Russell of Melrose MA

HEALY Edward W of Manchester NH & HANNON Catherine A of Manchester NH int 3 May 1960 by GEORGE B Healy of Lennox MA

HEATH C Wilbur of Worcester MA & TRIPP Inez of So Royalston MA int 28 Aug 1935 by GEORGE E Heath of Worcester MA

HEDGE Elliott R of Brookline MA & ROGERS Elaine of New York NY int 2 Sep 1940 by PETERSON Abbott of Brookline MA

HEDSTROM Carl Hjalmer of Fitchburg MA & SWANBERG Clara of Worcester MA int 29 Mar 1948 by MILTON C Berg of Gardner MA

HEIGHAM Albert P of Brighton MA & JEWELL Martha of Wolfeboro NH int 19 Apr 1947 by ROBERT H Heigham of Wiscasset ME

HENDERSON Donald of Medford MA & THOMPSON Dorothy of Hanover NH int 3 Jun 1952 by ALEXANDER Henderson of Medford MA

HENDERSON Herbert James of Mansfield MA & THOMPSON Jane of Chester NH int 25 Aug 1952 by MONTGOMERY Marshall of Lakeworth FL

HENDERSON James of Miami FL & DUSTAN Marcia of E Barrington NH int 21 Jul 1960 by EARL E Hain of No Plainfield NJ

HENDERSON John B of Needham MA & LEARY Catherine T of Portsmouth NH int 10 Jul 1941 by LEARY John F of Portsmouth NH

HENDERSON Robert of Winchester MA & FULLER Mary of Rye Beach NH int 23 Aug 1940 by NEAGLE Richard of Malden MA

HENDRICK Lloyd M of Pocasset MA & LADD Arline M of Derry NH int 4 Jun 1943 by IRVING J Enslin of Litchfield CT

HENDRICK Paul of New York NY & CROWELL Nancy of Litchfield NH int 5 Nov 1941 by WILLIAM J Ballou of Chester VT

HENLEY Zenas Richard of Manchester NH & SCOTT Louise Marie of Belfast ME int 9 Jul 1956 by NORTON A M of Kansas Cty MO

HENNESSY Brian Patick of Greenfield NH & THOMPSON Anne Eliz of Nahsua NH int 20 Jun 1957 by RICHARD W Duncanson of Bennington VT

HERBERT Louis V of Manchester NH & BERNIER Constance of Manchester NH int 21 Mar 1959 by NOURY Eugene of Lowell MA

HERBST Arthur L of Pittsburg PA & GINSBURG Lee of Newton Ctr MA int 9 Jul 1958 by ROLAND B Gittlesohn of Boston MA

HERLIHY Timothy Jerome of Wakefield MA & DOYLE Barbara Ann of Hampton NH int 9 May 1955 by JOSEPH W Higgins of Ipswich MA

HERRIOTT D Paul of Cranston RI & AHRUNDT Joy of Nashua NH int 1 Aug 1952 by D Paul Herriott of Cranston RI

HERRMARM Ernest F of Adams MA & BROWN Mary E of Deerfield NH int 8 Aug 1936 by TILTON C H Bouton of St Peterburg FL

HERSON Harold of Waterville ME & PEABODY Clara of Waterville ME int 24 May 1934 by WILSON Arthur E of Providence RI

HERZOG Richard Arthur of Beverly MA & WORTMAN Jane Margaret of Portsmouth NH int 30 May 1952 by C Basil Harris of Kittery Pt ME

HEWEL William of Keene NH & DOMINA Anne of Keene NH int 20 May 1959 by JOHN Joseph Crowley of Roxbury MA

HEWINS Alfred of Allston MA & BULLARD Mary of Boston MA int 25 Sep 1946 by NOSS Frederick B of Andover MA

HEWITT Peter M of Cambridge MA & SCHOEPF Luan of Dublin NH int 18 May 1954 by SMITH Charles of Cambridge MA

HEYMANS Francis of Salem NH & CONNOLLY Eleanor Virginia of Chelmsford MA int 10 Dec 1954 by HARLIE E Goodwin of Methuen MA

HEYWOOD Ruel of Franklin MA & BUCKAMAN Hazel Mrs of Franklin MA int 26 Jul 1932 by MARRON Regnald K of New Castle NH

HICKOK Frederick C of Andover MA & KELLER Roberta I of Manchester NH int 4 Aug 1939 by HERMAN C Johnson of Andover MA

HILCHEY Ernest of Boston MA & NICHOLS Ruth E of Warner NH int 12 Sep 1953 by H Dubois of Newport VT

HILDRETH Lucian of NH & NELSON Ellen of NH int 12 Sep 1939 by TRACY Olin B of Melrose MA

HILL Carrington W of Boston MA & DUERR Margaret Ellen of Templeton MA int 30 May 1935 by OTTO Eugene Duerr of Fitchburg MA

HILL Charles H of Warner NH & BROWN Alice L of Warner NH int 23 May 1949 by SMITH Harry of Lowell MA

HILL David S of Gales Ferry CT & PHILBRICK Nancy of Epping NH int 23 Jan 1957 by LAURENCE M Hill of Griswold CT

HILL Donald of Walpole NH & DEXTER Dolores Mae of Putney VT int 26 Oct 1956 by NORMAN R Farnum Jr of Holyoke MA

HILL Edward Joseph of Springfield MA & WESTHEAD Audrey of Greensboro NC int 13 May 1957 by LAWRENCE L Dugin of Providence RI

HILL Geo Ensign of ? New York NY & PIKE Constance of Pike NH int 12 Aug 1936 by NEFF Edgar R of Arden NC

HILL George Edward of Cambridge MA & ENSTIS Leslie of Brookline MA int 29 Aug 194 by TROWBRIDGE Cornelius of Chestnut Hill MA

HILL William F of Dedham MA & NEWELL Ethel Grace of Dedham MA int 20 Sep 1938 by DANIEL I Gross of Athol MA

HILTON Clarence of Lynn MA & SMITH Grace M of Raymond NH int 10 Jun 1946 by SMITH Chellis V of Raymond NH

HINGSTON William J of Charlestown MA & BATCHELDER Rosamond of Raymond NH int 25 May 1950 by MILLER Herbert E of Raynham MA

HINOJOS Sil of ? & CURTICE Doris M of ? int 28 Aug 1944 by C Leslie Curtice of Bass River MA

HIX Clarence E Jr of Durham NC & SWEET Elizabeth L of Chicago IL int 18 Aug 1936 by SWEET William W of Chicago IL

HOAG David of Old Lyme CT & HERSON Geraldine of Rochester NH int 12 Jul 1954 by WM Dixon Hoag of Old Lyme CT

HOAR Richard Edwin of Winchendon MA & WOODWARD Elloine Eliz of Dublin NH int 13 Sep 1934 by CLINTON Brockway of Hingham MA

HOBBS Stillman of Great Neck Long Island NY & DAVIS Helen E of Hollidaysbury PA int 1 Aug 1958 by KIRKE W Davis of Barrington NJ

HOCHNELL Robert Edwin of Needham MA & BONNER Mary Eliz of Toledo OH int 8 Aug 1951 by NOBLE Charles C of Syracuse NY

HODGDON George Samuel of Portsmouth NH & DAVIS Milly Lou of Portsmouth NH int 7 Aug 1945 by FRANK B Chattenton of Cambridge MA

HODGDON Herbert E of Wolfboro NH & KIRKLAND Patricia of Wolfboro NH int 5 Jul 1948 by J J Hutchinson of Lyndonville VT

HODGE Russe of Salem NH & HULMER Virginia G of Salem NH int 16 Dec 1938 by ARCHIE H Crowley of Methuen MA

HODGIN Thomas W of York ME & JUNKINS Ruth A of Rye NH int 13 Sep 1949 by MAYO Harold E of Phil PA

HODSDON Grant William of Ctr Ossipee NH & TURNER Florence Eliz of Malden MA int 30 Jun 1933 by EARLE B Cross of Rochester NY

HOEY Homer of Marlboro MA & BURBANK Edna of Fitchburg MA int 30 Jul 1930 by JOSEPH Atkinson Colonel of Boston MA

HOFFMAN Donald of Concord MA & UHLER Jane of Concord MA int 23 May 1957 by CLAYTON Brooks Hale of Boston MA

HOGAN Wm Elias of NY City & BUTLER Helen E of W Swanzey NH int 28 Aug 1934 by JOHN S Keating of Chestnut Hill MA

HOLAR John of Bellows Falls VT & LAMPHERE Jean of Woodsville NH int 7 Oct 1957 by ROBERT S Kerr of Bellows Falls VT

HOLDEN Edward Chauvenet of Brookline MA & JARVIS Dorothy B of Brookline MA int 20 May 1935 by CHIDLEY Howard of Winchester MA

HOLDEN William Henry of W Peterboro NH & PESARCZYK Poronislass of W Peterboro NH int 1 Oct 1929 by TOBIN John F of Altamont NY

HOLDSWORTH Raymond of Lynn MA & HALE Ester of Fitchburg MA int 3 Aug 1928 by PEASE Howard A of Fitchburg MA

HOLLEY Ernest of Manchester NH & DESILETS Germaine of Manchester NH int 22 Jun 1936 by EDWARD Desilets of St Hyacinth CAN

HOLMAN Paul of Leominster MA & DOAN Isabel of Winchester MA int 11 Jun 1926 by FRANK L Doan of Winchester MA

HOLMES Frank H of Wellesley MA & LISK Mildred E of Newton MA int 4 Mar 1947 by GEORGE O Ekwall of Waltham MA

HOLROYD Thomas Fletcher of Lawrence MA & DOERR Virginia Mae of Salem NH int 18 Apr 1950 by FAY Lincoln Gemmell of Lawrence MA

HOLST Wm Henry of New London NH & GOODWIN Gretchen M of New London NH int 26 Jul 1956 by MATHEWS C R of Parkeesbury W VA

HOMAN Charles G of Manchester NH & ANDERSON Olive of Manchester NH int 30 Apr 1926 by HOOPER R Goodwin of Lawrence MA

HOOD Warren of Danvers MA & HITCHOCK Wilhelmina of Danvers MA int 5 Aug 1935 by KENNETH R Henley of Danvers MA

HOOVER Waren G Jr of Jacksville FL & PARENT Florence Norma of Woodstock NH int 4 Aug 1947 by WOODBURY Josephe E of Somerville MA

HOPKINS Philip G of Cleveland OH & TATEM Elizabeth L of Cleveland OH int 2 Sep 1947 by HERBERT Houghton of Deerfield MA

HOPSWOOD Harold G of Litchfield NH & DRIVER Helen L of Nashua NH int 25 Apr 1950 by DRIVER Geo H of Billerica MA

HORLACKER David Edmund of Carlisle PA & STITZEL Marie Cleveger of Carlisle PA int 1 Jun 1953 by AMOS B Horlacher of Carlisle PA

HORN Frank Wilbur of Brookline MA & WILLIAMS Emily Morton of Brookline MA int 13 Aug 1945 by TRAUB Warren E of New Haven CT

HORNER James Richey of Concord NH & NEDEAU Barbara Elaine of Concord NH int 15 Jun 1948 by LAURENCE H Blackburn of Lowell MA

HORNSTRVA Frank Haig of Antrim NH & GRIFFIN Joanne of Antrim NH int 1 Aug 1952 by MEES Matt of Stroughton MA

HORTON Douglas of Randolph NH & McAFEE Mildred Helen of Wellesley MA int 23 Jul 1945 by GEORGE William Brown of Summit NJ

HORTON Ivan of Milan MI & STEBBINS Phyllis of Milan MI int 4 Sep 1953 by SPIDELL Curry M of Milan MI

HORTON Wm Francis Jr of Charlestown NH & NELSON Sarah Jean of Charlestown NH int 12 Aug 1954 by WATSON Albert P of Tynsboro MA

HORVATH Steven Michael of Lakewood OH & DILL Elizabeth of Arlington MA int 28 Aug 1940 by WEATHERLEY Arthur of Lincoln ME

HOSHOR James Clay Jr of Alberqueque NM & NEWHALL Anne of New Hampton NH int 8 Sep 1952 by CLAYTON Brooks Hale of Boston MA

HOSMER Charles B Jr of Alexandria VA & PRUGH Jeralyn of Goffstown NH int 11 Dec 1955 by THEODORE L Clapp of West Newton MA

HOUDE Raymond Louis of Nashua NH & BOUTHILLIER Laurette of Nashua NH int 20 Aug 1937 by J A Desmarais of St Hyacinthe CAN

HOUGHTON David of Walpole NH & PHELPS June of Walpole NH int 26 May 1960 by NORMAN R Farnum Jr of Holyoke MA

HOULE Ernest of Manchester NH & CHAMPAGNE Marie Irene of Manchester NH int 16 Jun 1939 by EMERY Champagne of Manchester NH

HOULE Paul Emile of Manchester NH & DESAULNIERS Yvonne J of Manchester NH int 18 Aug 1948 by MELANSON Athanas of Shaivingan Fall Pq

HOURI Han Raymond of Dover NH & WENTWORTH Joan Leanne of Dover NH int 25 Sep 1958 by MAYRAND Stephen of Engadine MI

HOWARD Ernest of No Sutton NH & CHADWICK Geraldine of New London NH int 22 Jul 1943 by JOHN C Hatch of Lebanon Springs NY

HOWARD Henry Raymond of Boston MA & PUCKETT Serdena A of Nashua NH int 31 May 1948 by TAYLOR Robert J of Boston MA

HOWD Salmon Giddings of New York NY & DAWES Francina D of Roxbury NH int 2 Nov 1932 by ROBBINS Howard C of Palisades NY

HOWE John of Concord NH & KUCH Robin Graves Mrs of Concord NH int 4 Nov 1960 by CARL B Bare of Newport RI

HOWELL Raymond E Jr of Mt Vernon NY & ELLIS Fay of Carbondale PA int 13 Nov 1954 by RAYMOND E Howell Sr of Cortland NY

HOWLAND Elmer Le Roy of Portsmouth NH & BUZZELL Marian Sarah of Somersworth NH int 1 May 1939 by FRANK A Kelly of St Johnsbury VT

HUBBARD Crescins G of White Plains NY & NUSSBAUM Jean of New York NY int 1 Aug 1950 by JULE Ayers of Wilkes Barre PA

HUDON Normand Albert of Berlin NH & DUCHESNAYE Beatrice of Berlin NH int 23 Jan 1950 by LEMIEUX Arthur of Attleboro MA

HUDSON Shaw of Hopedale MA & MASON Wilma A of Hopedale MA int 28 Jul 1933 by MASON John of Somerville MA

HUDSON William C of Newton MA & KNIGHT Marian O of Wellesley MA int 2 Sep 1938 by STANLEY Ross Fisher of Hanover MA

HULL John B of Dover NH & BROWN Gertrude of Dover NH int 10 Aug 1937 by JOHN D Hull of Haverhill MA

HUMPHREY Flloyd B of Pasadena CA & CLAPP Susan W of Meredith NH int 21 Jun 1955 by SAADAH Mournier of Woodstock VT

HUNT Javis Jr of N Attleboro MA & NIMS Judith Catherine of Manchester NH int 17 Aug 1956 by WORSTER Harold O of Foxborough MA

HUNT Victor Austin of Chester NH & ROBERTSON Betty Lou of Chester NH int 15 Jul 1957 by ROGERS Howard of Naugatuck CT

HUNTLEY Robert of Boston MA & MURPHY Joan of Boston MA int 1 Sep 1955 by LESLIE William R of Brookline MA

HURLEY John Randall of Wakefield MA & MERRILL Judith Mary of Concord NH int 8 Jul 1959 by HURLEY Wilfred of Boston MA

HUSE Wendell Orrin of Stafford NH & SAINTGEORGE Cora-Ann of Pittsfield NH int 9 Jun 1959 by Lester Holmes of Alfred ME

HUTCH Alexander of Princeton NJ & LANCASTER Mary of Princeton NJ int 25 Jul 1938 by WILLIAM F Howe of Somerville MA

HUTCHINS Oscar B of Portsmouth NH & MORTON Ementrude of Portsmouth NH int 9 Mar 1960 by REED Waller M of W Kennebunk ME

HUTCHINS Vivian Foster of Detroit Michigan & DUTCHER Anne Van Wart of Arlington NJ int 9 Jul 1930 by WILLIAM Coombe of Arlington NJ

HUTCHINSON Donald Stuart of Boston MA & OGILVY Heather Ann of Boston MA int 4 Aug 1960 by HILES James R of Boston MA

HUX Robert Earl of Durham NH & STONE Elizabeth Alice of Tilton NH int 5 Jun 1953 by EDEARD G Ernst of Bangor ME

IGNATOVICZ Adam of Exeter NH & LUZEN Mary of Exeter NH int 29 Apr 1930 by ORANOVSKY V of Salem MA

ILLSLEY Donald Raymond of Nova Scotia & COLCORD Shirley Ann of Atkinson NH int 3 Jul 1950 by FREDERICK R Bruce of Nyack NY

ILSLEY Charles Ferdinand of Milwaukee WI & CARROLL Leslie of Miami FL int 28 Aug 1957 by F Craighill Brown of New Haven CT

INGALLS Carlton Sidney of W Epping NH & DOWNING Eleanor Ruth of Plaistow NH int 25 Feb 1942 by SMITH Chellis V of Hyde Park MA

INGALLS Richard of Newton NH & LOVERING Sandra of Salem NH int 12 Jan 1960 by TEED Kenneth R of E Long Meadow MA

INGERSON H Stewart of Providence RI & SMITH Ethel A of Canton RI int 25 Aug 1938 by MAURICE E Barrett of Norwich CT

IRISH Perley of Conway NH & MERRILL Patti of No Conway NH int 2 Aug 1957 by CHARLES L Durgin of Rangeley ME

IVES Gerard M of New York NY & TALCOTT Ruth Pratt of New York NY int 13 Aug 1938 by NOYES Morgan P of Mont Clair NJ

JAANS Richard of Haverhill MA & CUSHMAN Elizabeth of Hampton Beach NH int 13 Apr 1937 by CLARK T Browell of Haverhill MA

JACKSON Harry B of Lebanon NH & HAZEN Doris of Lebanon NH int 3 Jan 1935 by JOHN W Barker of Athol MA

JACKSON Stanley of Lebanon & WALDO Doris of Lebanon int 19 Jul 1929 by FREDERICK G Chutter of Mystic CT

JACQUES Romeo L of Somersworth NH & MEREAULT Marceline S of Rochester NH int 19 Aug 1959 by TANGUAY Ovid of Biddeford ME

JAMROG John J of Manchester NH & BARTULA Helen of Manchester NH int 24 Jun 1930 by STASZ Ladeslaus of Port Henry NY

JANELLE Jeanne Adrienne of Manchester NH & SOUCY Jean Charles of Manchester NH int 13 Jun 1955 by PANNETON Paul E of Wakefield MA

JAQUITH William H of Andover MA & FREDERICK Virginia W of Dorchester MA int 2 Jul 1948 by SHATTUCK Gardine H of Boston MA

JARBEAU Norbert of W Warwick RI & JEAN Marguerite of Nashua NH int 15 May 1942 by L Lucien Jean of W Warwick RI

JAROSZ Andrew of Manchester NH & DANIS Doris P of Grasmere NH int 1 May 1951 by LEAIENWORTH Lynn of E Orange NJ

JASINSKI Frederick M of Manchester NH & KALESZ Judith May of Manchester NH int 17 Sep 1955 by STEJZER Ferdinand of Lowell NH

JEAN Adelard of Nashua NH & CARON Stella of Nashua NH int 23 Dec 1936 by L L Jean of Nashua NH

JEAN Lionel of Nashua NH & LaBOUNTY Lucille of Nashua NH int 25 Jun 1949 by JEAN Rome of CAN

JEFFERSON Paul Edward of Omaha NB & STORY Edith Guild of Boston MA int 26 Aug 1953 by VON-DER-SUMP Frederic of Lantan FL

JEFFERSON Robert of Nashua NH & FOSTER Frances of Nashua NH int 18 Sep 1937 by LAWRENCE L Barber of Arlington MA

JEFFRIES Charles H of St Cloud FL & HADLEY Mary C of Wilmington MA int 24 Jun 1952 by MAXFIELD Otis A of Wilmington MA

JEFTS Charles Albert of Langdon NH & CHANDLER Daisy Bell of Langdon NH int 28 Aug 1927 by HENRY B Bryan of Jersey City NJ

JENKINS Arthur Bayard of Hartford CT & EATON Eunice Florence of Hartford CT int 5 Sep 1927 by SAMUEL R Colladay of Hartford CT

JENKINS Daniel O of Pleasant Valley PA & FLANDERS Jane A of Weare NH int 5 Jul 1955 by POLIN Daniel K of New York NY

JENKINS Ernest Jr of Bedford NH & EVARTS Barbara of Hooksett NH int 8 Aug 1945 by MATCHETT Wilbur of Inwin PA

JENKINS Ronald Elliott of Watertown MA & SMITH Nora Joyce of N Conway NH int 1 Jun 1953 by DURGIN Chas of Rangeley ME

JENNESS Roger Franklin of Dover NH & LITTLEFIELD Dorothy Jae of Rochester NH int 12 Aug 1947 by WM J Davis of Salisbury MA

JENNESS William R of Rye NH & VOLKMANN Priscilla of Rye NH int 26 Jul 1949 by HAROLD S Hannum of St Johnsbury VT

JENNINGS Bernard M of Winchester NH & HILL Emily M of Winchester NH int 21 Dec 1939 by WALKER Edgar R of Waltham MA

JENNINGS Roy Elliot of Haverhill MA & TUCKER Elizabeth of Wolfeboro NH int 9 Jun 1958 by SCOTT N Harlan of Downsville NY

JENOVESE Fredrick of Concord NH & GILMAN Carrie of Concord NH int 4 Nov 1940 by MICHAEL A Jenovese of Worcester MA

JENOVESE James Michael of Concord NH & THERIAULT Priscilla of Nashua NH int 6 Jul 1959 by MICHAEL A Genovese of Leominster MA

JESSOP Lionel of Brooklin MA & CUSHING Alvilda of Brooklin MA int 23 Aug 1933 by VALENTINE Lloyd H of Lynn MA

JEWETT Charles C of Vero Beach FL & RIESE Helen M of Melrose MA int 20 Aug 1955 by CARL A Glover of Pawtucket RI

JEWETT Kenneth E of Shorn NH & WOOD Charlotte of Kingston NH int 19 Jul 1949 by SPERRY Willard L of Cambrige MA

JILLETTE Arthur Geo Jr of Stoneham MA & WHITE Janet Downs of Ossipee NH int 23 May 1960 by PIERCE John of Melrose MA

JODOIN Conrad of Manchester NH & BERGERON Eugenie of Manchester NH int 22 Aug 1935 by P O Bergeron of Clyde KS

JOHN Franklin H of Newton MA & PIERCE Sybil of Concord NH int 11 Aug 1945 by PATTERSON George F of Farmington MA

JOHNSON Albert Hallier of Hopedale MA & GILL Frances Margaret of Melrose MA int 26 Jun 1937 by CROSS Earle B of Rochester NY

JOHNSON Chester of W Concord NH & ADAMS Helen of Chester VT int 6 Jun 1952 by VINCENT E Johnson of Deep River CT

JOHNSON Donald Ephraim of Portland ME & GOULD Jane of Ossipee NH int 19 May 1954 by JOHN B S Fitzpatrick of Thomaston ME

JOHNSON George L of New York NY & ROLLINS Ferne of Dover NH int 17 May 1948 by LESTERLE Holmes of Alfred ME

JOHNSON Kenneth Wm of Winchester NH & TARBELL Elva Amaret of Winchester NH int 17 Jul 1945 by GEORGE T Carle of Park Ridge IL

JOHNSON Leon K of Melrose MA & MacDONALD Caroline of Stoneham MA int 29 Oct 1934 by ROBBINS Doug of Lowell MA

JOHNSON Leroy of No Sutton NH & VANDEBURG Elsie M of No Sutton NH int 21 Sep 1939 by CLARK Wm J of Watervleiet NY

JOHNSON R Quentin of Arlington MA & PRYER Sylvia of Ashland NH int 14 Sep 1942 by SEIDENSPINNER Chas of Providence RI

JOHNSON Richard Clancy of E Rochester NH & PHILBROOK Jean Wilma of E Rochester NH int 20 Jun 1947 by FRANK B Chatterton of Cambridge MA

JOHNSTON Lawrence M of Hartford CT & MARDEN Margaret Arlene of Newton NH int 25 Aug 1953 by VIALL John S of Arlington MA

JOHNSTON William B of Malden MA & LEWIS Mary C of Lebanon NH int 1 Jul 1947 by WILLIAMS Clyde D of Greenfield NH

JONES Frank N of Newburyport MA & SAARI Ilini of Fitzwilliam NH int 1 May 1934 by CHARLES W Cooper of Akron OH

JONES George W of Somerville MA & STEVENS Rosamond of New York NY int 16 Nov 1950 by WEBSTER Arthur of Salem MA

JONES Jean Paul Jr of Miami FL & BALDWIN Elizabeth of Bradenton FL int 4 Aug 1940 by WILLIAM D Barnes of Salem CT

JONES Jerry of Lamesa TX & KENT Gloria of Hampton Fallsh int 11 May 1959 by MARTIN Paul T of Wentham MA

JONES Lawrence J of Lynn MA & FALKINS Dorothy of Lynn MA int 26 Aug 1946 by FRANKLIN Ellis of Cambridge MA

JONES Ralph E Jr of Stamford CT & FAIRBANKS Ann of Newport NH int 26 May 1954 by WILBUR I Bull of Waterford ME

JONES Wm McPheeters of Port Auprine Haiti & BETCHLEY Helen Louise of Melvin Village int 7 Sep 1933 by WALKER Raymond E of No Attleboro MA

JOOKER Edwin Wilson of Littleton MA & BEAL Pauline Bird of Suncook NH int 29 Jun 1946 by J Wesley Ingles of Lewiston ME

JORDAN Bernard Harvey of Governors Island NH & STOCK Harriet M of Concord NH int 15 Aug 1946 by JULE Ayers of Kingston PA

JORGENSON Arthur M of Winthrop MA & JONES Evelyn Marjorie of Portsmouth NH int 10 Aug 1938 by MANGLEDOIFF L P of Providence RI

JOSTED Oscar C of Wellesley MA & OSBORN Louise of Montclair NJ int 5 Jul 1950 by WILLIAMS Clyde A of Farmingham MA

JOY Alfred Raymond of Keene NH & BARNARD Ellen Erma of Manchester NH int 10 Sep 1930 by EDWIN Joy of Boston MA

JOYCE Kevin A of Manchester NH & SWANSON Audrey M of Sanford ME int 12 Sep 1958 by EDWARD J Keating of Worcester MA

JUDD Justus E of Royalston MA & SHINE Lucille of Royalston MA int 25 Apr 1957 by MORRILL Frederick L of Southboro MA

JUDD Stuart of Waterbury CT & CLOSE Edna of Waterbury CT int 1 Jul 1944 by LAURIN Sven A of Amesbury MA

KAHLE Kenneth M of Dorchester MA & McLEAN Margaret M of Newton NH int 5 Sep 1958 by TRASK Harry E Jr of Haverhill MA

KAITZ Robert Murray of Cheles MA & JONES Barbara of Malden MA int 17 Jul 1950 by WEINBERG Charles of Malden MA

KARMERIS William of ? & GRIGORACOS Kathryn of ? int 14 May 1941 by ARCHBISHOP Christopher of Lowell MA

KARNACEWICZ Michael A of No Walpole NH & CANTLIN Margaret D of Keene NH int 3 Jun 1960 by FRANCIS A Hickey of Fairfax VT

KATSALIS Timothy of Manchester NH & TULGREN June M of Manchester NH int 31 May 1950 by WILLIAM B Fowler of Arlington MA

KAUFMAN Richard of Lancaster PA & BECHOK Mary of Claremont NH int 21 Aug 1950 by PINKHAM Robert of Westbrook ME

KAULBACK George of Haverhill MA & BAKER Ethel A of Westerville NH int 20 Jan 1941 by MORRIN Thomas M of Westeville (Hampstead) NH

KAVANAS Peter of Manchester NH & MAIDONI Anastasia of Norwich CT int 17 Sep 1927 by T P Comuntzis of Brooklyn NY

KAY James Hutchinson of Baltimore MD & DRAPER Marion Hoffman of Baltimore MD int 13 Jun 1941 by SPEERS Guthrie of Baltimore MD

KEARNEY Wm F of Manchester NH & DOLPH Barbara M of Boston MA int 25 Jul 1957 by TANGNEY Edward J of Quincy MA

KEEFE Philip C of Dover NH & WALLACE Ann of Rochester NH int 1 Aug 1947 by WALLACE Anothy of Highland Falls NY

KEELER Duane T of Pembroke NH & WELLS Norma M of Epsom NH int 24 May 1948 by MASON John of Walpole MA

KEELER Ralph Jr of Canterbury NH & HILDRETH Lucille of Boscawen NH int 24 Jun 1940 by RALPH W Keeler of Brooklyn NY

KEELEY Charles Finning of Nashua NH & EVERETTE Carroll Eliza of Nashua NH int 27 Jun 1958 by RILEY Edward J of Malden MA

KEENAN James A Jr of Waterbury CT & CRANE Mary Louise of Rye Beach NH int 17 Aug 1957 by RICHARD J Dowling of Worcester MA

KEENE Charles W of Salem NH & FOSTER Julia of Meuthen MA int 18 Aug 1945 by GEORGE T Beecher of Methuen MA

KEEZER Carter Diamond of Plaistow NH & STALKER Muriel Mary of Plaistow NH int 25 Oct 1933 by CHARLES H Havice of Cambridge MA

KEIR Harold Perry of Whitefield NH & JONES Marilyn Ellen of Boston MA int 25 Apr 1944 by J Heisse Johnson of Madison NJ

KEIRSTEAD C Fraser of Fitchburg MA & POTTER Marcia of Leominster MA int 17 Dec 1949 by CHARLES W Keirstead of Chicago IL

KELLER Otto Pitman of Laconia NH & DRISKO Caroline of Laconia NH int 2 Jun 1939 by REED George Hale of Winchester NH

KELLEY Isaac R of No Adams MA & MEADER Edith A of Falmouth MA int 1 Apr 1941 by MEADER Leon B of Charleston ME

KELLEY James Wilson of Boston MA & BRIGGS Marjorie Eselle of Gorham NH int 6 Oct 1941 by E Wilson Kelley of Pittsburgh PA

KELLEY Richard G of Salem NH & FARR Mary of Salem N int 22 Jun 1942 by LANGE Richard R of Methuen MA

KELLEY Robert Wayne of E Hartfort CT & HAZEN Raelene of Hartford CT int 23 May 1960 by SMITH Clayton F of Hartford CT

KELLEY Ronald Croyden of Woodsville NH & NICKERSON Ruth Barbara of Malden MA int 29 May 1947 by ADRIAN T English of Providence RI

KELLNER Robert L of Onset MA & WILSON Thelma of Wolfeboro NH int 26 May 1958 by LESLIE H Kellner of Onset MA

KELLY Joseph of Brighton MA & WAGNER Alma of Manchester NH int 29 Sep 1936 by MATTHEW C Duggan of Boston MA

KELLY Joseph Mry of Boston MA & BARRETT Anny Mary of Concord NH int 27 Jun 1946 by PHILIP C M Kelley of No Easton MA

KELTON Frank B of Camp Forrest Tenn & CRAWFORD Louise Clara of Hooksett NH int 29 Nov 1943 by LEE D Bergsman of Boston MA

KENDALL James Andrew of Gilsum NH & FISK Eunice Mae of Gilsum NH int 2 Nov 1955 by BRADLEY Chas A of Coventry CT

KENNEY Joseph of Manchester NH & LEDDY Joan of Epping NH int 9 Aug 1949 by JOSEPH J Dion of Detroit MI

KENT David Richard of Wellesley MA & MARSHALL Cynthia Alice of Manchester NH int 27 Jun 1960 by Harold W Garmon of Boston MA

KENTZ Frederick Jr of Summit NJ & O'BRIEN Rita of Manchester NH int 1 Feb 1946 by O'BRIEN Patrick M of Newark NJ

KERR Robert John of Boston MA & SANBORN Jean of Danville NH int 12 Mar 1956 by WEBSTER Arthur of Salem MA

KERSHNER Robert W of Scranton PA & SCHNEIDER Ruthanne of Scranton PA int 26 Jun 1935 by HENRY H Crane of Scranton

KESSARIS Kenneth James of Beverly MA & SCOTT Nancy Mabel of Beverly MA int 6 Jul 1952 by WEBSTER Arthur of Salem MA

KEZER Fayette Wm of Derry NH & HIGGINS Martha Gorham of Salem NH int 3 Oct 1933 by ROBBINS Clarence G of Methuen MA

KIACH Ray R of Springfield MA & RANDALL Mary Janet of Troy NY int 10 Aug 1937 by RYDER Ernest R of Troy NY

KIELY John Blaise of Holyoke MA & CROTEAU Claudette of Keene NH int 5 Aug 1958 by SHEEHY Donald F of Lorton VA

KIENAN Avery Norbert of Berlin NH & GEARY Mary Elizabeth of Portsmouth NH int 18 Jul 1934 by JAMES E Geary of Gloucester MA

KIERMAN Joseph of Philadelpia PA & RACKETT Cecila M of E Jaffery NH int 16 Aug 1926 by WALTER A Kierman of Douglaston NY

KIERSTEAD George A of Newton NH & LEWIS Mabel of Newburyport MA int 29 Sep 1952 by ERNEST L Allan of Merrimack MA

KILBURN Floyd Homer of Andover NH & GARDNER Ruth of Moultonboro NH int 24 Aug 1940 by HUGH C Burr of Rochester NY

KILEY James of Lawrence MA & HOLLAND Eileen of Manchester NH int 16 Sep 1954 by DANIEL F Cronin of Lowell MA

KILHAM Peter of Boston MA & BREEZER Fran of Tamworth NH int 24 Dec 1934 by POWELL F C of ?

KILMISTER Percy of W Concord NH & BRIGGS Marion of Concord NH int 13 Jul 1927 by A Earl Kernahan of W Somerville MA

KIMBALL Harrison of Troy NH & PIISPANEN Stella of Keene NH int 13 Sep 1939 by TIBBETTS Charles M of Lawrence MA

KING Anthony J of Charlestown MA & THOMPSON Marjorie of Rutland MA int 22 Jul 1959 by LANG Stephen C of Somerville MA

KING Arthur Clark of Wonalancet NH & WALKER Edith Catharine of Tamworth NH int 6 May 1939 by PEASLEE Arthur W of Providence RI

KING Charles George of Colchester VT & CURRIER Emma Ellen of Alstead NH int 15 Apr 1933 by THOMAS Leroy Crosby of Waterbury CT

KINNEY Wayne of Atkinson NH & KILBURN Jean of Atkinson NH int 1 Aug 1958 by WEBB Theodore A of Haverhill MA

KINSON Ernest Richard of Charlestown NH & BRADISH Ruth Irma of Charlestown NH int 2 Jun 1955 by WATSON Albert P of Tyngsboro MA

KINTER William B of Pittsfield VT & HILSON Anne of Exeter NH int 9 May 1947 by PERKINS Palfrey of Boston MA

KINYON George Dana of Bellows Falls VT & BURNHAM Evelyn of Henniker NH int 27 May 1931 by ROUNDY Rodney of Portland ME

KIRK Leo of Burlington VT & RUBEOR Marion of Hinsdale NH int 23 Dec 1950 by MULLIGAN W R of Burlington VT

KIRSCH Richard E of Lowell MA & WICKLUND Phyllis Barbar of Lowell MA int 23 Sep 1957 by SCALISE Victor of Lowell MA

KIRWAN Richard J of Hampton NH & BLAKE Deborah E of Hampton NH int 14 Oct 1952 by J Osborne Crowe of Ipswich MA

KIRWIN John Francis of Omaha NB & BANCROFT Persia Helen of West Newton MS int 10 Jul 1945 by DANA M Greeley of Boston MA

KLOWEON William of Holyoke MA & PASTUSZENSKI Eva of Hinsdale NH int 18 Sep 1934 by PRODNAM Michael of So Deerfield MA

KNAPP Richard Allen of Ossipee NH & DAVIS Carmen Roberta of Jackson NH int 20 May 1954 by WOOD Nathan of Arlington MA

KNIGHT Ainsworth Jr of W Rindge NH & WHIPPIE Della of Rindge NH int 8 Sep 1958 by H Frederick Brown of Jamaica Plain MA

KNOTTS J Franklin of Boston MA & TITUS Mary Julia of W Medford MA int 1 Aug 1947 by LEWIS O Hartman of Boston MA

KNOWLES Royce Adin of Binham ME & SNELL Roberta Helen of Skowhegan ME int 30 Jun 1953 by SNELL Charles Jerold of Manchester MA

KNUDTON Edwin H of Rutherford NJ & HUCKINS Josephine of Plymouth NH int 12 Jun 1930 by CHRISTIAN W Knudten of Chicago IL

KOCH Henry John Jr of New York & GRAVES Robin McGregor of Concord NH int 19 Jul 1941 by COLLINS Patrick of Newton MA

KOEHLER Richard L of Duxbury MA & STURGEON Beulah M of Stoneham MA int 2 Aug 1954 by PIKE Carroll M of Melrose MA

KOHN Eugene of Omaha NB & GREENBERG Judith of Omaha NB int 20 Feb 1959 by JULIUS Kravetz of New York NY

KOLF Thomas of Dorchester MA & GIREN Pauline of Berlin NH int 7 Sep 1956 by MURPHY Thomas F of Tewksbury MA

KOLLIGIAN Haig Charles of W Haven CT & LITTLE Reta Mary of Errol NH int 25 Jul 1947 by ROBERT Haldane of Madison ME

KOLODNEY William of W Hartford CT & STARR Ellen of W Hartford CT int 14 Jul 1955 by SPEERS Theodore C of New York NY

KOLODZIEJ Ted of Manchester NH & OSBORNE Mary of Pittsfield NH int 1 Jul 1957 by PENN Bruce E of Whitehouse NJ

KRAMER Howard Gray of Ossipee NH & SMITH Ruth Frances of Ossipee NH int 26 Aug 1940 by J Gordon Carey of Roslindale MA

KRAUSE George Russell of Barnstead NH & AYER Emelyn Florence of Sherburne NY int 25 Feb 1945 by ROUNDY Rodney of Portland ME

KRAUSE James of Winchester NH & THOMPSON Evelyn of Winchester NH int 20 Jun 1940 by GEORGE Truman Carl of Chicago IL

KRUGER Charles of Carlisle PA & YANEZ Carmen Milda of Manchester NH int 4 Aug 1953 by LINCKS Howard J of Roslindale MA

KRUSIEWESKI Alexander of Winchester NH & SOLASZ Rose Victoria of Winchester NH int 18 May 1926 by TETAU Valentine of Springfield MA

KRVEMER Richard J of Fort Wayne IN & MILLS Patricia of Cape Eliz ME int 15 Nov 1957 by McNEIL Nichols J of Portland ME

KRZYWICKI Bronislaw of Lawrence MA & KMIEC Irene of Salem NH int 1 Sep 1949 by JOHN F Kasprzyoki of Lawrence MA

KUISISTO Allan Andrew of Durham NH & MARSH Evelyn Josephine of Laconia NH int 17 Jul 1951 by ANTTI Oskar Knnuusisby of Peabody MA

KUJANPAA Arthur of Fitchburg MA & MAKI Edna of Fitchbury MA int 5 Sep 1942 by ANDREW Groop of Fitchburg MA

KULPA John Joseph of E Hartford CT & KAESER Louise Mae of W Hartford CT int 16 Jun 1950 by WALLACE G Fiske of W Hartford CT

KUNYEON Ernest M of Newport RI & BARE Horince W of Newport RI int 17 Aug 1942 by CARL Brenton Bare of Newport RI

L'HEUREUX Chanel Joseph of Lawrence MA & DIONNE Agnes Dorothy of Nashua NH int 1 Jun 1948 by FR Forestier of Chelsea MA

LABER Alfred W of Newport NH & HODGES Evelyn Miriam of Greenland NH int 21 Apr 1953 by NICKERSON Ivan L of Springfield MA

LABRANCHE George M L of New York NY & MUNRO Kathleen Patricia of Wolfeboro NH int 15 Aug 1949 by NOBLE Charles C of Syracuse NY

LABRANCHE Raymond of Newmarket NH & CONNOR Jeannette Edith of Newmarket NH int 14 Aug 1958 by W D Connor of CAN

LABRIE Arthur of Nashua NH & MAYNARD Doris of Nashua NH int 19 Oct 1950 by PERE Gerard Labrie of Montreal CAN

LABRIE Francis of Manchester NH & BESSE Ruth Lillian of Londonderry NH int 8 Jul 1952 by BESSE Jos of Warwick RI

LACKEY Phillip of Winchester NH & MINER Dorothy of Winchester NH int 25 Jul 1939 by IVER M Johnson of Winchester NH

LAFRANCE Arthur of Manchester NH & BENNERT Susan E of Manchester NH int 23 Jun 1960 by DONALD E Bossart of Amherst MA

LAFRANCE Robert of Berlin NH & FILLION Therese of Berlin NH int 22 May 1959 by NORMAND A Fillion of Lowell MA

LAGASSE Richard of Sandown NH & STOREY Edith M of Sandown NH int 1 Aug 1948 by SULLIVAN James L of Dorchester MA

LAHEY Wilfred E of Weare NH & DREWRY Ruth I of Weare NH int 27 May 1939 by OLIVER M Frazer of Worcester MA

LAKIN Seymour of Roxbury MA & AUERBACH Edith of Franklin NH int 4 Feb 1943 by LEWITTES Rabbi Wendell of Dorchester MA

LAMMERT Martin of Saint Louis MO & THOMPSON Alice Cornelia of Concord NH int 26 Apr 1948 by FORD Geo M of New York NY

LAMPHIER Edward Andrew of Dorchester MA & AHERN Elizabeth Ann of Concord NH int 29 Jul 1953 by ROBERT L Ahern of Pittsfield MA

LAMPREY Philip of Lowell MA & STONA Diane of So Berwick ME int 24 Jun 1959 by JOHN S Bankosky of W Barnstable MA

LAMPRON Shirly W of Loudon NH & TIBBETTS Ester Elaine of Loudon NH int 21 May 1956 by TIBBETTS Benjamin D of Waterville ME

LAMSON Herbert Day of Exeter NH & SUMMERFIELD Rosalie A of Phil PA int 5 Aug 1926 by ARTHUR C Baldwin of Phil PA

LANDAU Irving I of Windham NH & COHEN Lena of Boston MA int 11 Nov 1943 by BENJAMIN L Grossman of Roxbury MA

LANDINI Urban Titus of Somerville MA & THOMPSON Charlotte Anne of Claremont NH int 5 Jun 1951 by DAVID R Covell Jr of Cleveland OH

LANDRY Albert of Somersworth NH & FORTIER Irene of Somersworth int 7 Jul 1931 by EDWARD Laliberte of Sherbrooke Province of Quebec CAN

LANDRY Richard Earl of Nashua NH & RENAULT Lorraine Ann of Nashua NH int 21 Oct 1957 by RENAUD Oliver J of Natick MA

LANE Caryl L of E Swanzey NH & BROWN Nancy of Keene NH int 6 Sep 1960 by LEWIS William W of ?

LANE Edward J Jr of Taunton MA & RAWSON Patricia of Intervale NJ int 7 Aug 1947 by SIBLE H Norman of New York NY

LANE Robert D of Boston MA & NICHOLS Nadene of Brookline MA int 10 Dec 1946 by PARK Charles E of Boston MA

LANE Wendell E of Anchorage AK & CHAMPAGNE Rita T of Manchester NH int 14 Jun 1957 by EDWARD Desilets of CAN

LANE William Kenneth of Keene NH & DODDS Betsy of Keene NH int 21 Jun 1951 by PREWITT C R of New Rochelle NY

LANG Hallett Churchill of Boston MA & KUNHARDT Rosemary Joan of Francestown NH int 24 Aug 1948 by NOMAN D Goehring of Milton MA

LANGDELL Merritt R of Manchester NH & EASTMAN Lena H of Manchester NH int 12 Sep 1927 by MILFORD R Foshay of Lynn MA

LANGELIER Robert Armand of Auburn ME & NADEAU Carmen Marie of Manchester NH int 4 Aug 1952 by PEPIN Napoleon of Sherbrook CAN

LANSEY Jean of Manchester NH & CLEMENT Juliette of Manchester NH int 28 Jun 1935 by PAUL Lacroix of CAN
LAPLANTE Ralph of Keene NH & SHINE Carmen of Keene NH int 13 May 1957 by RENE J L of Washington DC
LAPOINTE Alphonse of Somersworth NH & FORTIER Jeannette of Somersworth NH int 17 May 1953 by VACHON Claude of Natick MA
LARMON Russell Raymond of ? & JOHNSON Katharine G of ? int 16 Nov 1938 by ARCHIBALD Black of Montclair NJ
LAROCHE Joseph of Manchester NH & LEMIRE Lorraine R of Manchester NH int 8 May 1952 by PAUL E Marquis of Lowell MA
LAROSA Richard Domenic of Colliers W VA & BELANGER Elaine of Nashua NH int 7 Nov 1959 by WILFRID Belanger of Lowell MA
LARSEN Harry Richard of Boston MA & BARROWS Julia of Atkinson NH int 16 May 1956 by SWANSON Theodore N of W Roxbury MA
LARTER Edward Alan of Lowell MA & OLNEY Margaret Lucia of Lowell MA int 7 Jul 1930 by PENNEY Hugh of Lowell MA
LASKARIS Nicholas of Strafford NH & KARAHELAS Mary of Dover NH int 20 Jul 1938 by KALAPOIHAKI John of Boston MA
LASKEY George D Jr of Newton NH & FOWLER Audrey of Amesbury MA int 22 Dec 1960 by GUY M Judkins of Palmer MA
LASTINE James L of Bridgeport CT & CASSILY Miriam of Dover NH int 9 Sep 1959 by L Jermome Lastine of MD
LATVA Paul Edwin of Wendell NH & BAXTER Joan of Newport NH int 17 Sep 1948 by ALFRED J N Henriksen of Augusta ME
LAURIN Sven A of Amesbury MA & CRONK Gertrude M of Salem NH int 15 Jul 1948 by QUIMBY Herbert F of Jamaica Plain MA
LAVERDUE Elphege of Nashua NH & DESROSIERS Rose Aimee of Nashua NH int 17 Jun 1929 by LAVERDUE Gilbert of Montreal CA
LAVERY Donald Francis of Manchester NH & AREL Louise Lucille of Manchester NH int 24 Aug 1956 by PEPIN Napoleon of Sherbrooke CAN
LAWLOR Charles Francis of Bellows Falls VT & POWERS Catherine E of No Walpole NH int 20 Jun 1946 by LAWLOR Brendan of Hubertus WI
LAWRENCE Raymond W Dr of Staten Island NY & BATCHELDER Helen L of Landon NH int 14 Apr 1949 by READ Alden A of Newport RI
LAWSON Alexander S of New Hyde Park NY & TIPPING Evelyn Dorothy of Claremont NH int 25 Jul 1947 by SCANBLER S A of E Corinth VT

LAWSON Charles Judson Jr of Newton MA & HUBBARD Joan of Nashua NH int 16 Jun 1942 by RAY A Eusden of Newton MA

LAZARIO Roland of Keene NH & SHINE Valeria of Keene NH int 14 Sep 1955 by RENE Launce of Lewiston ME

LEACH Arthur David of Litchfield NH & HOPWOOD Marjorie Shirly of Nashua NH int 11 Mar 1953 by GEORGE H Driver of Marblehead MA

LEAVER Eugene of Newport NH & FAIRBANKS Jeanne of Newport NH int 2 Oct 1945 by WIETING Gilbert W of Lawrence MA

LEAVITT Edmund F of Manchester NH & BOISVERT Dori T of Manchester NH int 6 Sep 1952 by RICHARD Ferdinard R of Natick MA

LEAVITT Russell H of Concord NH & MERRILL Edith W of Deland FL int 15 Jun 1948 by GEORGE B Dean of New Hampton NH

LEBLANC Paul A of Manchester NH & LANOIE Doris D of Manchester NH int 1 Feb 1957 by MARQUIS Paul E of Lowell MA

LEBLANC Alire of Derry NH & BRUNELLE Lorraine of Derry NH int 2 Sep 1948 by LEPOLD Burnelle of Cambridge MA

LEBRUN Paul of Manchester NH & DUPONT Lucille of Manchester NH int 15 Feb 1960 by GEORGE Dupont of Lowell MA

LECOMPTE Roger Edward of Concord NH & LANDRY Louise Marie of Concord NH int 25 Jul 1958 by LANDRY Leo P of Pittsfield MA

LECROIX Edmond R of Berlin NH & LAVIGNE Olive Helen of Berlin NH int 29 Jul 1954 by LAVIGNE Sabin of St John CAN

LEDDY John S of Epping NH & McKNIGHT Loretta H of Epping NH int 30 Aug 1948 by JOHN B E Dion of Haverhill MA

LEE Robert Edward of Jamaica Plains MA & KNOX Mildred Alice of Concord NH int 25 Aug 1939 by KNOX Fred R of Chester VT

LEFEFVRE Yolande of Manchester NH & NICKNAIR Jean Louise of Eagle Lake ME int 29 Jun 1960 by NICKNAIR Donald L of Washington DC

LEHOULLIER Alphee A of Portsmouth NH & RIVAIS Laura M of Portsmouth NH int 19 Jul 1932 by LeHOUILLIER Alban of So Natick MA

LEHOULLIER Raymond of Somersworth NH & FORTIER Lucie of Dover NH int 2 Oct 1944 by LeHOUILLIER Alban of Natick MA

LELAND Hollis L of Columbus OH & EMERSON Rosamond of Durham NH int 19 Jul 1937 by HARLIN M Campbell of Bellow Falls VT

LEMAN Russell J of Salem MA & HAYDEN Gertrude M of Lynn MA int 8 Jul 1930 by JEFFRAS Charles W of Melrose MA

LEMAY Adrien of Manchester NH & PAQUETTE Marie Jeanne of Manchester NH int 14 Mar 1953 by MAURICE Desfasses of CAN

LEMAY Bernard M of Los Angeles CA & PARADES Jacqueline of Manchester NH int 12 Jul 1947 by LeMAY Lionel of Attleboro MA

LEMAY Gabriel J of Hartford CT & VALLIERIES Adrienne of Manchester NH int 10 Mar 1945 by VALLIERIES Jean Joseph of Lowell MA

LEMAY Guy L of Manchester NH & CARPENTIER Martha A of Manchester NH int 11 Dec 1936 by LeMAY Lionel of Attleboro MA

LEMAY Paul of Manchester NH & BEAUDET Cecile of Manchester NH int 23 Oct 1945 by GERARD Beaudet of Quebec CAN

LEMAY Romeo R of Manchester NH & POIRIER Gertrude of Manchester int 8 Aug 1958 by LeMAY Lionel of Attleboro MA

LEMIEUX Joseph Alfred of Berlin NH & DELISLE Marie Germaine of Berlin NH int 15 Jul 1946 by LEMIEUX Arthur E of Attleboro MA

LEMIEUX Roger of Manchester NH & DUPONT Marcelle of Manchester NH int 28 Jan 1957 by DUPONT George of Lowell MA

LEMIRE Charles R of Manchester NH & LISOTTE Claire of Manchester NH int 16 Nov 1951 by MARQUIS Paul E of Lowell MA

LEMIRE Rene G of Manchester NH & BRAGG Joan E of Manchester NH int 15 Nov 1956 by MARQUES Paul E of Lowell MA

LENZ Ernest O of Manchester NH & CRAWFORD Thelma of Hookset NH int 7 Nov 1941 by BICKET Willard of Ctr Lovell ME

LEONARD Frank Gerald of Dedham MA & ANNIS Teresa Marguete of Dover NH int 6 May 1927 by WITTEMORE Francis Lee of Dedham MA

LEONARD John Dillon of New York NY & MORISON Beningna of Dobbs Ferry NY int 20 May 1959 by PARK Chas E of Boston MA

LEONARD William J of Nashua NH & MORGAN Alice K of Nashua NH int 17 Jul 1947 by SCANLON Francis W of Holyoke MA

LEONARDI Howard of Nashua NH & O'NEIL Eileen of Nashua NH int 7 Jun 1941 by T F Curry O'Neil of Lowell MA

LEONE Ralph Huston of Sunapee NH & MILLER Hope Johnson of Sunapee NH int 23 Jul 1949 by ADAMS Sydney of Auburndale MA

LEPPER Richard W of Morrisville VT & STONE Carolyn M of Exeter NH int 10 Jun 1947 by SMITH Charles W F of Wellesley MA

LERASSEUR Oliver Pierre of Hooksett NH & JANELLE Marie Anne of Manchester NH int 9 Jan 1947 by EITENNE M Janelle of Three Rivers CAN

LESLIE George Evans Jr of So Hampton NH & HOLMSTROM Janice Hope of So Hampton NH int 20 Aug 1951 by SAWYER Roland D of Ware MA

LESLIE William Seaton of Amesbury MA & BROCK Joanne Elizabeth of Hopkinton NH int 3 Sep 1958 by KEECH William T of Acton MA

LESSLIE Gordon G of Boston MA & MAHMOT Maxine of Concord NH int 4 Jun 1959 by ARTHUR W Lesslie of Middletown CT

LEVASSEUR Donald of Manchester NH & BELASKI Helen of Manchester NH int 21 Aug 1957 by GILLE J Boily of CAN

LEVESQUE Joseph Alfred of So Hampton NH & DIXON Nancy Priscilla of So Hampton NH int 19 Mar 1954 by LUDEKING Charles W of Amesbury MA

LEVESQUE Raymond of Nashua NH & BEAULIEU Madeleine of Nashua NH int 10 Mar 1948 by FRANCOIS R Boudreau of Manville RI

LEVET William B of Bronaville NY & SMITH Margaretta A of Deering NH int 26 Aug 1932 by BEAVEN Albert W of Rochester NY

LEVY Norman of Boston MA & McLAUGHLIN Barbara of Manchester NH int 29 Jun 1956 by LEON M Adkins of Nashville TN

LEWANDOWSKI William of Derry NH & SENTER Patricia of Derry NH int 24 Jul 1948 by CHARLES S Johnson of Baltic CT

LEWIS David Ray of Scotia NY & WALTER Frances of Campton NH int 27 May 1958 by LEWIS A Ray of Scotia NY

LEWIS Myron Richardson of Littleton NH & TINKER Janet Dunbar of Wolfboro NH int 5 Jul 1955 by THOMPSON Frederick of Portland ME

LEYSON Robert Allan of Lynn MA & WEELER Shirley of Exeter NH int 16 Oct 1958 by SCHWARZCHILD S of Lynn MA

LIBBY Owen Harold of Alstead NH & HARRINGTON Ruth E of Alstead NH int 10 Jul 1950 by HERBERT R Houghton Jr of Deerfield MA

LIBBY Rufus A of No Hampton NH & MUDGETT Flora E of Ctr Sandwich NH int 12 Jun 1928 by TRACY Olin B of Skowhegan ME

LIDSTONE Ralph L of Rollingford VT & DAVIS Mildred C of Walpole NH int 3 Jun 1931 by OLA R Houghton of Wallingfort VT

LIGHT Howard Amos of Claremont NH & CARRIEL Loraine M of Claremont NH int 14 Nov 1940 by McCOLLESTER Lee S of Tufts College MA

LIGHTNER Cass of ? & GRIGGS Cornelia Preston of ? int 8 Jul 1943 by LATHROP John H of Windsor VT

LINDENLAUB John of Cambridge MA & HART Deborah of Wolfeboro NH int 16 Aug 1957 by CHALMERS Coe of Hartford CT

LINDERHOLM Bruck Edgar of Blegrade MN & FISHER Muriel Elliot of Manchester NH int 11 May 1948 by J Edward Elliot of Stockbridge MA

LINDI Walter J of W Hartford CT & DODSON Beatrice E of Hartford CT int 24 Jul 1950 by PARKER Fletcher of Hartford CT

LINEHAN Jerome Ignatius of Pride Crossing MA & MULLEN Mary Sexton of Concord NH int 7 Jan 1942 by LINEHAN Daniel of Weston MA

LINTS Donald of Quincy MA & PILLSBURY Virginia of Derry NH int 5 Feb 1954 by PILLSBURY Leonard H of Melrose MA

LIQUE Philip Anthony of White River Jct VT & LEE Miriam Isabelle of W Lebanon NH int 4 Aug 1960 by LEONARD J Gaspie of So Lancaster MA

LITTLE Gardner C of Newburyport MA & MERCIER Georgiana of Haverhill MA int 21 Aug 1937 by JUS D Hull of Haverhill MA

LITTLEFIELD Joseph D of Penacook NH & ANDRESEN Elsie F of Boscawen NH int 8 Jun 1946 by EDWIN P Anderson of Providence RI

LOCHMAN Wilson D of Waltham MA & WRIGHT Miriam O of Waltham MA int 8 Dec 1949 by ERNEST A Brown Jr of Waltham MA

LOCKE Edward A Jr of Boston MA & STRATTON Mildred Y of Nashua NH int 15 Jun 1935 by A J Archibald of West Somerville MA

LOCKE Robert S of Pittsfield NH & DUDLEY Sylvia of Gilmanton NH int 29 Sep 1958 by OSBORN Donald L of Randolph VT

LOHNES Maurice W of Portsmouth NH & CLEARY Ruth Jail of Portsmouth NH int 18 Mar 1948 by WILSON H J of Wilmington NC

LOMBARD Everett Fisher of Epsom NH & HAGGETT Hazel Ethel of Pembroke NH int 19 Oct 1940 by SAMBORN Arthayer Jr of Woodville MA

LOOMIS Robert Forbush of Antrim NH & HALE Helen of Antrim NH int 10 Oct 1946 by HERBERT Hitchen of W Newton MA

LOONIS Russell of Hydenville MA & SULLY Katherine of Berlin NH int 28 Jun 1951 by WHIPPLE L Bryon of N Hampton MA

LORD Francis Edmond of Manchester NH & BOURASSA Jeanne of Manchester NH int 17 Nov 1947 by LEMIEUX Arthur E of Attleboro MA

LORD George T of Cambridge MA & HESSER Gladys of Manchester NH int 3 Oct 1929 by THOMAS Chalmers of Boston MA

LOTHROP James H of W Hartford CT & ROWELL Virginia of Newport NH int 19 May 1958 by CLARK Clarence of York ME

LOTTER Leroy William of Mt Vernon NY & HOLMAN Arline Nellie of Mt Vernon NY int 13 Jun 1932 by CHASE Loring of Rumford RI

LOVE Lawrence R of Hanover NH & BUTMAN Dorothy of Orford NH int 15 May 1937 by CHARLES F Atkins of Fairlee VT

LOVELOCK Michael of Springfield VT & PRAKATAINA Olga Adeline of Keene NH int 7 Nov 1946 by FEDETZ Nich of Springfield VT

LOVERING Ernest Jr of Boston MA & HOLT Elizabeth Cabot of Dublin NH int 15 Jun 1937 by JAMES Edgar Gregg of Waterbury CT

LOWTHERS William of Stoneham MA & BAYEK Diane of Plaistow NH int 19 May 1959 by RICHARD T Coughlin of Stoneham MA

LOZEAN Edgar of Nashua NH & BEAUDET Rachel of Nashua NH int 30 Apr 1936 by G E Bergeron of Haverhill MA

LOZOWSKI Walter of Claremont NH & STAPLETON Katherine of N Walpole NH int 3 Oct 1950 by ORZECH Paul of W Rutland VT

LUCAS Donald Harold of Guppey WV & WILSON Gayle Pamelia of Dexter ME int 16 Aug 1960 by BENSON Howard E of Kittery ME

LUCE Wesley Downs of Riverhead Long Island NY & SPENCE Elizabeth M of Nashua NH int 24 Jun 1946 by TERRELLE B Crum of Edgewood RI

LUDEMANN Henry A Lt of Katonah NY & MICHEL Irene of Rochester NH int 8 Jan 1952 by EMILE A Brochu of New York NY

LUFKIN Chauncey Forbush of Rye NY & HEARD Elizabeth of Manchester NH int 30 Jun 1953 by STEPHEN T Crary of Northhampton MA

LULFKIN Harold of Acworth NH & BURNHAM Shirley Marie of Alstead NH int 27 May 1946 by HERBERT R Houghton Jr of Troy NY

LULL Clifton of ? & GRAY Mrs of Grafton NH? int 21 Jul 1948 by HAROLD W Buker of Lynn MA

LUND Bartlett of Lancaster NH & CARRIEL Shirley of Claremont NH int 14 Jul 1944 by JOHN P Garfield of Taunton MA

LUND Forest Colburn Jr of E Hartford CT & SMITH Ellen Marie of Wolfeboro NH int 31 Oct 1956 by HARVEY O Carter of Lynn MA

LUND Ralph Arnold of Watertown CT & LUND Ruth Almida of Lancaster NH int 3 Feb 1945 by JOHN W Haynes of Pawtucket RI

LUSSIER Maurice G of Manchester NH & BILODEAU Madeleine S of Manchester NH int 20 Jun 1955 by BILODEAU Geo M of CAN

LYNCH Edward Joseph Jr of Freeport Long Isl NY & HALLIGAN Ann Pauline of Concord NH int 9 Feb 1959 by JOHN P Halligan of Chicago IL

LYONNAIS Paule Eugene of Manchester NH & ROWELL Jean Emily of Manchester NH int 4 Aug 1953 by LYONNAIES Emery of Lowell MA

MAAZ Francis of Nashua NH & GLIDDEN Marguerite of Nashua NH int 25 Aug 1947 by ROCK Paul M of Malden MA

MAC Michael Grant A of Boston MA & WILCOX Ruth C of Boston MA int 3 Jun 1938 by FRANK G Hagemann of Westwood MA

MACCORMAC Harry H of E Wakefield NH & WALLEY Doris A of Farmington NH int 4 May 1960 by POTTER Lenwood of Dennis MA

MACDONALD Donald of Manchester NH & HUNKINS Charlotte of Auburn MA int 19 Apr 1937 by MAY Edred of Leominster MA

MACDONALD Donald of Towanda PA & GILBERT Rita of Philadelphia PA int 22 Jun 1931 by HERBERT E Benton of Philadelphia PA

MACDONALD Gordon Warren of Candia NH & MALONEY Alice Mary of Candia NH int 5 May 1948 by JACKSON Samuel A of Boston MA

MACDONALD Mendon of Manchester NH & BROWN Elizabeth Cheney of Ashland NH int 16 Jun 1953 by SPEERS Theodore C of New York NY

MACDONALD Walter Grant of Watertown MA & NASON Eleanor of Bradford MA int 14 Sep 1927 by CLARK T Brownell of Haverhill MA

MACEK Victor of Manchester NH & BETLEY Phylis of Manchester NH int 17 Sep 1947 by MACEK Joseph of Phonenixville PA

MACEY Richmond of Concord NH & GRENIER Diane of Concord NH int 2 Jan 1952 by JOSEPH J Deschesnes of Fitchburg MA

MACINTOSH Gordon Wm of Stamford CT & PRUGH Beverly Dallas of Goffstown NH int 21 Dec 1956 by CLAPP Theodore L of W Newton MA

MACK Alexander Cpt of Rutland VT & ITRAIN Jean of Manchester NH int 16 May 1927 by MARSHALL Stephen of Boston MA

MACK Harold of Ayer MA & HARRIS Kathleen of Fitchburg MA int 18 Aug 1949 by ROBERT E Baggs of Watertown MA

MACKAY Ora Robert of Malden MA & DeFORREST Eunice of Dedham MA int 7 Oct 1932 by RANDALL Ulysses S of Everett MA

MACKERRON A Allan of Dedham MA & LOMBARD Valerie of Keene NH int 22 Aug 1944 by WILLIAMS Ralph W of Dedham MA

MACKIC George Albert of Newburyport MA & STEVENS Florence May of Union NH int 22 Apr 1946 by STANLEY E Anderson of Newburyport MA

MACLEE William of Exeter NH & MASON Dorothy of Epping NH int 24 Aug 1933 by SIMPSON James C of Watertown MA

MACMURDO James of Cleveland OH & WILKINSON Lily of Manchester NH int 15 Sep 1932 by JOSEPH Atkinson of Boston MA

MACPHERSON Wallace C of Claremont NH & PATTEN Jeanet of Claremont NH int 10 Apr 1953 by MacPHERSON Robert of Dorchester MA

MACUKEWICZ Francis E of Hillsboro NH & CODY Priscilla Ann of Hillsboro NH int 1 Feb 1956 by JOSEPH Feeley of Dedham MA

MACWILLIAMS Robert Geo of Waltham MA & HORNEBECK Elizabeth of Waltham MA int 23 May 1941 by WALKER Edgar R of Waltham MA

MADDIX Forrest N Jr of Brookline MA & HARRINGTON Lois Eleanor of Natick MA int 18 Jul 1946 by FREDERICK W Alden of Natick MA

MADOR Eusebe of Pittsburg NH & PAQUETTE Suzanne of Pittsburg NH int 11 Jun 1958 by ALBERT Drouin of CAN

MAGANSON Joseph of Wilton NH & ABBOTT Marjorie of Wilton NH int 27 Jun 1948 by A Harold Dale of Billerica MA

MAGEE Mr of Fitchburg MA & HOWES Barbara of Fitchburg MA int 3 Aug 1921 by ARTHUR Hopkinson of Fitchburg MA

MAGUNSON George A of Exeter NH & HAZEN Pauline E of Exeter NH int 23 Sep 1939 by CHARLES W Frye of Amesbury MA

MAHAR Harold of Colebrook NH & HANSELL Blanche of Colebrook NH int 30 Sep 1940 by CHANDLER Alex L of Sandwich MA

MAHONEY David Wm of Bridgewater CT & LAMY Constance M of Manchester NH int 8 Oct 1957 by LAMY Roland M of Leborgne Haiti

MAHONEY William of Portland ME & LUCAS Ellen of Portsmouth NH int 20 May 1954 by JOSEPH E Houlilian of Portland ME

MAILLOUX Diadonne of New Bedford MA & BROUILLETTE Aurore P of Manchester NH int 12 Dec 1933 by MAILLOUX Paul of La Patril CAN

MAIN Frederick Hall of Holyoke MA & KNOX Margaret Faxton of NY City NH int 10 Aug 1948 by LOVETE Sidney of New Haven CT

MAIN James W of Groveton NH & DEARBORN Mary of Woodsvile NH int 20 Jun 1938 by NICKERSON E H of Groton VT

MAJOR Armand J of Manchester NH & JULIEN Pauline of Manchester NH int 15 Jul 1950 by EUGENE Dion of New Bedford MA

MALCOLMSON John of Brookline MA & BENNETT Mary of Dover NH int 22 Apr 1958 by SHAUB Robert C of Clinton MA

MALENFANT Donald R of Nashua NH & CLAVEAU Rita G of Nashua NH int 9 Dec 1955 by PARADIS Robert M of Lowell MA

MALLARY Raymond Dewitt of Bradfort VT & PIERCE Grace Evelyn of Brooklyn NY int 16 Apr 1947 by PIERCE Gordon D of Brooklyn NY

MALLOY James Anthony of Brookline MA & CHRISTENSEN Carol Joan of Rye NH int 9 Jun 1958 by MADISON James F of Annapolis MD

MALONE Harold John of New Britain CT & ROBINSON Beverly Helen of Loudon NH int 20 Jun 1950 by BERNARD D Killeen of Hartford CT

MANNA Salvatore of No Hanover MA & BACON Shirley Alice of Jefferson NH int 21 Jun 1950 by HAROLD M Frye of St Johnsbury VT

MANNING Francis of Manchester NH & CALLAHAN Rita G of Manchester NH int 11 Apr 1949 by KIERCE Jos of Dorchester MA

MANSEAU Henry Leon of Gardner MA & COLEMAN Dorothy A of Londonderry NH int 20 Aug 1956 by JAMES A Benson of Weston MA

MANSELL Richard L of Stoddard NH & MURDOCK Jean E of Alstead NH int 10 Oct 1953 by STETSON Clifford R of Springfield VT

MANSFIELD James Scott of New York NY & LAWTON Sarah Corneilia of Plainfield NJ int 12 Jul 1937 by PARK Charles E of Peterboro NH

MANTER George Ducan of Worcester MA & DEARBORN Katherine F of Greenland NH int 28 May 1940 by MANTER John G of Upton ME

MARCEAU Joseph Donald of Pawtucket RI & WILLETT Violet Louise of Lincoln NH int 28 May 1949 by ROSAIRE Croteau of Lincoln NH

MARCHAND Donald P of Manchester NH & LAMARRE Doris Ann of Manchester NH int 5 Nov 1953 by THERRIEN Jean Maurice of Montreal CAN

MARCHAUD Charles of Cambridge MA & O'CONNELL Mary D of Cambridge MA int 10 Jun 1957 by LYNCH Daniel G of Boston MA

MARCHEWKI Edward Paul of Lebanon NH & MORIN Lucille Marie of W Lebanon NH int 17 Jul 1958 by O'BREADY Maurice of Sherbrooke CAN

MARCOTTE Onil J of Berlin NH & PERRON Marie Anne of Berlin NH int 16 Jul 1956 by MARCOTTE Huber of Saskatchewan CAN

MARCOUX Lawetta of Nashua NH & VAILLANCOURT Adrian of Nashua NH int 21 Nov 1944 by VACHON Gerard of Alexandria Bay NY

MARCOUX Noel of Nashua NH & PELLETIER Lorette of Nashua NH int 28 Aug 1950 by CARL J Heon of Franklin PA

MARDEN Ralph C of Reading MA & HINDON Constance of Reading MA int 3 Mar 1937 by MURPHY William T of Reading MA

MARDIGIAM Gilberte of Manchester NH & BOGHOSIAM Antranig of Concord NH int 26 Jun 1953 by CAREN Gdanian of Lowell MA

MARK Bernard F of Hampton Falls NH & BLATCHFORD Gertrude E of Hampton NH int 18 Mar 1939 by WEYMOUTH Donald B of Clinton MA

MARLATT John W of Amherst NH & SPILLMAN Janet of Amherst NH int 30 Jul 1954 by GORDON J Kirk of Somerville MA

MARQUIS Felix of Nashua NH & KIRKORIAN Evelyn M of Nashua NH int 27 Sep 1954 by LEONARD Boucher of Lowell MA

MARQUIS Leo of Nashua NH & BELANGER Edith of Nashua NH int 10 May 1943 by WILFRID Belanger of Lowell MA

MARRO Albert Carmine of Claremont NH & SAMSON Alberta of Claremont NH int 6 Jun 1960 by PETER D Falco of Burlington VT

MARTEL Joseph Ernest of Manchester NH & SAINTPIERRE Marie Ida of Manchester NH int 30 Jun 1931 by StPIERRE Gustave of Manchester NH

MARTIN Joseph Timothy of Staten Island NY & TARIFF Denise Cecile of Berlin NH int 16 Aug 1957 by TARDIFF Arthur J of Plattsburg NY

MARTIN Leroy Harrison of Greenfield MA & NICHOLS Hazel Sheldon of Spofford NH int 21 Aug 1950 by PAUL H Chapman of Greenfield MA

MARTIN Paul H of Biddeford ME & CARON Camille of Manchester NH int 19 Jan 1957 by GERARD C Doyon of Waterville ME

MARTINE Lawrance of Wollaston MA & WEVER Dorothy of Portsmouth NH int 15 Aug 1944 by WEBSTER Arthur of Salem MA

MARTINEAU Victor of Manchester NH & ROUX Jeannette of Manchester NH int 2 Jul 1935 by EDWARD Desilts of Hyacinth CAN

MARX Arthur G of Langdon NH & SPURR Eleanor F of Clinton NY int 1 Aug 1959 by SARGENT Robert A of So Berwick ME

MARXTEN John Calvin of Salem NH & DICKEY Ruth Edna of Salem Depot NH int 29 Jul 1955 by MAGOON Earle Jr of Gray ME

MASON Don F of New York NY & MILLER Madelyn C of Brookline MA int 8 May 1931 by CHESTER H Howe of Lynn MA

MASON Robert of Attleboro MA & MacPHEE Louise of Sharon MA int 15 Apr 1960 by STRICKLAND Freeman of Andover MA

MATCHETT Wilbur J of Bedford NH & JENKINS Margaret of Bedford NH int 13 Feb 1937 by JAMES L Grazier of Cardiff MD

MATHER Cedric L of Jacksonville IL & FOSTER Phyllis E of Merrimack NH int 30 Apr 1942 by ALDEN Drew Kelley of New York NY

MATHER Eugene H of Brookline MA & PARKER Florence E of Boston MA int 7 Jun 1930 by HARRIS G Hale of Marblehead MA

MATHEY George R of Littleton NH & WEBB Sheila of Palm Beach FL int 19 Apr 1951 by TEISEN Tage of Palm Beach FL

MATTHEWS George of Methuen MA & TABBURSH Elizabeth of Haverhill MA int 18 Aug 1951 by SCHROG Oswald O of Haverhill MA

MATTIE Edward J of Unionville CT & GRIM Elizabeth Lewis of New Haven CT int 10 Jul 1942 by SCOTT Philip G of New Haven CT

MAXFIELD Leland L of Milton NH & BRONSON Elizabeth Z of Boston MA int 19 May 1938 by J Winfield Bronson of Brooklyn NY

MAXWELL Allen Bruce Jr of Boston MA & ADAMS Helen Frances of Exeter NH int 3 Sep 1947 by WYPE Gregory F of Patterson NJ

MAXWELL Joseph E of Wakefield MA & MAXWELL Annie R of Malden MA int 20 Jul 1934 by ALLEN W Clark of Brookline MA

MAXWELL Ralph of Concord NH & STREET Ellen E of Concord NH int 26 Aug 1936 by W N Gleason of Reading MA

MAXWELL William A of Winchester NH & COBURN Gwenith E of Winchester NH int 8 Jul 1960 by EDGAR Flory of New Preston CT

MAY Louis H of Brunswick ME & ATHERTON Emily G of Winchester NH int 8 Sep 1942 by GEORGE Truman Carl of Chicago IL

MAYNARAD Louis of Dover NH & CAYLE Mary of Somersworth NH int 2 Aug 1940 by MAYNARD Paul of S Natick MA

MAYNARD Lionel of Dover NH & KELLEY Eileen of Dover NH int 10 Jun 1940 by MAYNARD Paul of Natick ME

MAYO Lawrence Ralph of Littleton Co & O'HARA Gail of Lyme NH int 10 Aug 1960 by GEORGE O Ekwall of Waltham MA

MAYRAND Henry of Dover NH & BOURQUE Lorrain of Dover NH int 3 Nov 1941 by MAYRAND Stephen of Natick MA

MAZZEO Frank Anthony of Millbury MA & PREVOST Joan Volande of Keene NH int 21 Jul 1959 by NOLIN Joseph A of Attleboro MA

MCADAM Alan Hugh of Brighton MA & LACAILLADE Madeleine of Nashua NH int 13 Sep 1947 by EUGENE W Kierman of Brighton MA

MCADAMS Leon H Jr of Westminster MA & RICH Genera Arlene of Deering NH int 16 Jul 1940 by YEAPLE Whitney S K of Westminster MA

MCALLISTER John J of Manchester NH & NADEAU Yvette of Manchester NH int 1 May 1952 by PEPIN Napoleon of Sherbrooke CAN

MCCABE Bernard Joseph of Manchester NH & O'TOOLE Mary Ann of Manchester NH int 20 Jun 1941 by NEALON Thomas J of Fresno CA

MCCANDLES Robert of Cambridge MA & NAGLE Joanne of Bel mont MA int 27 May 1947 by ROSE Cecil H of Boston MA

MCCARATHY John Gratton of Brockton MA & FONTAINE Fleurette Z of Pembroke NH int 13 Feb 1946 by McCARATHY Dennis V of Randolph MA

MCCARTER Henry B of So Boston MA & DIONNE Jeanette of E Jaffrey NH int 1 Nov 1944 by McCARTER Frederick T of Boston MA

MCCARTHY John Thomas of Newton MA & COTE Lina of Manchester NH int 4 Apr 1945 by FRANCIS E Connors of No Chelmsford MA

MCCAULEY Harold J of Oreland PA & BASTON Alice S of Ardsley PA int 6 Jun 1958 by McCAULEY Arthur R of Hatsboro PA

MCCLARE William Henry of Portsmouth NH & KELLY Margaret Grace of Concord NH int 23 Jun 1954 by JAMES F Kelly of Ipswich MA

MCCLARY Louis Edward of Bellows Falls VT & PHEUR Anna Frances of N Walpole NH int 28 Mar 1946 by PHEUR William F of Clarks Summit PA

MCCLAY Earle Henry of Ctr Harbor NH & GRAMLING Benadette H of Ctr Harbor NH int 2 Sep 1948 by ALLAN K Chalmers of Newtonville MA

MCCORD William M of Pittsburg PA & COLBY Gladys Irene of Litchfield NH int 2 Dec 1946 by PRITCHARD Welbam M of Fairbury IL

MCCORMACK James of New Haven CT & McCORMACK Carol of Portsmouth NH int 25 May 1959 by McCORMACK Francis of Ashland VA

MCCORMACK Stewart Vernon of Milford NH & CARLISLE Marjorie C of Concord NH int 19 Aug 1940 by FREDERICK R Knox of Chester VT

MCDANIELS Donald Melvin of New Castle NH & AMAZEEN Tania Elsie of New Castle NH int 8 Sep 1960 by RAYMOND W Bowsen Jr of Lee MA

MCDONALD Raymond J of Watertown MA & McSHANE Ellen Jane of Waltham MA int 10 Aug 1953 by REDDEN John J of Huron MI

MCDOUGAL Bouton of Chicago IL & KURNER Winnifred L of Melrose MA int 8 Aug 1941 by FRED S Buschmeyer of Washington DC

MCFADEN Joseph Edward of W Hartford CT & SWEENEY Bertha May of E Jaffrey NH int 22 Apr 1933 by BRUCE W Cronmiller of So Hadley MA

MCFARLAND Richard of Framingham MA & MARCOTTE Mary Jane of Nahsua NH int 7 Jun 1956 by CORNELIUS F Kelly of Butler NJ

MCGARY Malcom C of Rindge MA & VERGURST Joanne Marie of Dedham MA int 21 Jun 1949 by JOSEPH Barth of Alva ME

MCGEGAR Robert G Jr of Washington DC & MARCY Conitana of Newton MA int 29 May 1939 by CHARLES M Crooks of Lexington MA

MCGILL Frederick T Jr of Newton MA & FREDERICK Virginia L of Boston MA int 1 Aug 1931 by ADELBERT L Hudson of Dorchester MA

MCGINLEY Bruce of Whitefield NH & BAILEY Barbara of Whitefield NH int 3 Jul 1957 by R S Cummings of Wallingford CT

MCGRATH John Alfred of Gloucester MA & JEWETT Isabel M of Concord NH int 28 Mar 1930 by JOHN R Copplestone of Amesbury MA

MCGRATH Marshall C of Rochester NH & PIKE Carolyn Estelle of Rochester NH int 31 May 1951 by WRIGHT George T of Encampment WY

MCKAY Ian H of N Chelsmford MA & STEWART Catherine of Chelmsford MA int 12 Dec 1935 by THOMAS Percy E of Lowell MA

MCKAY Ralph C of Pembroke NH & BAILEY Ruth of Hooksett NH int 14 May 1943 by WILLIAM F Ineson of Pembroke NH

MCKEE Richard Gray of W Chester VA & THOMAS Louise Gordon of Laconia NH int 6 Aug 1929 by McKEE William Thompson of W Chester VA

MCKEON Frank of New Haven CT & BRISSE Jeanne Adele of Laconia NH int 26 May 1948 by P A Brisse of Evansville IN

MCKINNEY William Lord of Manchester NH & PURGESS Victoria of Andover NH int 29 Oct 1925 by PATTERSON George T of Wollaston MA

MCLAUGHLIN Ralph of Pittsfield NH & HASELTINE Elizabeth H of Reeds Ferry NH int 17 Jun 1931 by LEON M Adkins of Delmar NY

MCLEAN Harold Clifton of Salem NH & DODGE Priscilla A of Candia NH int 23 Aug 1944 by HENRY J Chandler of Boston MA

MCLEOD Neil Roderick of Upper Montclair NJ & BONTHRON Mary Louise of Detroit MI int 2 Jul 1932 by H Montrimer Gesner Jr of E Orleans MA

MCLURE C George of Boltonville VT & LITTLE Patricia of Monroe NH int 24 Nov 1945 by WOODWORTH Arthur of McIndoe Falls VT

MCMASTER Harry of Kittanning PA & McELWAIN Annie of Kittanning PA int 21 Oct 1957 by WESLEY Dixon of Levittown PA

MCNALLY John Brown of Berlin NH & HANSCON Delorose Jean of Portsmouth NH int 18 Aug 1954 by MORRIS Thuman B of Warsaw IN

MCNAMARA Paul of W Lebanon NH & MAYRAND Madeline of Hanover NH int 6 Sep 1950 by MAYRAND Paul of Augusta ME

MCNARMA Richard of Suncook NH & SAINTJEAN Joan E of Suncook NH int 13 Nov 1953 by STAHL Roland of Storrs CT

MCNEILL Wright of Lebanon NH & ACKERMAN Ruth of Lebanon NH int 22 Sep 1927 by McCASKILL John J of Fort Kent ME

MCQUEENY Owen James of Manchester NH & BOISVERT Carmen Suzane of Manchester NH int 10 Apr 1957 by MARIANO Gagnon of Requena Peru

MCQUILLEN Maurice of Manchester NH & GLAVIN Catherine of Manchester NH int 15 Sep 1952 by O'LEARY D M of Brooklyn NY

MCQUILLEN Robert C of New Boston NH & SCRIBNER Priscilla Jean of Dublin NH int 25 Aug 1947 by BENJAMIN F Andrews of Columbus OH

MCWILLIAM Robert T of Garden City NY & HAZALTON Phyllis of Hanover NH int 20 Jun 1942 by LAWRENCE Hayward of Newburyport MA

MEADER Donald of Rochester NH & GRAY Elizabeth of Rochester NH int 6 Jul 1949 by REID Wilbur L of Windsor PA

MEADER Elwyn Marshall of Rochester N & PARK Virginia Alleson of Pittsfield NH int 11 Jul 1938 by SWETMAN John A of Norwick CT

MEAGHER James W of Hubbardston MA & WOOD Betty Jean of Templeton MA int 21 Jul 1954 by PAIGE Donald E of Gardner MA

MEEKER Norman of Somerville MA & RICE Mary of Malden MA int 27 Jul 1936 by WILLIAM H Duvall of Malden MA

MEFFERT William Frank of Wolfeboro NH & BRUCE Patricia Ann of Rochester NH int 17 Jun 1958 by WIEGAND Dudley of W Newbury MA

MERCER Paul of Nashua NH & BERRY Marjorie of Providence RI int 19 Jul 1949 by WRIGHT Donald of Providence RI

MERCER Paul Sands of Nashua NH & LUND Audrey G of Hollis NH int 6 Oct 1948 by WESTON A Cate of No Adams MA

MERRIFIELD Raymond of Newton NH & WILSON Vera L of Kingston NH int 27 May 1946 by WILSON William J of Jay NJ

MERRILL George F of Hampton Falls NH & LUDGATE Louise N of Bartlett NH int 5 Aug 1958 by SULYOK Kalm of W Barnet VT

MERRILL Robert B of Cleveland OH & LLOYD Cythia of Exeter NH int 12 Feb 1952 by RUTHREDGE Lyman V of Boston MA

MERRRILL Clarence W of Salem NH & SPENCER Helen Johnson of Salem N int 20 Sep 1948 by LAURIN Sven A of Amesbury MA

MESSIER Roland of Somersworth NH & TANGUAY Rachel of Somersworth NH int 4 Feb 1954 by TANGUAY Ovid of Biddeford ME

METHOT Frank D of Claremont NH & LOCH Elfriede of Claremont NH int 6 Aug 1952 by PHILIPPE Methot of Quebec Cty CAN

MEWING Stewart B of New York NY & YOUNG Helen Voorhees of Newport NH int 8 Jun 1945 by WAMSLEY Frederic of New Rochelle NY

MEYER Andrew Gill of Waltham MA & HASKELL Sarah Brockman of Farmington NH int 12 Jul 1955 by MYLES D Blanchard of W Carthage NY

MICHAUD Leo of Somersworth NH & BRETON Gracia E of Somersworth NH int 7 May 1954 by TANGUAY Ovid of Biddeford ME

MICHAUD Paul of Manchester NH & LAPIERRE Ruth of Manchester NH int 17 May 1948 by UBALD Clement of Montreal CAN

MICHNICEWICZ Steven of Bellows Falls VT & LINSDSTROM Mary E of No Walpole NH int 20 Apr 1950 by PHEUR William F of Bedford MA

MICHOLS Bruce of Dover NH & TRUE Eleanor Carol of Lee NH int 4 Oct 1955 by LESTER Holmes of Alfred ME

MILAM Arthur Wilson of Jacksonville FL & GUIDER Elizabeth of Littleton NH int 22 Sep 1953 by SHEEHY Maurice of Washington DC

MILES William J of Central Falls RI & STERNDALE Beverly of Kittery ME int 10 Jul 1952 by WILLIAMS Geo B of So Haven MI

MILLER Coleman of Marlboro MA & SAULL Leora of Woburn MA int 6 Feb 1930 by JOSEPH Atkinson of Boston MA

MILLER Fred H of Newport MA & LEWIS Jeannette of Sprinfield MA int 3 Aug 1933 by McCOLLESTER Lee S of Tufts College MA

MILLER George Franklin of Fitzwilliam NH & HANSON Pauline Isabel of Gilsum NH int 20 Mar 1942 by SMITH Henry F of Medford MA

MILLER John of Brattleboro VT & HUDSON Arvilla of Hinsdale NH int 15 Sep 1951 by CHARLES L Austin of Queens Village NY

MILLER Olivar Walker of Ludlow MA & BAYLISS Olive Ida of Cornish NH int 28 Jun 1938 by F P Daniels of Winsdor VT

MILLER Robert W of Kensington NH & BOWLIN Roberta A of Seabrook NH int 15 Jun 1942 by SAWYER Roland D of Ware MA

MILLER Ross James of Twin Falls Idaho & LEE Nancy Jean of Lancaster NH int 14 Feb 1958 by J Donald Hughes of Boston MA

MILLER William George of Bolton MA & HOKINS Dorothy Ina of Melrose MA int 22 Jul 1953 by CLARENCE W Fuller of Melrose MA

MILLIGAN Harold of New York NY & ROSEN Marjory Mount of New York NY int 13 Sep 1941 by A Edwin Keigioin of New York NY

MILSTONE Edward of Lawrence MA & KENNETH Rebecca of Lawrence MA int 4 Oct 1956 by TWERSKY Norman of Lawrence MA

MINER Paul Wesley of Fishkill NY & DORAN Sally of Bristol NH int 1 Feb 1947 by MINER F Theodore of Fishkill NY

MINOR Paul E of Keene NH & MELLON Audrey of Hillsboro NH int 18 Aug 1945 by FRANK A M Coad of Brockton MA

MITCHELL Alexander of Claremont NH & BERDECKI Mary of Claremont NH int 2 Sep 1937 by MATYSUK Demian A of New York NY

MITCHELL Bernard of Concord NH & GIBBS Lois of Lancaster NH int 4 Jun 1954 by J Evangeline Barney of Framingham MA

MITCHELL Jonathan N of Middletown OH & CHIDLEY Barbara of Winchester MA int 24 Jul 1940 by CHIDLEY Howard of Winchester MA

MITCHELL John F of Worcester MA & BLENDER Mary Evelyn of Worcester MA int 29 May 1940 by MORGAN Walter A of Worcester MA

MITCHELL Nathaniel of Boston MA & FISHER Edna of Malden MA int 26 Sep 1945 by MINICH Rob L of Malden MA

MITCHELL Ralph W of Keene NH & ROLLINS Natalie of Keene NH int 29 Jun 1948 by ROY W Battenhouse of Cambridge MA

MITHCHELL Samuel P of Danville VA & PETTIGREW Blanche E of Portsmouth NH int 26 Nov 1929 by ISAAC Higginbotham of Wollaston MA

MIVILLE Maurice G of Manchester NH & CARRIGAN Lillian of Manchester NH int 27 Jun 1945 by MIVILLE Luke of Manchester NH

MOFFAT Piermont of New York NY & GREW Litta Cabot of Manchester NH int 15 Jul 1927 by SLATTERY Charles L of New York NY

MOFFATT Charles of Fitchburg MA & WILDER Gertrude C of Fitchburg MA int 12 Apr 1929 by HENRY Rees Jones of Ashburnham MA

MOLLICA John J of Waltham MA & BROGAN Nancy Mary of Concord NH int 4 Apr 1960 by McDERMOTT James of Techmy IL

MONAHAN Thomas J of N Strafford NH & KINIRY Martha Ann of Lancaster NH int 25 May 1959 by McAULIFFE Wm J of Notre Dame IN

MONBLEAU David H of Malden MA & THOMPSON Sally of Henniker NH int 10 Aug 1951 by MONBLEAU Charles of Malden MA

MONTGOMERY Hugh of Boston MA & HOWLAND Esther of New Haven CT int 17 Jun 1930 by MONTGOMERY James A of Phil PA

MONTGOMERY Hugh of Portsmouth NH & HOPCRAFT Trever of Warner NH int 3 Dec 1934 by MONTGOMERY David of West Roxbury MA

MONTIGNY Robert E of Nashua NH & COTE Denise J of Nashua int 2 Jun 1955 by PARADIS Robert M of Lowell MA

MONTY Richard J of Alstead NH & BOSS Hermont A of Alstead NH int 21 Dec 1949 by SULLIVAN Joseph L of Hartford VT

MOODY Roger of Wolefeboro NH & HANEY Virginia of Ossipee NH int 6 Jul 1953 by SANBORN Arthayer of Woonsocket RI

MOONEY Robert of Concord NH & COTTON Nancy Jane of Laconia NH int 26 May 1958 by ROCHE Edmund J of Charlettown CAN

MOORE Arthur of Brookline MA & THOMAS Minnie of Somerville MA int 14 Aug 1929 by GEORGE Heath of Malden MA

MOORE Arthur Merrill of Hamilton MA & BROWN Sarah Witherell of So Hampton NH int 31 Dec 1946 by MURCHIE H John of Amesbury MA

MOORE Jon B of Madbury NH & WOODWARD Nancy of Dover NH int 20 Aug 1955 by LESTER C Holmes of Alfred ME

MOORE Kenneth Thomas of Middlebury VT & REYNOLDS Dorothy Elizah of Peterborough NH int 12 Aug 1953 by WALKER T Hawley of Middlebury VT

MORAN Leonard of Manchester NH & SCANNELL Margaret of Manchester NH int 13 Aug 1952 by SCANNELL Leonard of London Eng

MORELAND James of New London NH & LEWIS Margaret of Jamaica Plains MA int 30 Jun 1954 by IVANYI Alexander of Lancaster MA

MORETTI Daniel of Cranston RI & FITZSIMON Judith of Keene NH int 10 May 1960 by JAMES A Fitzsimon of Newport RI

MORGAN Donald of Hartford CT & PRINCE Margaret Ethel of Lake Forest IL int 19 Aug 1942 by PRINCE Herbert W of Lake Forest IL

MORI Albert Henry Jr of Garden Ct NY & WYMAN Dorothy Ann of Loudon NH int 8 Jun 1953 by WATSON Albert P of Tyngsboro MA

MORIEARTY William E of Boston MA & O'BRIEN Terese M of Manchester NH int 1 Aug 1950 by O'BRIEN Abbott Patrick of Newark NJ

MORIN Ernest of Greenville NH & VAILLANCOURT Paule J of Greenville NH int 27 Aug 1952 by RINE J Joyal of Amesbury MA

MORIN Gerald Richad of Nashua NH & DESMARAIS Leona Yvonne of Nashua NH int 30 Jul 1956 by PONTIEX L Lussier of Saskatchen CT

MORIN Joseph Robert of Manchester NH & BRASSARD Pauline Rita of Manchester NH int 25 Jun 1959 by THIBODEAU J A of Nicolet CAN

MORIN Oscar of Hooksett NH & BERNARD Laurette of Manchester NH int 22 Aug 1946 by HENRY Bernard of Montreal CAN

MORISON John Hokins of Peterboro NH & DANTAS Olga Desouza of Brazil int 21 Jul 1944 by PARK Charles E of Boston MA

MORISON Robert S of Peterboro NH & REMPEL Beningna of Cambridge MA int 17 Dec 1936 by PARK Charles E of Boston MA

MORNEAU Walter of Hudson NH & CRAIGNAN Irene J of Manchester NH int 27 Mar 1945 by MORNEAU John Paul of Aroostook Jct CAN

MORRELL George M of Keene NH & HUCKINS Glory F of Keene NH int 10 May 1950 by STRATHERN Leslie G of Fitchburg MA

MORRELL Nathan E of ? & GREEN Barbara Ann of ? int 14 Dec 1946 by ARCHIE H Crowley of Lawrence MA

MORRIS J Theodore of Scranton PA & SCHLAGER Ruth Anne of Scranton PA int 26 Jun 1935 by HENRY H Crane of Scranton PA

MORRISETTE Philippe R of Manchester NH & VAILLANCOURT Therese R of Manchester NH int 15 May 1952 by PELLETIER Nestor R of Marlboro MA

MORRISON Stanley of Weare NH & FELCH Claire M of Henniker NH int 28 Jul 1933 by McKINNEY W L of Bridgewater MA

MORSE Ira Herbert of W Roxbury MA & MAHONEY Julie Burke of Warren NH int 5 Mar 1931 by G Albert Higgins of Lawrence MA

MORSE Percy I of Merrimack NH & LOVEJOY Mabel B of Exeter NH int 20 May 1930 by POLING Daniel A of Deering NH

MORSE Richard H of Haverhill MA & BARTLETT Hazel L of Haverhill MA int 4 Aug 1937 by JOHN D Hull of Haverhill MA

MORSE Roger Alfred of Saugerties NY & SMITH Mary Lou of Laconia NH int 13 Sep 1951 by LOVERUDE Otto R of ?

MORTLAND Donald F of Searsport ME & HAMILTON Jacqueline of Laconia NH int 15 Aug 1956 by DONALD W Henderson of So Windham ME

MOSSON Francis of Salem NH & MELVIN Claire of Lawrence MA int 5 Dec 1960 by McNAMARA Eugene P of Lawrence MA

MOTT Peter of Washington DC & SCHIOT Gail of Portsmouth NH int 13 Jul 1956 by SAYRE Francis B Jr of Washington DC

MOTYLEWSKI Stanley of Nashua NH & HARGRAVES Doris M of Nashua NH int 29 Sep 1949 by L A Hargraves of Anniston AL

MOULTON Edward Allis of Belmont MA & HACKETT Marilyn Jane of Hampton NH int 12 Aug 1959 by JOHN P Fitzsimmons of Belmont MA

MOWATT Herman H of Lynn MA & METCALF Daphice of Ctr Sandwich VT int 30 Jun 1949 by SARGENT Geo P T of New York NY

MULLEN Alfred L of Milton MA & SHORTELL Brenda of Manchester NH int 12 Aug 1960 by SHORTELL Thomas E of Quincy MA

MULLEN Bernard G of Manchester NH & HARTSHORN Jessie of Milford NH int 28 Apr 1950 by JUDE T Cahillane of Newark NJ

MUN William C of Concord NH & HAYDEN Barbara of New Castle NH int 24 Aug 1948 by ROUNER Arthur A of Brooklyn NY

MURHAGH Leo of Dracut MA & BOURASSIA Eugenie of Manchester NH int 16 Sep 1935 by IRA J Bourassa of Sherbrooke CAN

MURPHY Arthur Thomas Jr of E Hartford CT & GAMBLE Mary J M of Portsmouth NH int 5 Aug 1952 by ARTHUR L Dunnigan of W Lynn MA

MURPHY Edward of Boston MA & CHRISTIE Marjorie of Boston MA int 16 Aug 1937 by C Irving Fletcher of Dorchester MA

MURPHY Francis Richard of Manchester NH & BEAULIEU Doris Irene of Manchester NH int 14 May 1959 by EMILE E Archambault of Boston MA

MURPHY George E of Coxsackie NY & DENNIS Ruth of Rochester NH int 19 Mar 1958 by EDWIN K Gechney of Stoneham MA

MURPHY James E of Gorham NH & MECKLENS Dorothy Ella of Durham NH int 10 Aug 1939 by MECKLIM Norman J of Crescent City FL

MURPHY Richard L of Boston MA & WHITCOMB Josephine Ann of Fitzwilliam NH int 25 Apr 1949 by PRESTON Richard G of Worcester MA

MURPHY Richard Wesley of Campton NH & WEED Margaret Aber of Lowell MA int 10 Aug 1934 by RATCLIFF John C of Tufts College MA

MURPHY Walter George of W Roxbury MA & KEYES Elaine F of Quincy MA int 7 Jun 1945 by WING Charles A of Quincy MA

MUZZEY Everett of Laconia NH & GAGE Irene of Laconia NH int 26 Jul 1957 by EDWARD J Gorman of Newton MA

NADEAU Ernest of Manchester NH & SOUCY Cecile of Manchester NH int 6 Aug 1947 by HENRI Cote of Rimouski Quebec CAN

NADEAU Joseph L of Somersworth NH & ROY Therese of Somersworth NH int 2 Jan 1948 by NADEAU Rolana A of Fitchburg MA

NADEAU Roer George of Berlin NH & NOLET Lorraine Eleanor of Berlin NH int 26 Apr 1954 by STANISLAS Bolduc of Montreal CAN

NADEAU Wilfrid of Manchester NH & ROY Eva of Manchester NH int 28 Jul 1925 by NAPOLEON Pepin of CAN

NAGEL Robert H of Albany NY & FROLICH Marjorio of Stinson Pond int 15 Aug 1940 by CHARLES O Farrah of Newton Highland MA

NALLY Judson Clayton of Kennebunk ME & BRENNAN Mary Frances of Kennebunkport ME int 20 Feb 1943 by JAMES A Johnson of Kennebunkport ME

NANUTT Vendermoon of Scarisdale NY & LAW Mary Sue of Caledonia IL int 21 Jul 1947 by MONTGOMERY Marshall F of Lake Worth FL

NAVIAS Robert A of Schenectady NY & KAUFMAN Elaine of Rochester NH int 24 Jun 1951 by RUTHREDGE Lyman of Boston MA

NEEDHAM Joseph Garton of Brandon VT & BEVERSTOCK Eleanor Nina of Keene NH int 10 Aug 1933 by J Varror Gaston of Bedford MA

NELSON Aubrey Wayne of Washington DC & SHAW Katherine Emma of Lebanon NH int 7 Sep 1950 by MACASKILL John of Ronsayville CA

NELSON John Herbert of Hampton Falls NH & THOMPSON Isabelle of Exeter NH int 16 Nov 1938 by WINSLADE Taplin J of N Tewksbury MA

NELSON Ronald F of Charlestown NH & LALIBERTE Margaret of Charlestown NH int 28 Nov 1960 by LALIBERTE Joseph of Sherbrooke CAN

NEOS George of Manchester NH & TRANTAFILON Fotini of Manchester NH int 9 Dec 1935 by THEODORON Theo of Lowell MA

NESBITT Walter John Jr of Concord NH & MACK Grace Eliazabeth of Bow NH int 23 May 1951 by RAYMOND J Bean of Chester PA

NESBITT William John of Rochester NH & CREGO Frances Fletcher of Rochester NH int 15 Apr 1942 by FELLOW Leroy W of Haverhill MA

NEWCOMB Harvey P of Swampscott MA & ORIORNE Priscilla of Swampscott MA int 29 Aug 1929 by ROBERT Campbell Jr of Swampscott MA

NEWCOMBE Ernest Edward of Keene NH & BOWER Jean Elizabeth of Keene NH int 26 May 1948 by ROY W Battenhouse of Cambridge MA

NEWTON Carson Jay of Conway NH & JANES Elizabeth W of Conway NH int 21 Jul 1945 by A W Altenbern of Hardwick MA

NEWTON Kenneth H of Cambridge MA & BEEDE Frances Melcher of Meredith NH int 29 Nov 1933 by LORD Augustus W of Providence RI

NICHOLAS James E of No Adams MA & MacKENZIE Jenne F of Lawrence MA int 18 Jul 1957 by MacKENZIE R W E of Lawrence MA

NICHOLS Ernest Gilbert of Hudson NH & DAMERY Leda Marie of Hudson NH int 26 May 1953 by G Earl Daniels of Cambridge MA

NICHOLS Howard Dr of Haverhill MA & O'CONNOR Margaret M of Haverhill MA int 22 Jul 1933 by CHARLES E Dunn of Rutherford NJ

NICHOLS Lane Alfred of Brattleboro VT & HUDSON Cherolyn Edith of Hinsdale NH int 13 Jul 1957 by CHARLES L Austin of New Canaan CT

NICHOLS Rodman A of Salem MA & FIMPLE Mildred of Brookline MA int 2 Jul 1949 by BRADFORD E Gale of Salem MA

NICHOLS Theodore of W Swanzey NH & DAVIS Greta Marlee of Hinsdale NH int 21 May 1951 by W B Higgins of So Lancaster MA

NICHOLS William H of Lexington KY & BURWELL Elizabeth B of Cambridge MA int 12 Aug 1936 by J Lester Hawkins of Boston MA

NICKERSON Thomas Drake of Belmont MA & CUSHMAN Jane of Laconia NH int 4 Jun 1956 by WILLIAM T Knapp of Hartford CT

NICOLAISEN H Edward of Brookline MA & DANIELS Hope of Plainfield NH int 5 Dec 1939 by FRANCIS P Daniels of Windsor VT

NICOLL Robert T of Andover MA & TEWKSBURY Gladys E of Derry NH int 19 Aug 1940 by HERMAN C Johnson of Andover MA

NILSON Gerbert T of Lexington MA & LEWIS Elizabeth of Lexington MA int 4 Oct 1955 by TAYLOR Floyd J of Lexington MA

NITZBURG Stanley of New York NY & THAYER Patricia V of New York NY int 23 Sep 1960 by THAYER A Greene of Amherst MA

NIXON John Victor of Cleveland Height OH & ANNOS Catherine Louise of Wolfeboro NH int 23 Aug 1948 by JOHN W Annas Jr of Syracuse NY

NONNEMACHER William of Dublin NH & SHONK Louis Whilennore of Dublin NH int 20 Aug 1956 by WHITTEMORE Francis L of Dedham MA

NORMAN Eric A of Woodstock CT & ANDERSON Gertrude of Manchester NH int 14 May 1943 by F A Erickson of Worcester MA

NORSTRAND Hans Donald of Boston MA & HARDY Marion of Brookline MA int 11 Jul 1936 by EDWIN N Hardy of Greenwich CT

NORTH Robert H of Nashua NH & TAYLOR Geraldine of Billerica MA int 26 Dec 1944 by JOHN W Brigham of Billerica MA

NORTHRUP David H of Lenox MA & DODGE Patricia of Brookline MA int 3 May 1959 by NORTHRUP Arthur B of Lenox MA

NORTON George Paul Jr of Fitchburg MA & WHITING Barbara of Wilton NH int 13 Aug 1940 by EDWARD Perry Daniels of Concord MA

NORTON Robert E G of Desmoines IA & WEST Johanna Scott of Warner NH int 28 May 1957 by HARRY F Booth of Norton MA

NOTTINGHAM Wayne B of Rindge NH & VanBERKUM Eveline E of Ithaca NY int 9 Nov 1953 by BENJAMIN Bradford of Gardner MA

NOURY Leonard of Manchester NH & JOLICOEUR Doris Irene of Bedford NH int 4 Nov 1948 by RICHARD Ferdinand of Natick MA

NOWACKI Leo T of Bedford MA & PETTES Barbara R of Orange NH int 1 Jun 1956 by Richard W Gregore of Bedford MA

NUTTER Edward H of Epsom NH & YEATON Glenna of Epsom NH int 21 Nov 1952 by FRANK J Coleman of Cranston RI

NYHUS Paul Luther of Winger MN & LUNDBLAD Ellen J of Berlin NH int 22 Jul 1960 by MYHUS H E of Winger MN

NYSTEDT George of Tamworth NH & HILL Nema T of Providence RI int 6 Sep 1957 by DALLAS R Gillespie of Clinton CT

O'BRIEN Donald M of Keene NH & STINSON Mary Ann of Richmond NH int 4 Aug 1960 by MacKENZIE Robert W E of Lawrence MA

O'BRIEN Joseph P of Manchester NH & DOHERTY Celia A of Manchester NH int 3 Jul 1950 by O'BRIEN Patrick E of Newark NJ

O'BRIEN Raymond of Natick MA & PARO Carol A of Wilton NH int 8 Oct 1957 by JOSEPH P Burke of Lawrence MA

O'CONNOR John Joseph Jr of New York NY & PARE Jane Arline of Manchester NH int 21 Dec 1954 by O'NEILL Reginald F of Weston MA

O'DONNELL Richard J of Wells Beach ME & PARENT Patricia H of Salmon Falls NH int 7 Jun 1951 by SHEVENELL R H of Dover NH

O'NEAL Edward of Schenectady NY & ERKI Mary Jane of Derring NH int 24 Jul 1946 by POLING Daniel A of Phila PA

O'NEILL John of Manchester NH & THIBODEAU Doris E of Manchester NH int 3 Aug 1960 by WILLIAM F Donovan of So Boston MA

O'NEILL John Patrick of Manchester NH & O'BRIEN Margaret Louise of Manchester NH int 24 Sep 1959 by DANIEL J Doyle of Lynn MA

OLIVER Albert I Jr of Lewiston MA & POOLE Barbara F of New London NH int 2 Jun 1942 by OLIVER Albert I of Lewiston ME

OLIVER Robert Norris of Corpus Christi TX & BROWN Olive Louise of Winchester MA int 16 Apr 1948 by HAMILTON M Gifford of Newton MA

OLSIN Arthur of Somerville MA & BIRD Catherina of Dorchester MA int 3 Aug 1928 by PUTLEDGE Lyman V of Dedham MA

OLSON Norman Hugo of Virginia Beach VA & SAUNDERS Barbara Ann of Gilford NH int 20 Aug 1958 by JULE Ayers of Wilkes Barre PA

ORMISTON James of Watertown NY & WILEY Mary Ellen of Watertown NY int 5 Sep 1958 by DON R Boyd of Watertown NY

OSBORNE Earl C of Pembroke NH & HART Dorothy E of Bennington NH int 29 Sep 1929 by BYINGTON Edwin H of W Roxbury MA

OSBORNE Kilby Page of Brooklin MA & HOBSOM Katharine B of Haverhill MA int 20 Jun 1927 by NEHIMIAH Boynton of Newton Ctr MA

OSBOURNE Roland Vainey of Haverhill MA & TAYLOR Minerva Jane of Haverhill MA int 23 Jan 1946 by PROUDFOOT Raymond S of Haverhill MA

OSGOOD Ralph R of Meredith NH & CAMPBELL Blanch of Franklin NH int 24 Aug 1935 by EVERETT Moore Baker of Providence RI

OTIS Edward Osgood of Boston MA & HILTON Charlotte James of Boston MA int 6 Jul 1925 by HENRY Knox Sherrell of Boston MA

OUELETTE Albert Eugene of No Attleboro MA & PARISEAU Helen Frances of Manchester NH int 23 Apr 1954 by LUKE M Chabot of Biddeford ME

OUELLETH Gabrielle of Nashua NH & DESGAGNE Rene of St Michel Quebec CAN int 12 May 1945 by OUELLETTE Lucien of Joliette Quebec CAN

OUELLETTE Gerrard Jr of Nashua NH & JEAN Yvonne of Nashua NH int 23 Feb 1956 by OUELLETTE Lucien of Quebec CAN

OVERSTREET Howard Joseph of Warrenvile IL & TESSIER Shirley Eleanor of Fitchburg MA int 30 Aug 1954 by WHITNEY Walter F of Sarasota FL

OWEN Earl Dana of Whitefield NH & WRIGHT Margaret W of Whitefield NH int 30 Jul 1925 by THOMAS S Cline of New York

PACKARD Dana Lawrence of Cambridge MA & LIVERMORE Ruth Cushing of Malden MA int 18 Apr 1937 by RICE Austin of Wakefield MA

PACKARD Hubert of Cambridge MA & FORD Anita of Peterboro NH int 18 Jun 1934 by MATHEW J Flaherty of Arlington MA

PACKARD Stillman A of Newington NH & NUTTER Beverly of Kittery ME int 17 May 1954 by NELSON John E of Island Falls ME

PAGE Donald Austin of Chester NH & GARLAND Barbara Ann of Newton Highland MA int 29 May 1953 by MILFORD Grant Chandler of Boston MA

PAGE Harold George of Seabrook NH & McINTOSH Gertrude of Seabrook NH int 21 Jun 1954 by OVERMAN C Vauhn of Biddeford ME

PAGE Lincoln of Woodsvile NH & LORD Esther of Melvin Village NH int 27 Jul 1933 by WALKER Raymond E of N Attleboro MA

PAGE Ralph of Nelson NH & NOVAK Ada of New York NY int 22 Oct 1945 by BRADFORD Gale of Salem MA

PAGE Richard of Lawrence MA & LONG Dorothy of Lawrence MA int 15 Sep 1953 by SMITH Norbert W of Methuen MA

PAGE Royal of Loudon Ridge NH & MOORE Phyllis of Loudon Ridge NH int 5 Jun 1942 by STONE George S of Waterbury VT

PAIGE Dean of Bennington NH & ROBIE Jacquelyn of Langdon NH int 18 May 1959 by STRICKLAND Freeman of Andover MA

PALMER Charles Wayne of Indianapolis IN & GORDON Priscilla of Jaffrey NH int 18 Feb 1959 by CHARLES A Engvall of Medford MA

PALMER Mauford L of Littleton NH & CALLAGHAN Annette R of Kezar Falls ME int 8 Jun 1932 by A A Callaghan of Kezar Falls ME

PALMER Vincent of Milton MA & MacKAY Lucie Cable of St Louis MO int 25 Aug 1939 by PHILIPS Z B of Washington DC

PANNETON Ernest R of Manchester NH & DUCHARME Frances of Manchester NH int 10 May 1956 by PANNETON Paul E of Wakefield MA

PANTINOS James of Claremont NH & CATSAM Olga of Newport NH int 31 May 1938 by ARCHBISHOP Christopher of Lowell MA

PAPACONSTANTINOU George of Manchester NH & ZAHOPOULOU Demetra of Manchester NH int 8 May 1942 by ARCHBISHOP Christopher of Lowell MA

PAQUETTE Roland Joseph of Portsmouth NH & WEST Madeleine G of Portsmouth NH int 2 Sep 1939 by IRA J Bourassa of Sherbrooke CAN

PARE Alphonse of Manchester NH & NORMAND Irene of Manchester NH int 14 Apr 1930 by VERONNEAU A of Lowell MA

PARE Andre Joseph of Nashua NH & BELANGER Therese Annete of Nashua NH int 2 Nov 1946 by VERONNEAU A of Lowell MA

PARKER Carlos Everette of Haverhill MA & LANGLEY Frances S of Plaistow NH int 24 Aug 1943 by MARSHALL Benj of Haverhill

PARKER Howard E of Sunapee NH & SANBORN Barbara P of Newport NH int 11 Aug 1953 by EDWARD G Harris of Phil PA

PARKER Willard H of Amherst NH & McDEVITT Myrtle of Lake Worth FL int 9 Sep 1955 by LEBOSQUET John E of Greenfield MA

PARKHURST Ralph Edward of Peterborough NH & CUMMINGS Marjorie of Peterborough NH int 28 Aug 1930 by HENRY S Ives of Newberry VT

PARKS Lincoln John of Pomfret CT & SCHAS Phyllis Anne of Manchester NH int 2 Aug 1950 by PARKES Robert H of Pomfret CT

PARLEEE William Alden of Stoneham MA & DAWE Ruth Amanda of Stoneham MA int 24 Apr 1957 by LEONARD J Gaspie of Malden MA

PARMENTER Robert of Manchester & MASON Catharine of Concord NH int 7 Jun 1944 by BREWSTER William of Southborough MA

PARRISH Edward of New York NY & BRUSH Joan of Dublin NH int 26 Jun 1935 by SUTER John W Jr of New York NY

PARRY Russell E of Westminster VT & KATHAN Edna Carie of Walpole NH int 26 Aug 1937 by PIKE Carroll M of White River Jct VT

PARSON Kenneth of N Hampton MA & BEAN Phyllis of Warner NH int 16 Apr 1953 by WHIPPLE L Byron of N Hampton MA

PARTISS Richard Gordon of CT & LANGLEY Ethel Frances of Dover NH int 5 Oct 1931 by CLINTON W Carvell of No Andover MA

PARTRIDGE Edward John of Bainbridge NY & WALCOMB Marion Eliz of W Chesterfield NH int 17 Jun 1937 by WILLIAM A Esterbrook of Thetford VT

PATCH George Nicholas of Meriden CT & SANBORN Winifred of Springfield MA int 11 Oct 1943 by J Osborne Crowe of Pepperell MA

PATERSON Arthur E Jr of Middleton CT & SHERMAN Helen Elizabeth of Franklin NH int 18 May 1946 by PATERSON Arthur E of Middleton CT

PATRICK John Wm of Rye NH & MacCALLUM Priscilla J of Hampton NH int 10 Sep 1951 by MacCALLUM George of Zanesville OH

PATTEE John Joseph of New Hampton NH & HART Marilyn Mae of Meredith NH int 18 Jul 1960 by VanSTRIEN David of Weeks Mills ME

PATTEN William E of Boston MA & BATES Florence of Brighton MA int 22 Aug 1943 by S W Anthony of Brighton MA

PAUL George Le Roy of Hampton NH & PURINGTON Frances Mae of Hampton NH int 12 Apr 1955 by PAUL George H of Pittsfield VT

PAULEU Wayne of Fort Wayne IN & WIGGINS Miriam of Portsmouth NH int 21 Aug 1934 by VINCENT Wm Nesbit of Fort Wayne IN

PAYNE John Thomas of Saco ME & TARR Ruth Harrison of Biddeford ME int 21 Mar 1951 by RALPH Edward Kyper of Saco ME

PEABODY Ernest W of Rochester NH & PERRY Ruth Eliz of Milton NH int 1 Apr 1947 by SPENCER Eugene of Kennebunk ME

PEACE Leonard of Swanton VT & DANIELS Joyce M of Hillsboro NH int 11 Aug 1959 by POLIN Daniel K of New York NY

PEARSON Woodring Dr of New York & FRENCH Mary Elizabeth of Nashville TN int 15 Jun 1940 by ELMER T Clark of Nashville TN

PEBBLES Carl J Jr of Concord NH & HOIT Pansy of Concord NH int 7 Aug 1947 by H Thayer Johnson of Salt Lake City FL

PECK Dexter Belnap of Newtown CT & WOOD May Lydia of New York NY int 12 Jun 1930 by GEORGE F Clover of New York NY

PEDERSEN Elmer Anders of Malden MA & MORSE Alice Pomeroy of Haverhill MA int 26 Nov 1946 by KENDIG B Cully of Haverhill MA

PEELETIER Amedee O of Nashua NH & BEAULIEU Jacqueline G of Nashua NH int 24 Jun 1946 by FRANCOES R Boudreau of Manville RI

PELLETIER Philip H of Portage ME & BOLD Lorraine G of Caribou ME int 24 May 1950 by HORATIO N Hapworth of Mechanic Falls ME

PELLETIER Roger A of Nashua NH & LeMAY Theresa Marie of Nashua NH int 21 Sep 1949 by MANDLER Omer N of Pomfret CT

PEMNINGTON Harry F of Brookline MA & BEMIS Esther A of Manchester NH int 14 Sep 1927 by MILFORD R Foshay of Lynn MA

PENDLETON Charles of Chicago IL & THORP Millicent Johnson of Manchester NH int 28 Apr 1942 by THORP Almus M of Columbus OH

PENDLETON George of W Springfield MA & WOOD Alice W of Arlington MA int 30 Jul 1954 by WOOD Nathan of Arlington MA

PERKINS Leland F of Cleaviston FL & LEE Iva Jennings of Auburn NY int 5 Aug 1931 by FREDERIC W Fitts of Boston MA

PERKINS Melvin Stanley of Keene NH & MOORE Dorothy H of Keene NH int 6 Sep 1944 by SELLARS Fred of Staten Island NY

PERKINS Robert of Hartford CT & STEARNS Lucielle of Hinsdale NH int 21 May 1946 by WILSON Kilgore of Hartford CT

PERKINS Robert E of Loudon NH & IDA Flora I of Swansey NH int 16 Jun 1934 by SWETNAM John A of New London CT

PERKINS Walter Poling of Newton NH & RUNDLETTE Joanne S of Amesbury MA int 26 Apr 1956 by LUDEKING Charles W of Amesbury MA

PERKINS William A of Keene NH & MAJOR Claire of Keene NH int 21 Aug 1957 by RINE J Joyal of Amesbury MA

PERRIN Lloyd C of Worcester MA & MORTON Louise of Hinsdale NH int 23 Jul 1947 by EUGENE L Biddle of Deerfield MA

PERRY Ernest A of Ossipee NH & KNOX Gwendolyn of Ossipee NH int 21 Dec 1948 by ROBERTS Carlye B of Attleboro MA

PERRY Rolland Leo of Manchester NH & VACHON Carolyn Ann of Manchester NH int 6 Aug 1947 by VACHON Alexander of Ottawa CAN

PERRY Stanton of Newport NH & PLOTNER June of Newport NH int 6 Sep 1955 by HOBERT W Blanchard of Indian Lake NY

PETERS Edward M of Medford MA & SHATTUCK Bernice A of Nashua NH int 19 Jun 1929 by DETHLEFS Louis C of Medford MA

PETERS John Henry of New Bedford MA & SKINNER Anne of No Dartmouth MA int 9 Jun 1942 by LESLIE C Greeley of New Bedford MA

PETERSON Carl Lyle of Amesbury MA & BLAKE Ruth Mae of Amesbury MA int 10 Oct 1928 by MOORE John of Amesbury MA

PETERSON Morill A of Boston MA & HAWSKINS Leona A of Portsmouth NH int 15 Aug 1932 by RICKER Albert E of Eliot ME

PETERSON Paul Wm of Manchester NH & COOPER Beverly June of Manchester NH int 11 Mar 1954 by WENZEL Enwald C of So Norwalk CT

PETERSON Walter of Rochester NH & HIRD Elizabeth Thurgood of E Wolfeboro NH int 9 Nov 1958 by ROSS Cannan of Newton MA

PETRY Jonathan Devere of San Diego CA & HAMBLET Patricia Clark of Windham NH int 24 Mar 1959 by ROBERT P Barnes of Methuen MA

PELLETIER Oscar of Franklin NH & TARDIF Alma of Laconia NH int 5 Aug 1939 by HILIARE M of Montreal CAN

PFAB Vincent of Atlanta GA & BRUNO Caroline of Tilton NH int 19 Dec 1955 by PLAB Charles B of Lafayette LA

PFEFFER John Lorenz of Narberth PA & WEMYSS Jane of Lancaster NH int 3 Jun 1942 by GIBSON Bell of Wynnewood PA

PHELIBOTTA Norman of N Wilbraham MA & CROSS Phyllis H of Palmer MA int 21 Jun 1947 by MUCH Kenneth A of Springfield MA

PHELPS Bernard of Danbury NH & PERONTO Gladys Grace of Webster NH int 18 May 1953 by ALAN G Keith of Livermore Falls ME

PHELPS Robert of Andover NH & KILGORE Audrey of Andover NH int 17 May 1950 by LUPTON Dilworth of ?

PHILBRICK Frank Allen of Auburn CA & KNIGHT Mary Lucinda of Concord NH int 1 Sep 1938 by HERBERT Knight of Hamden CT

PHILBRICK James Wm of Brookline MA & AYER Sarah Eleanore of Chicago IL int 30 Jul 1929 by GARDNER Wm E of Boston NH

PHILLIP Chares Edwin of New York NY & GLORE Joyce Ridley of Brookline MA int 2 May 1955 by MARTIN J Arthur of Norton MA

PHILLIPS Edgar of Providence RI & MUSSER Anna Mary of Peterboro NH int 13 Sep 1944 by PROUDFOOT Raymond S of Haverhill MA

PHILLIPS Jack C of Cincinnati OH & FRADD Marjorie of Manchester NH int 5 Feb 1950 by MAYNARD Erville of Albany NY

PHINNEY Charles of Orange MA & BANKS Cora of Orange MA int 5 Jul 1952 by WALLACE C Fiske of ?

PICHETTE Gaston of Manchester NH & BELAND Leona of Lynn MA int 22 Nov 1954 by MURPHY Romeo of Lowell MA

PICK Kenneth of Melrose MA & MASON Elinor M of Brookline MA int 25 Jul 1939 by MASON John of S Walpole NH

PICKMAN Anthony P of Bedford MA & LORING Alice Page of Chocorua NH int 17 Sep 1941 by LEONARD Fenney of Weston MA

PIDGEON John A of Andover MA & SHEPARD Judith of So Deerfield H int 23 Jul 1951 by SMITH Henry B of Andover MA

PIECUICK Walter C of Manchester NH & POLO Dorothy Blanche of Lynn MA int 30 Oct 1941 by STASZ Ladeslaus of Port Henry NY

PIERCE Ernest L Jr of Quincy MA & BENTLEY Phyllis I of Methuen MA int 7 Oct 1941 by NICHOLS Reginald of Methuen MA

PIEROG Juleires of No Andover MA & NORRIS Mary of Dover NH int 16 Dec 1949 by NORRIS Ronald of Union City NJ

PIETROWSKI Joseph of Manchester NH & SYPEK Mary of Manchester NH int 22 Jul 1925 by LADISLAUS Stasz of Port Henry NY

PIKE Lawrence of Manchester NH & ROKES Ida Mae of Manchester NH int 23 Jan 1958 by KENNETH A Batchelder of Revere MA

PIKE Lloyd Franklin of Dover NH & WILLIAM Alice Marie of Barrington NH int 19 Jun 1941 by ROBBINS William J of Somerville MA

PIKE Richard G of Nashua NH & COLLINS Virginia of Nashua NH int 31 May 1939 by REID Wm R of Pepperell MA

PIKE Roland Seth of Milton Mills NH & DREW Carolyn Mary of Union NH int 12 May 1947 by SMITH Burton B of Lynn MA

PILLSBURY Richard Alton of St Johnsbury VT & BEDELL Patricia of Monroe NH int 24 Apr 1953 by JAMES J Hutchinson of Lyndonville VT

PILLSBURY Warren of Derry NH & WHITCOMB Jean Ellen of Derry NH int 5 Aug 1950 by PILLSBURY Leonard H of Randolph VT

PINARD Bertrand of Manchester NH & BEDARD Lucienne of Manchester NH int 21 Feb 1946 by PAUL Cote of Natick MA

PIPER Armand of Manchester NH & DUCHAIME Clarie of Manchester NH int 7 Jul 1952 by EMILE Boucher of Manchester NH

PIPER Lester Irving of Lynn MA & STEARNS Barbara of Lynn MA int 17 Jul 1947 by ROWE Gard L of Lynn MA

PIPER Roland of Concord NH & KNOX Lutie E of Concord NH int 12 Nov 1946 by FREDERICK R Knox of Chester VT

PIRUSSE Jean of Manchester NH & VALLIERE Margurite of Manchester NH int 9 May 1955 by ROLAND Blouin of Verdun CAN

PITCAIRN Laren of Bryaathyn PA & BOWLES Mary Anne of Plymouth NH int 9 Sep 1957 by PITCAIRN Theodae of Athyn PA

PITCHER Raphael C of Keene NH & WHIPPLE Grace L of Keene NH int 9 Jul 1925 by H Sumner Mitchell of Burlington VT

PITTMAN Robert H of Wilton NH & PACKARD Penelope of Wilton NH int 15 Jun 1955 by WILLIAM Henry Francis of Woodstock NY

PIXLEY Wendell Irving of So Stratford VT & BROCKWAY Margaret L of Lyme Ctr NH int 14 May 1949 by FREDERICK R Knox of Chester VT

PLANTE Norman A of Goffstown NH & BOULAY Rachel L of Manchester NH int 6 Mar 1957 by C Edouard Desilets of CAN

PLOUF Henry J Jr of Litchfield NH & CROWELL Judith of Litchfield NH int 27 Oct 1938 by WILLIAM J Ballou of Chester VT

PLUANER Willard of Portland ME & MARKS Elizabeth H of Portland ME int 13 May 1926 by DANIEL I Gross of Portland ME

PLUMER Melvin Ellsworth of Boston MA & ADAMS Mary of Dennis MA int 18 Aug 1954 by PLUMER Stanley of Dennis MA

POIRRIER Henry A of Laconia NH & WOODWARD Marcella F of Laconia NH int 2 Jun 1949 by FRANK J Coleman of Cranston RI

POLIN Claude of Paris France & DERR Anne F of Waban MA int 22 Aug 1960 by THOMAS S Derr of San Francisco CA

POLLARD Frederick of Nashua NH & UNDERHILL Jean of Nashua NH int 25 Oct 1948 by MILLER Fred H of Brattleboro VT

POMERY William L of Brookline VT & HART Mary A of W Chesterfield int 9 Jun 1958 by LEINING Fred C of Brattleboro VT

POOLE Alan W of Fall River MA & DeMENA Gloria of N Plainfield NJ int 17 Jul 1931 by WILSON Arthur E of Fall River MA

POPE Conard C of Cleveland OH & PHILLIPS Katherine C of Cleveland OH int 21 Aug 1929 by FREDERIC M Adams of Cleveland OH

PORTER Angus Mackay of New York & HENEAGE Sylvia Stearns of Hanover NH int 19 Jun 1931 by SPENCER Burton of Hanover NH

PORTER Reginald of Cambridge MA & STEARNS Eleanor of Canterbury NH int 22 May 1933 by DWIGHT W Hadley of Winchester MA

POSK Robert Simeon of Athol MA & JOYNT Anastasia Josephine of Peterboro NH int 24 Jun 1955 by CHARLES L Callahan of Maryknoll NY

POTTER Carl of Martinsville VA & COTTON Katherine E of Rochester NH int 13 Jul 1951 by HARRY G Ford of Columbus OH

POTTER Frederic J of Hartford CT & LILLEY Elizabeth Ann of Hartford CT int 24 Jul 1936 by PARKER Fletcher D of Hartford CT

POTVIN Henry A of Portsmouth NH & THOMAS Helen of Milford NH int 26 Sep 1940 by MOORE John Ward of Methuen MA

POTVIN Victor of Claremont NH & VEILLEUX Lorraine of Claremont NH int 19 Feb 1960 by VEILLEUX V J of Chicago IL

POULIOT Maurice of Lowell MA & LAMONTAGNE Blanche of Lowell MA int 17 Oct 1950 by ALDOR Boisvert of Manchesmanville RI

POWELL Monte Benton of Seattle WA & EASTMAN Diane Diadem of Fryeburg ME int 9 Jul 1956 by HORACE W Briggs of Fryeburg ME

POWELL Ralph Duke Jr of Keene NH & RICHARDSON Nancy of Marlboro NH int 14 Jul 1950 by MARSHALL Eck of Evanston IL

POWERS Hobart G of Brookline Village NH & BLACKWOOD Alice Louise of Fitchburg MA int 23 May 1952 by PRICE E Bruce of Fitchburg MA

POWERS Rodney C of Braintree MA & SHUTE Jane of Malden MA int 8 May 1939 by W Harold Deacon of Fall River MA

POWERS William Roy of Mt Vernon & SMITH Barbara Helen of Kensington NH int 12 Nov 1952 by SAWYER Roland D of Ware MA

PRATT Harris of Concord NH & COLBY Helen Abbott of Concord NH int 19 Nov 1929 by PRATT Willard of Boston MA

PRATT Robert of Newport NH & JOHNSON Patricia of Newport NH int 24 Jan 1954 by WENTWORTH Albert of St Johnsbury VT

PRENTICE Ronald H of So America & KAULBACK Helen of Malden MA int 18 Sep 1947 by MINICK Roly L of Malden MA

PRESCOTT Edwin H of Portland ME & DOIR Evelyn of E Rochester NH int 14 Nov 1938 by PRECOTT E H of Middleboro MA

PRESCOTT Lloyd of Lebanon NH & OSBORN Allison of Keene NH int 15 Jun 1959 by OSBORN Donald L of Randolph VT

PRESTLY John of Boston MA & GAY Adeline of Boston MA int 13 Aug 1930 by CHAUNCEY W Goodrich of Brunswick ME

PRESTON Lee of Manchester NH & HOLT Marion of Malden MA int 22 Jun 1928 by HENRY H Crane of Malden MA

PREVOST George E of Keene NH & BOISVERT Jeanne of Manchester NH int 10 May 1956 by J A Dutil of CAN

PRICE George of Scranton PA & CURRIER Eleanor Frances of Belmont NH int 9 May 1945 by NUTTER Harold W of Searsmont ME

PRICE George of New Boston NH & MOATT Dorothea of Exeter NH int 2 Apr 1934 by SCAMMON John H of Weston MA

PRICE James Ludlow of Woburn MA & PERRY Julia Elizabeth of Keene NH int 11 May 1959 by LEWIS William W of Arlington MA

PRICE Richard of Towson MD & CLARK Joy of Hampton NH int 25 Jan 1957 by ROBERT W Gallaway of Towson MD

PRICE Sidney Warren of Malden MA & FLAGG Jacqueline of Warner NH int 7 May 1954 by MONBLEAU Chas of Malden MA

PROCTOR William H of Brattleboro VT & BUDD Katherine of Charlestown NH int 19 Nov 1929 by MILTON S Czatt of Brattleboro VT

PROPER Richard of Keene NH & ROBINSON Roberta of Keene NH int 15 Aug 1952 by C Barnard Chapman of Providence RI

PROULX Oscar of Manchester NH & BOUCHARD Georgianna A of Manchester NH int 21 Apr 1958 by ALFRED Bouchard of CAN

PROVANDIE Paul Hector of Melrose MA & BOYNTON Priscilla of Portsmouth NH int 14 Oct 1936 by JOHN A Hainer of Phil PA

PROVENCAL Warren E of Concord NH & JENOVESE Angelina of Concord NH int 14 Nov 1944 by MICHAEL A Jenovese of Worcester MA

PROVENCHER Roland of Manchester NH & BOUCHER Corrine of Manchester NH int 10 Jul 1931 by HENRI J Goudreau of Crowley LA

PROVOST Simone of Manchester NH & JANELLE Alexia of Manchester NH int 21 Nov 1946 by NAPOLEON J Gilbert of Three Rivers CAN

PTODZIK Adolf of Manchester NH & MACEK Angela of Manchester NH int 13 Sep 1930 by MACEK Joseph of Shenandoah PA

PUTNAM Augustus of Boston MA & TWITCHELL Lucy B of Boston MA int 6 Jun 1938 by PERKINS Palfrey of Boston MA

PUTNAM Frederick L of Yarmouth MA & LOUD Shirley L of Dennis MA int 28 Jan 1958 by PUTNAM Stanley T of Dennis MA

PUTNAM N H of Hancock NH & SPRAGUE Elizabeth of Hancock NH int 10 Mar 1951 by RUTHREDGE Lyman of Boston MA

PUTNEY Alande Charles of Keene NH & EMERSON Elizabeth J of Fitzwilliam NH int 7 Sep 1934 by MITHCHELL H Summer of Sanford ME

QUELLETTE Arthur of Lowell MA & GARIEPY Beatrice of Pelham NH int 24 Aug 1935 by J Avila Gariepy of CAN

QUIMBY Bernard G of Northwood NH & ALLEY Virginia of W Josesport ME int 15 Jun 1940 by L L Glazier of Arkport NY

QUIMBY Walter E of Freemont NH & JACKSON Elizabeth of Amesbury MA int 19 Jun 1950 by LUDEKING Charles W of Amesbury MA

QUINCY David S of Manchester NH & KEARNEY Elizabeth of Manchester NH int 4 Apr 1949 by TANGNEY Edward J of Revere MA

QUINLAN John M of Amherst MA & KENTFIELD Joyce M of Amherst MA int 15 Aug 1958 by THAYER A Greene of Amherst MA

QUTERBRIDGE Yeaton of Bermuda & SCHUKE Roxana W of Cornish NH int 12 Jan 1947 by TEISER T of Old Bennington VT

RADFORD Frederick C of Melrose MA & BENNETT Rebecca of Saugus MA int 1 Apr 1959 by H Osgood Bennett of Manchester CT

RAFFERTY John of Baltimore MD & BARBIN Mary Eleaine of Exeter NH int 8 Jul 1959 by STROUP Edmond J of Westminster MD

RAICHE William of Nashua NH & MIGNAULT Marguerite of Nashua NH int 26 Feb 1951 by MIGNAULT Leonard of CAN

RAILSBACK Edward Neal of Newtonville MA & VARNEY Barbard Shepard of Rochester NH int 2 Aug 1938 by EDGAR L Bell of Norwich CT

RAINER Ralph of Kittery ME & MABY Betty of Kittery ME int 11 May 1950 by PARMBEY Chester W of Bristol CT

RAMBACH John Scott of Newton MA & KINGMAN Ann of Worcester MA int 12 Jun 1957 by CLINTON W Carvell of No Andover MA

RAMSPOTT Gordon of Rehoboth MA & GRAVES Janet of Derry NH int 13 Sep 1949 by WHITE Lester P of Gill MA

RANCOURT Henri Willie of Berlin NH & ROY Pauline Annette of Berlin NH int 29 Jun 1954 by ROLAND Becotte of CAN

RANDALL Edward of Haverhill MA & KERSHAW Grace of Newton NH int 27 May 1946 by WILSON William J of Jay NY

RANDALL Paul of Needham MA & SHORTELL Elizabeth Ann of Lancaster NH int 21 Sep 1950 by SHORTELL Thomas E of Newton MA

RANDALL Robert of Peabody MA & CRANDALL Prudance of Salem MA? int 18 Aug 1941 by FRANK A Crandall of Salem MA

RANLET John of Meredith Ctr NH & WHEELER Thelma of Laconia NH int 29 May 1943 by JOHN W Baggs of Portland ME

RANSDALL Laird of Meredith NH & ROGER Barbara of Meredith NH int 13 Jul 1949 by RALPH E Davis of Maplewood NJ

RAU Leonard of Belmont NH & BAILEY Patricia of Manchester NH int 14 Nov 1957 by PETTY Meuell C of Lynn MA

RAY Donald George of Manchester NH & GREENE Jo Ann of Goffstown NH int 1 Aug 1956 by PLOWRIGHT J A H of Birchton CAN

READ Eliphat Northrup of New York NY & CARTER Florence Evelyn of Malden MA int 8 Sep 1926 by HAROLD C Abbott of Malden MA

READ Richard W of Cambridge MA & ENEBUSKE Clara of Cambridge MA int 29 Aug 1927 by SAMUEL A Eliot of Boston MA

READ Stanley Ellery of Chicago IL & TANNER Alice Hartman of Littleton NH int 8 Aug 1935 by READ G Ellery of Sherbrook CAN

READ Thayer Gilman of Merrimack NH & WILSON Alice Jane of Manchester NH int 12 Sep 1941 by EARLE A Brooks of Newton MA

REAL Richmond W of Syracuse NY & PRELLER Carol Ann of Nashua NH int 18 Apr 1959 by MURPHY Joseph P of W Medford MA

REDDY John of E Jaffrey NH & O'NEIL Katherine of E Jaffrey NH int 10 Jul 1939 by PARKER George G of Spencer MA

REDFERN Robert of Berlin NH & SAINTLAURENT Edmonde of Berlin NH int 9 Aug 1950 by EDMOND Hache of Waterville ME

REDSTONE Norman K of Cranston RI & TUFTE Louise of Cranston RI int 10 Nov 1945 by LUTHARD N Eid Providence RI

REED William Ernest of Manchester NH & DONNELLY Margaret Agne of Manchester NH int 12 Jun 1946 by REED Paul J of Denver CO

REENERT Carl of Manchester NH & WOODS Margaret of Keene NH int 15 Aug 1933 by NOONAN Matheu K of Fayettville NC

REGAN George J of Manchester NH & CONWAY Mary M of Manchester NH int 18 Nov 1955 by O'BRIEN Francis A of Lowell MA

REICH Robert J of Hamden MA & JENNINGS Norma Jane of Lawrence MA int 31 Aug 1960 by RYAN Edwin L of Methuen MA

REICH Walter Edwin of New Jersey & HEMPHILL Priscilla R of Warren NH int 14 Jun 1935 by CHARLES L Fowler of Lowell MA

REID David of Melrose MA & TAIT Lucy of Chester NH int 11 Sep 1943 by PERRY M Blankenship of Peabody MA

REID Fergus Jr of York Harbor ME & SEABURY Etheldreda W of Kittery Pt ME int 15 Jun 1930 by SILVER H Percy of Bedford Hills NY

REID Wilmont P of Hartford CT & PLAISTED Patricia of Hartford CT int 15 Jan 1959 by SMITH Donald E of Hartford CT

REMILLAD Donald of Manchester NH & VALLIERIES Liona of Manchester NH int 16 Aug 1942 by VALLIERIES Jean Jospeh of Lowell MA

REMILLARD Gerard Henry of Manchester NH & BOURASSA Shirley Mae of Manchester NH int 25 Mar 1952 by IRA J Bourassa of CAN

REMY Azarias of Claremont NH & BLANCHARD Alexandrine of Claremont NH int 11 Aug 1956 by REMY C E Roland of Warwick

REMY Joseph Richard of Claremont NH & BLANCHARD Marie Rachael of Claremont NH int 21 Jun 1947 by REMY Roland of Providence RI

RESTUCCIA Carmelo of Belmont MA & DESILETS Carmelle P of Manchester NH int 31 Aug 1956 by C Edouard Desilets of CAN

REUNING Walter of Manchester NH & WOHLGEMUTH Wanda of Manchester NH int 22 May 1929 by THOMAS Fred W of Pawtucket RI

REYNOLDS Arthur Dana of Lyndeborough NH & CUMMINGS Marion Leona of Lyndeborough H int 11 Aug 1944 by RICHARD P Carter of Suffield CT

REYNOLDS Eldwin L of Brentwood NH & DUDLEY Elizabeth of Brentwood NH int 15 Sep 1949 by ROSE Wm Wallace of Lynn MA

RHINES Robert of Ridgewood NJ & MINER Constance of Ridgewood NJ int 3 Aug 1960 by GEORGE L Knight of Brooklyn NY

RHOADA John P of Gettsbury PA & OTT Janet F of Gettysburg PA int 13 Aug 1941 by OTT John W of Hagerstown MD

RICE Arthur Eugene of Odessa TX & BUDGE Wanda Jean of Raymonville TX int 16 Aug 1946 by McPHERSON Walter A of Ridgefield NJ

RICE George A of Mt Sunapee NH & GREGORY Margaret M of Mt Sunapee NH int 31 Oct 1952 by HOBERT W Blanchard of Indiana Lake NY

RICE Leo of Winchester NH & NURMI Linda of Brattleboro VT int 14 Oct 1959 by ROBERT J Harding of Brattleboro VT

RICE Robert of Newtown CT & RAMSEY Julia of Walpole NH int 1 Jun 1956 by NORMAN R Farnum Jr of Holyoke MA

RICE William B of Melrose MA & LINDSEY Elizabeth of Marblehead MA int 14 Aug 1931 by SNOW Sidney B of Chicago IL

RICHARDS Howard of Atkinson NH & ELLISON Mary Elizabeth of Haverhill NH int 15 Sep 1941 by WELSH Clement W of So Groveland MA

RICHARDSON James of Cambridge England & HULBURD Lucy W of Exeter NH int 14 Jul 1949 by PARK Charles E of Boston MA

RICHER Andrew R of Manchester NH & ZIMMERMAN Joan G of Manchester NH int 4 Dec 1959 by FREEMAN Strickland of Andover MA

RICK Gordon B of Hillsboro NH & THOMPSON Clara L of Hillsboro NH int 17 Aug 1939 by YEAPLE Whitney S of Rochester NY

RIDLON Wendell of Baldwin ME & KNIGHT Virginia of So Windham ME int 26 Aug 1944 by GERALD W Beals of So Windham ME

RIHL David Perry of Lebanon NH & PALMER Jean Eleanor of Lebanon NH int 17 Apr 1958 by WALTER H Beckwith of Vincentown NJ

RILEY William M of Somersworth NH & LEARY Mary L of Portsmouth int 21 Aug 1939 by LEARY John F of Portsmouth NH

RINCIARI Frank of Medford MA & BOLDUC June of Laconia NH int 29 Apr 1960 by ARMAND P Fortin of St Johnsbury VT

RINDEN Paul A of Concord NH & TARRANT Constance of Manchester NH int 2 May 1958 by RINDEN Arthur O of New York NY

RINES James Perley of Fitchburg MA & YORK Elaine English of Statesville NC int 31 May 1951 by STRATHERN L G of Fitchburg MA

RING Charles W of Charlestown NH & PARKS Dorris M of Charlestown NH int 14 Dec 1931 by JOHN Emerson of Bridgeport VT

RING Raymond of Epsom NH & REID Bessie of Epsom NH int 1 Jul 1930 by SIMMONS Arthur S of Willimington MA

RIPLEY Samuel Horace of Braintree MA & RAYMONE Blance Shirley of Derry NH int 16 Aug 1957 by ROBERT W Henderson of Belmont MA

RIREMILLARD Maurice A of Manchester NH & SOUCY Lorraine Theresa of Manchester NH int 25 Nov 1952 by MARQUIS Paul E of Lowell MA

RIVARD Rolland of Manchester NH & CHAPUT Octavie of Manchester NH int 8 Sep 1938 by PELLERIN H P of Three River CA

ROBERTS Henry Edson of Conway NH & CARLISLE Nancy Eliz of Conway NH int 31 Jul 1939 by FREDERICK R Knox of Chester VT

ROBERTS J Bruce of Rochester NH & RYAN June of Rochester NH int 21 May 1957 by EDWARD J Carney of Lawrence MA

ROBERTS Stephen J of Rollinsford NH & MAYRAND Gertrude of Dover NH int 3 Sep 1948 by MAYRAND Stepher L of Buckport ME

ROBICHAUD Leo of Berlin NH & RODERICK Olive of Berlin NH int 29 Aug 1938 by TAYLOR Earl L of Dannemora NY

ROBIE Lloyd of Hookseet NH & BURBANK Dorothy of Hooksett NH int 3 Jul 1941 by WILLARD A Bicket of Center Lovell ME

ROBINSON Cecil J of Swanzey NH & JONES Dorothy of W Swanzey NH int 22 Dec 1941 by PEARSON Roy M of Amherst MA

ROBINSON Edward H Jr of Seward AK & KNIGHT Ruth Elva of Seward AK int 30 Mar 1959 by LEON M Flanders of Greenlawn NY

ROBINSON Fred of Springfield MA & LARSON Bonnie of E Longmeadow MA int 14 Apr 1960 by TEED Kenneth R of E Longmeadow MA

ROBINSON John W of Greenwich CT & BATTEN Helen of Bristol NH int 7 Jun 1954 by MANZELMANN Richard of Greenwich CT

ROBINSON Leon of Westbrook ME & DAVIS Gladys R of Portland ME int 19 Aug 1929 by LOWE Ralph F of Augusta ME

ROCHE Ralph M of Malden MA & HOLMES Beverly of Alstead NH int 30 May 1959 by SHEPPARD Walter of Attleboro MA

ROCKETT John Alexander of Rockville Ctr NY & BURGESS Abby of Providence RI int 20 May 1956 by SCHACHT Robert H of Providence RI

ROCKHOLT Donald of Manchester NH & MALETTE Lorraine of Manchester NH int 28 May 1957 by M Flanagan of Lowell MA

RODERICKS Francis J of Lawrence MA & WELLS Irene H of Lawrence MA int 8 Jun 1940 by ROBBINS Clarence G of Chelsea MA

RODERID Charles Edward of Boston MA & DOOLE Constance Allyn of Laconia NH int 26 Jun 1958 by FRANCIS X Dooley of Brookline SD

RODGERS George C of Cambridge MA & WELLS Virginia of Enfield NH int 11 Jul 1934 by JOHN H Barber of Athol MA

ROE Fred of Greensboro MD & WARFIELD Barbara of Gorham NH int 1 Nov 1945 by DANA E Klotzle of Wellesley MA

ROGERS Avard D of Syracuse NY & FRENCH Patiricia of Hudson NH int 5 Jun 1958 by TOZER Arnold W of Manchester CT

ROGERS Donald P of Springfield MA & WALES Frances Beaman of Cambridge MA int 11 Jul 1952 by PENNINGTON Leslie T of Chicago IL

ROGERS George A Jr of Hudson NH & BURNHAM Natalie L of Pittsfield NH int 24 Nov 1945 by STANLEY E Anderson of Newburyport MA

ROGERS Kenneth Melzard of New London CT & HOLMES Edna of Gilford NH int 22 Jul 1941 by BARTHOLMEN James I of Strafford Springs CT

ROGERS Philip Carlye of Dover NH & BEANE Cecily Swan of Keene NH int 17 Sep 1956 by MEURY Edward W of Wellesley MA

ROHDE Arthur L of Brattleboro VT & BOND Christine L of Brattleboro VT int 24 Apr 1953 by MILLER Fred H of Brattleboro VT

ROLLS Stanley P of Toronto CAN & GOODWIN Agnes Muriel of Boston MA int 22 Jul 1949 by WILLIAM H Hormel of Boston MA

ROLSTON Parker Andrew of Greenland NH & JACKSON Elizabeth Jane of Greenland NH int 27 Mar 1951 by C Basil Harris of Kittery Point ME

ROMAN Benjamin of Alstead NH & FREAD Catherine of Alstead NH int 4 Aug 1932 by MARSHALL Benjamin T of Worcester MA

ROMANO Anthony W of White River Jct VT & MORIN Rose Marie of W Lebanon NH int 19 Aug 1955 by O'BREASELY Maurice of Sherbrook CAN

RONAN Edward of Newburyport MA & CONNORS Catherine of Somersworth NH int 7 Mar 1934 by SULLIVAN Edward S of No Chelmsford MA

RONDEAN Robert G of Salem NH & THOMPSON June of Salem NH int 7 Jun 1956 by LYNCH John W of Bedford MA

RONDEAU Burton E of Chesterfield NH & STODDARD Patrice Edna of Chesterfield NH int 8 Sep 1952 by MILLER Fred H of Brattleboro VT

RONDEAU Ramon of Salem NH & BAILEY Alice B of Salem NH int 8 Aug 1957 by LYNCH John W of Bedford MA

ROSE Kurt Eugene of W Newton MA & AVERY Marguerite L of Boston MA int 26 Jul 1952 by WALLACE G Fiske of W Hartford CT

ROSENVINGE Norman of Boston MA & GILBERT Deborah of Winchester MA int 19 Aug 1940 by CLIFTON Brewer of New Haven CT

ROSS Donald W of Springfield MA & ROYS Priscilla of East Kingston int 16 Aug 1937 by PAGE Frederick H of Waltham MA

ROSS Howard Persing of Sunapee NH & LEWIS Barbara of Keene NH int 14 May 1958 by CHARLES C Austin of Worcester MA

ROSS Walter Albert Jr of East Kingston NH & GILMAN Julia Eliz of Suncook NH int 5 Jun 1948 by ADAMS Z Arnold of Roslindale MA

ROUSSEAU Gordon of Exeter NH & DURETTE Pauline of Manchester NH int 17 Oct 1960 by ROBERT Durette of Natick MA

ROUTSIS John of Lowell MA & KAPSALIS Helen of Nashua NH int 5 Aug 1941 by ARCHBISHOP Christopher of Lowell MA

ROWE Harold of York ME & FENTON Carlene E of Atkinson NH int 17 Oct 1955 by LYON Walter W of Ward Hill MA

ROWE Harry P of Wynnwood PA & ANDRESS Charlotte of Newton MA int 26 Aug 1937 by MERRILL Randolph of Newton MA

ROWE Philip A of Portsmouth NH & VINKS Julie E of Brockton MA int 15 Aug 1931 by TOMKINS Floyd W of Rye Beach NH

ROWE Raymond Nelson of Chesterfield NH & THOMAS Gladys Ruffer of Brattleboro VT int 26 Jun 1953 by MILLER Fred H of Brattleboro VT

ROWLEY Harold Frederick of West Wareham MA & JONES Olive Nellie of Easton NH int 30 Aug 1927 by VANNAH Guy Linwood of Marblehead MA

ROY Bernard Daniel of Dover NH & DAVY Sylvia Agnes of Dover NH int 2 Nov 1957 by WILLIAM H Johnson of So Berwick ME

ROY Edward David of Amesbury MA & CHAPMAN Alice Elizabeth of Rochester NH int 30 Aug 1958 by LEONARD Gaspie of Amesbury MA

ROY John Paul of Rochester NH & LANGELIER Gloria Rachel of Rochester NH int 4 Jan 1947 by ROY Louis Philip of Quebec CAN

ROY Klaus George of Newton MA & BOTT Priscilla Ardelle of Jamaica Plain MA int 23 Jul 1951 by WHITNEY Hale of Boston MA

ROY Leo Joseph of Manchester NH & GRENIER Therese Juliett of Manchester NH int 12 Jun 1950 by SARTO Grenier of Keogami CAN

ROY Rene O of Berlin NH & CLOUTIER Bertha A of Berlin NH int 12 Jun 1950 by ROY Roger of Bucksport ME

ROY Thomas of Manchester NH & BRENTON Juliette of Manchester NH int 20 May 1932 by W J Giroux of Manchester NH

RUCKSTICKH Charles of Mason NH & MOISON Muriel of Groton MA int 30 Jun 1950 by MATTOCK Henry of Ayer MA

RUEST Normand of Lowell MA & BELANGER Rita of Nashua NH int 6 Aug 1956 by RUEST Sylvio of Salem MA

RUFFLE Ronald Harrison of Jaffrey NH & ROYCE Marie of Jaffrey NH int 1 Sep 1954 by REYNOLDS Levering Jr of Andover MA

RUONAVAARA Nathan of Mohawk MI & FELLMAN Miriam of E Barrington NH int 15 Aug 1957 by PAUL A Heidiman of Laurium MI

RUSSELL Jason L of Saugus MA & QUINBY Ruth Norwell of Saugus MA int 19 Jun 1933 by VOSSEMA Hendrick of Medford MA

RUSSELL Paul Raymond of Hinsdale NH & POWERS Sally of Hinsdale int 12 Aug 1958 by HOWARD E Hood of Hinsdale MA

RUSSELL Robert of Contoocook NH & ROWELL Marion of Contoocook NH int 17 Oct 1952 by WOLFF Richard A of Lynn MA

RUTHDREDGE John M of Dedham MA & VALENTIN Wilma Gordon of Jamaica Plains MA int 19 May 1941 by RUTHREDGE Lyman of Dedham MA

RUTHERFORD David Rea of Thompsonville CT & COOK Marilyn Joyce of Bartlett NH int 1 Mar 1960 by HORACE W Briggs of Fryeburg ME

RYAN Frank N of Peterboro NH & BAGLEY Anna S of Peterboro NH int 31 Mar 1934 by ERNEST W Eldridge of Ashby MA

RYDUARSKY Frank C of Roxbury MA & MELSKY Rose D of Claremont NH int 13 Apr 1938 by MATOLINA Joseph J of Bethpage Long Island NY

SAAVOIE Simoine of Manchester NH & VALLIERIES Adrien of Manchester NH int 2 Nov 1941 by VALLIERIES Jean Joseph of Lowell MA

SABINE Gardner Blake of Boston MA & CABOT Thea Handasyd of Dublin NH int 28 Jun 1949 by WHITNEY Hale of Boston MA

SAIA Joseph of New Bedford MA & CARON Lucille L of Manchester NH int 2 Apr 1947 by J R Benson of Brooklyn NY

SAINT AMANT Roger of Berlin NH & HUDON Lorraine J of Berlin NH int 12 Jun 1957 by LEMIEUX Arthur E of Montreal CAN

SAINT GERMAIN Robert M of Manchester NH & GAUTHIER Lillian M of Manchester NH int 11 Jan 1960 by PANNETON Paul E of Medford MA

SAINT LAURENT Paul Leo of Epping NH & GAGNON Jeannette Louise of Manchester NH int 29 May 1950 by ANTONIO Gangon of Calixa CAN

SAINT LAURENT Philippe L of Manchester NH & GUILLEMETTE Lucille M of Manchester NH int 7 Jul 1950 by L J Boissonneault of Haverhill MA

SAINT PIERRE Aurelien of Manchester NH & MARCHAND Elizabeth of ? int 10 Aug 1936 by ST Pierre Gustave of Manchester NH

SAKOVICH Matthew of Claremont & OSTROWSKI Sophie of Claremont int 11 Jul 1952 by NYKIEL John of So Boston MA

SALSBURY Harold of Manchester NH & BALDWIN Emily W of Manchester NH int 29 Sep 1936 by JOHN B W Day of Wilton NH

SANBORN E Russell of Concord NH & HARRIS Mary of Concord NH int 21 Jun 1930 by LEROY W Coons of Boston MA

SANBORN Joh Webster of Andover MA & PERKINS Alice May of Dover NH int 10 Oct 1933 by ROBERT W Coe of Brookline MA

SANBORN John Leonard of Durham NH & PERCIVAL Janice Ann of Durham NH int 5 Sep 1957 by WHYTE James Rae of Mt Hermon MA

SANDERSON Charles of Roxbury MA & MARTELL Helen of Somerville MA int 25 Jun 1932 by BRADFORD H Burnham of Boston MA

SANFORD Clarence of Canton MA & WILDER Lillian of Hancock NH int 21 Jul 1933 by J Arthur Edwards of Plymouth MA

SANFORD John C of CT & SANDERS Elizabeth L of Newmarket NH int 3 Jun 1947 by SCHOFIELD Russell G of Belmont MA

SANFORD Stephen Joseph of Walpole MA & COLLIER Elizabeth of Concord NH int 12 May 1957 by SANFORD Edgar L of Westboro MA

SANGER Hobart of Wollaston MA & HICKS Esther of Wollaston MA int 15 Sep 1954 by ERNEST R Bradley of Lowell MA

SARGENT Kenneth of Exeter NH & KNOX Mary L of Dover NH int 17 May 1949 by WENDELL P Knox of Vinalhave ME

SARGENT Richard of Lebanon NH & SCOTT Lillian of Elkins NH int 31 Aug 1934 by HUBERT D Jones of New Haven CT

SAVCHUCK Victor Jr of Boston MA & THOMPSON Christine of Boston MA int 7 Aug 1950 by FERRIS Theo P of Boston MA

SAVIN Edward A Jr of Philadelphia PA & UKLE Sandra D of Montgomery PA int 28 Jun 1960 by C Ransom Confort of Philadelphia PA

SAVINO Isidore of Worcester MA & JENOVESE Caroline of Concord NH int 1 Apr 1946 by MICHAEL A Jenovese of Worcester MA

SAWYER Donald Frederick of Brooklyn NY & OLIVER Alice Louise of Lisbon NH int 25 Jun 1925 by J M Wathen of Woonsocket RI

SCARINGI Gene Rev of Providence RI & WARD Dorothea Robinson of Chocorua NH int 11 Jun 1948 by GRANVILLE G Bennett of Providence RI

SCHARAR Edward R of Scranton PA & YULE Anne C of Scranton PA int 18 Aug 1936 by HENRY H Crane of Scranton PA

SCHAWTZ William of Scranton PA & JONES Eleanor of Taylor PA int 28 Jun 1936 by HENRY H Crane of Scranton PA

SCHELL Hans F of Waltham MA & ANDERSON Pauline of Stoneham MA int 30 Aug 1958 by JAMES L Hayward of Arlingon MA

SCHINDLER Alexander M of Worcester MA & ROSENBLUM Rhea of Manchester NH int 14 Sep 1956 by JOSEPH Klein of Worcester MA

SCHLICHTE John Daniel of Boston MA & BERRY Jean of Medford MA int 31 May 1960 by SCHLICHTE Geo A of Gloucester MA

SCHLICKMAN Henry of Hudson MA & BOURK Virginia A of Manchester NH int 13 Dec 1950 by DANAIEL F Cronin of Natick MA

SCHLOTH Wilhelm Gerorge of Manchester NH & COLBATH Lois Ann of Dover NH int 20 Aug 1948 by MORGAN Walter A of Worcester MA

SCHRAMM August Jr of Flushing NY & RICHARDS Jean Harriet of White Plains NY int 22 Aug 1931 by STREET William Dana of White Plains NY

SCHROEDER Herman of Brooklyn NY & BARNES Elizabeth of Cambridge MA int 5 May 1938 by RAY A Eusden of Newton MA

SCHULTZ Clifford Stanley of Wilton NH & WARREN Barbara E of Lyndeboro NH int 20 Jul 1954 by RICHARD P Carter of Suffield CT

SCHWEITMAN John B of Newport Kty & BROWN Janet Ingersell of Newton Highland MA int 8 Aug 1941 by ROBERTS Ben of Brandon VT

SCIDLER Baxon F of London England & ASHBROOK Lucy J of Phil PA int 5 Jul 1939 by VINCENT C Donovan of New York NY

SCOTT Frederick G of Newburyport MA & RICARD Rachel of Nashua NH int 15 Feb 1955 by LAWRENCE F Keefe of Newburyport MA

SCOTT Walter B of Deerfield NH & FERGERSON Carolyn H of Epping NH int 2 Jun 1930 by TILTON C H Bouton of St Petersburg FL

SCRIMSHAW Nevin S of Wauwatosa WI & GOODRICH Mary W of Middletown CT int 14 Aug 1941 by CORNELIUS Kruse of Middletown CT

SCRUTON Frank John of Farmington NH & PHELPS Pauline Eliz of Webster NH int 31 May 1946 by J Osborne Crowe of Pepperell MA

SCUDDER Thayer of Woodbury CT & DRINKER Mary Eliza of Fitzwilliam NH int 7 Aug 1950 by THEODORE P Ferris of Boston MA

SEAGREN Stuart T of Stanford CT & OSTROWSKI Mary of Claremont NH int 31 Jul 1952 by NYKIEL John of So Boston MA

SEAMAN Robert of Nashua NH & MAILHOT Jacqueline of Nashua NH int 4 Oct 1956 by PARADIS Robert M of Lowell MA

SEARLES Kenneth of Mt Vernon NH & GILSON Joyce of Wilton NH int 7 Nov 1957 by PHILIP C Johnson of Manchester MA

SEARS Walter Edwin of Quincy MA & MacDONALD Mary Jean of Springfield NH int 16 Aug 1948 by DAHL Geo of New Haven CT

SEARS Walter H of Newton MA & STOCKIN Eleanor C of Concord NH int 27 Jul 1926 by EDWARD C Camp of Watertown MA

SEATER Robert Paul of Watertown SD & FRANK Hilda R of Hyde Park MA int 26 Jun 1948 by OWEN George W of Hyde Park MA

SEAVER Thomas Wm of Portsmouth NH & PIKE Frances Jean of Portsmouth NH int 5 Jul 1934 by SEAVER Thomas C of Jersey City NJ

SEAVEY Walter A of Rochester NH & HARTLEY Alice Maude of Rochester NH int 22 Aug 1929 by ALBERT W Jefferson of Lynn MA

SEELEY Richard Arthur of Phil PA & CRAM Sherideth Diana of Pittsfield NH int 8 Jul 1959 by JAMES W Faulkingham of Hudson Falls NY

SEIBERT Edwin R of New York NY & CASS Rachel of Amherst NH int 17 Sep 1929 by M T Anderson of Hubbardston MA

SEIBERT John Robert of Columbus OH & REHL Dorothy Elizabeth of Columbus OH int 14 Aug 1948 by SHERIDAN W Bell of Delaware OH

SEISEL Max of Brooklyn NY & LYNCH Irene of Hill NH int 7 Aug 1936 by FRED B Ford of Lee Rochelle NY

SENGISTER James of Buffalo NY & LAMBERT Mary of Cambridge MA int 26 Jun 1953 by MURDUCK Elmer H of Cambridge MA

SENNEVILLE Richard of Manchester NH & ROY Rose Aline of Manchester NH int 20 Mar 1956 by GOERGE Bilodeau of CAN

SENTER Richard L of Manchester NH & LAMBERT Marcelle of Manchester NH int 16 May 1960 by WILLIAM W Campbell of Bangor ME

SERROTI Gilbert of Detroit MI & BRAY Sally of Detroit MI int 17 Aug 1959 by HENREY A Crane of Detroit MI

SEUFERT Robert Allen of Nutley NJ & SMITH Janice Christine of New Hampton NH int 7 Feb 1953 by LINN Creighton of Flemington NJ

SEVERN Donald Wesley of New York NY & SIDES Natalie of New York NY int 8 Mar 1941 by WALTER R Ferris of Easton MD

SEVIGNY Raymond of Goffstown NH & LABRANCHE Dolores of Manchester NH int 13 Jun 1955 by PANNETON Paul E of Wakefield MA

SEWALL Samuel of Saco ME & OSTRANDER Audrey of Raymond NH int 2 Sep 1941 by TRAFTON Roy M of Leominster MA

SHAFER Thayer C of Durham NH & PEARSON Ann Carol of Hooksett NH int 15 Nov 1957 by ROWLAND C Adams of Springfield MA

SHAKA James Athan of Manchester NH & BEAN Jacqueline H of Erroll NH int 11 Jun 1951 by ROBET Haldane of Madison ME

SHARRON Frederick James of Gardner MA & LEVEILLE Rolande of Manchester NH int 4 May 1951 by BASIL Corbett of Trenton NJ

SHATTUCK Daniel Jr of Jaffrey NH & ALLEN Travis of Jaffrey NH int 27 Jun 1960 by GEORGE E Jaques of Jewett City CT

SHAW Ernest Edward of Salem Depot NH & FOSTER Christine E of Salem Depot NH int 27 Jun 1958 by SHAW E Leslie of Lawrence MA

SHAW Richard Maurice of Laconia NH & BARTLETT Janet Elaine of Claremont NH int 7 Sep 1955 by ERNEST A Brown Jr of No Andover MA

SHEAHAN William Joseph of Lakoda NB & POLASKI Patricia Jean of Winchester NH int 6 Jun 1955 by POLEWACZYK Stanley of Shemokin PA

SHEFIELD Lawrence J of Hanover NH & DALHEN Marjorie Hughes of Sunapee NH int 26 Jun 1936 by HOWARD Chidley of Winchester MA

SHEHAN Robert of Baltimore MD & WARD Judy of Manchester NH int 10 Jul 1959 by SHEHAN Lawrence J of Bridgeport CT

SHEPARD Robert Land of ? & ALLEN Phyllis of ? int 13 Jun 1951 by WILLIAM F English of Norwood MA

SHEPHERT Francis Harold of Tilton NH & HORNE Marjorie Althea of Tilton NH int 16 Jul 1941 by CHESTER H Howe of ?

SHERRIDAN William Earl of Concord NH & GLNRY Elaine Marjorie of Rochester NH int 4 Aug 1948 by JOHN L Holden of Peachman VT

SHERWIN John Pershing of Arlington MA & RUTHERFORD Janet Colburn of Arlington MA int 2 Jul 1946 by RAYMOND S Hall of Boston MA

SHEVENELL Alfred G of Dover NH & EYRES Cleo of Dover NH int 7 Aug 1942 by SHEVENELL R H of Natick MA

SHIBLEY George Peter of Dover NH & RUTHERFORD Ann Julie of Barrington NH int 7 Aug 1957 by FRANCIS J Gilday of Boston MA

SHIELDS Lawrence R of Ayer MA & PRIOR Camilla E of Baldwinville MA int 9 Jul 1936 by LEVY Lawrence E of Chicopee Falls MA

SHILLINGHAW Clifford of Pleasantville NY & MARX Frances Eleanor of New York NY int 30 Jul 1958 by STETSON Clifford R of Springfield VT

SHIPMAN Carl of Burlington VT & LaROUCHE Claudia of Boston MA int 18 Apr 1957 by POWERS Robert J of Burlington VT

SHOEFFEL Michael of Hanover NH & WHITE Catherine Ann of Hanover NH int 4 Nov 1957 by WHITE John J of White Chester CT

SHORT Frederick Edward of Columbus OH & MCGARY Jo Ann of Columbus OH int 4 Aug 1948 by JOSEPH Barth of Almma ME

SHORT Howard Elmo of Springfield MA & DUNCAN Margaret of Concord NH int 8 Jun 1935 by ELMER E S Johnson of Hereford PA

SHUFELT Edwin Rufus of Sandown NH & LOUD Edith of Boston MA int 13 Jun 1946 by MERRILL Randolph of Newtonville MA

SIBLEY Charles Herbert of Worcester MA & CALDER Janet of Boston MA int 25 Aug 1955 by ENGVALL Charles A of Medford MA

SIERAKOWSKI John of Salem MA & PIOTROWSKAR Ladislava of Manchester NH int 22 May 1937 by STASZ Ladeslaus of Port Henry NY

SILBER Eli of Haverhill MA & RAINE Hilda of Salem NH int 29 Dec 1933 by JACOB M Cohen of Lawrence MA

SILEO Nicholas G of Chester PA & POTEAT Nida P of Lewisburg PA int 7 Jul 1949 by POTEAT Gordon of Lewisbury PA

SILK Thomas Wesley of Ithaca NY & DODGE Mary Bowden of Whitefield NH int 19 Aug 1953 by PEALE Norman V of NY NY

SILVA Anthony Edward of So Portland ME & SULLIVAN Patricia Ann of Dover NH int 6 Jan 1958 by FENNEY Daniel of Portland ME

SILVER Ralph of Newmarket NH & HARVEY Alma of Newmarket NH int 4 Jun 1945 by SCHOFIELD Russell G of Belmont MA

SIMMERS Henry P of Andover MA & BERNIER Adrienne of Nashua NH int 2 Jun 1944 by WILFRID Belanger of Lowell MA

SIMMINS Charles W Jr of Palm Beach FL & BOLLEN Lois Sinclair of Melrose MA int 12 Jun 1947 by SPRING C of Melrose MA

SIMON Walter Michall of Marlboro MA & ANGELL Millie Blanche of Marlboro MA int 1 Sep 1956 by SCHADEGG Multon F of Arlington MA

SIMONDS Franklin of Los Angeles CA & JOHNSON Ada H of New Hampton NH int 28 Jul 1925 by OLIN B Tracy of Norway ME

SIMPSON Richard F of Louisville KY & REGGIO Janet Josephine of Chesham NH int 10 Aug 1949 by DAN Huntington Fenn of Boston MA

SINCAVAGE William of Girardville PA & WILLETT Jo-Ann of Lincoln NH int 16 Apr 1959 by RASAINE Curteau of CAN

SINOTTE Arthur of Concord NH & JENOVESE Joanina of Concord NH int 23 Nov 1946 by MICHAEL A Jenovese of Worcester MA

SKANTZE Walter Harold of Alton NH & ROBERTS Florence of Gilmanton NH int 21 Aug 1957 by OSBORN Donald L of Northfield VT

SKILLEN James Don of Brooklyn NY & CROFT Beatrice Harriet of Claremont NH int 12 Dec 1940 by SCHAFF Lester of Mansfield PA

SKILLIN Dean B of So Bend IN & HAINES Dorothy of Hanover NH int 25 Jun 1952 by SKILLIN Carl D of Hardwick VT

SKOFIELD Herman of New Boston NH & PHIPPS Jane of Walpole NH int 15 Jun 1948 by JAMES A Dailey Jr of West Medway MA

SLADE Marshall Perry of Mt Kisco NY & COOLIDGE Bertha of Boston MA int 12 Aug 1933 by FREDERICK R Griffin of Phil PA

SLATTERY Patrick F of Bellows Falls VT & MCNAMARA Elizabeth F of No Walpole NH int 16 Sep 1929 by LAWRENCE R Cain of Fairfield VT

SLAYMAN Howard of Brookline NH & BARNEY Margaret of Dublin NH int 14 May 1935 by PARK Charles E of Boston MA

SLAYTON Carroll Leland of Concord NH & TEBBETTS Ina Letita of Concord NH int 15 Jun 1931 by J M Hatch of Montpelier VT

SMART Earl Thomas of Portsmouth NH & FOYE Marion Alemeda of Kittery ME int 1 Sep 1933 by OLSEN Frederic of Kittery ME

SMEAD Claude M of Putney VT & CURTIS Margaret Frances of W Swanzey NH int 6 Apr 1949 by PEIRY Carroll E of Barret VT

SMILEY Gilbert of Brookline MA & McKINNEY Elizabeth R of Derry NH int 16 Dec 1929 by TYLER Barrett P of Brookline MA

SMITH Albert Joseph Jr of Wakefield MA & PARKINSON Dorothy Ann of Derry NH int 10 Jul 1958 by LOUMER W G of Amherst MA

SMITH Arthur Leroy of Dover NH & JENNESS Phyllis Louise of Dover NH int 3 Jun 1947 by JAMES A Coney of No Berwick ME

SMITH Benjamin J of Laconia NH & DINSMORE Thelma of Laconia NH int 4 Aug 1927 by EUGENE D Dolloff of Boston MA

SMITH Carl Ellsworth of Raymond NH & LANE Eloise Frances of Hampton NH int 28 Jul 1925 by TRACY Olin B of ?

SMITH Charles Wesley of Raymond & CRAM Vivian Frances of Raymond int 9 Aug 1925 by EVARTS Pond Rev of Deerfield ME

SMITH Douglas of Marshfield VT & BECKER Lois of Hanover NH int 12 Aug 1959 by LOREN House Jr of Norwich VT

SMITH Frank Chalmers of Detroit MI & GILBERT Katharine of Winchester MA int 19 Aug 1940 by CLIFTON Brewer of New Haven CT

SMITH Fred of Quincy MA & EASTMAN Dorothy Evelyn of Intervale NH int 25 Jul 1932 by DANIEL Evans of Intervale NH

SMITH Frederick L of Grantwood NJ & STRAWN Nona of Jersey City NJ int 18 Jul 1949 by MONTGOMERY Marshall of Lake Worth FL

SMITH Glenn H of Rochester NH & HUCKINS Edith M of Rochester NH int 16 Apr 1951 by REID Wilbur L of Wrightsville PA

SMITH Harold R of So Hampton NH & DIXON Elizabeth Elaine of So Hampton NH int 27 Jun 1945 by MURCHIE H John of Amesbury MA

SMITH Herbert W of Deering NH & DAVIS Elizabeth M of Deering NH int 18 Jul 1958 by POLIN Daniel K of New York NY

SMITH R Bruce of Schenectady NY & RADCLIFF Catherine of E Kingston NH int 7 Apr 1958 by SMITH Delbert B of Schenectady NY

SMITH R Bruce of Schenectady NY & REDCLIFF Catherine of E Kingston NH int 12 Apr 1958 by NICHOLS Vernon Charles of Alexandria NY

SMITH Ralph Fairfield of Keene NH & WATSON Emily B of Keene NH int 25 Jul 1938 by MITCHELL H Summer of Sanford ME

SMITH Roland Kendall of Rye NH & PHILBRICK Costance Ann of Rye NH int 12 Jun 1958 by ROBBINS Wm J of Glen Cove ME

SMITH Ross George Jr of Derry NH & TIBBETTS Frances of Derry NH int 4 Jul 1940 by TRACY Olin B of Melrose MA

SMITH Russell of Kittery Point ME & HANLON Elsie Cecilie of Wollaston MA int 11 Aug 1938 by REID John of Peabody MA

SMITH Sidney of Baltimore MD & LEONARD Edith H of Exeter NH int 1 Sep 1948 by SMITH Charles T of Wellesley MA

SMITH Sydney of Lynn MA & MAYNIHAN Cornelia of Newton MA int 23 May 1935 by M A Kapp of ?

SMITH William Alfred of Sharon VT & KELLEY Helen Elizabeth of Lebanon NH int 7 Jun 1929 by CHUTTER Fred G of Mystic CT

SMITH William Marsden of Epsom NH & PEASLEE Dorothy of So Pittsfield NH int 31 May 1950 by CONEY James A of No Berwick ME

SNAIR Richard Bruce of Conway NH & CHILDS Elizabeth of Boscawen NH int 16 Sep 1957 by LeVOY Herbert E of Swampscott MA

SNOW John Gardner of Cambridge MA & SAWYER Ethel May of Dorchester MA int 10 Apr 1931 by A Z Conrad of Boston MA

SNOW Richard F of Winchendon MA & SAWYER Margurite of W Rindge NH int 17 Sep 1927 by A Z Conrad of Boston MA

SNYDER Donald Bertram of Boston MA & LANGMAID Rosamond of Boston MA int 21 Sep 1956 by WHITNEY Hale of Boston MA

SNYDER John of CA & FERRY Virginia of Cambridge MA int 10 Jun 1942 by TROWBRIDGE Cornelius of Newton MA

SNYDER Luther H of Washington DC & GUSTAFSON Gladys V of Concord NH int 24 Sep 1937 by SNYDER Henry W of Washington DC

SOCIETRO Rosaris Louis of Milford NH & FORBES Roberta F of Nashua NH int 26 Sep 1938 by JOHN R Copplestone of Haverhill MA

SOLOMON Howard A of Worcester MA & SAXTON Alice G A of Worcester MA int 27 Aug 1928 by MILFORD Foshay of Lynn MA

SOPAL John of Manchester NH & DUVAL Francoise of Manchester NH int 4 Sep 1952 by THIBAULT Ethelbert of Manchester NH

SOUCY Real Emile of Manchester NH & CHAMPAGNE Denise Marcea of Manchester NH int 24 Aug 1960 by JOSEPH Etienne of Ottawa CAN

SOUCY Roger Alphonse of Sanbornville NH & PARKER Beverly Eloise of Tamworth NH int 12 Aug 1950 by LINGDBERG Dagamar of Kesar Falls ME

SOUTHMAYD Robert of Manchester NH & ADAMS Anna of Manchester NH int 11 Jun 1951 by H Norman Korb of Roxbury MA

SOUTHMAYD Walter of Manchester NH & BARTON Dorothy of Manchester NH int 11 Jun 1951 by H Norman Korb of Roxbury MA

SOUTHOFF Herbert of Swarthmore PA & WOLFE Helen of Lyme NH int 10 Oct 1943 by THURSBY Irvin G of Milford CT

SPALDING Roland S of Fitchburg MA & AMSDEN Esther May of Nashua NH int 4 Jun 1925 by JUDSON Lewis Cross of Fitchburg MA

SPALLINO Charles of ? & CRAY Barbara of No Walpole NH int 10 Aug 1946 by C F Cray of Barre VT

SPAN Warren Richard of Springfield VT & KENNEDY Beatrice Alice of Woodsville NH int 18 Jun 1931 by MARTN Eldon H of Springfield VT

SPAULDING Menley of Sanford ME & WITQEL Claire S of Wells ME int 11 Mar 1959 by PALMER Warren S of Sanford ME

SPELLMAN John P of Somersworth NH & GRADY Catherine A of Dover NH int 15 Apr 1950 by LEWIS Delmage of Pittsfield MA

SPENCER Donald H of Rochester NY & DALZEL Geraldine of Rochester NY int 5 Feb 1957 by HUGH Fleming of Chelsea MA

SPENCER Duncan M of Beford Hill NY & CLARK Louisa H of Dublin NH int 25 May 1953 by PARK Charles E of Boston MA

SPENCER Oscar L of Fall River MA & LEWIS Bertha C of Fall River MA int 16 Aug 1933 by THOMAS Albert C of Fall River MA

SPICER Jack Leonard of Washington DC & BROWN Mary Drake of Rye Beach NH int 5 Jul 1939 by FRERDINAND Q Blanchard of Cleveland OH

SPOERL Howard of Bath ME & TILDEN Dorothy of Galesbury IL int 11 Jun 1929 by MARSHALL Harold of Boston MA

SPRAGUE Atherton Hall of Northampton MA & WHITTEMORE Marion Helen of Newport NH int 9 Jun 1925 by FRED Erick D Hayward of Meuthen MA

SPRAQUE Walter of Fremont NH & ROULEAU Dona of Atkinson NH int 13 Aug 1959 by CLAY Terry of Oakdale ME

SPROULE Harold G of Nashua NH & WITHYAM Mavis E of Nashua NH int 16 Nov 1933 by EDWARD A Durham of Haverhill MA

STAIRS Mr of CAN & KELLEY Florence of Newton NH int 25 May 1949 by PALMER Ralph of Mansfield MA

STALTER Lawrence E of Park Ridge NJ & NUTTER Dorothy of Salmon Fall NH int 14 Nov 1935 by STEPHEN P Brownell of Wells ME

STANLEY John R of Cambridge MA & JANETOS Barbara of Dover NH int 18 Oct 1955 by METAXAS Arthur J of Cambridge MA

STANTON Edwin Mills Jr of New York & PATERSON Joan of New York int 2 Jul 1946 by TRUEBLOOD Roscoe E of Cohasset MA

STANTON Robert L of Manchester NH & GELINAS Claudette G of Manchester NH int 9 Feb 1959 by MAURICE Gelinas of Washington DC

STAPLES Paul Cutter of Boston MA & BEER Joanne G of Jamacia Plains MA int 1 Jun 1951 by RUTHREDGE Lyman of Boston MA

STARIE John H of Tilton NH & RICHARDSON Dorothy A of Franklin NH int 21 Jul 1938 by STARIE John W of Glover VT

STARK Robert Lawrence of Goffstown NH & FLANDERS Emmy Lou of Weare NH int 22 Jul 1938 by OLIVER M Frazer of Worcester MA

STARR Arnold of Newton MA & REINGOLD Thelma of Newton MA int 15 May 1959 by ROLAND B Gittlesohn of Boston MA

STEARNS Horace of Charlestwon NH & CAMPBELL Jean of Springfield MS int 1 Aug 1938 by HARLIN M Campbell of Bellows Falls VT

STEARNS John Francis of Manchester NH & MIVILLE Josephine V of Manchester NH int 24 Aug 1933 by ROY A F of Cleveland OH

STEDFAST Elmer H of Medford MA & TAATJES Eleanor of Medford MA int 7 Sep 1950 by MEIKLE Rober W of Medford MA

STEINKA Frederick Henry of Fitzwilliam NH & STONE Kathleen Watson of Fitzwilliam NH int 22 Jul 1951 by LEONARD W Fowler of Athol MA

STEPHANNON Glenn H of Clayton MO & CLARK Gail of Parkville MO int 14 Apr 1939 by STEPHENSON Geo W of Talcottville CT

STEPHEN Henry George of Torrington CT & MUDGETT Dorothy of Littleton NH int 25 Jun 1928 by ROBINSON Alson H of Plainfield NJ

STEPHENSON Leigh of Gilford NH & JONES Patricia of Belmont NH int 2 Jun 1953 by J Evangeline Barney of Framingham MA

STETSON John M of Urbana IL & PATTEE Sarah of Bristol NH int 11 Aug 1925 by WILLIAM D Beach of North Woodstock NH

STETTLEBACK Arne E of Williams Bay WI & PIXLER Constance L of Medford MA int 25 Aug 1949 by PIXLER Wellington C of Medford MA

STEVENS Edward of Pelham NH & LYNEE Mary A of Pelham NH int 20 Jun 1934 by AMBROSE Bailey of Lowell MA

STEVENS George S of Whitefield NH & SAMPSON Margaret of Jefferson NH int 25 May 1953 by SAMPSON Antoine of Sherbrooke CAN

STEVENS Herbert of Brentwood NH & ELDREDGE Rosalie of Stratham NH int 20 Oct 1959 by DONALD B Morris of ?

STEVENS Norman of Candia NH & AMRON Helen of Candia NH int 23 Aug 1946 by HENRY J Chandler of Boston MA

STEVENSON Roland Chester of Westminster MA & BEATON Hazel Jean of Winchester NH int 26 May 1952 by OLSEN Enock of Danbury CT

STEWART Arthur of Durham NH & GUFFITHS Sadie Marion of Durham NH int 20 Aug 1930 by CLINTON W Carvell of No Andover MA

STEWART Robert of Scotia NY & WHITFORD Frances of Crown Pt NY int 19 Jul 1940 by PELON J Charles of New York NY

STIGUM Egel of Hanover NH & CARR Judith of Wolfeboro NH int 14 Sep 1956 by LYONS Donald H of Waltham MA

STILES Leo K of So Manchester CT & YOUNG Elsie M of Dover NH int 29 Jun 1927 by EARLE B Cross of Rochester NY

STILES Walter H of Exeter NH & JOHNSON Ellen May of Intl Fall ME int 11 Feb 1946 by MAYWOOD William of Haverhill MA

STOCKWELL Bryant of Royalston MA & DIAMOND Eva of Peterboro NH int 19 Jun 1941 by LEONARD W Fowler of Maynard MA

STODDARD Gerald of No Haverhill NH & PHELPS Priscilla E of Webster NH int 9 Sep 1943 by J Osborne Crowe of Pepperell MA

STODDARD Robert of Woburn MA & MORGAN Dianne of Freedom NH int 8 Sep 1959 by TJAARD G Hommes of Arlington MA

STOKES Gilbert of Wolfeboro NH & MILLER Lillian Dorothy of Wolfeboro NH int 22 May 1942 by MARSHALL Benjamin of Haverhill MA

STONE Albert Edward Jr of Mt Pocono PA & WOODBURY Grace Holt of Bedford NH int 1 Jun 1954 by STONE Albert E of Mt Pocono PA

STONE Chester Frank of Winchester NH & GEE Retta May of Winchester NH int 26 Sep 1934 by WALKER Edgar R of Waltham MA

STONE Earle of Harvard MA & WASHBURN Alice of Mason NH int 20 Sep 1937 by JAMES T Berry of Stratton ME

STONE Ernest George of Nashua NH & ATKINSON Mona Jean of Nashua NH int 13 Jul 1956 by TRACY Olin B of Buffalo NY

STONE Gilbert Gordon of Attleboro MA & BILLINGS Nancy of Wellesley MA int 13 May 1954 by SAMUEL S Johnston of Wellesley MA

STONE Rex Langdon Jr of Fort Fairfield ME & CANFIELD Nancy Alice of Ft Fairfield ME int 17 Jun 1944 by NELSON Canfield of Fort Fairfield ME

STOPYRA Walter of Lawrence MA & KURTA Helen of Nashua NH int 1 Aug 1949 by STOPYRA Alfter of Ellicot City MD

STOREY Harold of Newton Jct NH & DAVIS Dorothy of Newton Jt NH int 25 Aug 1941 by WILSON William J of Gainesville NY

STOUT Gerald J of ? & ASH Lydia of Lisbon NH int 28 Jun 1932 by RICHARD J H E of Ellenbury NY

STROBER Gerald of Brooklyn NY & MEDVIDDOFSKY Leah of Keene NH int 20 May 1960 by PFEIFFER Charles of Beverly MA

STROCK Henry Blaine Jr of New Castle PA & HAYES Lois Irene of Dover NH int 17 Oct 1952 by STROCK John Henry of Oak Lane PA

STROUD Ronald of Boston MA & SAINTCLAIR Costance of Tilton NH int 14 Aug 1941 by STROUD Arthur D of Boston MA

STRUBE Henry William of Lawrence MA & BRYAR Arlene Grace of Laconia NH int 6 Apr 1940 by ZABRISKIE Howard of Cranston RI

STURTEVANT Robert Allen of Greenland NH & CARROLL Elizabeth Anne of Portsmouth NH int 12 Jun 1948 by J Tremayne Copplestone of Boston MA

STUTZMAN Guy G of New Bedford MA & JENNISON Lucinda Mary of Milford NH int 4 Oct 1929 by WOLFE G Edgar of Milford MA

SULLIVAN Charles Sumner of Plainfield NH & HALL Bertha of Brookline NH int 23 Jul 1935 by REV J Irving Fletcher of Dorchester MA

SULLIVAN Harold Martin of Orono ME & TESSIER Julette Claraie of Manchester NH int 6 Jul 1953 by LETORNEAU Francis of Orono ME

SUNDERLAND Jesse Earl of Georgia VT & COLBY Marion Gertrude of Danville NH int 19 May 1930 by W C Chappell of Pittsburgh PA

SUTHERLAND Norman Blake of Essex Jct VT & JOBES Sarah Ann of Newport NH int 9 May 1956 by SNELLING Robert A of Essex Jct VT

SWAN Eugene L Jr of New York NY & BLAINE Katherine of New York NY int 25 Aug 1951 by LOVETT Sidney A of New Haven CT

SWANSON Everett of Waterbury CT & HOUGHTON Harriett of Waterbury CT int 27 Aug 1932 by DAVID P Gaines of Waterbury CT

SWEENEY Hubert J B of Manchester NH & SOUCY Pauline L of Manchester NH int 8 Sep 1958 by MARQUIS Paul E of Lowell MA

SWEENY Richard of Park Ridge IL & GAGNON Martha of Nashua NH int 3 Jun 1952 by PAUL F Izzo of Worcester MA

SWEETMAN Floyd of Rumney & MARSHALL Janet H of Bedford int 13 Oct 1925 by THOMAS Frank W of Bedford MA

SWENSON Lennart A of Somerville MA & KNOWLTON Idella J of Boscawen NH int 17 Apr 1945 by PARKER Asa M of Wellesley MA

SWETT Fred Kitfield of Swanzey NH & MAYO Frances Leone of Framingham MA int 10 Jun 1944 by ROBERT Lee Dutton of Holden MA

SWIFT Richard W of Sugar Hill NH & DEAN Gertrude of Canton MA int 21 Jul 1960 by ZDENEK Bednar of Canton MA

SWINNERTON Carl P of Ctr Harbor NH & MARSHALL Nathalie E of Henniker NH int 22 Aug 1935 by TRACY Olin B of Melrose MA

SYKES William W of Windham NH & CALQUHOM Harriet E of Andover MA int 22 Sep 1932 by WALKINS C R of Fort Moultrie SC

SZOIO Rederick of W Medford MA & LAMPREY Arlen E of Wakefield MA int 7 Apr 1958 by SAWYER Roland D of Weare MA

TAMBLING Preston P of USN Base Portsmouth NH & FULLER Gertrude of Lawrence MA int 3 Jun 1930 by SIMPSON James C of Watertown MA

TANGUAY Roland of Somersworth NH & CHASSE Jeannette of Rochester NH int 24 Jun 1957 by TANGUAY Ovid of Biddeford ME

TANGUAY Valmoe of Somersworth NH & RIGAZIO June Lorraine of Rochester NH int 4 May 1957 by TANGUAY Ovid of Biddeford ME

TAPLEY Roland of Boston MA & BENNINK Augusta H of Wellesley MA int 16 Jun 1959 by ROY A Eusden of Newton MA

TAPLIN John of Wellesley MA & BALDWIN Virginia of Wellesley MA int 4 Jul 1939 by PROCKER T Hayes of Wellesley MA

TAPPAN Robert Morse of Darien CT & PIERCE Eleanor Frances of Hampton NH int 16 Apr 1957 by M Sargent Desmond of Danbury CT

TAQUE Robert of Rochester NH & CANNEY Jean of Somersworth NH int 18 Dec 1953 by PENDLETON Charles of Bethel ME

TARDIF Armand G of Laconia NH & DUMAIS Marguerite of Laconia int 11 Jul 1938 by TARDIF Hilary M of Biddeford ME

TARDY Archie L of Laconia NH & CATIN Marie Jeanne of Laconia NH int 6 Aug 1940 by MARIE Hilaire of Biddeford ME

TARLSON George W of Laconia NH & WILD Winifred J of Jackson NH int 25 Oct 1951 by POELHEMUS Oscar M of Haverhill NH

TARLTON Lorrin of Watertown NH & WHEELOCK Olive of Fitzwilliam NH int 21 Jun 1934 by EDWARD C Camp of Watertown MA

TARR Arnold Bernard of Dover NH & MILES Wanda Gail of Sanford ME int 4 Sep 1959 by SUMMER V Ward of Sanford ME

TATER Bruce of Fitchburg MA & JOSEPH Ann of MA int 10 Jun 1957 by SCHWAITZ Albert B of Fitchburg MA

TATRO Glenyth Maynard of Keene NH & TARBOX Marilyn Theresa of Keene NH int 26 Jun 1956 by ERNEST A Hogan of Providence RI

TAWA Anthony of Boston MA & SEVERANCE Ella Jane of Pembroke NH int 20 Oct 1949 by SHAKER A J of W Roxbury MA

TAYLOR Edward Story of Cambridge MA & RATHBONE Constance Mary of Palmer MA int 23 Jul 1931 by FREDERICK R Griffin of Walpole NH

TAYLOR L Roland Jr of Keene NH & HOLBROOK Susan C of Keene NH int 6 Oct 1959 by J Edison Pike of Andover MA

TAYLOR Oliver of Rindge NH & SWIFT Carleen of Rindge NH int 4 Oct 1954 by H Frederick Brown of Brighton MA

TAYLOR Wm Simpson of Peterboro NH & WRIGHT Louise H of Peterboro NH int 26 Aug 1959 by PARK Charles E of Boston MA

TEGER John Edgar of Arlington Heights MA & OLIVER Jean Ellaine of Rochester NH int 29 May 1951 by HVEZDON V Kafka of Harvard MA

TELLIER Robert of Manchester NH & LAVALLEE Estelle of Manchester NH int 10 Aug 1953 by LeMAY Lionel of Attleboro MA

TEPPER Ernest John of Concord NH & JENOVESE Dorothy M of Concord NH int 17 Apr 1953 by MICHAEL A Genovese of Leomister MA

TERESKO Walter P of Graniteville MA & LUCAS Claire Lucille of Nashua NH int 2 Nov 1957 by MULLIGAN Paul F of Graniteville MA

THAYER Hollis K of Brooklyn NY & READ Florence E of Brooklyn NY int 2 Aug 1935 by SIMMONS Franke E of Whitefield NH

THAYER James Edgerley of Alton NH & PERKINS Beulah Louise of Farmington NH int 25 May 1934 by WATSON Albert P of Wilton ME

THAYER Philip Chandler of New Ipswich NH & CALDWELL Helen Frances of New Ipswich NH int 19 Sep 1928 by PRESCOTT George J of Cambridge MA

THAYER William of New Ipswich NH & TOKO Patricia of New Ipswich NH int 31 Jul 1951 by CLAPP Edward T of Portland CT

THERRIAULT Ralph of Nashua NH & DESJARDINS Lorraine of Nashua NH int 28 Feb 1951 by MAURCIE Desjardins of CAN

THERRIEN Roland of Nahsua NH & HUDOW Jacquline of Nashua NH int 4 Aug 1949 by RUEST Sylvio of Dracut MA

THIBAULT Richard of Wellesley MA & LeBRUN Shirley of Lebanon NH int 11 Mar 1959 by LeBRUN Donald of Techny IL

THIBAULT Roland A of Greenville NH & LaFLAMME Marjorie of Manchester NH int 30 Jul 1953 by C Edouard Desilets of CAN

THIBODEAU Alex of Manchester NH & SCOTT Caryl of Manchester NH int 13 Dec 1960 by QUININ N Robert of Alexandria VA

THOMAS Alan R of Upper Darby PA & SPRENGLING Uni A of Sandwich NH int 27 Sep 1957 by KANE Jos of Harrisburg PA

THOMAS Harold Jr of Boston MA & RUSHIT Mary of Cambridge MA int 8 Sep 1959 by HARRIS Barbour of Quincy MA

THOMAS Stanley W of Gorham ME & STEVENS Dorothy L of Kingston NH int 4 Jun 1949 by THOMAS Hayward of Gorham ME

THOMPSON Charles C of Westwood MA & COOPER Barbara E of Rochester NH int 23 May 1941 by THOMPSON A Roy of Westwood MA

THOMPSON George K of Cambridge MA & RANDALL Eunice L of Watertown MA int 6 Oct 1948 by HOLLIS M French of Woods Hole MA

THOMPSON Lovell of Boston MA & SIMONDS Katharine of Snowville NH int 10 Aug 1929 by CHARLES L Adams of New Cannan CT

THOMPSON Merrill Willis of Cape Porpoise ME & GRAY Evelyn Vesta of Dover NH int 7 Mar 1951 by LESTER C Holmes of Alfred ME

THOMPSON W Paul Jr of Binghamton NY & LESSIG Sarah Wylie of Binghamton NY int 22 Aug 1955 by THOMPSON W Paul of Binghamton NY

THOMPSON William Norris of Nashua NH & MARTIN Ruth Pauline of Nashua NH int 2 Nov 1928 by E A Durham of Haverhill MA

THORNDIKE David of Brookline MA & MOREAU Marguerite of Jaffrey Ctr NH int 18 Sep 1955 by J Donald Johnston of Deerfield MA

THORNTON Edwin of Townsend VT & GRAY Edith Nana of Rochester NH int 12 Sep 1932 by PAIGE Wesley A of Riverside RI

THORON Gray of Boston MA & CLARK Mary Dwight of Dublin NH int 1 Jun 1939 by PARK Charles E of Boston MA

THORPE Gordon Dodge of Manchester NH & TAYLOR Bessie Clara of Goffstown NH int 20 Feb 1945 by ARTHUR E Gregg of Cornwall Bridge CT

THORUP William Barrett of Boston MA & LOWELL Murial of Warner NH int 26 May 1937 by AYERS Wm B of Wollaston MA

THUNBERG Jon of Canterbury NH & WHITE Mary Francis of Manchester NH int 8 Aug 1957 by HOWARD L Brooks of Arlington VA

THURSTON E Mr of Exeter NH & NICHOLS Glendel of Pittsfield NH int 7 Oct 1937 by GEO Lee Fish of Newburyport MA

THYNG Charles Lt of Barnstead NH & THOMPSON Beryle of Winchester NH int 2 Jun 1941 by GEORGE Truman Carl of Chicago IL

TIBBETTS Arthur P of Rye NH & BROWN Shirley D of Rye NH int 23 Aug 1948 by FRANK B Chatterton of Cambridge MA

TIBBETTS Merrick Sawyer of Keene NH & EDSON Elizabeth Harding of W Lebanon NH int 31 Aug 1950 by ROBERT James Harding of Jeffersonville VT

TIERNEY David B Jr of Milford NH & McLEOD Joan of Milford NH int 24 Jul 1956 by WILLIAM S Gooch of Kittery Point ME

TIGER Melvin A of Poughkeepsie NY & HAMILTON Barbara M of Winchester MA int 12 Jul 1955 by SNOOK John Jr of Winchester MA

TILESHAN Fredisic M of Dorchester NH & LEAVITT Elizabeth of Exeter NH int 28 Aug 1929 by TOMKINS Floyd W of Phil PA

TILESTON Harry W of Jamaica Plains MA & MOORE Brenda of Boston MA int 10 Sep 1948 by MORGAN Walter A of Worcester MA

TILSON Claude D of Manchester NH & SANDER Magda Nelson of Manchester NH int 24 Sep 1952 by WEINLICK John R of Bethlehem PA

TILTON John Havemeyer of Littleton NH & SEIDLER Marjory D of Littleton NH int 23 Aug 1949 by ZUCKERMAN Harvie of New York

TILTON Robert Owen of Berlin NH & LAVIGNE Ceale Claire of Berlin NH int 22 Apr 1953 by LAVIGNE Sabin of St Jean CAN

TITUS Elwood Owen of Silver Springs MD & WALZ Doriss of Belmont MA int 12 Jun 1951 by TITUS Harry of Rochester NH

TOBEY John Burgoyne of Barre VT & FINNEY Elizabeth Anne of Concord NH int 15 Apr 1957 by AHERN Richard of W Springfield MA

TOBIN Richard S of Manchester NH & DANEY Mary Catherine of Manchester NH int 24 Sep 1930 by FRANCIS X Downey of Boston MA

TOLLEY James Roscoe of Northumbeland PA & LEWIS Lucy Strong of Brooklyn NY int 12 Jul 1932 by LEWIS Frederick of Brooklyn NY

TOLMAN Raymond E of Swanzey NH & RICE Loraine of Winchester NH int 14 Oct 1959 by ROBERT J Harding of Brattleboro VT

TOMKINS Ira of Winthrop ME & HICKS Evangelyn of Canaan NH int 25 May 1954 by LINDBERG Carl O of Framingham MA

TOMLINSON James S of So Portland ME & STERLING Constance E of Piales Island ME int 27 Aug 1934 by ROUNDY Rodney of Portland ME

TOMOU George of Nashua NH & VASIOTIS Anthoula of Nashua NH int 20 Jan 1941 by ARCHIBISHOP Christopher of Lowell MA

TOMPKINS Coles F Jr of Salem MA & NESBITT Florance Aimee of Lynn MA int 24 Oct 1952 by EARLE M Hand of Hudson MA

TOMPKINS Wallace E of Springfield MA & PICKRELL Elizabeth M of Springfield MA int 14 Jul 1949 by WALTER A Aschenbach of Springfield MA

TORNROSE William Frederick of Salisbury MA & SADLER Marcia Lea of Evanston IL int 7 Aug 1957 by CORNELIUS Baker of Evanston IL

TOTMAN Ralph Wright of Walpole NH & FREAD Dorothy Rawson of E Alstead NH int 17 Aug 1931 by MARSHALL Benjamin of Worcester MA

TOUSSAINT Raymond of Salmon Falls NH & LeHOULLIER Bertha of Somersworth NH int 16 Aug 1947 by LeHOULLIER Gaston of Lowell MA

TOWLE James William of Chester NH & DEARBORN Virginia J of Chester NH int 21 Oct 1949 by FREDERICK L Harrison of Orange MA

TOWLE Paul Roger of Rocchester NH & TOMPSON Eleanor Jane of Rochester NH int 14 Jun 1960 by ROBERTS Carlye B of Worcester MA

TOWLE Vernon Ervin of Bennington NH & WILSON Rachael Anne of Bennington NH int 16 May 1941 by OSBORNE Earl C of No Berwick ME

TOWLE Winslow B Jr of Stamford CT & CHASE Ruth Anita of So Sutton NH int 15 Aug 1944 by TUCKER Francis S of Conshohocken PA

TOWNES Charles Hard of New York NY & BROWN Frances of Berlin NH int 23 Apr 1941 by HILDA Libby Ives of Portland ME

TOWNSEND Paule Storrs of Lebanon NH & RADCLIFFE Marie G of Oak Park IL int 3 Jun 1946 by RADCLIFFE Lynn J of Oak Park IL

TOZER Arnold W of Hudson NH & ALGER Georgina of Middleboro MA int 9 Jun 1949 by JAMES P Berkeley of Newton Ctr MA

TRACY Stephen P of Meriden CT & LOUGEE Dorothy E of Milton NH int 11 Aug 1933 by WATSON Albert P of Wilton ME

TRAER James Robert of Woburn MA & BOUSFIELD Jean of Wilmington MA int 7 Apr 1958 by RICHARD E Harding of Wilmington MA

TRASK Richard J of Lowell MA & LORING Alma V of Westville NH int 12 May 1951 by RICHARD Ferdinand of Natick MA

TRAUTMAN Gerald H of Ontario CA & TUCKER Doris J of Bronxville NY int 12 Jul 1934 by EMERY L Bradford of Boxford MA

TREAT Donald F of Detroit MI & TALBOT Anne of Keene NH int 31 May 1949 by TREAT Rober Eddy of Detroit MI

TREDINNICK Frank A Jr of Wakefield MA & OTTO Emily M R of Concord NH int 30 Sep 1943 by RICE Austin of Wakefield MA

TREIVS Charles of Hyde Park MA & VILES Lilla Frances of Hyde Park MA int 19 Jul 1935 by MacDONALD Forrest of Hyde Park MA

TREMBLAY Bertrand of Manchester NH & CHAMPAGNE Ange Laure of Manchester NH int 5 Aug 1938 by EMERY Champagne of Manchester NH

TRENT James Edward of Bradford MA & CROSSMAN Margarette of Hampton Falls NH int 22 May 1945 by A Beverly Crossman of Worcester MA

TREVENA Ronald of Lisbon NH & CHURCH Priscilla of N Haverhill int 22 Feb 1960 by MYRON W Dodds of No Haverhill NH

TRICKEY Charlotte of Milton NH & STEWART Glenn W of E Rochester NH int 23 Jun 1939 by ROSE Wm Wallace of Lynn MA

TRIPP Edwin Webster of Farmington NH & TWITCHELL Anne of Farmington NH int 7 May 1959 by JOHN H Jordan of Sanford ME

TROJANO Harold of Meredith NH & WHITE Marjorie of Meredith NH int 13 Sep 1945 by RONALAD S Bezanson of Portland ME

TROMBLEY Alexander S of Lancaster PA & NELSON Barbara of Concord NH int 10 Aug 1934 by TROMBLEY Clifford G of Lancaster PA

TROWBRIDGE Alexander B of Winter Park FL & BOVINGDON Louise Thorne of Lake Forrest IL int 3 Jun 1942 by A Graham Baldwin of Andover MA

TROWBRIDGE Robertson of Morristown NJ & SAGENDORPH Lorna of Dublin NH int 9 May 1956 by TROWBRIDGE Cornelius of Morristown NJ

TRUMBULL Philip of New Boston NH & CAMPBELL Pauline Fraser of Dublin NH int 7 Jul 1942 by SUTER J W Jr of New York NY

TRUSLOW James of Whitinsville MA & KENDALL Anna Deigh of Sanbornville int 21 Jun 1930 by CHARLES E Cutchinson of E Orange NJ

TUBE Fred Napolean of Nashua NH & TANGUAY Eugene of Nashua NH int 30 Apr 1930 by PAUL Demangeleere of Boston MA

TURCOTTE Henry of Manchester NH & TONYIN Marcella of Manchester NH int 26 Jun 1935 by HENRI Goundreau of Manchester NH

TURGEON Alcide of Dover NH & HOUDE Yvonne of Dover NH int 19 Jul 1935 by TURGEON M R of Lewiston ME

TURGEON Andre of Somersworth NH & HOUDE Beatrice of Dover NH int 25 Sep 1939 by TURGEON M R of Lewiston ME

TURGEON Joseph of Dover NH & DROLET Jeanne Anita of Somersworth NH int 16 Jul 1937 by TURGEON M R of Lewiston ME

TURNER Garner Clyde of Keene NH & WELLS Virginia of Cambridge MA int 2 Aug 1941 by WILLIAM E Gardner of Nantucket Island MA

TURNER Stanley Heywood of Harvard MA & MALLEY Elizabeth M of Dover NH int 20 Aug 1929 by ROBERT W Coe of Brockton MA

TUTTLE Ronald of Wilton NH & PARO Mary Lou of Wilton NH int 5 Jun 1950 by JOSEPH P Burke of Brighton MA

TUTTLE Rufus Clarke of Orange MA & WOOD Hazel of New London NH int 4 Jun 1930 by VANBUSKIRK G Bennett of Orange MA

TWITCHELL E B of Hanover NH & DAVIS Anne of Hanover NH int 13 May 1954 by PLAGENZ George R of Boston MA

TWOMBLOY Phillip Norton of Winchester MA & HOUSER Betsy Tenney of Belmont MA int 18 Jul 1949 by DONALD B Fitzsimmons of Winchester MA

TWOMEY James F Jr of Willimantic CT & CLARK Paulita U of Concord NH int 13 Aug 1931 by RAYMOND F Conlon of Burlington VT

TWOMEY William of Moultonboro NH & STUTTERMAN Alice of Danvers MA int 6 Jun 1951 by McMANEES Frederick of Brighton MA

TYLER Callin E of Richmond VA & WEBB Louise Harries of Newmarket NH int 26 Apr 1943 by SCHOFIELD Russell G of Belmont MA

TYLER David B of Holden MA & STOHLBERG Lois of Holden MA int 1 Mar 1957 by HARTLEY T Grandin of Holden MA

TYLER Henry Augustus of Wakefield MA & LANEN Jane Jackson of Melrose MA int 29 May 1929 by RICE Austin of Wakefield MA

UHLENDORF Carl Fredrick of Somerville MA & KENT Elizabeth of Somerville MA int 10 Aug 1934 by SAMUEL R Dont of Shenandoah PA

ULINE Kenneth H of Lyme NH & BULL Marion Ruth of Lyme NH int 18 Jun 1947 by WILBUR Bull of Waterford ME

UNDERWOOD Raymond of Washington DC & HARRIS Freda Louise of Meredith NH int 16 Jul 1931 by THOMAS J Cate of Malden MA

UPTON Frederick of Gorvanda NY & WALL Hazel of Portsmouth NH int 13 Sep 1946 by TEDFORD Willis E of Corenna ME

UTZ Cornelius of New York NY & AUGUSTINUS Dogmar of New York NY int 15 Aug 1942 by FODNEY W Roundy of Portland ME

VACHON Lawrence of Berlin NH & CARON Louise of Berlin NH int 12 Jun 1952 by VACHON Claude of Natick MA

VACHON Raymond P of Somersworth NH & DUBOIS Marguerite of Rochester NH int 15 Oct 1948 by M E Chartrand of Lewiston ME

VACHON Roland of Somersworth NH & LANSFACON Yvonne of Somersworth NH int 6 Apr 1945 by VACHON Gerard of Alexandra Bay NY

VAILLANCOURT Paul of Manchester NH & LAMBERT Rita of Manchester NH int 22 Oct 1956 by J A Gonthier of Attleboro MA

VALLEE Donald Gerard G of Manchester NH & GAUTHIER Jeanette R of Manchester NH int 22 Sep 1951 by ALPHONSE Houle of Lowell MA

VALOIS Joseph of Trois Rivers Quebec CAN & PROVENCHER Yvonne of Manchester NH int 2 Nov 1928 by VALOIS C O of St Cuthbert Quebec CAN

VALZ Deno Gris of Andover MA & TRRNTINA Erma of Milford NH int 26 May 1931 by LOUIS I Beldon of Hartford CT

VAN Buskirk Lawrence H of E Rochester NH & LANGMAID Norma Julia of E Rochester NH int 8 Aug 1949 by ERNEST L Harvey of Richmond ME

VAN Note William G of Artanter NJ & POLING Rachael K of Deering NH int 19 Oct 1929 by POLING Daniel A of NY

VANBEUSCHATEN Wm Henry of West Park NY & HADLEY Dorothy Marie of Concord NH int 27 Jul 1934 by LYFORD Richard T of Bula Cynayd PA

VANDURSEN Lawrence R of Scranton PA & VORIS Virginia of New York NY int 18 Jun 1931 by HENRY H Crane of Scranton PA

VARNEY Albert of Alton NH & PALMER Barbara of Alton NH int 18 Apr 1951 by CHARLES Austin Earle of St Johnsbury VT

VATCHER Earl A of Hancock NH & WILDER Pansy May of Hancock NH int 23 Jul 1930 by J A Edwards of Central Falls RI

VERMILYE Peter H of Long Island NY & MITCHELL Lucy M of Walpole NH int 20 Sep 1950 by ROONEY E J of St Johnsbury VT

VERNON Robert Carey of Poland Springs ME & HAYES Carolyn of New London NH int 14 Apr 1949 by VERNON P L of Poland Springs ME

VEZINA Herve N of Gardner MA & NOEL Rachel E of Nashua NH int 3 Aug 1940 by S J Desautels of Chicopee Falls MA

VICKERY William of Rochester NH & SMITH Natalie of Rochester NH int 31 Jul 1950 by REID Wilbur L of Windsor PA

VINCENT Alfred of Seattle WA & VIENS Gabrielle of Manchester NH int 23 Jan 1942 by VINCENT Clarence of Glenview IL

VINCENT Frank W Jr of Concord MA & BOYDEN Mary Lydia of Winchester MA int 15 Aug 1938 by VINCENT Harold G of Barton VT

VINCENT Lee of Goffstown NH & ZELLER Janet Goodwin of Dunbarton NH int 28 May 1953 by PAYNE John Howard Jr of Gardner MA

VIOLETTE Vernon of Portsmouth NH & WOOLHULL Roberta of Portsmouth NH int 3 Jan 1957 by VIOLETTE Chanel of Boston MA

VOGLER Charles Colburn of Wellesley MA & THORPE Sarah Eliz of Nashua NH int 27 Jul 1954 by NASH Norman B of Boston MA

VOLPE John Willard of Brockton MA & HAYES Nancy Louise of Boston MA int 6 Jun 1960 by MANN George Jorma of Mills ME

VonWEAVER Donald of Bloomington IN & STEVENS Ella May of Epping NH int 18 Aug 1960 by PENDER James E of Jamaica Plains MA

VORCE Welcome H of Keene NH & DeBERNAIDO Christine M of Keene NH int 23 Jul 1948 by MARTIN Michael of Oklahoma City OK

VOSBURGH Charles Vernon of Bellow Falls VT & PELTON Marian Louise of Bellows Falls int 22 Aug 1949 by GARDNER D Cottle of Bellows Falls VT

VOSE Atherton C of Brookline MA & DALES Barbara Jane of West Newton MA int 21 May 1936 by MERRILL Boynton of West Newton MA

VOTER John Gilbert Jr of Methuen MA & FORREST Elizabeth Jean of Pelham NH int 10 Oct 1953 by SUNDBERG Albert Jr of Lynn MA

WAFER James Wilson of Littleton NH & FISHER Priscilla of Keene NH int 23 Oct 1952 by C Barnard Chapman of Providence RI

WALDO Abner Morrison of Ashland NH & BROWN Bertha of Ashland NH int 4 Oct 1958 by SPEERS Theodore C of Speers NY

WALKER John E of Epping NH & OEHNE Valla E of Sarasota FL int 26 Jul 1949 by CLINTON W Carvell of No Andover MA

WALKER Joseph of New Jersey & COLBURN Naomi of New London NH int 10 Dec 1947 by HAROLD W Cuker of Lynn MA

WALKER Joseph Alcott of Newmarket NH & TRUESDALE Mildred of Lewiston ME int 5 Sep 1925 by CLINTON W Carvell of No Andover MA

WALKER Nelson of Portsmouth NH & NORNWELL Priscilla of Portsmouth NH int 22 Aug 1946 by THORP Almus of Columbus OH

WALKER Walter Wills of New London NH & SCHUCKER Judith of New London NH int 9 Sep 1955 by ARTHUR Hopkinson of Greenfield MA

WALL John S of East Kingston NH & GIFFORD Patricia of East Kingston NH int 18 Oct 1958 by RAYMOND J Cosseboom of Framingham MA

WALLACE Robert Alan of Brookline MA & BURNAP Jean Cameron of Greenvile NH int 16 Jan 1957 by BENJAMIN F Andrew of Lunenburg MA

WALLACE William of Sandwich NH & MORGAN Faith of Sandwich NH int 31 Jul 1950 by EDWARD Hale of Framingham Ctr MA

WALLACH John Michael of Newburgh NY & LOVETT Eileen of Franconia NH int 20 Jul 1940 by JOHN W Dunn of Brooklyn NY

WALLIS Malcom of Patterson NJ & SAMPSON Phyllis H of Providence RI int 8 Jul 1940 by SAMPSON Wallace of Laconia NH

WALSH Frank J of Manchester NH & CRETES Dorothy G of Manchester NH int 3 Sep 1954 by LAMY Roland M of Leborgne Haiti

WALSH Hollis O of Melrose MA & FLANDERS Elizabeth of Brentwood NH int 12 Aug 1930 by WHITE O J of Watertown MA

WALTON Alfred of Keene NH & GRUBE Velma of Keene NH int 9 Jan 1957 by C Barnard Chapman of Providence RI

WALTON Richard T of Alton NH & DETSCHER Dorothy Ann of Wolfeboro NH int 9 Aug 1952 by NOBLE Chas C of Syracuse NY

WAMPLER Garry R of Pottstown PA & NOURY Claire G of Nashua NH int 7 Mar 1960 by NOURY Eugene of Lowell MA

WARD Erwin Walter of Alstead NH & DUSTIN Mirian Anne of Alstead NH int 16 Jun 1953 by STETSON Clifford R of Springfield VT

WARD Frank of New York NY & MANGUISE Mildred of New York NY int 14 Aug 1929 by A Edwin Keigwin of New York NY

WARD Parker V of Nashua NH & EVERETT Mary of Nashua int 14 May 1943 by MARKHAM Thomas F of Lowell MA

WARDELL Roderick of Binghamton NY & TEMPLE Frances of Portsmouth NH int 23 Feb 1951 by OUTLAW Ging of Hyde Park MA

WASHBURN Guy Porter of ? & SUOMINEN Laila of ? int 17 Jun 1937 by MYRON W Adams of W Townsend MA

WASILEWSKI Joseph J of Portsmouth NH & HOWARD Phyllis of Portsmouth NH int 19 Jul 1946 by NASON Philip S of Cortland NY

WASLASKE Peter of Athol MA & PADUCHAK Olga of Hindsdale NH int 22 Jun 1936 by MICHAEL Boberski of So Deerfield MA

WATSON Albert S of Washington DC & GREENE Margaret Chase of Washington DC int 29 Jul 1947 by LEAMON John H of Cambridge MA

WATSON Eugene S of Madison NH & JORDAN Maeville E of Cape Eliz ME int 11 Dec 1952 by NATHANAEL M Guptill of Newton MA

WATSON James B of Boston MA & STENDEN Marian of Putnam CT int 25 May 1928 by LOVETT Sidney A of Boston MA

WEAVER Joseph M of Wheaton IL & AUBEST Marian L of Middlebury VT int 5 Jul 1938 by A Aubert of Wallingford VT

WEBBER Bernard Allen of Hillsboro NH & CHEEVER Hannah Amanda of Boston MA int 15 Nov 1945 by FRANK A M Coad of No Abington MA

WEBBER Everett Heath of Concord NH & KNOX Jean Elizabeth of Concord NH int 25 Aug 1952 by FREDERICK R Knox of Chester VT

WEBLE Aman R Jr of Manchester NH & WHITNEY Leona of Derry NH int 30 Apr 1957 by KENNETH A Batchelder of Revere MA

WEEKS Ashley of Malden MA & ROBARGE Alysse of Malden MA int 9 Aug 1929 by HENRY H Crane of Scranton PA

WEEKS William Richard of Greenland NH & HOLLEY Marion Evelyn of Greenland NH int 7 Nov 1941 by ROBERT S Hall of Fort Slocum NY

WEISMAN Douglas Carl of Hudson NH & BERRY Bonnie Lou of Cleveland OH int 5 Oct 1960 by BRANSWELL Crawford of Lowell MA

WELCH Robert W of McIndoes VT & BURT Jan Marie of Bath NH int 30 Apr 1959 by PAUL D Bobbitt of Weels River VT

WELCH William F of Manchester NH & BRODERICK F Louise of Manchester NH int 9 Jun 1953 by JOHN A Broderick of Brighton MA

WELDON George F of Lawrence MA & MULLEN Agnes of Manchester NH int 17 Oct 1925 by GEORGE A Egan of Force PA

WELLS Neil A of Epsom NH & YOUNG Dorothy A of Concord ME int 10 May 1946 by MASON John of So Walpole MA

WELSH John J of Manchester NH & COYCE Helen R of Manchester NH int 30 Aug 1933 by FRANCIS X Downey of Boston MA

WENTWORTH Charles B of Newton NH & INGALLS Mildred Frances of Newton NH int 14 May 1929 by JAMES G Beveridge of Milford MA

WENTWORTH Norman of Haverhill MA & NICHOLS Natalie of Atkinson NH int 27 Aug 1927 by ROBERT Campbell Jr of Swampscott MA

WEST Ernest F of E Kingston NH & CARTER Elizabeth M of Exeter NH int 18 Aug 1926 by EDWARD A Dodd of Hyde Park MA

WEST Ralph of Chichester NH & HANCOCK Beverly Dianne of Webster NH int 31 Jul 1953 by ROBERT Decker of Anthony RI

WEST William Henry Jr of New York NY & HANEY Hope Stephenson of New York NY int 22 Aug 1938 by MILLS Charles S of Hartford CT

WETMORE George Henry of Fitzwilliam NH & FLANDERS Marion G of Plaistow NH int 20 Jun 1933 by SMITH Chellis V of Hyde Park MA

WETMORE Walter Charles of Concord NH & SATURLEY Florence A of Concord NH int 6 Jun 1951 by OLNEY S B of Portland ME

WETZEL John K of Allentown PA & CANN Alice Miller of PA int 11 Jun 1957 by WELSH A Augustus of Bethlehem PA

WEYENS Wayne Elmer of Chicago IL & GOSS Muriel E of Quincy MA int 13 Aug 1946 by TAYLOR Malcolm of Brookline MA

WEYMOUTH Donald B of Hampton Falls NH & MOODY Olive of Concord NH int 17 Oct 1932 by PERCY A Kilmister of Norwich CT

WHATMOUGH Seddon Jr of Salem Depot NH & WILD Marion Jean of Salem Depot NH int 2 Jul 1951 by ROBERT E Drew of Methuen MA

WHEAT Gerald S of Moravia NY & GASS Katherine Janette of Conway NH int 25 Jun 1953 by LEA Fergus of Brighton ME

WHEELER Bernard L of Derry NH & BARTLETT Cynilla O of Derry NH int 27 Apr 1938 by JAMES M Cubie of Saugus MA

WHEELER Coburn T of Peterboro NH & ROLLINS Betrica of Newport NH int 8 Jun 1936 by RAIBLE Obert of Greenfield MA

WHEELER Nyron of Claremont NH & MARCOTTE Pauline Marie of Claremont NH int 25 May 1959 by GERARD H Brochu of Burlington VT

WHELDEN Frank M of Grafton MA & CALL Edith of W Newton MA int 15 Jul 1955 by TURRELL Stephen W of Grafton MA

WHILES William of Antrim NH & CRANE Mildred E of Washington NH int 24 May 1951 by MONBLEAU Charles of Malden MA

WHITCOMB Paul Eugene of Keene NH & ROWE Josephine Mary of Charlestown NH int 2 Jul 1932 by AUGUSTINE Jones of Springfield VT

WHITE Erskine N of Winchester MA & LUTZ Eileen Eugenie of Warner NH int 26 Oct 1949 by WALLACE W Anderson of Portland ME

WHITE Webster W Jr of New Hampton NH & OSGOOD Shirley H of Nashua NH int 15 Mar 1946 by EDWARD G French of Johnson VT

WHITELAW David L of Snyder NY & EATON Nancy Wells of Hillsboro NH int 4 Feb 1955 by MONBLEAU Charles of Malden MA

WHITMAN Donald of Drewsville NH & KEMP Barbara of Alstead NH int 30 May 1951 by MARSH George B of Perkinsville VT

WHITMORE Henry Jr of W Newton NH & CHASE Grace M of Concord NH int 3 Sep 1929 by WHITMORE Holmes of Milwaukee WI

WHITTINGHILL Maurice of Hanover NH & CUMMINGS Doris of Hanover NH int 25 Aug 1932 by A W Clark of Chestnut Hill MA

WICKURT Clifford J Dr of Baltimore MD & FROST Marie Elizabeth of Baltimore MD int 14 Aug 1943 by STAFFORD Russell Henry of Boston MA

WIDDER David Vernon of Harrisburg PA & AMES Vera Adela of Saskatchewan CAN int 24 May 1939 by MILES Hanson of Weston MA

WIEGAND Allen P of Worcester MA & WATTENFELLS Ingrid of Burlington VT int 23 May 1956 by WIEGAND Dudley of W Newbury MA

WIGGIN Donald Otis of Belmont NH & PATTERSON Lois Ruth of Sanbornton NH int 24 Apr 1957 by WILLIAM T Keech of Acton MA

WILEY Howard R of Salem MA & JACKMAN Pauline Frances of Salem MA int 1 Mar 1927 by LYON Charles W G of Salem MA

WILHELM Bobby La Van of Concord NC & GEROULD Mary of Franklin NH int 13 Oct 1947 by HOOFER R Goodwin of Bethel VT

WILKINS Samuel of Wayland MA & VINCENT Letitia of Wayland MA int 19 Aug 1943 by EMERSON F Blodgett of Newton Ctr MA

WILLEY Cedric of Newport NH & WADHULL Joan F of Newport NH int 13 Jun 1958 by MacLEOD Robert J of Stoughton MA

WILLEY Floyd of Manchester NH & CUNNINGHAM Helen E of Manchester NH int 17 Dec 1934 by LAWRENCE L Barber of Arlington MA

WILLIAMS Clifford of Canterbury CT & CHASE Joanne of Laconia NH int 15 Aug 1952 by STUBS Henry W of Canterbury CT

WILLIAMS Edmund S of Boston MA & SMITH Doris of Hudson NH int 17 Oct 1934 by WESTNEAT Arthur S of Boston MA

WILLIAMS Edward Karl of New York NY & HARLOW Bettine Martha of New York NY int 5 Jul 1954 by NOBLE A Grant of Willamstown MA

WILLIAMS Fred of Westiminster VT & MacLANE Marion of Alstead NH int 11 Jul 1951 by MARSH George B of Perkinsville VT

WILLIAMS Fred of Watertown MA & TAYLOR Maureen of Brighton MA int 10 Jun 1955 by JOHN R Ferris of Phila PA

WILLIAMS Paul Albion of Brookline MA & MORGAN Kathryn of Lisbon NH int 23 Aug 1938 by WATHEN John M of Blackstone MA

WILLIAMS Wallace J of New London NH & SPAULDING Marilyn Rose of New London NH int 18 Jul 1952 by McCONNELL James W of Liverpool NY

WILLIAMSON Robert W of Norwood MA & COLBY Margaret C of Claremont NH int 24 Sep 1929 by OSMOND P Hoyt of Monticello NY

WILLIAMSON William L of Atlanta GA & CORDWELL Alice of Berlin NH int 9 Jul 1956 by DELPHAS S Barnett of Whitinsville MA

WILLIS Robert of Auburndale MA & McCARTHY Mary of Concord NH int 12 May 1954 by McCARTHY Mary of Newton MA

WILSON Earle Craig of Hanover NH & JENNEY Arlene Lois of Plainfield NH int 5 Aug 1942 by FREEMAN Jenney of Syracuse NY

WILSON George Henry of Alstead NH & WILSON Rena Amelia of Lunenburg VT int 17 Apr 1959 by ISADORE H Fox of Cambridge VT

WILSON Guy of Durham NH & WHIPPEN Carolyn of Durham NH int 13 Feb 1945 by LAURENCE W C Emit of Winthrop MA

WILSON Hoyt Weber of Walpole NH & CLARK Muriel of Brooks ME int 10 Apr 1942 by ROBERT M L Holt of Amherst MA

WILSON Philip C of Tuftonboro NH & LEACH Isabel B of Tuftonboro NH int 26 Jun 1947 by MORGAN Garfield of Lynn MA

WINDLE Albert Wm of So Berbick ME & TEBBETTS Ethel of So Berwick ME int 11 Dec 1935 by WILLARD M E of So Berwick ME

WINTER Clark of Ogunquit ME & JAMESON Lois of Branford CT int 23 Aug 1946 by STEWART George of Dublin NH

WITHEE Kenneth of Boston MA & LITTLEFIELD Caroline of Hampstead NH int 1 Jun 1936 by FRANK E Drew of Peabody MA

WOOD Clarence A of Meredith NH & WILLIS Florence of Meredith NH int 15 Jan 1937 by ERNEST C Herrick of Newton Ctr MA

WOOD H Edward of Fairhaven MA & GRANT Marjorie B of Winchester MA int 23 Jun 1936 by PARKER Wm H of Fairhaven MA

WOOD Robert of W Lebanon NH & BISHOP Martha L of W Lebanon NH int 16 Jun 1950 by WILLIAMS Ed of White River Jct VT

WOOD William Bliss of Arlington MA & WALLIN Josephine M of Deerfield NH int 3 Apr 1938 by WOOD Nathan of Arlington MA

WOODBURY Robert Isaac of Topsfield MA & DANA Marjorie Odell of Topsfield MA int 9 Aug 1929 by TRACY Olin B of Skowkegan ME

WOODRUFF Bliss of Randolph NH & DAVIS Marian of Randolph NH int 23 Aug 1952 by MULLER Kenneth D of East Stoneham ME

WOODRUFF David of Concord MA & TIBBETTS Janett of Milton NH int 25 Jul 1960 by MAXFIELD Leland L of Newton MA

WOODWARD Andrew L of Lyme NH & LAWSON Bertha Eva of Lyme NH int 8 Jun 1948 by MOORE Rutherford of So Royalton MA

WOODWARD Donald E of W Franklin NH & PATTON Beverly Ann of Tilton NH int 18 May 1956 by STILES Dennis Jr of Corning NY

WOODWARD Harold Walter of Franklin NH & CLINE Louise Elaine of Franklin NH int 17 Oct 1952 by MONTGOMERY Marshall of Lake Worth FL

WOOLSTENHULME Lynn J of Camp Lejeune NC & MOBBS Marjorie Louise of Kensington NH int 7 Oct 1952 by SAWYER Roland D of Ware MA

WORRELL William Ballard of Salisbury NH & RAYMOND Phyllis Ann of Salisbury NH int 3 Nov 1955 by WILLIAM H Johnson of So Berwick ME

WORTHEN Harold Palmer of Elkins NH & GODSHALK Avis Spencer of Elkins NH int 28 Sep 1948 by SMITH Meredith P of Marblehead MA

WOTT Ralphp William of Franklin & SIMOND Marion Edith of Boston int 19 Jan 1926 by PALLADINO Frederick of Boston MA

WRIGHT Augustus of Portland ME & ROGER Eleanor of Amesbury MA int 22 Aug 1952 by LUDEKING Charles W of Amesbury MA

WRIGHT David of Nashua NH & JEAN Jeannie of Nashua NH int 8 Mar 1959 by F X Caron of Quebec CAN

WRIGHT Elanc Rust of Alton NH & PRESCOTT Minnie Nelson of Natick MA int 23 Aug 1932 by B F Gustin of No Amherst MA

WRIGHT Hastings Kemper of Winchester MA & HOWELL Nancy Elizabeth of Birmingham MI int 17 May 1954 by JOHN W Ellison of Winchester MA

WRIGHT Lawrence W Jr of Concord NH & LAUNEY Mary of Concord NH int 22 Jun 1937 by HERBERT H Knight of Hamden CT

WRIGHT Robert J of White Plains NY & PETTY Nancy V of NH int 9 Nov 1935 by WRIGHT Charles O of White Plains NY

WRIGHT William Stearns of Pembroke NH & FARNUM Mary Elizabeth of Pembroke NH int 5 Aug 1949 by EARLE L Buchin of Virginia MN

WURTH Walter Albert of Maplewood NJ & SHULTIS Ruth of So Newbury NH int 27 Oct 1930 by BENJAMIN P Browne of Winchester MA

YARID Charles M of Arlington MA & SLATER Janet of Lowell MA int 7 Sep 1960 by SHAHIN Michael C of Lowell MA

YAW Clio James of Portsmouth NH & BARNETT Elizabeth Ann of Portsmouth NH int 18 Oct 1956 by GEORGE R Bates of Amesbury MA

YEAGER William L of Corwall NY & WOLFE Alice Louise of Pittsford NY int 17 Aug 1938 by MERRILL Boynton of W Newton MA

YEATON Theodore E of Epsom NH & FOWLER Marjorie E of Epsom NH int ul 1945 by MASON John of So Walpole MA

YLINEN Elmer E of Troy NH & WIINIKKA Ann of Marlboro NH int 17 May 1954 by TOIVO A Esala of Fitchburg MA

YORK Franklin of Concord NH & WELCH Louise of Concord NH int 17 Jun 1946 by BEYER Richard T of Springfield VT

YORK Henry of Bretton Woods NH & TEW Josephine of Bretton Woods int 10 Sep 1929 by TEW Maurice of Scranton PA

YORK John W of Kensington NH & STACY Jessie E of Exeter NH int 14 Aug 1944 by SAWYER Roland D of Ware MA

YOUNG Elmer E Rev of Candia NH & ANDERSON Barbara of Candia NH int 13 Jun 1953 by CHARLES A Bray of St Johnsbury VT

YOUNG Harvey C of Catskill NY & SAWYER Muriel of Warner NH int 10 Jul 1940 by ALEXANDER L Chandler of Sandwich MA

YOUNG Robert of Newington NH & MERRILL Lucy of Greenland NH int 27 Oct 1958 by M Sargent Desmond of CAN

YOUNG Wesley of Pepperell MA & ARMSTRONG Charline of Brookline NH int 5 Jul 1939 by LUPIEN Edmond D of Pepperell MA

YOUNG William C of Strafford NH & WHITTIER Charlotte C of Strafford NH int 18 Aug 1936 by ALVIN C Bacon of Natick MA

YUILL Arthur Graham of Manchester NH & MINDT Helen Milda of Pembroke NH int 11 Apr 1942 by EARLE S Buchin of Cedar Grove NJ

ZAEDER John Philip of Erie PA & THAYER Sylvia Louise of Farmington NH int 17 May 1958 by HENRY J Keating of New Rochelle NY

ZAIKIS Sylvester of Dorchester MA & UTKA Josephin of Nashua NH int 30 Sep 1948 by ANTHONY Bruzas of Hartford CT

ZIARKO Albert of Detroit MI & DULA Helen of Detroit MI int 6 Sep 1960 by HENRY H Crane of Detroit MI

ZIEGRA Louis Richard Jr of Deep River CT & STEVENSON Alice of Jaffrey NH int 20 Apr 1953 by FRED I Cairns of Hamilton CAN

ZILA Albert Vincent of Cedarhurst NY & PERKINS Frances Marjoria of Ctr Harbor NH int 6 Aug 1951 to Allan Knight Chalmers of Boston MA

ZILCH Normand of Newport NH & L'ETOILE Roberta of Claremont NH int 17 Nov 1949 to J A Dutil of E Brewster MA

This index lists the surnames of the brides listed in the text.

ABBOT, 50 52 56 57 67 78 80 84
ABBOTT, 17 21 29 49 51 58 64 67 72 75 76 80 81 85 146 173
ACKERMAN, 179
ADAMS, 3 44 58 64 67 69 119 139 158 176 195 212
AHERN, 165
AHRUNDT, 151
AILIN, 48 70
ALDRICH, 127
ALEXANDER, 130 146 147
ALGER, 221
ALLARAD, 143
ALLEN, 37 39 82 96 99 208
ALLEY, 197
ALLIN, 61
ALLISON, 30 59 85
AMAZEEN, 177
AMBROSE, 31 55 87 88
AMES, 8 53 229
AMRON, 214
AMSDEN, 212
ANDERSON, 38 67 153 187 206 232
ANDRESEN, 170
ANDRESS, 203
ANDREWS, 40 148
ANGELL, 210
ANGER, 143
ANNIS, 168
ANNOS, 187

ANSDEN, 5 31
ARCHER, 36
AREL, 124 166
ARGUIN, 115 124
ARLIN, 56 72 81
ARMSTRONG, 113 147 232
ARNOL, 37
ARNOLD, 38
ARSENAULT, 98 121 129 139
ASH, 215
ASHBROOK, 206
ASHE, 124
ASHLEY, 131
ASLIN, 55
ATHERTON, 176
ATKINS, 39
ATKINSON, 215
ATTWOODEE, 36
ATWOOD, 14 53 106
AUBEST, 227
AUERBACH, 165,
AUGUSTINUS, 223
AUSTIN, 54 56 133
AVERY, 89 203
AYER, 12 13 16 33 48 90 163 193
AYERS, 10 108
AZARIAN, 132
BABB, 61 71 145
BACHELDER, 78 90 143
BACON, 38 63 174
BADGER, 43
BAGDASARIAU, 109

BAGLEY, 35 204
BAILEY, 30 31 39 56 76 87 178 198 203
BAKER, 44 55 63 68 72 91 160
BALCH, 97
BALDASARO, 99
BALDWIN, 44 48 55 57 88 108 159 205 217
BALL, 27
BALLARD, 88
BAMISTER, 123
BANCROFT, 163
BANKS, 193
BARBER, 39
BARBIN, 198
BARE, 164
BARKER, 15 18 28 68 75
BARNARD, 159
BARNES, 206
BARNETT, 231
BARNEY, 135 210
BARRETT, 45 123 124 161
BARRON, 108
BARROW, 37
BARROWS, 166
BARTHOLOMEN, 16
BARTLETT, 4 5 25 43 46 184 208 228
BARTON, 212
BARTOW, 97
BARTULA, 157
BASSETT, 118
BASTILLE, 113
BASTON, 177
BATCHELDER, 4 19 32 136 152 166
BATES, 3 6 21 50 73 191
BATTEN, 201
BAXTER, 166
BAYEK, 171
BAYLEY, 38
BAYLISS, 181
BEACHAM, 25
BEACHMAN, 11

BEAILIEU, 138
BEAL, 159
BEAN, 65 78 101 190 208
BEANE, 202
BEARD, 1
BEARDSLEE, 33
BEATON, 131 214
BEAUCHAIN, 109
BEAUCLAIR, 132
BEAUDET, 168 171
BEAUDOIN, 104
BEAULIEU, 101 169 184 191
BECHOK, 137 160
BECKER, 211
BECKMAN, 106 142
BECKNER, 137
BEDARD, 194
BEDELL, 194
BEEBE, 106
BEEDE, 186
BEER, 213
BEERNAERT, 102
BELAND, 143 193
BELANGER, 166 175 190 204
BELASKI, 169
BELCHER, 148
BELDEN, 104
BELKNAP, 63 80
BELL, 105
BELLIVEAU, 115
BELLVUE, 98
BEMIS, 192
BENNERT, 164
BENNET, 54 89
BENNETT, 9 21 126 137 147 173 197
BENNINK, 217
BENTLEY, 194
BENTON, 109
BERDECKI, 181
BERGERON, 96 158
BERLE, 51 116
BERNARD, 183
BERNIER, 151 210

BERRY, 21 34 125 179 206 227
BERTAND, 128
BESSE, 164
BETCHLEY, 159
BETLEY, 172
BEVERSTOCK, 185
BIBEAU, 123
BICKFORD, 14 31
BIDWELL, 111
BILLINGS, 215
BILODEAU, 171
BIRD, 188
BISHOP, 39 148 230
BISSONNETTE, 129
BIXBY, 11 21 71
BLACK, 143
BLACKBURN, 87
BLACKLEY, 39
BLACKWOOD, 196
BLAINE, 216
BLAIS, 110
BLAISDELL, 3
BLAKE, 3 12 37 38 56 63 104 162 192
BLANCHARD, 37 49 54 55 199
BLASDEL, 12 19
BLASDELL, 56
BLATCHFORD, 175
BLAZO, 23
BLENDER, 181
BLISH, 132
BLISS, 126 150
BLODGET, 72
BLODGETT, 28 75 84
BLOUNT, 106
BLOZO, 23
BLUNT, 35
BOARDMAN, 58
BOGHOSIAM, 175
BOHANAN, 117
BOHANON, 74
BOHON, 36
BOIS, 126
BOISE, 46

BOISVERT, 95 167 179 196
BOIVIN, 95
BOLD, 191
BOLDUC, 200
BOLLEN, 210
BOLLES, 150
BOLTON, 122
BOND, 19 202
BONNER, 152
BONTHRON, 179
BOODY, 13
BORDEN, 117
BORVEN, 37
BOSS, 182
BOTT, 204
BOUCHARD, 103 197
BOUCHER, 138 197
BOULAY, 195
BOULGER, 96
BOURASSA, 170 199
BOURASSIA, 184
BOURK, 206
BOURQUE, 176
BOUSFIELD, 221
BOUTELLE, 117
BOUTHILLIER, 154
BOUTIN, 88
BOUTON, 3 6 22 23 74 75
BOUTWELL, 140
BOVINGDON, 222
BOWDITCH, 97
BOWEN, 123
BOWER, 186
BOWERS, 5
BOWLES, 194
BOWLIN, 181
BOX, 36
BOYCE, 112
BOYD, 69 95
BOYDEN, 224
BOYNTON, 33 91 197
BRACKET, 47
BRACKETT, 111
BRADBURY, 32

BRADISH, 162
BRADLEY, 7 16 46 62 66 72 74
BRADSTREET, 38
BRAGG, 84 168
BRAGON, 119
BRAM, 46
BRASSARD, 183
BRAY, 208
BREED, 65 144
BREEZER, 162
BREMER, 97
BRENNAN, 185
BRENTON, 204
BRETON, 103 180
BREWSTER, 103
BRIANT, 37 60
BRIDGE, 36 135
BRIDGES, 65
BRIEN, 140
BRIGGS, 161 162
BRIGHAM, 23
BRIMBLOCOM, 62
BRINGHAM, 60
BRISSE, 178
BRITLES, 99
BROCHU, 110
BROCK, 169
BROCKWAY, 104 194
BRODERICK, 227
BRODEUR, 100
BROGAN, 182
BRONSDON, 48
BRONSON, 176
BROOKS, 16 34 65 76 83 86 91 110
BROUILLET, 147
BROUILLETTE, 173
BROWN, 14 19 26 28 30 33 35 38 48 52 54 57 65 70 71 73 77 83-85 88 94 97 127 134 136 139 140 146 151 152 155 165 172 182 188 206 213 219 221 225
BROWNELL, 113

BRUAMT, 83
BRUCE, 123 179
BRUNELLE, 110 167
BRUNO, 193
BRUSH, 190
BRYANT, 17 40 69 91
BRYAR, 216
BRYER, 110
BRYNE, 112
BUCKAMAN, 151
BUDD, 196
BUDGE, 200
BULL, 223
BULLARD, 21 29 71 108 151
BULLOCK, 35 148
BUMFORD, 116
BUNKER, 16 17 95 107 129
BUNTIN, 48
BUNZELL, 23
BURBANK, 147 153 201
BURGESS, 202
BURLEY, 59
BURNAP, 226
BURNHAM, 27 43 109 162 171 202
BURPEE, 54 57
BURPEY, 82
BURRELL, 116
BURT, 227
BURTON, 109
BURWELL, 186
BUSH, 138
BUSS, 60 73
BUSWELL, 20
BUTFINCH, 37
BUTLER, 9 38 40 47 153
BUTMAN, 22 170
BUTTERS, 44 59
BUZZELL, 155
BYAM, 25 60 74 76 78
CABOT, 38 204
CAFREY, 69
CAGNE, 145
CAIRNS, 135

CALDER, 209
CALDWELL, 102 218
CALL, 228
CALLAGHAN, 189
CALLAHAN, 102 174
CALLEY, 29
CALQUHOM, 217
CAMPBELL, 121 132 188 214 222
CANFIELD, 215
CANN, 228
CANNEY, 217
CANNON, 127
CANT, 37
CANTLIN, 160
CAPEN, 43 47 62 81
CAPRON, 65
CARBONNEAU, 98
CARBOTT, 40
CARDINAL, 123
CAREY, 1
CARLETON, 15
CARLISLE, 177 201
CARLTON, 8 20
CARON, 66 114 122 157 175 204 223
CARPENTER, 20 38 84 88
CARPENTIER, 168
CARR, 23 25 35 86 215
CARRIEL, 169 171
CARRIER, 23 150
CARRIGAN, 181
CARROLL, 156 216
CARTER, 32 43 45 64 70 72 74 76 90 96 106 198 227
CASEY, 102
CASS, 6 25 118 207
CASSILY, 113 166
CASWELL, 36 102
CATE, 2 144
CATIN, 217
CATSAM, 190
CAULE, 64 79
CAVANAUGH, 131

CAYLE, 176
CEDAR, 148
CELMENT, 11
CENTER, 78
CHADWICK, 1 28 30 37 44 51 86 91 155
CHAFE, 6
CHAFFEE, 121
CHAFFIN, 58
CHALMERS, 149
CHAMBERLAIN, 127
CHAMPAGNE, 140 154 165 212 221
CHANDLER, 9 44 45 52 54 56 71 73 75 77 82 86 157
CHANEY, 2 9 14 17 28 32
CHAPLIN, 33
CHAPMAN, 10 39 59 138 203
CHAPUT, 201
CHARLES, 10
CHARPENTIER, 141
CHASE, 6 14 20 35 39 51-53 56 74 77 136 141 221 228 229
CHASES, 12
CHASSE, 217
CHATELIER, 131
CHATMAN, 36
CHAUVIN, 129
CHEEVER, 227
CHELLIS, 117
CHENET, 32
CHENEY, 32 37 106 117
CHETEMAN, 125
CHEVEN, 77
CHIDLEY, 181
CHILDS, 212
CHMIELEWSKI, 146
CHRISTENSEN, 174
CHRISTIE, 184
CHURCH, 222
CHUTE, 104
CHUTTER, 98
CIFFORD, 17

CILLEY, 6
CLAPP, 155
CLAPS, 6
CLARK, 3 19 46 55 77 78 83 97 98 100 137 146 196 213 214 219 223 230
CLARKE, 61 117 145
CLARKSON, 40
CLAVEAU, 173
CLEARY, 110 170
CLEASBY, 4 53
CLEASLEY, 48
CLEAVES, 2
CLEMENS, 38
CLEMENT, 2 16 18 62 75 106 166
CLIFFORD, 8 15 20 64
CLINE, 231
CLISBY, 65
CLOSE, 159
CLOUGH, 5 40 135
CLOUTIER, 204
COBB, 106
COBURN, 176
CODY, 173
COFFIE, 8
COFFIN, 38 40 53 55
COGSWELL, 10 71
COHEN, 165
COLBATH, 206
COLBURN, 225
COLBY, 13 27 40 52 62 64 79 101 139 177 196 216 230
COLCORD, 156
COLE, 70
COLEMAN, 95 140 174
COLLIER, 107 205
COLLINGS, 7
COLLINS, 4 36 38 53 194
COMBS, 73 79
CONANT, 107
CONCERN, 7
CONKLIN, 122
CONNER, 49
CONNOLLY, 151
CONNOR, 164
CONNORS, 1 202
CONWAY, 199
CONY, 78
COOK, 52 105 204
COOLIDGE, 85 210
COOMBS, 37 79
COOPER, 118 192 219
CORBETT, 99
CORDWELL, 230
CORLIS, 60 80
CORLISS, 50
CORNWELL, 119
COSTELLO, 145
COTE, 106 114 177 182
COTTON, 134 182 195
COUGLIN, 121
COUREHESUE, 119
COURNING, 119
COUTURE, 102
COVERS, 15
COX, 119
COYCE, 227
CRADOCK, 37
CRAFTS, 146
CRAIGNAN, 183
CRAM, 3 23 85 207 211
CRANDALL, 198
CRANE, 136 160 228
CRAWFORD, 161 168
CRAY, 83 213
CREGO, 186
CRETES, 226
CRIMBELL, 70
CRITTENDON, 96
CROCKER, 40
CROFT, 210
CRONK, 148 166
CROOKS, 148
CROOMS, 36
CROSBY, 2 47 49 53 91 113 135
CROSS, 39 193

CROSSMAN, 222
CROTEAU, 126 161
CROWELL, 151 195
CROWNINGSHIELD, 40
CRUIKSHANK, 140
CUMMINGS, 139 190 200 229
CUMMINS, 38 147
CUNNINGHAM, 24 35 229
CURRAN, 101
CURRIER, 3 12 32 63 139 162 196
CURRY, 56
CURTICE, 64 152
CURTIS, 66 79 210
CUSHING, 11 158
CUSHMAN, 156 186
CUTLER, 19
CUTTER, 10 22 46 47 53 54 64 69 73 74 82 87
CUTTING, 88
DAHL, 122
DALE, 46
DALES, 225
DALHEN, 208
DALZEL, 213
DAM, 25
DAME, 3 16
DAMERY, 186
DAMON, 50 57
DANA, 29 85 230
DANE, 47 115
DANEY, 220
DANFORD, 49
DANIELS, 44 68 186 191
DANINSON, 5
DANIS, 116 157
DANTAS, 183
DARLING, 81 127
DAVENPORT, 35 39 125
DAVIDSON, 15 49 105 122
DAVIS, 2 7 9 10 13 18 20 25 27-29 31 34 39 49 57 60 71 135 137 143 152 153 163

DAVIS (continued)
169 186 201 211 215 223 230
DAVISON, 91
DAVY, 203
DAWE, 190
DAWES, 155
DAY, 76
DEAN, 19 59 69 216
DEARBORN, 52 173 174 221
DEBERNAIDO, 225
DEFOREST, 150
DEFORREST, 172
DELAHANTY, 97 139
DELISLE, 168
DELOREY, 129
DEMENA, 195
DEMERITT, 2 9 28 30 54
DEMPSEY, 147
DENNIS, 37 138 184
DENNISON, 15
DEPIERREFEU, 141
DEROCHEMONT, 94
DEROCHES, 121
DEROSSEAU, 87
DERR, 195
DESAULNIERS, 155
DESBOIS, 119
DESCLOS, 139
DESGAGNE, 189
DESHARMAIS, 106
DESILETS, 153 199
DESILLETS, 140
DESJARDINS, 127 218
DESMARAIS, 183
DESROCHERS, 102 123 144
DESROSIERS, 166
DETSCHER, 226
DEXTER, 152
DIAMOND, 215
DICKERSON, 20
DICKEY, 175
DIEHL, 132

DILL, 154
DIMOND, 49 67 85
DINSMORE, 17 31 67 88 211
DIONNE, 164 177
DIXON, 169 211
DOAN, 153
DODDS, 165
DODGE, 37 38 50 57 178 187 209
DODSON, 170
DODWELL, 100
DOE, 5
DOEG, 5
DOELE, 123
DOERR, 153
DOHERTY, 187
DOIR, 196
DOLE, 39 98 102 139
DOLLOFF, 24 80
DOLPH, 160
DOLTON, 11 32
DOMINA, 151
DONAHOE, 143
DONNELLY, 199
DOOLE, 202
DOON, 119
DORAN, 112 181
DORR, 37
DORRITY, 24
DOTSON, 101
DOUILLETTE, 133
DOW, 9 11 13 15 22 26 37 53 57 58 62 64 112
DOWN, 8 95
DOWNING, 156
DOWNS, 78
DOYEN, 56
DOYLE, 151
DRAKE, 76 128
DRAPER, 93 160
DREW, 34 52 97 130 194
DREWRY, 164
DRIGGS, 147
DRINKER, 207
DRISKO, 160
DRIVER, 35 154
DROLET, 222
DROUIN, 149
DUBE, 103 104
DUBOIS, 223
DUCHAIME, 194
DUCHARME, 146 189
DUCHESNAYE, 155
DUCLOS, 128
DUDLEY, 30 170 200
DUERR, 152
DUFRESNE, 120
DUGUAY, 106 138
DUHAINE, 129
DULA, 232
DUMAINE, 101
DUMAIS, 217
DUN, 51
DUNBAR, 125
DUNCAN, 209
DUNCKLEY, 49
DUNKLEE, 82
DUNLAP, 45 108
DUPONT, 167 168
DURANT, 35 149
DURETTE, 203
DURGIN, 18
DUSTAN, 151
DUSTIN, 26 226
DUSTON, 32
DUTCHER, 156
DUTTON, 23
DUVAL, 212
EASTAM, 81
EASTMAN, 12 44 52 56 58 59 62 64 65 72 75 87 150 165 196 211
EATON, 6 8 11 13 14 16 18 21 22 29 31 65 75 80 82 107 157 228
EDGERLY, 76
EDSON, 219
EDWARD, 148

EDWARDS, 7 15 122
ELA, 44 75
ELDREDGE, 214
ELIOT, 41
ELLINGWOOD, 53
ELLIOT, 21 44 55 60 72 82
ELLIOTT, 21 53 55 57 61 74 95
ELLIS, 155
ELLISON, 5 128 200
EMERSON, 2 12 17 18 22 25 32 61 81 167 197
EMERY, 1 5 30 44 49 59 63 70 71 75 78 86 125 129
EMMONS, 38
ENEBUSKE, 198
ENILSEY, 37
ENRIGHT, 137
ENSTIS, 152
ERICKSON, 132
ERKI, 188
ERKIS, 133
ESTABROOK, 75
EVANS, 6 126
EVARTS, 157
EVERETT, 226
EVERETTE, 160
EVES, 70
EWEN, 63
EYRES, 209
FABYAN, 24 30
FAIRBANK, 144
FAIRBANKS, 13 132 135 159 167
FAIRCHILD, 135
FALKINS, 159
FANAN, 39
FARETRA, 136
FARLAND, 71
FARMER, 149
FARNHAM, 19 37
FARNSWORTH, 150
FARNUM, 44 50 53 66 72 74 80 83 231
FARR, 161

FARRAN, 67
FARRAR, 8 36
FARRINGTON, 98
FAUCHER, 129
FAULKNER, 150
FAVOR, 57
FAY, 79
FECTEAU, 121
FEISE, 109
FELCH, 1 45 183
FELLER, 20
FELLMAN, 204
FELLOWS, 62 109
FELTCH, 67
FENTON, 113 203
FERGERSON, 207
FERGUSON, 130 149
FERLAND, 135
FERNALD, 17 94 136
FERREN, 100
FERRIN, 45
FERRY, 212
FEWKES, 128
FIELD, 112
FIFE, 50 133
FIFIELD, 8 68 79 133
FILLION, 116 164
FIMPLE, 186
FINNEY, 220
FISH, 48 83
FISHER, 113 169 181 225
FISK, 10 17 57 67 71 80 82 85 120 161
FISKE, 4 24 48 76
FITTS, 37 124
FITZSIMON, 182
FLAGG, 196
FLANAGAN, 118
FLANDERS, 14 16 33 37 45 50 62 67 70 82 85 90 106 114 157 214 226 228
FLEMING, 109 130
FLINK, 133
FLINT, 113

FLOOD, 7
FOGG, 11 22 26 88 105
FOLENSBEY, 4
FOLLANSBEE, 14
FOLSOM, 10 69 127
FONTAINE, 177
FORBES, 3 212
FORD, 189
FORREST, 95 225
FORTIER, 145 165-167
FORTIN, 12 145
FOSS, 8 58 78 80 107 112
FOSTER, 17 27 28 62 65 82 83 105 139 157 160 176 208
FOURNIER, 111 120
FOUST, 55
FOWLER, 147 166 232
FOX, 2 36 44 52
FOY, 136
FOYE, 210
FRADD, 193
FRANCE, 147
FRANCIS, 137
FRANK, 207
FRANKS, 105
FRASEY, 38
FREAD, 202 221
FREDERICK, 123 157 178
FREEZE, 107
FRENCH, 1 22 27 45 47 48 65 77 81 105 121 134 140 191 202
FROLICH, 185
FROOG, 15
FROST, 61 133 147 229
FROSTER, 38
FRYE, 81
FULLER, 151 217
FULLINTON, 23
GAGE, 27 34 132 185
GAGNON, 98 119 122 205 216
GALE, 60 72
GALLAGHER, 125
GALLUP, 144

GAMACHE, 127
GAMBLE, 184
GAMCHE, 125
GANELL, 47
GARABEDIAN, 94
GARDNER, 36 113 116 145 146 162
GARFIELD, 54 148
GARIEPY, 197
GARLAND, 40 48 189
GARVIN, 79
GARY, 69
GASKILL, 102
GASS, 228
GATH, 97
GAUDREAULT, 114
GAUTHIER, 136 205 224
GAVDENS, 126
GAY, 12 109 196
GAZES, 96
GEARY, 162
GEE, 215
GELINAS, 213
GEORGE, 23 35 45 54 73 74
GEROULD, 229
GERRISH, 38 72
GIBBS, 181
GIFFORD, 225
GIGUERE, 126
GILBERT, 172 203 211
GILE, 9 43
GILES, 27 63
GILL, 50 66 145 158
GILLINGHAM, 103
GILLMAN, 57 85
GILLMORE, 46 57 63 78 82
GILMAN, 4 5 78 83 137 141 158 203
GILMORE, 16
GILSON, 207
GINSBURG, 151
GIREN, 163
GLASS, 6
GLAVIN, 179

GLIDDEN, 39 83 144 171
GLNRY, 209
GLORE, 193
GLOVER, 2 8 45 71 74
GODDARD, 45
GODFREY, 36
GODIN, 111
GODSHALK, 231
GOING, 32
GOLDMAN, 142
GOLDSMITH, 38
GONTHIER, 104
GOODRICH, 207
GOODWIN, 11 32 40 87 153 202
GORDON, 81 117 131 189
GOSS, 228
GOSSELIN, 114
GOUBERT, 109
GOUDREAU, 120
GOUGH, 103
GOULD, 44 117 158
GOVE, 36 68 84
GOWIN, 13
GOWING, 24 32 91
GRADY, 213
GRAF, 134
GRAGG, 29
GRAMLING, 177
GRANGER, 95
GRANT, 36 99 108 127 131 134 145 149 230
GRATTON, 127
GRAVES, 123 163 198
GRAY, 141 179 219
GREELEY, 35
GREEN, 29 37 82 84 86 183
GREENBERG, 163
GREENE, 45 198 226
GREENLEAF, 33 39
GREENLIEF, 35
GREENOUGH, 4 25
GREENWOOD, 102
GREGOIRE, 126

GREGORY, 200
GRENIER, 172 204
GREW, 181
GRIFFIN, 2 22 65 88 154
GRIFFITH, 32 130
GRIGGS, 62 69 169
GRIGORACOS, 160
GRIM, 132 176
GROSS, 20
GROVER, 14 36 68
GRUBE, 226
GRUMMAN, 93
GUERTIN, 139
GUFFITHS, 214
GUIDER, 180
GUILE, 8
GUILLEMETTE, 205
GUSTAFSON, 212
HACKETT, 184
HADLEY, 21 77 91 157 224
HAGER, 41
HAGGETT, 170
HAHN, 96
HAILMAN, 112
HAINES, 47 57 84 210
HALE, 19 29 30 32 89 105 107 153 170
HALL, 15 26 28 31 34 50 56 60 80 87 98 99 111 121 136 137 216
HALLIDAY, 148
HALLIGAN, 171
HAM, 30 62
HAMBLET, 193
HAMBLETON, 73
HAMILTON, 10 22 111 126 184 220
HAMLIN, 148
HAMMER, 115
HANCADE, 101
HANCOCK, 86 227
HAND, 115
HANEY, 182 227
HANFORD, 122

HANLON, 211
HANNON, 150
HANSCON, 179
HANSELL, 173
HANSON, 2 22 32 129 180
HARDY, 80 103 187
HARGRAVES, 184
HARISSON, 9
HARKNESS, 84
HARLOW, 229
HARMON, 120
HARPER, 83
HARPPER, 37
HARRAN, 4
HARRIAM, 10
HARRIMAN, 10 12 13 15 26 28
HARRIMANA, 29
HARRINGTON, 169 173
HARRIS, 12 36 83 118 136 172 205 223
HART, 169 188 191 195
HARTFORD, 7 46
HARTHAN, 38
HARTLEY, 207
HARTSHORN, 110 184
HARVEY, 54 210
HASELTINE, 12 178
HASELTON, 11
HASKEL, 39
HASKELL, 49 150 180
HASKINS, 110
HATCH, 141
HATHORN, 27 81 84
HAWSKINS, 192
HAY, 25
HAYDEN, 167 184
HAYES, 15 99 215 224 225
HAYNES, 25
HAZALTON, 179
HAZEN, 156 161 173
HAZLETINE, 47 50
HAZZEN, 37
HEALEY, 132
HEARD, 171

HEATH, 15 27 28 74 76
HEDRICK, 125
HEMPHILL, 199
HENEAGE, 195
HENNESSEY, 107
HENRY, 24 99
HEON, 46 102
HERBERT, 65 82
HEREMAN, 28
HERRICK, 59
HERRON, 150
HERSEY, 25
HERSON, 152
HESSER, 170
HEWLIN, 39
HICKS, 205 220
HIGGINS, 161
HIGLE, 3
HILARD, 33
HILDRETH, 19 116 160
HILL, 55 56 68 72 77 78 89 97 146 158 187
HILLIARD, 29
HILSON, 162
HILTON, 89 188
HILYARD, 55
HINCH, 122
HINDON, 175
HIRD, 193
HITCHOCK, 154
HOAG, 86
HOBSOM, 188
HODGDON, 85
HODGE, 27 33 44 66 77 81 89 90
HODGEDON, 142
HODGES, 164
HODGS, 35
HOFFSEE, 146
HOGAN, 126
HOIT, 12 30 47 53 55 86 89 191
HOITT, 20 29
HOKINS, 181

HOLBROOK, 218
HOLCUME, 125
HOLLAND, 67 162
HOLLEY, 227
HOLLOWAY, 94
HOLMAN, 170
HOLMES, 99 123 201 202
HOLMS, 36
HOLMSTROM, 168
HOLT, 8 10 20 61 79 171 196
HOOD, 105
HOOK, 86
HOPCRAFT, 182
HOPWOOD, 167
HORNE, 208
HORNEBECK, 173
HORTON, 5 49
HOSMER, 24
HOUDE, 222
HOUGHTELING, 121
HOUGHTON, 106 216
HOULE, 107 123
HOUSER, 223
HOW, 77
HOWARD, 40 126 136 226
HOWE, 26 52 59 65
HOWELL, 231
HOWES, 173
HOWLAND, 182
HOYET, 9
HOYT, 3 16 89 117 137
HROYLE, 148
HUBBARD, 8 11 167
HUCKINS, 142 163 183 211
HUDON, 128 205
HUDOW, 218
HUDSON, 37 180 186
HUFF, 96
HUGGINS, 23
HUGHES, 118
HULBURD, 200
HULMER, 153
HUMPHREY, 1
HUNKINS, 9 14 172

HUNT, 12 39 59 77 80 90
HURLEY, 134
HUSE, 115
HUSSON, 110
HUTCHINS, 103 126
HUTCHINSON, 59 78
HYMAN, 98
IDA, 192
INGALLS, 50 71 143 227
INGERSELL, 36
INGRAHAM, 114
IRISH, 67
ITRAIN, 172
JACKMAN, 15 18 37 229
JACKSON, 17 22 37 197 202
JAMESON, 55 113 230
JANELLE, 168 197
JANES, 186
JANETOS, 213
JANVIN, 11
JAQUITH, 46 56 86
JARVIS, 153
JEAN, 5 157 189 231
JEFFERS, 17
JEFFERSON, 103
JEFFRY, 36
JENESS, 30
JENISON, 39
JENKINS, 10 175
JENNESS, 211
JENNEY, 230
JENNINGS, 199
JENNISON, 216
JENOVESE, 110 197 206 210 218
JEPSON, 124
JERDINE, 45
JESSEMAN, 108
JETTE, 95
JEWELL, 59 69 73 75 81 89 412 150
JEWETT, 7 82 89 137 178
JOBES, 216
JODOIN, 104

JOENSSON, 120
JOHNSON, 5 24 33 56 62 64 71 99 104 131 143 144 147 150 166 196 210 215
JOHNSTON, 132
JOINER, 147
JOLICOEUR, 140 187
JONES, 7 26 50 53 81 121 122 145 159 160 201 203 206 214
JORDAN, 226
JORGENSEN, 144
JOSEPH, 217
JOYNT, 195
JUDKINS, 128
JUDSON, 133
JULIEN, 173
JUNEAU, 138
JUNKINS, 153
KAAN, 127
KAESER, 164
KALESZ, 157
KAMILA, 116
KAPSALIS, 203
KARAHELAS, 166
KARPPI, 13
KASHULINE, 141
KATHAN, 190
KATZ, 143
KAUFMAN, 185
KAULBACK, 196
KAUPPI, 144
KEARNEY, 197
KEASEY, 47
KELLER, 152
KELLEY, 13 63 69 76 90 176 212 213
KELLOWAY, 107 149
KELLY, 90 110 120 177
KELSEY, 135
KEMP, 26 228
KENDALL, 63 222
KENISTON, 67 75
KENNEALLY, 120
KENNEDY, 12 119 213
KENNETH, 181
KENT, 47 74 85 125 159 223
KENTFIELD, 197
KERRNETT, 127
KERSHAW, 198
KEYES, 49 185
KEYS, 49
KIAH, 40
KIDDER, 3 100
KILBURN, 162
KILGORE, 193
KIMBALL, 5 13 24 31 32 52 53 55 58 61 67 68 70 71 79 80 87 88 91 114 125
KING, 39 102 144
KINGMAN, 198
KINGS, 66
KINIRY, 182
KIRKLAND, 153
KIRKORIAN, 175
KIRKPATRICK, 130
KITCHEN, 95
KIVELA, 138
KIVISTO, 93
KLOCK, 94
KMIEC, 164
KNEBEL, 112
KNEELAND, 46
KNIGHT, 18 20 27 108 155 193 200 201
KNOWLES, 47 58
KNOWLS, 43
KNOWLTON, 10 43 44 216
KNOX, 131 167 173 192 194 205 227
KONISHO, 134
KRAMER, 138
KRUMMES, 101
KUCH, 155
KUNHARDT, 165
KURNER, 178
KURTA, 215
L'ETOILE, 232

LABLE, 137
LABONTE, 54
LABONTIE, 75
LABOUNTY, 66 157
LABRANCHE, 208
LACAILLADE, 176
LACROIX, 119
LACY, 26 71
LADD, 7 18 20 22 151
LAFLAMME, 105 218
LAKE, 107
LAKEMAN, 38
LALIBERTE, 101 147 185
LALLY, 109
LAMARRE, 174
LAMBERT, 207 208 224
LAMONTAGNE, 195
LAMPHERE, 153
LAMPREY, 217
LAMY, 173
LANCASTER, 156
LANDRY, 100 167
LANE, 20 34 51 82 86 211
LANEN, 223
LANG, 18 51 52 54 75 75 84
LANGDON, 108
LANGELIER, 203
LANGLEY, 15 119 190
LANGMAID, 112 212 224
LANKEY, 134
LANOIE, 167
LANSFACON, 223
LANY, 15
LAPIERRE, 180
LAPLANTE, 120
LAPOINTE, 96 114 136
LARDEN, 111
LARIVIERE, 103
LARLEE, 93
LAROCHELLE, 146
LAROUCHE, 209
LARSEN, 149
LARSON, 201
LASCOMB, 35

LASSONDE, 111
LAUNEY, 231
LAVALLEE, 218
LAVIGNE, 96 167 220
LAVOIE, 105
LAW, 185
LAWLOR, 118
LAWRENCE, 11 31 46 48 84 88 130 138
LAWSON, 231
LAWTON, 174
LAZARUS, 121
LEACH, 230
LEARY, 151 200
LEATHERS, 19
LEAVITT, 16 66 71 82 91 220
LEBLANC, 120 121
LEBOSQUET, 77
LEBRUN, 218
LEDDY, 161
LEDREW, 150
LEE, 37-40 170 181 192
LEHOULLIER, 107 128 139 221
LEIGHTON, 4 23 131
LEJOY, 12
LEMAY, 100 191
LEMIEUX, 104
LEMIRE, 166
LEONARD, 211
LESSARD, 96
LESSIG, 219
LETORNEAU, 148
LEVASSEUR, 104 125
LEVEILLE, 208
LEWIS, 159 162 180 182 186 203 213 220
LIBBEE, 21
LIBBEY, 2 98
LICOLN, 59
LILLEY, 195
LINDH, 124
LINDQUIST, 115
LINDSEY, 200
LINGARD, 142

LINNALL, 95
LINSDSTROM, 180
LIONNE, 103
LISK, 153
LISOTTE, 168
LISTER, 118
LITCH, 83
LITTLE, 6 11 163 179
LITTLEFIELD, 16 123 146 157 230
LIVERMORE, 189
LLOYD, 180
LOCH, 180
LOCK, 63 85
LOCKE, 26 29 81
LOMBARD, 172
LONG, 28 39 189
LONGFELLOW, 39
LORD, 6 63 189
LORING, 113 147 193 221
LOUD, 197 209
LOUGEE, 96 221
LOVEJOY, 55 69 128 183
LOVELL, 140
LOVER, 150
LOVERING, 61 156
LOVETT, 226
LOVIT, 39
LOWELL, 39 137 219
LOWMAN, 141
LUCAS, 40 141 173 218
LUCY, 71
LUDGATE, 180
LUND, 171 180
LUNDBLAD, 187
LUNDSTROM, 130
LUNT, 36
LUSSIER, 134
LUTZ, 228
LUZEN, 156
LYFORD, 81 88
LYMAN, 136
LYNCH, 207
LYNEE, 214

LYON, 38
LYONS, 141
LYTLE, 124
MABY, 198
MACARTHUR, 133
MACCALLUM, 191
MACDONALD, 124 158 207
MACEK, 122 197
MACHIAN, 128
MACK, 185
MACKAY, 189
MACKENZIE, 186
MACKINNON, 121
MACLANE, 229
MACPHEE, 175
MACPHERSON, 149
MACVEAGH, 116
MAHMOT, 169
MAHONEY, 183
MAIDONI, 160
MAILHOT, 207
MAJOR, 125 192
MAKI, 164
MALETTE, 202
MALITSOS, 119
MALLEY, 222
MALONEY, 172
MANGIONE, 106
MANGUISE, 226
MANLEY, 95
MANN, 58
MANNING, 37 138
MARAY, 137
MARBLE, 116
MARCEAU, 112
MARCH, 36 38 41 73
MARCHAND, 205
MARCOTTE, 178 228
MARCOUX, 124
MARCY, 102 178
MARDEN, 18 44 85 159
MARDIN, 66 77
MARGRAF, 120
MARKS, 195

MAROIS, 124
MARONEY, 101
MARQUIS, 101 138
MARRITT, 149
MARSH, 137 164
MARSHALL, 9 28 80 83 103 161 216
MARSTON, 51 66 80
MARTELL, 205
MARTHES, 5
MARTIN, 54 57 95 98 128 219
MARX, 209
MASON, 85 106 155 172 190 193
MATSON, 144
MATTHEWS, 111
MATTON, 38
MAVRIC, 138
MAVRILLIS, 149
MAXFIELD, 94 117
MAXWELL, 176
MAYNARD, 66 76 85 102 131 164
MAYNIHAN, 212
MAYO, 216
MAYRAND, 129 179 201
MCAFEE, 154
MCALISTER, 99
MCALLISTER, 138
MCCARTHY, 230
MCCOLLESTER, 180
MCCORMACK, 177
MCCOY, 12 14
MCCRILLIS, 131
MCCURDY, 23
MCDEVITT, 190
MCDONALD, 109
MCDUFFEE, 95
MCDUFFIE, 4
MCELWAIN, 179
MCFARLAND, 22 49 61
MCGARY, 209
MCGRATH, 101 148
MCGREEVY, 100

MCINTOSH, 189
MCKAY, 104
MCKINLEY, 71
MCKINNEY, 210
MCKNIGHT, 167
MCLAUGHLIN, 169
MCLEAN, 159
MCLEOD, 219
MCMAHON, 119
MCNAMARA, 210
MCSHANE, 177
MCSKIMMON, 100
MCSWAIN, 134
MEACHAM, 133
MEADER, 161
MEARS, 58
MECKLENS, 184
MEDVIDDOFSKY, 215
MEHIER, 56
MELENDY, 91
MELLON, 181
MELSKY, 204
MELVIN, 184
MERCHETTI, 132
MERCIER, 170
MEREAULT, 156
MERRILL, 6 30 51 64 66 76 118 134 155 156 167 232
MERRITT, 130
MESENIE, 34
MESERVE, 24 25
METCALF, 184
MICHAUD, 105 140
MICHEL, 171
MIGNAULT, 102 198
MILES, 34 217
MILFORD, 36
MILLER, 29 40 84 96 133 137 144 168 175 215
MILLIKEN, 45 60 64
MILLS, 5 164
MILNER, 118
MILTON, 94
MINDT, 232

MINER, 164 200
MIRIAM, 79
MITCHELL, 130 224
MIVILLE, 214
MIXER, 91
MOATT, 196
MOBBS, 231
MOISON, 204
MONETTE, 110
MONTGOMERY, 70
MOODY, 7 18 41 72 73 79 142 228
MOONEY, 57
MOOR, 33
MOORE, 4 48 54 56 66 73 77 79 127 189 192 220
MOREAU, 219
MOREY, 101
MORGAN, 14 98 137 139 168 215 226 229
MORIN, 125 174 202
MORISON, 168
MORRIL, 74
MORRILL, 6 8 22 51 60 61 71 115
MORRIS, 34 111
MORRISON, 33 135
MORRISSEY, 107
MORSE, 35 50 63 191
MORTON, 156
MOSES, 80 98 130
MOULTON, 24 38
MOWER, 57 66
MOYNIHAN, 93
MUDGETT, 169 214
MUELLER, 147
MULLEN, 131 170 227
MULRDOCK, 78
MUNRO, 164
MURDOCK, 25 174
MURPHY, 10 121 155
MURRAY, 26
MUSSER, 193
NADEAU, 129 165 177

NAGLE, 177
NASON, 172
NAY, 52
NEAL, 51
NEDEAU, 154
NEEDHAM, 37
NEILAN, 112
NELSON, 63 94 97 152 154 222
NESBITT, 220
NEWCOMB, 122
NEWELL, 21 35 72 152
NEWHALL, 36 39 154
NEWTON, 70
NICHOLLS, 37
NICHOLS, 25 105 115 127 152 165 175 219 227
NICKERSON, 161
NICKNAIR, 167
NILES, 34
NIMS, 101 155
NOEL, 122 224
NOLET, 185
NOLETTE, 120
NORIS, 89
NORMAND, 142 190
NORNWELL, 225
NORRIS, 7 39 194
NORTHY, 36
NORTON, 98
NOURY, 226
NOVAK, 189
NOWELL, 149
NOYCE, 4
NOYES, 3 11 16 18 19 23 24 81 97
NOYS, 3 21
NOYSE, 21
NURMI, 200
NUSSBAUM, 155
NUTE, 10 18 116 119
NUTTER, 59 189 213
O'BRIEN, 161 183 188
O'CONNELL, 174

O'CONNOR, 186
O'DELL, 89
O'HARA, 176
O'LEARY, 129
O'NEIL, 168 199
O'TOOLE, 177
OAKES, 9
OBBEY, 39
ODELL, 24
OEHNE, 225
OGILVY, 156
OLDRIDGE, 39
OLIVER, 206 218
OLNEY, 166
OLSON, 141
ORDWAY, 3 56 89
ORIORNE, 186
ORNE, 39
ORRMAN, 37
OSBORN, 118 159 196
OSBORNE, 163
OSGOOD, 6 8 60 228
OSTRANDER, 208
OSTROWSKI, 205 207
OTIS, 2 17 130
OTT, 200
OTTO, 221
OUELLETT, 114
OUELLETTE, 111 124 145
PACKARD, 194
PADUCHAK, 226
PAGE, 3 9 21 25 28 50 59 64 114 132
PALMER, 6 16 19 132 200 224
PANNENTON, 94
PAQUET, 114
PAQUETTE, 167 173
PAQUIN, 104
PARADES, 168
PARE, 188
PARENT, 101 154 188
PARISEAU, 188
PARK, 179

PARKER, 30 72 86 87 93 94 99 131 142 176 212
PARKINSON, 211
PARKS, 201
PARO, 187 223
PARSON, 2
PARSONS, 134
PARTRIDGE, 121
PASTUSZENSKI, 163
PATEE, 23
PATERSON, 213
PATILLO, 146
PATRICK, 45 47
PATTEE, 214
PATTEN, 19 94 173
PATTERSON, 229
PATTON, 231
PEABODY, 31 151
PEAK, 77
PEARCE, 130
PEARL, 59
PEARSON, 37 118 208
PEASE, 19 135
PEASLEE, 16 22 136 140 212
PEASLEY, 6 7
PEAVEY, 125
PECK, 108
PEEK, 135
PELHAM, 37
PELLETIER, 174
PELTON, 225
PENDERGAST, 49
PENDEXTER, 19
PENN, 144
PENNEY, 113
PENNINGTON, 93
PENROD, 145
PEPEN, 3
PEPPER, 35
PERCIVAL, 205
PERKINS, 20 26 39 40 41 48 70 84 111 123 138 142 205 218 232

PERONTO, 193
PERRAULT, 138
PERRON, 174
PERRY, 14 130 191 196
PESARCZYK, 153
PETERS, 133
PETTES, 74 187
PETTIGREW, 181
PETTINGILL, 54
PETTY, 231
PHELPS, 154 207 215
PHEUR, 177
PHILBRICK, 32 39 62 69 85
    152 211
PHILBROOK, 158
PHILIPPY, 130
PHILIPS, 49 64
PHILLIPS, 5 109 116 195
PHILPOT, 107
PHIPPS, 210
PICK, 38
PICKERING, 27 37
PICKRELL, 220
PIERCE, 6 14 17 50 58 62 66
    76 134 158 173 217
PIISPANEN, 162
PIKE, 33 40 152 178 207
PILLSBURY, 4 38 68 70 87 170
PILSBERY, 41
PILSBURY, 36 69
PINARD, 100
PINDER, 73
PIOTROWSKAR, 209
PIPER, 4 13 45 47 54 55 65 69
    70 77 82 86 89 149
PIXLER, 214
PLAISTED, 199
PLAMER, 7
PLODZIK, 124
PLOTNER, 192
PLOWMAN, 124
PLUMMER, 7 15 25 60 137
POELMAN, 100
POIEIER, 129
POIRER, 148
POIRIER, 168
POLASKI, 208
POLING, 224
POLLAND, 32
POLLARD, 7 9 26 51 59 88
POLO, 193
POOL, 40
POOLE, 40 188
POOR, 4 23 47 131
PORCTOR, 45
PORTER, 41 44 46 106 120
POTEAT, 209
POTTALA, 110
POTTER, 3 4 9 21 46 48 54 56
    100 128 131 160
POTTLE, 61 79 89
POTTS, 145
POTVIN, 111
POWERS, 60 89 166 204
PRAKATAINA, 171
PRATT, 28 83 88 143
PRAY, 131
PRECSCOT, 38
PRELLER, 199
PRESCOTT, 61 78 83 231
PRESCUTT, 40
PRESTON, 114 140
PREVOST, 176
PRICE, 25
PRICHARD, 117
PRIEST, 50
PRINCE, 133 183
PRINGLE, 109
PRIOR, 209
PRIST, 12
PROCTOR, 45
PROVENCHER, 129 224
PRUGH, 154 172
PRYER, 158
PUCKETT, 155
PUDVAH, 97
PUENMAN, 140
PUFFER, 60 81

PUMROY, 66
PURCELL, 145
PURGESS, 178
PURINGTON, 191
PUTNAM, 83 120 149
PUTNEY, 14
QUIGLEY, 29
QUIMBY, 27 76 113
QUINBY, 204
RACKETT, 162
RADCLIFF, 211
RADCLIFFE, 221
RAINE, 209
RAMSEY, 200
RAND, 11 102
RANDALL, 117 142 161 219
RANTOUL, 97 118
RATHBONE, 217
RATT, 123
RAWSON, 165
RAY, 35 99 139
RAYMOND, 129 231
RAYMONE, 201
RAYNO, 144
READ, 117 218
REARDON, 119
REDCLIFF, 211
REED, 30 69 120
REGGIO, 210
REHL, 207
REID, 110 130 201
REINGOLD, 214
REINHARDT, 146
REMPEL, 183
RENAULT, 165
REYNOLDS, 26 32 107 182
RHODES, 127
RICARD, 206
RICE, 29 117 179 220
RICH, 176
RICHARD, 111 148
RICHARDS, 206
RICHARDSON, 39 77 100 117
   142 196 213

RIESE, 158
RIGAZIO, 217
RILEY, 134
RIMINGATON, 36
RINGSBURY, 66
RITCHIE, 120
RITZMAN, 125
RIVAIS, 167
RIVERS, 124
RIVIERE, 119
RLANBOIT, 139
ROADS, 36
ROBARGE, 227
ROBBINS, 62 123
ROBERGE, 103
ROBERTS, 115 210
ROBERTSON, 50 127 155
ROBIDAS, 143
ROBIE, 30 189
ROBINSON, 48 71 73 83 116
   143 149 174 197
ROBY, 47 82 112
RODERICK, 201
ROGER, 198 231
ROGERS, 40 59 80 116 150
ROKES, 194
ROLAND, 11
ROLFE, 48 63
ROLLINGS, 68
ROLLINS, 8 52 56 62 89 113
   115 123 145 147 158 181
   228
ROSE, 122
ROSEN, 106 181
ROSENBLUM, 206
ROSS, 48 84 88
ROSSI, 141
ROTCH, 133
ROULEAU, 213
ROUSSEAU, 98
ROUX, 175
ROWE, 24 228
ROWELL, 89 103 170 171 204
ROY, 7 113 141 185 198 207

ROYCE, 204
ROYS, 203
RUBEOR, 162
RUDELL, 122
RUGGLES, 96 98
RUNDLET, 63
RUNDLETTE, 192
RUNNELS, 70 80
RUSHIT, 218
RUSS, 86
RUSSEAU, 108
RUSSELL, 4 26 88 112 131 136
RUTHERFORD, 209
RYAN, 76 201
SAARI, 159
SABIN, 103
SABMAN, 38
SADLER, 220
SAGENDORPH, 222
SAINTCLAIR, 216
SAINTGEORGE, 156
SAINTJEAN, 103 179
SAINTLAURENT, 199
SAINTPIERRE, 143 175
SAMARA, 137
SAMPSON, 214 226
SAMSON, 109 127 145 175
SANBORN, 2 6 13 21 26 33 36-38 40 52 54 61 69 82 106 161 190 191
SANDER, 220
SANDERS, 13 39 61 205
SANDERSON, 64
SARGEANT, 144
SARGENT, 13 14 21 22 68 76 77 79 83 118
SATURLEY, 228
SAULL, 180
SAUNDERS, 188
SAVAGE, 36
SAVORY, 149
SAWTELL, 61
SAWYER, 7 12 18 29 31 66 88 106 108 116 140 212 232

SAXTON, 212
SAYER, 28
SCALES, 16 57 64 81
SCAMMON, 46 68
SCANNELL, 182
SCHAS, 190
SCHER, 132
SCHIOT, 184
SCHLAGER, 183
SCHMIDT, 115
SCHNEIDER, 134 161
SCHOEPF, 151
SCHOFIELD, 111
SCHOLNICK, 104
SCHUCKER, 225
SCHUKE, 197
SCHULTZE, 144
SCHURMAN, 134
SCOTT, 121 151 161 205 218
SCRIBNER, 179
SCRIPTURE, 31 126
SCRUTON, 95
SEABURY, 199
SEAVER, 109
SEAVEY, 26 46 66 72 85
SEAVY, 28
SEGOURNEY, 39
SEIDLER, 220
SENTER, 169
SESSLER, 112
SEVALL, 38
SEVERANCE, 4 11 29 33 128 217
SEYBOLD, 96
SHACKFORD, 38 47 91
SHADDUCK, 75
SHANDLER, 1
SHANNON, 19
SHARPLES, 105 137
SHATTUCK, 51 60 99 192
SHAW, 28 45 51 79 126 185
SHED, 18
SHEDD, 30
SHEDEL, 59

SHEPARD, 193
SHERBURNE, 81
SHERMAN, 191
SHINE, 159 166 167
SHONK, 187
SHORTELL, 184 198
SHUBURN, 67
SHULTIS, 231
SHUTE, 27 47 66 82 85 90 100 196
SIDELEAU, 113
SIDES, 208
SIDNEY, 115
SIEGLER, 108
SILLOWAY, 118
SILVER, 20 23 69 70 74
SIMARD, 125
SIMOND, 231
SIMONDS, 219
SIMONEAU, 143
SIMPSON, 68 72
SINCLAIR, 97
SIROIS, 100
SKEET, 40
SKILLAR, 108
SKINNER, 192
SLATER, 231
SLEEPER, 130
SLOWLEY, 28
SMALL, 24 96 127
SMART, 27 34 47 50 64 78 88
SMILEY, 46 147
SMITH, 8 11 12 16 17 19 20 23 31 32 37 44 46 55 57 58 68 70 74 89 95 96 112 112 115 119 123 125 133 136 148 149 152 156 157 163 169 171 184 196 208 224 229
SNELL, 4 29 163
SNOW, 31 87 128
SNYDER, 108
SOLASZ, 164
SOMERVILLE, 104
SOUCY, 157 185 201 216

SOUTHEN, 30 86
SOUTHER, 73
SPAULDING, 2 46 69 114 229
SPEED, 61 67
SPENCE, 171
SPENCER, 180
SPILLMAN, 175
SPOFFORD, 2 45 58 73 83 117
SPOONER, 142
SPRAGUE, 106 110 197
SPRENGLING, 218
SPURR, 175
SQUIER, 139
STACKPOLE, 17 18
STACY, 51 232
STALKER, 160
STANFORD, 37
STANIFORD, 36
STANLEY, 13
STANNEY, 39
STANWOOD, 13 93
STANYEN, 39
STAPLETON, 171
STARK, 9
STARLING, 39
STARR, 163
STAYAN, 59
STEARANS, 54
STEARNS, 27 83 192 194 195
STEBBINS, 154
STEELE, 94 121
STENDEN, 227
STEPHEN, 15
STEPHENS, 62 77 96
STERLING, 220
STERNDALE, 180
STERNS, 39
STEVEN, 6
STEVENS, 3 5 7 8 11 13 15 17 18 20 27 28 33 41 51 53 56 61 69 72 90 105 159 172 218 225
STEVENSON, 232
STEWARD, 126

STEWART, 23 75 93 102 178 222
STICKMEY, 47
STICKNEY, 37 49 53 59 60 74 80 84 86 120
STINSON, 187
STITZEL, 154
STOCK, 159
STOCKBRIDGE, 60 79 86
STOCKIN, 207
STOCKMAN, 36
STODDARD, 203
STOHLBERG, 223
STONA, 165
STONE, 4 100 156 168 214
STOREY, 164
STORY, 157
STOW, 74
STRATTON, 170
STRAW, 6
STRAWN, 211
STREET, 176
STREETER, 11 31 88 114
STURGEON, 163
STUTTERMAN, 223
SUCHOCKI, 146
SULLIVAN, 101 118 135 209
SULLY, 170
SUMMERFIELD, 165
SUOMINEN, 88 226
SWAFFIELD, 135
SWAIN, 12 21 36
SWAN, 36 51
SWANBERG, 150
SWANSON, 135 159
SWASEY, 39
SWEAT, 32 88
SWEATT, 23 31 53
SWEENEY, 129 178
SWEET, 36 37 152
SWIFT, 218
SWINNERTON, 40
SYKES, 131
SYLVAIN, 115 124
SYMONDS, 72 74
SYPEK, 194
SYPHERS, 108
TAATJES, 214
TABB, 38
TABBURSH, 176
TABOR, 97
TAIT, 199
TALBOT, 221
TALCOTT, 156
TANDY, 58 69 85
TANGUAY, 103 133 180 222
TANNER, 198
TARBAR, 135
TARBELL, 158
TARBOX, 39 217
TARDIF, 119 193
TARIFF, 175
TARR, 191
TARRANT, 201
TASKER, 20 23
TATEM, 154
TAYLOR, 15 52 78 97 99 107 187 188 219 229
TEBBETTS, 210 230
TEMPLE, 110 226
TESSIER, 119 189 216
TEW, 232
TEWKSBURY, 186
THAYER, 111 186 232
THERIAULT, 158
THIBAULT, 105 124
THIBODEAU, 188
THIMPLE, 38
THOMAS, 49 104 144 178 182 195 203
THOMPSON, 3 34 46 65 71 80 84 103 115 135 142 150 151 162 163 165 182 185 200 203 205 219
THOMSON, 38
THORN, 52 60 61 70
THORNDIKE, 65 87
THORNE, 143

THORP, 192
THORPE, 225
THURLIN, 13
THURSTON, 52 62 67
THWING, 37
THYNG, 142
TIBBETS, 80 230
TIBBETTS, 132 165 211
TILDEN, 213
TILTON, 68 112 116
TIMMINS, 40
TINKER, 169
TIPPING, 166
TITCOMB, 24 35 36 40
TITUS, 163
TOBEY, 99
TODD, 9 30 98 126
TOKO, 218
TOMPSON, 221
TONIS, 127
TONYIN, 222
TOTTEN, 120
TOWERS, 17
TOWLE, 28 31 59 85 117
TOWNER, 53
TOWNSEND, 27
TOWNSON, 72
TRACEY, 38
TRAKIMAS, 101
TRANTAFILON, 185
TRIPP, 150
TRRNTINA, 224
TRUE, 40 55 180
TRUELL, 108
TRUESDALE, 225
TRUSSELL, 7
TUCKER, 37 65 67 107 158 221
TUFFTS, 68
TUFTE, 199
TUFTS, 14 62
TULGREN, 160
TURCOTTE, 94
TURGEON, 101 124

TURNER, 33 64 74 90 153
TUTINGER, 138
TUTTLE, 9 10 40 61 79 113 136
TWILIGHT, 5
TWIP, 30
TWISS, 64 87
TWITCHELL, 146 197 222
TWOMBLEY, 19 25
TWOMBLY, 8 31 81
TYDEMAN, 94
TYLER, 57 65 87
UFFLEMAN, 141
UHLER, 153
UKLE, 206
UNDERHILL, 195
UNDERWOOD, 55 67
UPTON, 31
URAN, 81 90
UTKA, 115 232
VACHON, 105 192
VAILLANCOURT, 174 183
VALENTIN, 204
VALLIERE, 194
VALLIERES, 146
VALLIERIES, 168 199 204
VANBERKUM, 187
VANDEBURG, 158
VARNEY, 17 198
VARNUM, 26
VASIOTIS, 220
VASSAMILLET, 142
VEILLEUX, 128 129 195
VERGURST, 178
VICKERY, 70
VICSOUNT, 35
VIENS, 224
VILES, 221
VILOT, 5
VINCENT, 229
VINER, 40
VINKS, 203
VIRGIN, 2 16 30 63 65 70 73 75 79 86 87 143

VOLKMANN, 157
VON-DER-SUMP, 126
VORIS, 224
VUALPY, 36
WADHAMS, 114
WADHULL, 229
WADLEIGH, 16
WAGNER, 161
WAIT, 36
WAKEFIELD, 76
WALCOMB, 190
WALDO, 66 156
WALDRON, 68
WALES, 202
WALKER, 58 66 76 162
WALL, 223
WALLACE, 39 91 116 160
WALLEY, 172
WALLIN, 230
WALTEN, 135
WALTER, 169
WALZ, 220
WARD, 206 208
WARFIELD, 202
WARNER, 35
WARREN, 206
WASHBURN, 62 215
WASHER, 84
WASSON, 10
WATERMAN, 48
WATERS, 118
WATSON, 18 27 141 211
WATTENFELLS, 229
WATTS, 86 141
WAYMAN, 35
WEBB, 128 176 223
WEBBER, 61 80
WEBSTER, 15 21
WEED, 84 185
WEEKS, 53 79 85 105 142
WEELER, 169
WELCH, 104 112 232
WELLINGTON, 18 60 90

WELLMAN, 139
WELLS, 12 38 51 160 202 222
WEMYSS, 193
WENTWORTH, 2 29 67 110 115 118 120 155
WEST, 48 49 133 148 187 190
WESTERMAN, 122
WESTHEAD, 152
WESTON, 24 109 121
WESTWOOD, 103
WETHERBEE, 97
WEVER, 175
WHALEN, 140
WHEDDEN, 78
WHEELER, 41 72-74 89 147 198
WHEELOCK, 217
WHHITCOMB, 87
WHIDDEN, 89
WHIPPEN, 230
WHIPPIE, 163
WHIPPLE, 141 194
WHITAKER, 29
WHITCHER, 35
WHITCOMB, 14 62 130 147 184 194
WHITE, 1 10 24 31 38 90 123 132 158 209 219 222
WHITEHOUSE, 145
WHITELAY, 111
WHITFIELD, 76
WHITFORD, 214
WHITING, 108 120 187
WHITLAND, 67
WHITMARSH, 63
WHITNEY, 78 91 97 227
WHITON, 40
WHITTAKER, 17 84
WHITTEMORE, 128 213
WHITTERMORE, 45 51 99
WHITTIER, 232
WHITWELL, 40
WHYMAN, 99

WICKLUND, 162
WIGGIN, 13 32 50 54 58 66 68 71 90
WIGGING, 53
WIGGINS, 19 22 52 78 89 191
WIINIKKA, 232
WILCOX, 172
WILD, 40 217 228
WILDER, 4 49 53 87 182 205 224
WILEY, 188
WILKIN, 114
WILKINS, 26 48 51 75
WILKINSON, 172
WILLAND, 69
WILLARD, 1
WILLETT, 94 174 210
WILLEY, 2 9 48
WILLIAM, 194
WILLIAMS, 37 43 58 95 113 154
WILLINGTON, 90
WILLIS, 58 94 230
WILSON, 19 33 83 132 134 138 161 171 180 198 221 230
WING, 96
WINGATE, 51 75 86
WINKLER, 108
WINSLOW, 43
WITHYAM, 213
WITQUEL, 213
WIXON, 116
WOHLGEMUTH, 199
WOLF, 134
WOLFE, 212 232

WOLFERTZ, 133
WOLLEY, 122
WOOD, 16 51 55 90 136 158 179 191 192 223
WOODBURY, 54 215
WOODMAN, 8 24 41 113 127
WOODNONFF, 141
WOODS, 199
WOODWARD, 110 122 152 182 195
WOODWELL, 40
WOOLHULL, 225
WORMSEADE, 39
WORSTER, 77-79
WORTEN, 79
WORTH, 50
WORTHEN, 7 10 27
WORTHING, 45
WORTHLEY, 25
WORTMAN, 149 151
WOS, 114
WOSTER, 24
WRIGHT, 44 104 128 170 189 218
WYMAN, 183
YANEZ, 163
YATES, 100
YEATON, 75 187
YORK, 201
YOUNG, 10 24 140 180 215 227
YULE, 206
ZAHOPOULOU, 190
ZELLER, 224
ZIMMERMAN, 200

www.ingramcontent.com/pod-product-compliance
Lightning Source LLC
Chambersburg PA
CBHW071227170426
43191CB00032B/1065